XHTML and CSS Essentials for Library Web Design

Michael P. Sauers

Neal-Schuman Publishers, Inc.

New York

London

 Don't miss the companion Web site for this book, featuring sample coding, helpful additional resources, as well as updates from the author. Visit http://www.travelinlibrarian.info/writing/XHTML-CSS/ to download files and learn more about the latest in web design.

Published by Neal-Schuman Publishers, Inc.
100 William St., Suite 2004
New York, NY 10038

Printed and bound in the United States of America.

The paper used in this publication meets the minimum requirements of American National Standard for Information Sciences – Permanence of Paper for Printed Library Materials, ANSI Z39.48–1992.

Library of Congress Cataloging-in-Publication Data

Sauers, Michael P.
    XHTML and CSS essentials for library Web design / Michael P. Sauers.
        p. cm.
    Includes bibliographical references and index.
    ISBN 1-55570-504-9 (alk. Paper)
  1. Library Web sites—Design. 2. XHTML (Document markup language)— 3.
Cascading style sheets. I. Title

    Z674.75.W67S38 2006
    005.7'2—dc22

                                                        2004047429

For my parents,
I bet you wondered when I was going to get around to you.
Thanks for everything.

And for Laura,
although you were supposed to wait a little longer
for a dedication, I just couldn't leave you out of this one.
Who says having a language-geek for a best friend can't be useful?
Thank you for the past 18 years,
especially the three weeks you spent toiling on this manuscript.

Contents

PART I: XHTML Essentials

PART II: CSS Essentials

List of Figures

List of Tables

Preface

Librarians perform their jobs working closely with current standards, whether MARC or Z39.50 or LCSH or DDC. So why are most library Web sites created using HTML, a program not considered the current measure since at least 1999? Sticking with the out-of-date model seems to be the quick "don't fix what isn't broken" answer for many busy professionals. After all, isn't the job done if the page looks good when it pops up on a computer screen?

XHTML and CSS Essentials for Library Web Design contends that you shortchange the user if you design in a limited environment envisioning only desktop/laptop computers connected to one or two of the major browsers, such as Netscape Navigator and Microsoft's Internet Explorer. What about the next generation of popular browsers, such as Opera, Mozilla, Safari, and Firefox? And what about other platforms? Suppose a patron checks her library account using a Trēo600 cell phone/PDA—a terrific little gadget with a screen resolution of 64x64 pixels. Ever wonder what your site looks on a screen that size?

Back in 1999, the W3C—the World Wide Web Consortium, an international industry association that develops common protocols to promote WWW evolution and ensure its interoperability—stopped developing Hypertext Markup Language (HTML) and refocused its efforts on XHTML, an Extended XML-based language to create better Web pages. Cascading Style Sheets (CSS) are a feature of HTML in which you can create style templates that specify how different text elements (paragraphs, headings, hyperlinks, etc.) appear on a Web page. CSS has been a part of good design even longer than HTML. The bottom line? If your library site does not employ or underutilizes the latest markup language, you are performing unnecessary work. Incorporating CSS will save your design team literally hours of work. As an added bonus, CSS allows a greater consistency in your site's design and simply makes your pages reflect the modern and professional nature your institution wants to project.

Why is it so important to keep up with standards for users? If you're not using the current standards of XHTML and CSS, it is estimated that "99.9% of all Web sites are obsolete" (Zeldman, 2003). Providing access to information is a library's core mission. Undoubtedly you and your colleagues take pride in taking the time to organize and present the best information available. Shouldn't end users be able to take full advantage of your hard work? Utilizing current standards guarantees a patron easier access using any searching method.

ORGANIZATION

XHTML and CSS Essentials for Library Web Design is organized into three parts.

Part I, "XHTML Essentials," contains 11 chapters and covers all the nuts and bolts of this markup language, including history, syntax, and proper use.

- Chapter 1, "Introduction to XHTML," offers a brief history of markup from its earliest beginnings as SGML, through the development of HTML and the more recent introduction of XML and XHTML. It also supplies good reasons why you need to move from the older language to the newer.
- Chapter 2, "The Minimal Document," examines the standard information that must appear on every page to make it compliant.
- Chapter 3, "Basic Markup," examines key elements and attributes in an easy alphabetical arrangement. Each possesses a particular purpose, and none fall into any of the special categories of the remaining chapters.
- Chapter 4, "Hyperlinks," shows how to create links between documents and Web site and to other sites. It also illustrates how to install e-mail links within a particular file.
- Chapter 5, "Images," explains how to create imagemaps and insert images into text.
- Chapter 6, "Lists," introduces how to build in bulleted, numbered, or lettered lists.
- Chapter 7, "Tables," discusses how and when to use tables properly. It studies the code used for creating layout that organizes tabular data.
- Chapter 8, "Forms," delves into the creation of an online form to collect data from your users. This chapter demonstrates how to construct a sample ILL request form that automatically e-mails the collected information.
- Chapter 9, "Frames," explains how to divide up a user's window into multiple independent areas in order to view more than one document at a time.
- Chapter 10, "Metadata," talks about how to add information to documents to assist search engines and let other tools better index particulars.
- Chapter 11, "Validating Markup," deals with the W3C validator service. This feature is an essential tool for a Web designer writing with good, clean conventions because it checks code and makes sure it follows the rules of XHTML.

Part II, "CSS Essentials," contains ten chapters and covers the purpose, syntax, and proper use of cascading style sheets.

Zeldman, Jeffrey. 2003. *Designing with Web Standards* Indianapolis: New Rider.

- Chapter 12, "Introduction to CSS," discusses the logic behind this technology and why it is essential to use it when designing pages.
- Chapter 13, "CSS Mechanics," explores the basic syntax of writing proper CSS code and getting XHTML documents to pay attention to source instructions.
- Chapter 14, "Colors, Measurements and URLs," introduces how to specify colors, different units of measurement, and how to specify URLs when needed. It groups these three topics into a single chapter because they will have repercussions throughout the rest of the book.
- Chapter 15, "Formatting Text with CSS," reveals the basic properties of formatting content within a document. It includes manipulating font, text color, boldfacing, underlining and other features.
- Chapter 16, "The Box Model," launches a central concept in CSS and demonstrates how to control layout by making use of margins, padding, and borders.
- Chapter 17, "Links," deals specifically with hyperlinks.
- Chapter 18, "Lists," considers the part of CSS system that has an effect on the lists within your content. It includes examples suggesting original solutions for changing how to use lists.
- Chapter 19, "Forms," focuses on how to construct forms properly and present them in a logical and eye-pleasing manner.
- Chapter 20, "Positioning," combines concepts already discussed and takes them to the next level. It teaches how to create columns and introduces how to allow control within a document so that information appears regardless of placement in markup.
- Chapter 21, "Media Types," presents the concept of employing different styles depending on platform, such as seeing one style on screen but another printed style.

The companion Web site contains nine sources of reference documents and recommended instructions on how to move from HTML to XHTML.

NOTE: I suggest reading or reviewing the chapters in order, but I set up this guide so you can skip mastered subjects or be able to read just the chapters that interest you. Remember, if you come upon an unclear concept, you can always backtrack to a previous chapter.

I'm happy to try and answer any questions. Drop me an e-mail at *msauers@ travelinlibrarian.info* and I'll see what I can do for you.

You might also try posting your questions to WebDesign-L <www.webdesign-l.com/ >, XHTML-L <http://groups.yahoo.com/group/XHTML-L/>, and/or CSS-D <www.css-discuss.org/>. I participate in these lists along with hundreds of other experts in their respective fields.

I hope *XHTML and CSS Essentials for Library Web Design* inspires you to inventive site planning. I hope you enjoy the essentials and go on to learn more!

Acknowledgments

There are no small contributions in the writing of this book and I thank the following individuals and institutions:

Louise Alcorn, Katrina Anderson, the Arapahoe Library District, the Aurora Public Library, Jan Campau, Karen Coombs, the friends of the Aurora Public Library, Rosario Garza, Amy Helfman, Amanda Hollister, Lisa Holmberg, Susan Johns-Smith, Laura Martinez, Annemarie Meyer, and Mary Norman.

As a traveling trainer, I wrote parts of this book in many different locations. I extend my appreciation to the following people and places: the Denver International Airport, Phoenix Sky Harbor International Airport, Washington Dulles Airport, Chicago O'Hare Airport, Barnes & Noble (Reno, Nevada, Greece, New York, and Pittsford, New York), The Freighthouse Restaurant (Dodge City, Kansas), Starbucks (Aurora, Colorado, Reno, Nevada, and Greece, New York), Mom & Dad's house (Greece, New York), Home (Aurora, Colorado), the BCR offices (Aurora, Colorado), Louise's home (Des Moines, Iowa), and Starbucks and Borders (West Des Moines, Iowa).

PART I
XHTML ESSENTIALS

1

Introduction
to XHTML

Before we discuss just exactly what XHTML is and why you need to use it, a little background is in order. So, let me take you through a brief history of markup languages.

A BRIEF HISTORY OF MARKUP

IN THE BEGINNING

In the mid-1980s, when computers were first becoming the standard method of managing documents in a business environment, software developers determined that they needed a method by which to add code to documents in order for those documents to be read not only by humans, but also by the computers that were storing them.

Through the addition of such code, or markup, computers would be better able to retrieve documents based upon the context of the words for which a user was looking. In response to this need, the Standard Generalized Markup Language (SGML) was created. SGML is still used today, mostly in very large organizations that have immense document repositories that were built over the past 20 years. However, SGML is large and complex. One does not sit down for a few hours and learn how to write SGML. In many cases, when SGML is used, it is highly customized for the environment it is being used in.

Here is a sample SGML document:[1]

```
<FORM>"aak" # noun #1
 <GRAPHEMICS>
 <TYPE> "full"
```

```
<STATUS> officieel
</GRAPHEMICS>
<MORPHOLOGY>
<TYPE> "simpmorph"
 <FLECTION>
   <SPELLING> "aken"
<IRR>
 <CATEGORY> plural
</FLECTION>
<FLECTION>
 <SPELLING> "de"
 <CATEGORY> article
</FLECTION>
<FLECTION>
 <SPELLING> "mf"
 <CATEGORY> gender
</FLECTION>
</MORPHOLOGY>
<LU> "soort schip"
 <SYNTAX>
 <SUBCAT> "count"
</SYNTAX>
<SEMANTICS>
 <TYPE> "artefact"
<DEF_DIFF> "met een platte bodem voor vrachtvervoer over rivieren
     en kanalen"
<DEF_GENUS> "schip"
<SOURCE> "BVD"
<REFERENCE> "common"
<SHIFT> "noshift"
</SEMANTICS>
</LU>
</FORM>
```

THE WEB ARRIVES

In the early 1990s, Tim Berners-Lee of CERN, a physics lab in Switzerland, had an idea. He wanted to create a system that would allow him to distribute documents on the Internet. Although such systems already existed (of which Gopher was the most significant), Lee wanted to be able to link his documents together, allowing a user to jump from one document to another in a hypertext environment.

In order to do this, Lee knew that markup would need to be added to his documents so the computers could have a minimal level of understanding of the contents of the documents. Lee was aware of SGML but decided that it was just too complex for this task, so he took small parts of SGML and created the Hypertext Markup Language (HTML).[2] The first version of HTML was extremely basic compared to the markup we're used to today.

Here is a sample of an HTML 1.0 document:

```
<TITLE>HTML 1.0 document</TITLE>
```

```
<H1>HTML 1.0</H1>
<P>As you can see, there's not much to this document. More
details can be found on the <A href="http://www.w3.org/History/
19921103-hypertext/hypertext/WWW/MarkUp/Tags.html">W3C site</
A>.</P>
```

HTML 1.0 also included unordered and definition lists along with the ability to "high-light" text (which was quickly abandoned). You may notice that images were not in-cluded. That's because at this point, the Web was purely a text-only environment. It wasn't until the advent of the Mosaic browser that graphics were even considered as something the language needed to encompass.

THE RISE OF THE W3C

With the Web quickly becoming the standard method for document distribution on the Internet, Lee and others formed the World Wide Web Consortium (W3C) to help guide the development of the Web and its related technologies. In 1995, the W3C released the specifications for HTML 2.0. This version added several new items that we're familiar with today, including images, character encoding, the root element, head and body ele-ments, and the doctype statement. Here's an example of an HTML 2.0 document:

```
<!DOCTYPE HTML PUBLIC "-//IETF//DTD HTML 2.0//EN">
<HTML>
<HEAD>
<title>HTML 2.0 document</title>
</HEAD>
<BODY>
<h1>HTML 1.0</h1>
<img src="logo.gif">
<p>As you can see, there's not much to this document. More
details can be found on the <a href="http://www.w3.org/MarkUp/
html-spec/">W3C site</a>.</p>
</BODY>
</HTML>
```

THE BROWSER WARS, HTML 3, HTML 3+, AND HTML 3.2

Whenever I speak of the browser wars, I always picture myself as an old man talking to my grandchildren when they say, "Tell us about the war, Grandpa." Needless to say, al-though the browser wars have repercussions that still linger today, anyone who thinks that the Web as we know it now isn't stable was not around in the mid to late 1990s. Compared to that period, today's Web is extremely stable.

By 1996, Netscape Navigator was the dominant browser, but Microsoft also released its Internet Explorer browser. Both companies were vying for the dominant market share because they believed that whomever controlled the browser controlled the Web.

In an attempt to become the browser of choice, both of Netscape and Microsoft de-veloped browser-specific extensions to the current HTML standard. The folks at Netscape came up with elements such as `<background>`, `<frame>`, `<font>`, and `<blink>`.

Over at Microsoft, they created such elements as `<marquee>`, `<iframe>`, and `<bgsound>`. Meanwhile, the folks at the W3C were suggesting such elements as `<banner>` and `<fig>`. Consequently, developers started putting icons on their pages such as "best viewed in Netscape 3" or "best viewed in Microsoft Internet Explorer." (Some forward-thinking yet frustrated developers humorously used one that stated, "Best viewed in any browser.")

During this time of extreme developer confusion, several updates to HTML 2.0 were put forward. The two most significant of these were HTML 3.0 and HTML 3+. Both of these proposed standards included some of what each of the browser vendors were suggesting but neither proposal stuck.

So, in 1997 the W3C decided to reclaim control of the development of HTML and created HTML 3.2. What was significant about this standard was that the W3C took into consideration "current practices," accepting some of the vendor extensions into the standard while disposing of others. The HTML 3.2 standard included many new elements including `<script>`, `<meta>`, `<style>`, `<form>`, `<table>`, and `<center>`.

Here's our sample document updated to meet the HTML 3.2 standard:

```
<!DOCTYPE HTML PUBLIC "-//W3C//DTD HTML 3.2//EN">
<HTML>
<HEAD>
<title>HTML 3.2 document</title>
<style>
body {margin: 10%}
</style>
<meta name="description" content="A basic HTML 3.2 document">
</HEAD>
<BODY>
<h1>HTML 3.2</h1>
<img src="logo.gif">
<table width="600" border="1">
<tr>
<td>
<p>This document is looking much more similar to what we're
used to seeing today. More details can be found on the <a
href="http://www.w3.org/TR/REC-html32">W3C site</a>.</p>
</td>
</tr>
</table>
</BODY>
</HTML>
```

HTML 4.0 AND 4.01, THE END OF HTML

In 1999, the W3C released what would be the last version of HTML, 4.0 (quickly followed by HTML 4.01, which mostly fixed minor bugs in the documentation). According to the W3C, "HTML 4 extends HTML with mechanisms for style sheets, scripting, frames, embedding objects, improved support for right to left and mixed direction text, richer tables, and enhancements to forms, offering improved accessibility for people with disabilities."[3]

New elements in this version included `<acronym>` and `<abbr>`, `<col>`, and `<colgroup>` along with the accesskey, title, and lang attributes.

With some very minor tweaking, here is our sample document with a few of the HTML 4.01 elements and attributes added:

```
<!DOCTYPE HTML PUBLIC "-//W3C//DTD HTML 4.01//EN"
"http://www.w3.org/TR/html4/strict.dtd">
<HTML>
<HEAD>
<title>HTML 4.01 document</title>
<style>
body {margin: 10%}
</style>
<meta name="description" content="A basic HTML 3.2 document">
</HEAD>
<BODY>
<h1>HTML 4.01</h1>
<img src="logo.gif">
<table width="600" border="1">
<tr>
<td>
<p>This document is looking much more similar to what we're
used to seeing today. More details can be found on the <a
href="http://www.w3.org/TR/REC-html32"><abbr title="World Wide
Web Consortium">W3C</abbr> site</a>.</p>
</td>
</tr>
</table>
</BODY>
</HTML>
```

The reason that 4.01 was the final version of HTML was that the W3C was concurrently developing a replacement for HTML: XHTML.

THE RISE OF XML

In February 1998, the W3C announced the release of the eXtensible Markup Language (XML) 1.0 specification. Not intended as a replacement for SGML, it was "primarily intended to meet the requirements of large-scale Web content providers for industry-specific markup, vendor-neutral data exchange, media-independent publishing, one-on-one marketing, workflow management in collaborative authoring environments, and the processing of Web documents by intelligent clients. It is also expected to find use in metadata applications."[4] In other words, XML combined the ease of HTML with the power of SGML to allow groups and individuals to use markup in a Web environment to publish and exchange data.

Actually, XML is not a language; it is a metalanguage. Just as metadata is data about data, XML is a language for creating languages. What XML does is establish a set of rules for creating other languages. As long as the created languages follow the rules of XML, they are considered "XML-based" or "XML-compliant" languages. The benefit of this concept is that once multiple languages all follow the same set of core rules, the interoperability of those languages is increased.

Some examples of XML-based languages are XSL,[5] ThML,[6] MathML,[7] HR-XML,[8] and ETD-ML.[9]

THE ARRIVAL OF XHTML

In January 2000, the W3C announced the release of the XHTML 1.0 specification. At the most basic level, XHTML 1.0 is HTML 4.01 reformulated to follow the rules of XML, thereby allowing it to be compatible with all other XML-based languages.

Here is our sample document turned into XHTML:

```
<!DOCTYPE html PUBLIC "-//W3C//DTD HTML 4.01//EN"
"http://www.w3.org/TR/html4/strict.dtd">
<html>
<head>
<title>HTML 4.01 document</title>
<style>
body {margin: 10%}
</style>
<meta name="description" content="A basic HTML 3.2 document" /
>
</head>
<body>
<h1>HTML 4.01</h1>
<img src="logo.gif" alt="logo" />
<table width="600" border="1">
<tr>
<td>
<p>This document is looking much more similar to what we're
used to seeing today. More details can be found on the <a
href="http://www.w3.org/TR/REC-html32"><abbr title="World Wide
Web Consortium">W3C</abbr> site</a>.</p>
</td>
</tr>
</table>
</body>
</html>
```

As previously mentioned, the main benefit of XHTML is its compatibility with other XML-based documents. Unfortunately, unless you're working in an XML environment (which I assume most of you are not), this benefit is wasted on you. There is, however, another benefit to using XHTML; it forces you to write good clean code.

The rules of XML, though few, are significant and inflexible. A significant number of problems that Web pages have today can be traced back to the fact that many Web authors write the code to the browser. In other words, as long as it "looks right" in the browser, the job appears done. When you work in an XML environment, "looks right" is a good end result, but good clean code is a requirement.

THE RULES OF XML

Before we move on to creating our first XHTML document, allow me to review the five rules of XML. This is mainly for the benefit of those of you that are already familiar with HTML.

1. *XML is case-sensitive.*
   Due to this constraint, the W3C decided that XHTML must be written in lower case. In HTML, case did not matter.
2. *All elements must be closed.*
   In HTML, `</p>` was optional. In XHTML, if you open an element, you must also close it.
3. *Empty elements must also be closed.*
   Elements such as `<br>` and `<hr>` which in HTML have no closing element (`</br>` and `</hr>`) must be closed using the XML format of `<br />` and `<hr />`.
4. *All attributes must be fully formed.*
   Attributes such as `checked` and `noshade` (in forms and on `<hr>` respectively) have no values in HTML. In XHTML, all attributes must equal a value.
5. *Attribute values must be enclosed in quotation marks.*
   In HTML, quotation marks around attribute values were sometimes required and sometimes optional. XHTML always requires them, taking away the guesswork.

We'll be reviewing each of these in much more detail in the next chapter.

DISPLAYING VS. PARSING

Before we continue, we must address one behind-the-scenes difference between HTML and XHTML: displaying vs. parsing.

In the world of HTML, browsers have rules of how certain HTML instructions should be interpreted, resulting in the display that you're used to. This is why different browsers sometimes display your Web page differently. Those different browsers have different built-in rules.

However, in the XML world, since there are so many different languages that an author might use, it would be impossible for the browsers to have prewritten rules for displaying the markup. Therefore, XML documents are meant to be "parsed" first. Parsing is the act of comparing the document you wrote against the rules of the language you wrote it in. If an error is found, the parser should stop the job and report the line number on which the error was found. Yes, this might be considered harsh, but if you think of your document as structured data and not just as a Web page, the data should be checked to ensure it is formatted correctly, since incorrectly formatted data could cause problems down the line.

Documents written in XML-based languages (XHTML included) are not actually parsed in today's browsers. None of the current versions of Netscape, Mozilla, FireFox, Opera, or Internet Explorer contain parsers. They will treat your XHTML just like HTML and display your content accordingly. The important thing to keep in mind is that eventually, browsers will include parsers and then you will need to make sure your code is written in strict adherence to the rules of XHTML—no more sloppy coding. There are always ways to make sure you've followed the rules. We'll review that process in Chapter 11, "Validating Your Code."

Let's move on and start writing some XHTML.

NOTES

1. www.let.kun.nl/WBA/Content2/1.4.3_SGML_Example.htm
2. www.w3.org/TR/html401/intro/intro.html#h-2.3
3. Set dropped copy@msp5/
4. www.w3.org/Press/1998/XML10-REC
5. Extensible Style Language, www.w3.org/Style/XSL/
6. Theological Markup Language, www.ccel.org/ThML/
7. Math Markup Language, www.w3.org/Math/
8. Human Resources Markup Language, www.hr-xml.org/channels/home.htm
9. Electronic Thesis and Dissertation Markup Language, http://etd.vt.edu/etd-ml/

2

The Minimal
XHTML Document

Now that you have a good idea of where XHTML comes from and how it fits into the larger scheme of XML, let's take a look at the minimum amount of code an XHTML document needs.

THE XML PROLOG

Because XHTML is an XML-based language, the first line of code should be the XML prolog. (Please note that I say, "should be" and not "must be." I'll explain why later in the chapter.) The XML prolog is not technically part of your document. It actually sits outside your document (actually before your document) and announces to the parser which version of XML you are using to write your document.
The XML prolog looks like this:

```
<?xml version="1.0" encoding="utf-8"?>
```

You should note that the XML prolog looks very different from any other XHTML code. This is because it is not XHTML but raw XML code and is a direct instruction to the parser rather than a part of content or structure of your actual document. The XML prolog is contained within <? and ?> with xml as the element along with two attributes. The version attribute specifies which version of XML you are using to write your document. At the time of this publication, there was only one version of XML, 1.0, so this is your only choice. You should assume, however, that eventually there will be an XML version 2.0 you could use.

The `encoding` attribute indicates to the browser which character set you are using to write your document. In previous times I've used the value that specifies I'm using ASCII (also known as ISO-8859-1) to write my document. Another common value you may wish to use is UTF-8 (which was designed to be a replacement for ASCII), since it supports many more characters. Since UTF-8 is the updated option and one of the points of writing in XHTML is to be looking forward, I believe UTF-8 to be the better choice—it's the one I'll be using throughout this book.

Table 2.1 shows the values that you can use for your encoding and their matching character sets. For example, if you were writing your document in the Cyrillic alphabet, you would set the encoding to ISO–8859–5.

Table 2.1
Common Encoding Schemes

Encoding scheme	Number of bits	Notes
UCS–2	16	Unicode character set
UCS–4	32	Unicode character set in 32-bits
ISO–8859–1	8	Unicode Transformation
UTF–7	7	Unicode Transformation (for mail and news)
UTF–16	16, 32	Unicode that escapes 32-bit characters
ISO–8859–1	8	Latin alphabet (Western Europe and Latin America)
ISO–8859–2	8	Latin alphabet (Central and Eastern European)
ISO–8859–3	8	Latin alphabet (South Eastern European and Miscellaneous)
ISO–8859–4	8	Latin alphabet (Scandinavia and Baltic)
ISO–8859–5	8	Latin/Cyrillic
ISO–8859–6	8	Latin/Arabic
ISO–8859–7	8	Latin/Greek
ISO–8859–8	8	Latin/Hebrew
ISO–8859–9	8	Latin/Turkish
ISO–8859–10	8	Latin/Lappish/Nordic/Eskimo
ISO 10646	32	32-bit extended set (includes Unicode as a subset)
EUC-JP	8	Japanese using multibyte encoding
Shift_JIS	8	Japanese using multibyte encoding
ISO–2022-JP	7	Japanese using multibyte encoding for mail and news

IMPORTANT: Encoding is used to specify which character set you are using to write your whole document, markup and content, not the human language you are using to write your content. That is specified through the `lang` attribute that I will discuss later in this chapter.

DO YOU ACTUALLY NEED TO USE THE XML PROLOG?

As I mentioned earlier, the XML prolog should be entered as the first line of your document, since XHTML is an XML-based language. However, if you actually include the XML prolog in your code, you can cause your page to display incorrectly.

With the release of Microsoft's Internet Explorer 6.0, Microsoft finally considered that in previous versions, they had incorrectly implemented some of the CSS specifications, namely the Box Model (discussed in Chapter 16). Since many Web pages had been designed to account for implementation errors, Microsoft wanted to give the authors of those pages a way to circumvent the need for a necessary code correction. They created the now infamous "Quirks Mode."

By default, IE (beginning with Version 6) implements the CSS specification with a greater accuracy than previous versions, the fix of the Box Model being the biggest item. This is known as "Standards Mode." However, if the author of the page chooses, he or she can instruct IE to switch to "Quirks Mode," which includes the bugs from the previous version. One of the ways to invoke "Quirks Mode" is to include the XML prolog (or anything else for that matter) before the DOCTYPE statement. The result of this "Quirks Mode" is that if you include the XML prolog in your document, you significantly increase the chance that Internet Explorer will display your document incorrectly.

This is one instance in which rules and reality contradict. Luckily, leaving out the XML prolog will not cause any ill effects in any of today's browsers or any browsers in the foreseeable future. In all of the examples of this book, I will not be using an XML prolog. This does, however, create one potential problem. If you run your code through a validator, which we will be doing in Chapter 11, the validator will require you to indicate which encoding scheme you are using. There is, however, another way to indicate information—via metadata. I'll cover how to do this a little later in this chapter.

THE DOCTYPE STATEMENT

The DOCTYPE statement is the next (or more likely first) line of code that you need to insert into your document. Although this code has existed since the earliest version of HTML, it was generally considered optional, since browsers of the time were only designed to read HTML and nothing else. The other reason that they were optional is that no one ever bothered to run their code through a validator to see if they had written good, clean code. Since in XHTML, good clean code is a requirement rather than a goal, the DOCTYPE statement has now become a requirement as well.

Like the XML prolog, the DOCTYPE statement sits outside the document proper and looks a little different from normal XHTML code. Its purpose is to announce to the parser which version of which markup language you are using to code your document. There are DOCTYPE statements available for each of the versions of HTML and XHTML. All the other XML-based languages also have their own DOCTYPE statements.

The DOCTYPE statement serves an additional important purpose: to direct the parser to where it can look up the rules of the language, if necessary. For example, if you were sending a MathML document to a parser that had never before encountered MathML, it could, in theory, get the location of the rules file (known as the DTD or Document Type Definition), download it, and proceed to check the document against those rules.

RULES. REALITY: This is not what actually happens in today's browsers. Since these browsers do not contain parsers, they ignore the content of the DOCTYPE statement and follow their own sets of preprogrammed rules for dealing with the files they are sent, sometimes with appalling results. (Later in this chapter, we'll view the results of sending MathML code to IE6.)

So, if today's browsers virtually ignore the DOCTYPE statement, why should you bother including it? There are three reasons:

The first reason is forward compatibility. Eventually, the browsers will catch up with the technology and include parsers. When they do, you're not going to want to go back and add DOCTYPE statements to the thousands of pages in your library's Web site.

The second reason is the validator. When you finally reach the stage of validating your code (checking it for errors), you will need the DOCTYPE statement to tell the validator which markup language you're using and which set of rules to check your code against. If you don't, the validator won't bother to guess, nor will it bother to check your code.

The third reason is "Quirks Mode." If your DOCTYPE statement is missing (or incomplete), IE will dump your document into "Quirks Mode" and possibly misdisplay your page. This is not something most authors want to happen.[1]

BUT WHICH SUBTYPE OF XHTML?

We've decided that we're writing our document in XHTML but there's still one more decision to make before we start writing code: Which subtype of XHTML are we going to use?

Not only do you need to decide which markup language you're going to use (XHTML), which version (1.0, or 1.1), but also which subtype: strict, transitional, or frameset.

Let me introduce you to each of these, slightly out of order.

THE FRAMESET DOCTYPE

The frameset DOCTYPE is used when you are writing a frames-based document. We can safely assume that you will not need to do this for most of your site. I will cover frames in Chapter 9.

THE TRANSITIONAL DOCTYPE

The transitional DOCTYPE is the most flexible of the three subtypes. When you use the transitional DOCTYPE, you have the ability not only to use all the elements and attributes available in XHTML, but also to use a significant number of attributes that are left over from HTML (and a few HTML quirks). This gives authors additional flexibility and use of older code until they've learned the code that's replaced it. (In almost all cases the old attributes have been replaced with CSS code.)

THE STRICT DOCTYPE

The strict DOCTYPE is for hard-core code junkies. When you use the strict DOCTYPE, you are limited to the rules, only the rules, and nothing but the rules of XHTML. Anything in transitional left over from HTML is gone, and you must have a solid grasp of CSS in order to get your page to look anything like what you intend. The strict DOCTYPE is purely structural and contains almost nothing related to style at all.

In most cases, especially while you're getting started with XHTML and CSS, I recommend using the transitional DOCTYPE. Once you feel that you can code XHTML and

CSS in your sleep, then think about giving strict a try. Lastly, if you need to create frames, the frameset DOCTYPE is your only choice.

AND NOW, ON WITH THE CODE...

All three of the available XHTML DOCTYPE statements are similar, with only slight differences among them.

STRICT

```
<!DOCTYPE html PUBLIC "-//W3C//DTD XHTML 1.0 Strict//EN" "http:/
/www.w3.org/TR/xhtml1/DTD/xhtml1-strict.dtd">
```

TRANSITIONAL

```
<!DOCTYPE  html  PUBLIC  "-//W3C//DTD  XHTML  1.0
Transitional//EN"  "http://www.w3.org/TR/xhtml1/DTD/xhtml1-
transitional.dtd">
```

FRAMESET

```
<!DOCTYPE html PUBLIC "-//W3C//DTD XHTML 1.0 Frameset//EN" "http:/
/www.w3.org/TR/xhtml1/DTD/xhtml1-frameset.dtd">
```

Let's break them down and examine the components.

- `<!`

The opening tag.

- `DOCTYPE`

The element.

- `html`

The name of the language in which we are writing. (This has not been changed to "xhtml" to ensure backward compatibility. If you look at the DOCTYPE statements for other XML-based languages, you'll see more logical language names.)

- `PUBLIC`

The choices here are "PUBLIC" or "SYSTEM." Public languages are stored on remote computers and are written for anyone to use. System languages are generally stored on the same server as the document and are for private use. For example, if you wrote your own markup language for your use, you would set this option to "SYSTEM."

- `-`

The indicator of whether the organization that created the language is an ISO (International Standards Organization) member. "–" indicates it is not. "+" indicates it is.

- `//`

A subfield delimiter. "`//`" acts solely as a separator of information within the DOCTYPE statement, similar to the ‡ in a MARC record.

- `W3C`

The name of the organization that created the language. In this case it is the World Wide Web Consortium (W3C).

- `DTD XHTML 1.0 Transitional`

The official full name of the language.

- `//`

Subfield delimiter.

- `EN`

The human language identifier of the markup language. In this case, the language is English.

- `URL`

The address where the DTD file can be found should it be needed by the parser. (An incomplete URL will trigger "Quirks Mode" in browsers that use DOCTYPE switching.)

- `>`

The closing tag.

THE ROOT ELEMENT

Once you have written your DOCTYPE statement you must then give your document a basic framework in which all of your content will be included. The first part of that structure, the foundation of your document, is known as the root element. The root element is the element into which all other elements and their content will be placed. In an XHTML document the root element is `<html>`.

With a root element added, our document will look like this:

```
<!DOCTYPE html PUBLIC "-//W3C//DTD XHTML 1.0 Transitional//EN"
"http://www.w3.org/TR/xhtml/DTD/xhtml1-transitional.dtd">

<html>
```

```
</html>
```

You may be wondering why the root element isn't <xhtml>. This is one instance in which the authors of XHTML took pity on Web designers and decided to keep the same root element as used in HTML. This ensures that older browsers (and all current browsers) are able to read XHTML documents. Had the root element been changed to <xhtml>, there is a good chance that existing browsers would not understand it (since it was not part of the HTML specification) and would refuse to display any of the document's content.

The head element has one required attribute and two optional attributes. I'll cover the two optional attributes first.

THE LANG ATTRIBUTE

The lang attribute allows the author to specify the human language used to write the content of the document. The lang attribute can be used on any XHTML element to specify the language of that element's content. By adding this to the HTML element, we can indicate the language of the content of the entire document, since all content is contained within the root element.

```
<!DOCTYPE html PUBLIC "-//W3C//DTD XHTML 1.0 Transitional//EN"
"http://www.w3.org/TR/xhtml/DTD/xhtml1-transitional.dtd">
<html lang="en">
</html>
```

In this example I have indicated that the language being used in this document is English.

THE XML:LANG ATTRIBUTE

The xml:lang attribute allows you to specify which language you're using to write your XML code. This isn't used often. If used, it would look like the following example (in which I've also specified that I'm using English for my XML code).

```
<!DOCTYPE html PUBLIC "-//W3C//DTD XHTML 1.0 Transitional//EN"
"http://www.w3.org/TR/xhtml/DTD/xhtml1-transitional.dtd">
<html lang="en xml:lang="en">
</html>
```

THE XMLNS ATTRIBUTE

The attribute that must appear on the root element of an XML document—and consequently any XHTML document—is the namespace attribute: xmlns. The purpose of the namespace attribute is to uniquely identify which XML language you are using in your document. Once we add a namespace, our root element now looks like this:

```
<!DOCTYPE html PUBLIC "-//W3C//DTD XHTML 1.0 Transitional//EN"
"http://www.w3.org/TR/xhtml/DTD/xhtml1-transitional.dtd">
<html xmlns="http://www.w3.org/TR/xhtml" lang="en xml:lang="en">
</html>
```

I've added the xmlns attribute before the lang and xml:lang attributes, since markup convention has determined that traditionally required attributes are coded ahead of optional attributes. This is, however, not a requirement for good coding. As long as the element comes first, attributes may follow in any order. The value of xmlns is a URL. However, this URL doesn't point to a particular document. When namespaces were created, it was determined that there needed to be a way to *uniquely identify* each of the many different available namespaces. The easiest way was to use URLs, since they are already unique identifiers that people are accustomed to seeing. In other words, the URL in a namespace does not point to an actual resource. It is just a way to uniquely identify which namespace is being used.

It may appear to you that this purpose was served with the DOCTYPE statement. Well, yes, it was, but the namespace gives us flexibility beyond what the DOCTYPE statement does. In any single document there can be only one DOCTYPE. This statement should indicate the overall language, and which version of that language is being used to create the document. A single document can, on the other hand, include *more than one* namespace. This is the benefit of adding the namespace attribute. (It's also required for validation.)

For example, let's say that we have a document, written in XHTML, in which we need to include a complex mathematical formula. In the days of HTML, we would create the mathematical formula in one program, create a screenshot of the result, save it as an image, and include that graphic in our document as an image. Using the Math Markup Language (MathML)[2] we can use the speed benefits of text-based MathML to create the formula and present it within our XHTML document.

The first thing we need to do is to specify that our document will be using two different namespaces. To do this we add additional code to our root element.

```
<!DOCTYPE html PUBLIC "-//W3C//DTD XHTML 1.0 Transitional//EN"
"http://www.w3.org/TR/xhtml/DTD/xhtml1-transitional.dtd">
<html lang="en" xml:lang="en"
xmlns="http://www.w3.org/TR/xhtml"
xmlns:mml="http://www.w3.org/1998/Math/MathML">
</html>
```

What we have now declared is that our code is to be interpreted by the browser as XHTML unless it is preceded with mml:. (In that case it should be interpreted as MathML.) Now we need to add some content

```
<!DOCTYPE html PUBLIC "-//W3C//DTD XHTML 1.0
Transitional//EN" "http://www.w3.org/TR/xhtml/DTD/xhtml1-
transitional.dtd">
<html xmlns="http://www.w3.org/TR/xhtml"
xmlns:mml="http://www.w3.org/1998/Math/MathML" lang="en"
xml:lang="en">
<head>
<title>Multiple Namespace Example</title>
<meta http-equiv="Content-Type" content="text/html; charset=utf-
8" />
</head>
<body>
```

```
<h1>MathML/XHTML Example</h1>
<p>This is an example of MathML being used in an XHTML document</p>
 <mml:mrow>
 <mml:mi>A</mml:mi>
 <mml:mo>=</mml:mo>
  <mml:mfenced open="[" close="]">
   <mml:mtable>
    <mml:mtr>
     <mml:mtd><mml:mi>x</mml:mi></mml:mtd>
     <mml:mtd><mml:mi>y</mml:mi></mml:mtd>
    </mml:mtr>
    <mml:mtr>
     <mml:mtd><mml:mi>z</mml:mi></mml:mtd>
     <mml:mtd><mml:mi>w</mml:mi></mml:mtd>
    </mml:mtr>
   </mml:mtable>
  </mml:mfenced>
 </mml:mrow>
</body>
</html>
```

Next, we display the content in a browser that understands both XHTML and MathML. For this example, we'll use the Amaya browser from the W3C.[3] (Figure 2.1).

Figure 2.1   Our Hybrid XHTML/MathML Document as Displayed in Amaya

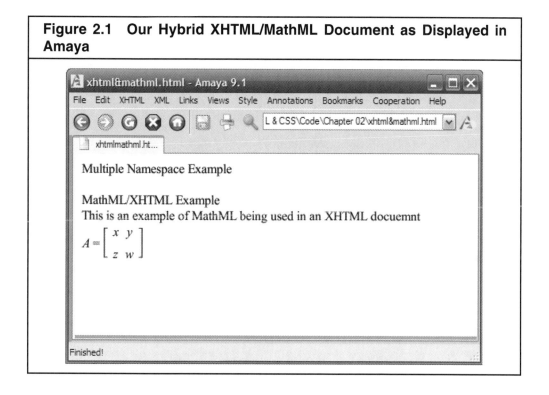

The trouble is, if you attempt to display this document in a browser that doesn't support MathML you'll get the following results (Figure 2.2).

Figure 2.2   Our hybrid XHTML/MathML Document as Displayed in IE6

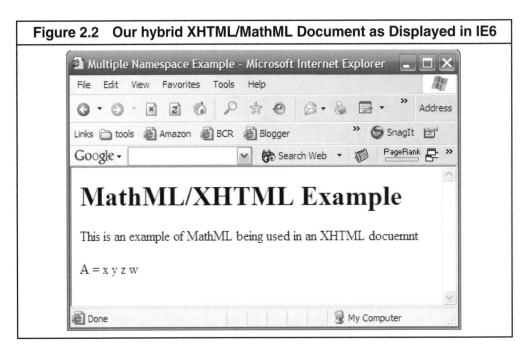

I must admit that I took the long way around to show you this example. There is another way to accomplish the same results with much less code. Since in my previous example, I have a *section* of my document that is written in another language I can move the MathML namespace from the document's root element down into the body of the document thereby eliminating the need to precede every element with mml. Take a look at the following revised code:

```
<!DOCTYPE html PUBLIC "-//W3C//DTD XHTML 1.0 Transitional//EN"
"http://www.w3.org/TR/xhtml/DTD/xhtml1-transitional.dtd">
<html xmlns="http://www.w3.org/TR/xhtml" lang="en" xml:lang="en">
<head>
<title>Multiple Namespace Example</title>
<meta http-equiv="Content-Type" content="text/html; charset=utf-
8" />
</head>
<body>
<h1>MathML/XHTML Example</h1>
<p>This is an example of MathML being used in an XHTML document</p>
<mml xmlns="http://www.w3.org/1998/Math/MathML">
<mrow>
 <mi>A</mi>
 <mo>=</mo>
 <mfenced open="[" close="]">
  <mtable>
   <mtr>
    <mtd><mi>x</mi></mtd>
    <mtd><mi>y</mi></mtd>
   </mtr>
   <mtr>
    <mtd><mi>z</mi></mtd>
```

```
      <mtd><mi>w</mi></mtd>
    </mtr>
   </mtable>
  </mfenced>
 </mrow>
</mml>
</body>
</html>
```

In this example, I've removed the MathML namespace from the `html` root element and placed it on an `mml` root element, closing the `mml` element at the end of the document. This creates a small section of code identified as MathML within my XHTML document.

You may still have one lingering question about why namespaces are necessary. In my previous examples, you can easily identify the XHTML and the MathML elements, although, most likely, all of the MathML elements are unfamiliar to you. So why can't the browser just "know" which elements belong to XHTML and which belong to MathML? In the examples I've provided, one might assume that it could. But (and this is the key), what happens if you have the same element name in *different* languages?

For example, in XHTML `<title></title>` indicates the title of the whole document. But, in the Bibliographic Markup Language (BibML)[4] `<title></title>` indicates "The text of the title of a section of a document or of a formal block-level element."

So in this case we have the same element with two different meanings. What if we used that element twice in one document without specifying to which markup language we were referring? The browser can't guess, so we need to specify. That is the ultimate purpose of XML's namespace attribute.

Your document now needs to be divided into two main sections: the head and the body.

THE DOCUMENT HEAD

Working on the same principle as the human body and thinking from the top, the head comes before the body. The element is `<head>` and is placed in between `<html>` and `</html>`. (I've left two blank lines within the head because I'll be going back and filling them in later.)

```
<!DOCTYPE html PUBLIC "-//W3C//DTD XHTML 1.0 Transitional//EN"
"http://www.w3.org/TR/xhtml/DTD/xhtml1-transitional.dtd">
<html xmlns="http://www.w3.org/TR/xhtml" lang="en" xml:lang="en">
<head>
</head>
</html>
```

The head of a Web document contains information about the document as a whole. As an analogy, think of a letter. The letter has a head and a body. The head of the letter contains information, including the date the letter was written, where the letter is coming from (the return address), and where the letter is going (the recipient's address). This is all information that describes the letter but is not the actual content of that letter. That content appears in the body. The same is true with the head of a Web document. It contains information about the document that is not part of the document's content.

The head of a Web document must contain one important piece of information—the document's title—and should also contain one other—the document's encoding scheme (since we're not specifying it in the XML prolog). The head can also include other information, such as metadata (covered in Chapter 10), style information (covered in the second half of the book), and scripts (not covered in this book).

THE DOCUMENT TITLE

In HTML, document titles were optional, though most Web authors rarely failed to include them. Since titles are crucial to Web documents, the XHTML creators decided to require this element for validation purposes. The element is `<title>`…`</title>`. I've added it to our sample document as follows:

```
<!DOCTYPE html PUBLIC "-//W3C//DTD XHTML 1.0 Transitional//EN"
"http://www.w3.org/TR/xhtml/DTD/xhtml1-transitional.dtd">
<html xmlns="http://www.w3.org/TR/xhtml" lang="en xml:lang="en">
<head>
<title></title>
</head>
</html>
```

Between the open and close title elements you need to enter some content—the text of your document's title. There are good titles and bad titles. Here are a few guidelines for writing good titles.

- *Titles should be descriptive of your document's content.*
  Though this seems like an obvious point, just think about some document titles you've seen in the past. For example, "Page One" is not a good title. It might give you the clue that you're on the first page of something but it gives no information about the content of the document.
- *Shorter titles are better than longer titles.*
  There is only so much space on the screen in which your title will be displayed. If it's longer than that space, most browsers will just cut off the excess portion, leaving it unreadable (or at least incomplete). Short and sweet solves this problem.
- *Keep bookmarks/favorites in mind.*
  When you set a bookmark (or favorite) for a site, some text magically appears to label that bookmark. That text is the page's title. (This is also why "descriptive and short" is a good title guideline. Don't you just love those bookmarks that take up half the screen width because they're so long?) Also, some browsers have automatically alphabetized their bookmarks. Therefore, a title like "Welcome to the Aurora Public Library" would be filed under "W" instead of a more appropriate "A."

Keeping these guidelines in mind, let's add some title text to our sample document.

```
<!DOCTYPE html PUBLIC "-//W3C//DTD XHTML 1.0
Transitional//EN" "http://www.w3.org/TR/xhtml/DTD/xhtml1-
transitional.dtd">
<html xmlns="http://www.w3.org/TR/xhtml" lang="en xml:lang="en">
<head>
<title>Acme Public Library</title>
```

```
</head>
</html>
```

Assuming I'm putting together my library's Web site from scratch and this is the first page I'm writing, it will probably be the home page. So why didn't I title it "Acme Public Library Home Page"? I believe that the phrase "home page" is way overused. I've found that most of my bookmarks are for home pages, so I don't need my bookmarks reminding me that it is a home page.

Additionally, in order to keep my titles consistent, I intend to start all of my titles on all of my pages the same way. Keeping with the title in my example I envision other titles like:

Acme Public Library—Reserves
Acme Public Library—Catalog
Acme Public Library—ILL
Acme Public Library—Hours
Acme Public Library—Borrowing Policy

For a real-life example, take a look at the titles on BCR's Web site at www.bcr.org.

Using this format, not only are my titles consistent across the entire site but they are descriptive of not only the site that contains them but also the content of the page I've bookmarked. Also, they'll all be filed together in alphabetized bookmark lists.

THE RETURN OF THE ENCODING SCHEME

In my earlier discussion of the XML prolog, I mentioned that there is a way to specify which encoding scheme your document uses without using the XML prolog.

The alternate method for indicating the encoding scheme is to specify it in a piece of metadata placed in the head of your document. (I will deal more with metadata, in Chapter 10. For now, I'll just give you the specifics for dealing with this one particular XHTML requirement.)

I've added the needed code on line six of the following example:

```
<!DOCTYPE html PUBLIC "-//W3C//DTD XHTML 1.0
Transitional//EN" "http://www.w3.org/TR/xhtml/DTD/xhtml1-
transitional.dtd">
<html xmlns="http://www.w3.org/TR/xhtml" lang="en" xml:lang="en">
<head>
<title>Mallville Public Library</title>
<meta name="HTTP-Equiv" content="text/html; content=utf-8">
</head>
</html>
```

Let me point out a few particular items about this code. The first is that, since attribute values are case-sensitive, the HTTP-Equiv must be typed in a mixed case as shown. Additionally, it may appear that I am violating the "if it follows an equal sign it must be enclosed in quotes" rule if you look at the equal sign that follows encoding. Actually, the pair of quotes starts after content= and ends after the 8. In other words, in this example, the equal sign following encoding is part of the value for content; encoding is not an attribute itself. If we were to place a quotation mark after content=, there would be an off number of quotation marks in the code (five to be exact), which would wreak havoc with a validator and possibly prevent your document from displaying in a browser, too.

THE DOCUMENT BODY

Lastly we need to give our document a body using the <body>...</body> element. The body contains all of the content of our document that we want displayed to our users in their browser. Here is our revised code:

```
<!DOCTYPE html PUBLIC "-//W3C//DTD XHTML 1.0
Transitional//EN" "http://www.w3.org/TR/xhtml/DTD/xhtml1-
transitional.dtd">
<html xmlns="http://www.w3.org/TR/xhtml" lang="en xml:lang="en">
<head>
<title>Mallville Public Library</title>
<meta name="HTTP-Equiv" content="text/html; content=utf-8">
<body>
</body>
</head>
</html>
```

Despite the fact that our document doesn't contain any actual content, this is a complete document. In fact, XHTML doesn't require that your document contain any content at all. Therefore this document is perfectly valid and complete as it is.

Let's take a look at it in a browser. (Figure 2.3).

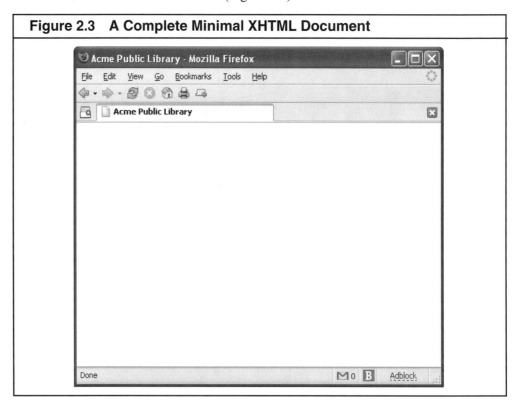

Figure 2.3   A Complete Minimal XHTML Document

There isn't much there, is there? The only way we know that our document is actually being displayed is the fact that the title of our document appears at the top of the window. (The blue bar at the top of a window is known as the "title bar. ") Any content of our document's body is displayed in the big whitespace taking up most of the browser's window. Since we've put nothing between open and close body, that area has nothing to display.

A COMPLETE MINIMAL XHTML DOCUMENT

So, after all that, let's review what the bare minimum is that you must have within an XHTML document in order to have a valid XHTML document.

```
<!DOCTYPE html PUBLIC "-//W3C//DTD XHTML 1.0
Transitional//EN" "http://www.w3.org/TR/xhtml/DTD/xhtml1-
transitional.dtd">
<html xmlns="http://www.w3.org/TR/xhtml" lang="en">
<head>
<title>My First XHTML Document</title>
<meta name="HTTP-Equiv" content="text/html; content="utf-8">
</head>
<body>
</body>
</html>
```

Line one is the `doctype` statement. I've chosen XHTML transitional. I've also decided not to include the XML prolog so as to avoid sending IE into "Quirks Mode."

Line two is my root element with the appropriate XML namespace and the optional language attribute.

Line three starts the head of my document.

Line four contains my document's title.

Line five contains the metadata specifying my document's encoding scheme.

Line six closes my document's head.

Line seven opens my document's body.

Line eight closes my document's body.

Line nine closes my root element and ends my document.

It isn't much, but it is a complete and valid XHTML Web page.

SOME COMMENTS ON HOW TO WRITE YOUR CODE

I wrote this chapter one evening after teaching my basic Web design class in Reno, Nevada. Early in that class, one of the librarians in the class asked me the following question based upon how I'd been presenting the material: When I write code in real life, do I fill in the starts and ends of elements and then go back and fill in the middle as I'd been presenting it to the class, or do I just sit down and start coding from beginning to end. The answer I gave the class has just as much application here. In many cases, when I'm coding a page in "real life" (i.e. ,when not teaching), I code from top down, opening elements, writing their content, and then closing them as appropriate. Of course, many of the Web pages I create regularly, especially those for BCR, have templates that have most of the basic code already written for me, and I just fill in the content in the middle. However, when I teach code, I teach it the way you've been experiencing it so far. I get the code in, opening and closing, and then go back and fill in the middle. In my ten years of teaching Web design, I've found that this is not only the best way to present the material in order for others to understand it, but also the best way to code until you've reached a level of comfort with and understanding of the code. Once you can code a whole page without having to look up any elements, attributes, or values, you're probably ready to give a top-down coding approach a try.

That being said, let's give our document some actual content.

NOTES

1. Several other current browsers also employ a "Quirks Mode"—not just Internet Explorer. So don't think that the problem is unique to Microsoft. I just used IE as my example since it's the only browser that also has a problem with the XML prolog. This is commonly known as DOCTYPE switching. For more information on which browsers use DOCTYPE switching check out the A List Apart article "Fix Your Site With the Right DOCTYPE" at www.alistapart.com/stories/doctype/.
2. MathML is intended to facilitate the use and re-use of mathematical and scientific content on the Web, and for other applications such as computer algebra systems, print typesetting, and voice synthesis. MathML can be used to encode both the presentation of mathematical notation for high-quality visual display, and mathematical content, for applications where the semantics plays more of a key role such as scientific software or voice synthesis. www.w3.org/Math/
3. www.w3.org/Amaya/
4. "BibML is an XML markup language designed to contain bibliographic information, particularly as content exported in Bibtex and Refer notations. BibML also contains content types from DocBook's , and as such may be considered an integration of the three sources." http://kmi.open.ac.uk/projects/ceryle/doc/docs/NOTE-bibml1.html

3

Basic XHTML Markup

Now that we have our minimal XHTML document, we need to give it some content. Your document may or may not contain a considerable amount of narrative content. For example, your library's home page may contain just a paragraph or two of narrative content and be mostly a picture of your library and some sort of menu system guiding users to the other pages in the site. Both the amount and type of content a document has will influence which elements and attributes you'll use.

Since the needs of one library's page may be markedly different from the needs of another, I will present you with the majority of XHTML elements in alphabetical order, rather than in order of perceived importance or relevance. If you are interested in reading about more commonly used elements first, then consider beginning with paragraphs and headings.

This chapter does not cover all XHTML elements. Some elements such as hyperlinks, images, lists, tables, and forms are more complex and are covered individually in future chapters. If you are new to XHTML, I would encourage you to get comfortable with using the elements covered in this chapter before moving on to the more complex elements. But first, let's talk about adding comments to your code.

COMMENTS

```
<!-- -->
```
Strict / Transitional / Frameset

Anything enclosed within the start (`<!--`) and end (`-->`) comment tags is hidden from the browser and also from search engines. (We'll explore the search engine feature of comments more when we get to the world of Cascading Style Sheets.) Comments are a holdover from the programming world. Many programmers are taught to document their code through the use of inline comments not only to explain the logic behind the code but also to pass along instructions to others who may also work on the program, either concurrently or in the future. The use of comments within markup code is inconsequential to many Web designers today. In most cases authors find it unnecessary to add comments to their code since markup is not as abstract as most programming languages. There are, however, a few situations for which I feel comments are highly appropriate.

The first case is in the use of a specific tool or site to generate content. By adding a comment to your code you give credit where credit is due. The following code shows this type of comment.

```
<!--
The following two paragraphs were generated using the Lorem
Ipsum Generator located at http://www.lipsum.com/
-->
<p>Lorem ipsum dolor sit amet, consectetuer adipiscing elit.
Duis vel enim ac urna mollis venenatis. Fusce dictum orci in
diam. Duis placerat, wisi et vehicula ultricies, erat leo molestie
nunc, et rhoncus turpis urna ut turpis. Morbi ultricies volutpat
tellus. Curabitur sodales consequat sapien. Sed placerat. Aliquam
luctus dolor at eros. Vestibulum tincidunt, lectus sit amet
luctus placerat, libero nunc pulvinar wisi, at condimentum tur-
pis nisl at ante. Quisque odio nibh, consequat et, sodales in,
posuere eu, est. Maecenas commodo. Donec placerat pede ac odio.
In vel ante.</p>
<p>Nam laoreet. Vestibulum ante ipsum primis in faucibus orci
luctus et ultrices posuere cubilia Curae; Integer congue. Etiam
magna ante, scelerisque id, volutpat ut, dapibus sit amet,
wisi. Curabitur lacus sapien, dapibus id, semper eu, pharetra
quis, magna. Nullam fermentum venenatis neque. Fusce pede ipsum,
feugiat nec, dictum et, molestie nec, ipsum. Etiam faucibus
suscipit pede. Aliquam justo. Duis risus. Vestibulum lobortis
augue ut magna. Aenean justo dui, venenatis in, aliquam vitae,
tempus et, pede.</p>
```

Additionally, you can use comments to temporarily remove information from a document. For example, if some of the information in your document is time-sensitive (maybe your library's summer hours are different from the rest of the year), you can include all the information within your document but only have the relevant information displayed depending on the time of the year.

The following code shows a section of a document that includes both the regular and summer hours of a library. In this case, the summer hours are not being displayed to the user.

```
<p>Hours:</p>
<ul>
<li>Mon–Fri 9am–7pm</li>
<li>Sat Noon–8pm</li>
<li>Sun Noon–5pm</li>
</ul>
<!--
<p>Summer Hours:</p>
```

```
<ul>
<li>Mon—Fri 9am—7pm</li>
<li>Sat Noon—5pm</li>
<li>Sun Closed</li>
</ul>
-->
```

Figure 3.1.   The Results of Commenting Markup in the Browser

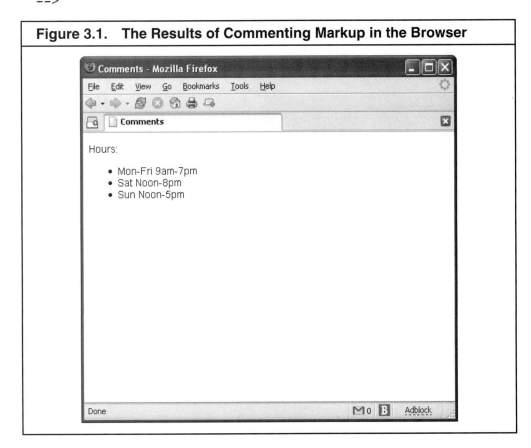

Once the summer comes along, you need only to move your comment markers, rather than retype the hours information.

In this instance you should notice that there is markup included within the comments. This is perfectly acceptable. Anything included within comment tags will be ignored both by the browser and by search engines.

When dealing with comments, it is important to keep in mind that although users cannot see the contents of your comments within the browser, they can still view the source code of your document and read any and all comments you have included. When writing information into comments, you don't want to include anything that you wouldn't want someone else to read.

ABBREVIATIONS

`<abbr>` . . . `<abbr>`
Strict / Transitional / Frameset

The `<abbr>` element indicates that its content is an abbreviation of something else. With the addition of the title attribute today's browsers will display the value of the title attribute as tip text.

```
<p>Welcome to the <abbr title="World Wide Web">WWW</abbr> Library Directory.</p>
```

Figure 3.2. The `abbr` Element

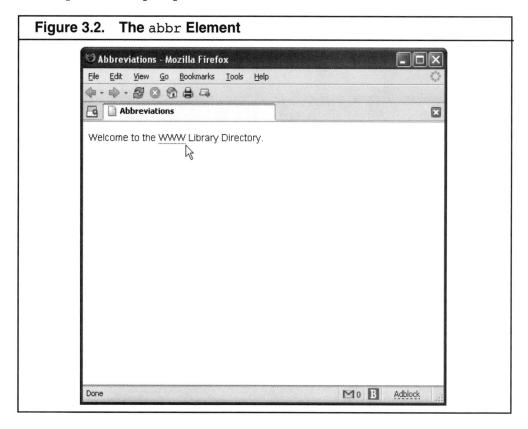

ACRONYMS

`<acronym>` . . . `<acronym>`
Strict / Transitional / Frameset

Similar to the abbreviation element, the `acronym` element indicates that its content is an acronym of something else. With the addition of the `title` attribute today's browsers will display the value of the title attribute as tip text.

```
<li><a href="http://www.awarecenter.org/">AWARE Center Homepage
&8212; <acronym title="HyperText Markup Language">HTML</acronym> Writers Guild</a></li>
```

Figure 3.3. **The** `acronym` **Element with the** `title` **Attribute Displayed as Tip Text**

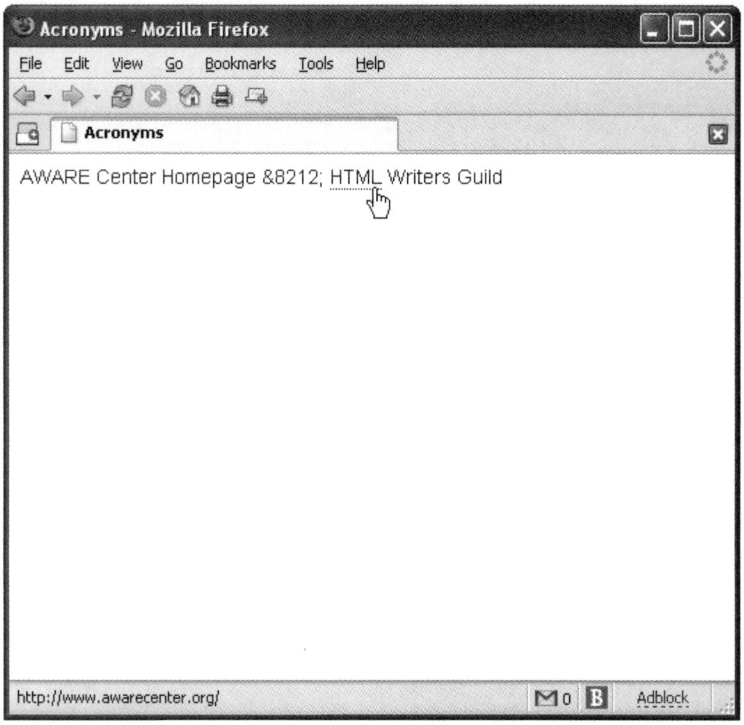

ADDRESSES

`<address> . . . </address>`
Strict / Transitional / Frameset

The `<address>` element is designed to enclose addresses and/or contact information on a page. By default, most of today's browsers will italicize the enclosed content. If you don't want your address information italicized, don't worry. Remember that we can always change the appearance of its conetnt using CSS.

```
<address>
123 Main St<br />
Anytown, CO 80014—1478<br />
(303) 555—6277<br />
(800) 555—1552<br />
Fax (303) 555—9787
</address>
```

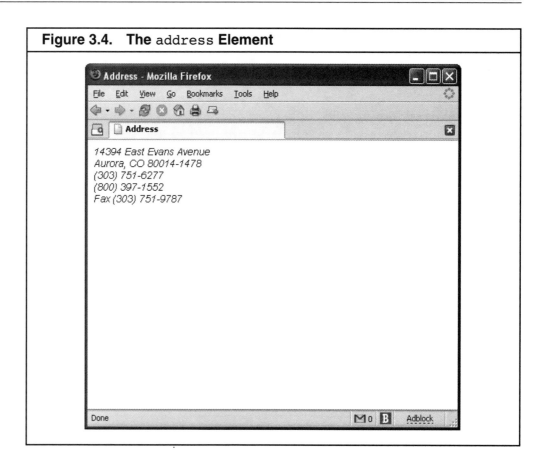

Figure 3.4.   The `address` **Element**

BOLD

`<b> . . . </b>`
Strict / Transitional / Frameset

The `<b>` element causes the contained text to be displayed in bold font in the browser. This element is available in the transitional doctype but not in the strict doctype as it is not a structural element. Use of `<b>` is discouraged and authors should use CSS instead.

```
<p>Several words in this paragraph have been <b>bolded for
effect</b>.</p>
```

Figure 3.5.   The bold Element

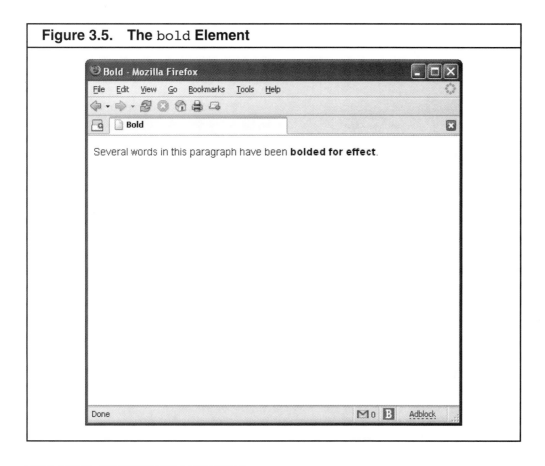

BIDIRECTIONAL ALGORITHM

```
<bdo> . . . </bdo>
```
Strict / Transitional / Frameset

The <bdo> element allows an author to override any default direction of a language and specify whether the content should be displayed left to right or right to left. The dir attribute specifies the direction via the "rtl" and "ltr" values.

```
<p>One of the words in this paragraph is <bdo dir="rtl">backwards
</bdo>.</p>
```

Figure 3.6.   The bdo **Element**

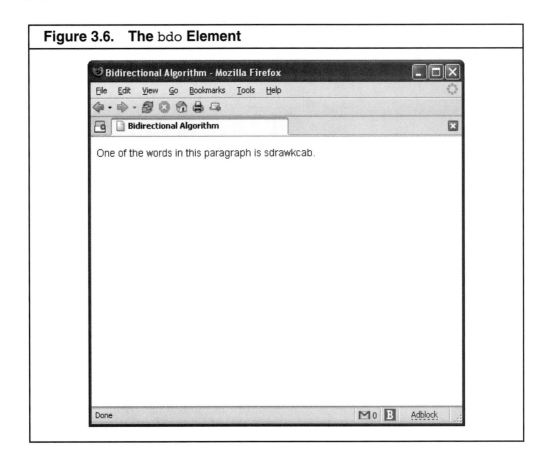

BIG TEXT

`<big> . . . </big>`
Strict / Transitional / Frameset

Content of the `<big>` element will be displayed to the user as one size larger than the current default size of the text. The size of the resulting text will depend upon multiple factors including, but not limited to, the default size of the text as set by the author and by the user's browser settings (Figure 3.7). For example, if the user is viewing your document in Internet Explorer, the default size of text is displayed as "medium" as set by IE. Big text will be displayed in the "larger" text size. If, however, the user has changed the default text size to "smallest," big text will be displayed in the "smaller" size (i.e., one size up).

Figure 3.7. The Firefox Text-Size Menu

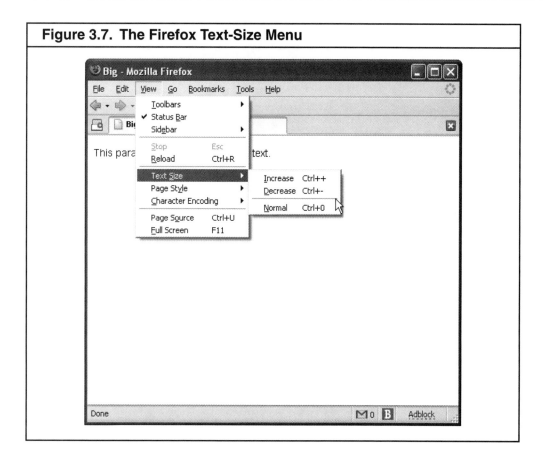

```
<p>This paragraph contains some <big>big</big> text.</p>
```

Figure 3.8.   The `big` Element

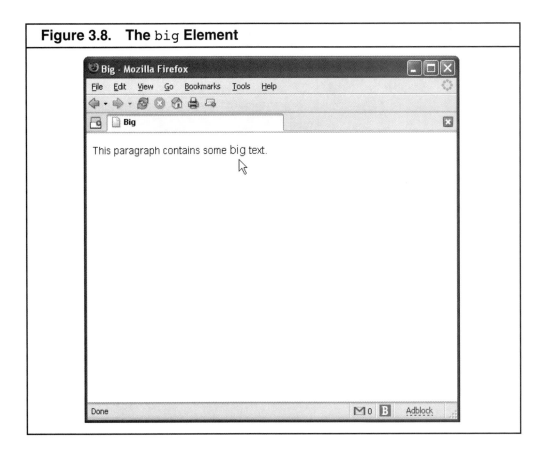

BLOCKQUOTES

`<blockquote> . . . </blockquote>`
Strict / Transitional / Frameset

According to *The Chicago Manual of Style*, a quote of "a hundred words or more—or at least eight lines—are set off as a block quotation." Unfortunately, this is another one of those elements that has been used for stylistic purposes over its structural roots by HTML designers of old, since in most browsers the default behavior of content contained within a blockquote is to increase the left and right margins of the text block by approximately 40 pixels. (This amount varies from browser to browser.) One common misunderstanding is that a blockquote "indents" the block from both sides. This is incorrect. As we will discuss further in Chapter 16, there is a material difference between an indent and a margin change. An indent affects only the first line of a block. A change of margin affects the whole block. Therefore a `<blockquote>`, by default, instructs the browser in a margin change, not an indent. Referring back to the structural purpose, a blockquote is intended to contain long quotes. Unfortunately, many designers have used the blockquote to simply change the margins of the block, regardless of whether the content of the blockquote is quoted text.

Remember that in XHTML, the intent is to specify the structure of the document only. If the content is not a long quote, it should be contained within a paragraph, not a blockquote. If you want to change the margins on that paragraph, that's what CSS is for. Do not use <blockquote> just to change a block's margin.

(Additionally the cite attribute allows you to specify the URL of the source document.)

```
<p>According to an article from Library Spot:</p>
<blockquote cite="http://www.libraryspot.com/spotlight/gates
foundation.htm"><p>In response to the increasing need for com-
puter skills and experience for success in one's education and
career, the Gates Foundation Library Program was established to
partner with public libraries across the country to provide low-
income communities with access to computers, the Internet and
digital information. Initially undertaken by Microsoft Corporation
in 1995 under the title Microsoft Libraries Online!, the Gates
Foundation Library Program was created in 1997 with a $200 mil-
lion cash commitment from Bill and Melinda Gates.</p></blockquote>
```

Figure 3.9. The blockquote Element

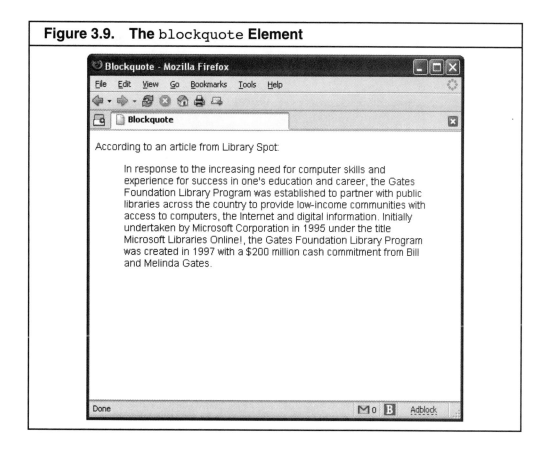

Longtime Web developers may find the use of the paragraph element within the blockquote element to be odd. Though today's browsers will allow you to leave the <p> element out of your code, it would be technically incorrect. Consider that your <blockquote> might contain multiple paragraphs. In that case, the need for the paragraph elements becomes more meaningful.

BODY ATTRIBUTES

```
<body> . . . </body>
```
Transitional / Frameset

I have already covered the <body> element in Chapter 2, but I have decided to repeat it here since there are attributes that can be added to control the appearance of your document. Additionally, none of these attributes appear in the strict DTD. Therefore, it is preferred that the effects be achieved through the use of CSS.

```
link=""
```

The link attribute specifies the color of hyperlinked text within your document (defaults to blue in today's browsers). The following code will result in all unvisited hyperlinks displaying in red.

```
<body link="red">
<p>Connect to <a href="http://odyssey.aurora.lib.co.us/">Odys-
sey</a> the online catalog of the Aurora Public Library.</p>
</body>
```

```
alink=""
```

The alink attribute specifies the color of hyperlinked text while active (defaults to blue in today's browsers). "Active" is defined in the visual world as the period during which the user's mouse has clicked on the link but the mouse button has not yet been released. The following example will have link text display green in this instance.

```
<body link="red" alink="green">
<p><a href="http://odyssey.aurora.lib.co.us/">Aurora  Public
Library</a></p>
</body>
```

```
vlink=""
```

The vlink attribute specifies the color of hyperlinked text after a link has been visited (defaults to purple in today's browsers). The following code will display the link in yellow once the link has been visited.

```
<body link="red" alink="green" vlink="yellow">
<p><a href="http://odyssey.aurora.lib.co.us/">Aurora  Public
Library</a></p>
</body>
```

```
background=""
```

The background attribute specifies that an image is to be used as a background for the document. Images used in this case will first display in the upper left corner of the page and repeat horizontally, then vertically, as necessary to fill the browser's window. Assuming this document is located at server root, the following code example specifies that the `background.gif` file located in the images directory to be used.

```
<body background="images/background.gif">
```

Figure 3.10. The `background` **Attribute on the** `body` **Element**

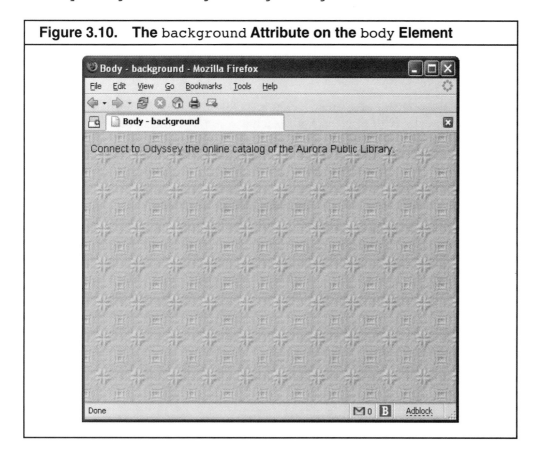

`bgcolor=""`

The `bgcolor` attribute specifies a color to be used as the document's background. (The default is white.) In this example, the background color has been set to a pale green.

```
<body bgcolor="#ccffcc">
```

Specifying color in XHTML

For those of you not already familiar with how to specify colors in HTML or XHTML, the first several examples I gave should have been relatively easy to decipher since I just named the specific color I wanted to use. However, the example for `bgcolor` may have been confusing.

In markup you have two different ways to specify color: by name or by hexadecimal notation. The following is a brief description of each.

Colors by name

There are 140 distinct colors that today's browsers will recognize by name. These include the colors (red, blue, green) along with several shades of each (aqua, deepskyblue, and magenta to name a few). Additionally there are some with very odd names such as linen, papayawhip, mistyrose, and thistle. A complete list of all 140 named colors can be found at www.oreilly.com/catalog/wdnut/excerpt/color_names.html.

Hexadecimal notation

You might assume (and you would be correct) that there are actually more than 140 colors to choose from. In fact, there are exactly 16,777,216 to choose from. Naming all 16-million-plus colors would be impossible, so an alternative was created. The issue becomes how to specify one of more than 16 million options in a code only six characters long. We accomplish this through base-16 (or hexadecimal) counting. Let's take a look at another example of color notation done using hexadecimal.

```
<body bgcolor="#33cc33">
```

First we include the '#' to indicate that we're using hexadecimal notation. We then need to include the six-character code. This code is broken down into three parts: the values for red, green, and blue, respectively. In this case, the value for red is "33," the value for green is "cc," and the value for blue is "33." Each value has a range from zero to 256. In hexadecimal notation, "33" is the same as 51 in "normal" or base-10 counting and "cc" is equivalent to 204. In essence, we are specifying that we want a red value of 51 out of 256, a green value of 204 out of 256, and blue value of 51 out of 256.

The following chart compares counting in base-10 and base-16:

Base–10	0,1,2,3,4,5,6,7,8,9,10,11,12,13,14,15,16,17,18,19,20, 21,22,23,24,25,26,27,28,29,30,31
Base–16	0,1,2,3,4,5,6,7,8,9,A,B,C,D,E,F,11,12,13,14,15,16,17, 18,19,1A,1B,1C,1D,1E,1F

You don't need to learn how to count in base-16. Almost any color chart online will provide the hexadecimal code necessary to replicate any color you choose.

"Web-safe" colors

Whenever you use color on a Web page, you run the risk that your user's monitor will not support some of the colors you've chosen. To minimize this risk, I suggest that you limit your color choices to what is known as the "Web-safe" color palette. This is a group of 216 colors that will be supported by the greatest number of devices. Though this problem is not as significant as it once was, it is still recommended that new authors stick to the Web-safe palette. For assistance, in selecting from the Web-safe palette and the respective hexadecimal notations, visit the VisiBone Webmater's Color Lab at www.visibone.com/colorlab/.

LINE BREAKS

```
<br />
```
Strict / Transitional / Frameset

Line breaks force the content immediately following the element to appear on the next line of the page. This is the equivalent of adding a hard return to a document in a word-processing program. Line breaks are empty elements, requiring the trailing slash to close them.

```
<p>This is an example of a line break.<br />
It is traditional to start the next line of text on a new line
in your code but this is not required.<br />You can run all of
your text and code together if you like.</p>
```

Figure 3.11. The br element

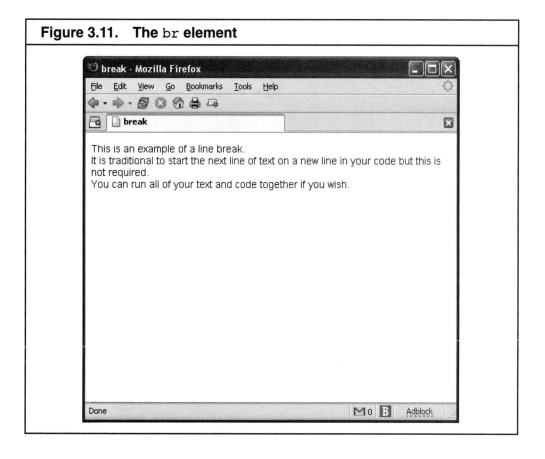

CLEAR

```
clear="right|left|all"
```
Transitional / Frameset

The clear attribute allows you to insert a line break that will not print any additional content until the specified left margin can be reached. (I will go into the use of this attribute in more detail in Chapter 5.)

CENTER

```
<center> . . . </center>
```
Transitional / Frameset

The center element centers all of its content. This element has been deprecated (marked for removal from the XHTML specification) in favor of using CSS to control alignment.

```
<center>
<p>The content of this paragraph will be centered.</p>
<p>The content of this paragraph will also be centered.</p>
</center>
```

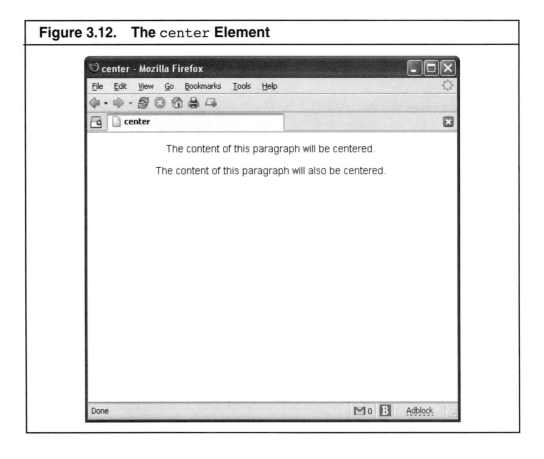

Figure 3.12.   The center **Element**

CITATIONS

```
<cite> . . . </cite>
```
Strict / Transitional / Frameset

The `<cite>` element is used to indicate that you are referencing something in regard to the surrounding text. Today's browsers will display `<cite>` content in italics.

```
<p>More information can be found in <cite><a href="http://
www.faqs.org/rfcs rfc2324.html">RFC 2324</a></cite>.<p>
```

Figure 3.13.　The `cite` element

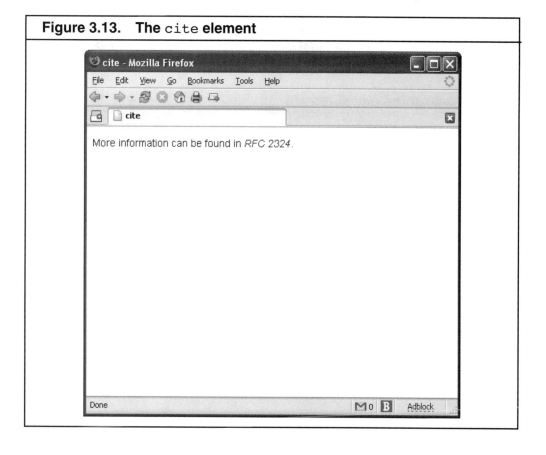

CODE

```
<code> . . . </code>
```
Strict / Transitional / Frameset

The <code> element is used to enclose sample code within a Web document. By default, today's browsers treat <code> content as they would any other content but switch to a mono-spaced font. The <code> element does not preserve whitespace as does the <pre> element.

```
<p>The following lines of JavaScript will display the date the
page was last updated.<br />
<code>document.write("This page has been updated: " +<br />
document.lastModified);</code></p>
```

Figure 3.14. The code **Element**

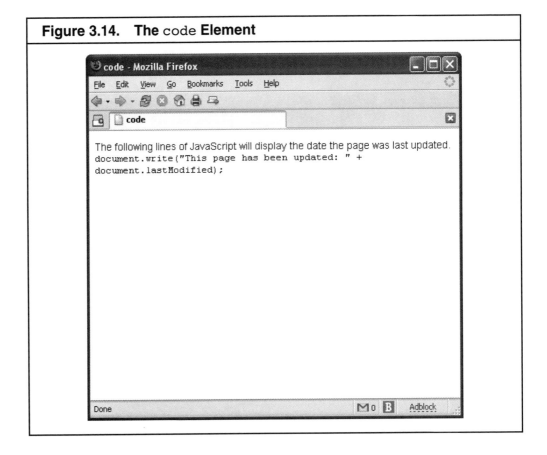

DELETED TEXT

```
<del> . . . </del>
```
Strict / Transitional / Frameset

Content contained within the `<del>` element is content that should be treated as if deleted from the document. Usually used in conjunction with the `<ins>` element, this element directs today's browsers to display this content as though it were struck through.

```
<p>The next meeting of the board is scheduled for <del>Wednesday</
del> <ins>Tuesday<ins>, April 13, 2004.</p>
```

Figure 3.15.   The del **Element**

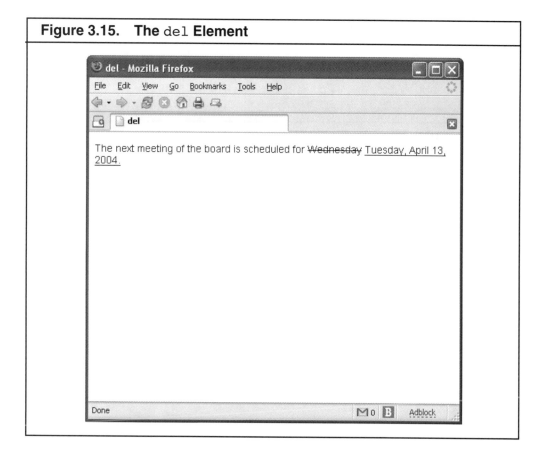

DEFINITION TEXT

`<dfn> . . . </dfn>`
Strict / Transitional / Frameset

According to the W3C, the `<dfn>` element "indicates that this is the defining instance of the enclosed term." On first read, this is a confusing definition to nearly anyone. What it really means is that the content of the `<dfn>` element is being defined within the context of the current portion of the document. For example, in the following paragraph, we are defining "Interlibrary Loan," so "Interlibrary Loan" should be contained with the `<dfn>` element. Today's browsers will italicize `<dfn>` content.

```
<p><dfn>Interlibrary Loan</dfn> is a service that allows you to
borrow materials from other libraries through this library. To
make an Interlibrary loan request you must first search the
library's catalog to make sure we do not already own the item.
</p>
```

Figure 3.16.   The `dfn` Element

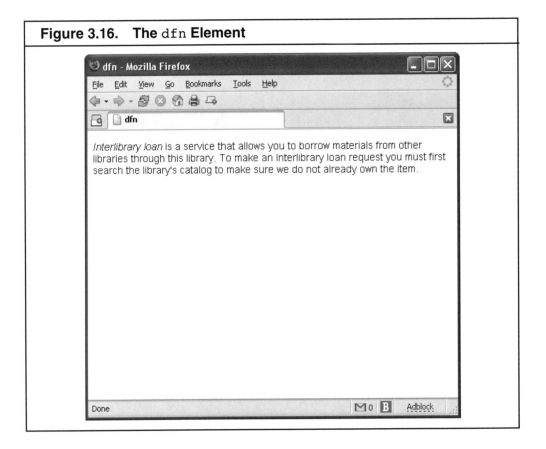

EMPHASIS

```
<em> . . . </em>
```
Strict / Transitional / Frameset

Content contained within the `<em>` element is considered to be emphasized. Today's browsers will usually italicize emphasized text. Many authors have never used `<em>` since it looks exactly like the results of the `<i>` (italics) element.

The use of the italic element does not describe the content of the element. It only provides instruction as to how the content should be displayed. If you are using the element for appearance only, you should use CSS instead of markup. (Also, `<i>` has been deprecated.)

The `<em>` element specifies that the content *has emphasis* (just as I've emphasized the last two words of the previous clause). The benefit of using `<em>` over `<i>` is that `<i>` locks your text into italics. Through the use of the more descriptive `<em>` you can either let the browser determine the appearance of the (usually italics) or use CSS to dictate the appearance directly.

```
<p>The &lt;em&gt; element specifies that the content <em>has
emphasis</em>.<p>
```

Figure 3.17.   The em Element

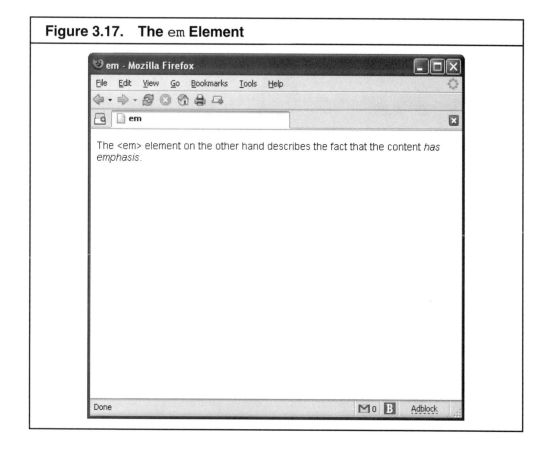

FONT CONTROL

```
<font> . . . </font>
```
Transitional / Frameset

The `<font>` element is the single element that emphasizes concept of "tag soup" that I talked about in Chapter 1. The main reason for this is that `<font>` is an inline element. Because of this, whenever you want to change to a different font, you must close the current font and open another one. In a document that contains multiple fonts (or font sizes or font colors), dozens of font elements can appear, quickly increasing the amount of code within a document. For this reason alone, you are always better off using CSS to control your fonts. That said, the element is still in regular use and I'm sure you'll come across it soon if you haven't already, so I'll give it much more attention than it deserves here.

Font is an inline element that will affect all of its content. The options that are available to you (all through attributes) are the font's face, color, and size.

```
face="font1,font2,font3, . . . "
```

The most common use for the `<font>` element is to change the font that is being used to display document. The font that is currently being used is known as the font's "face." The `face` attribute allows you to specify the name of the font that should be used on the content of the font element. For example:

```
<p>This paragraph will be in the browser's default font.</p>
<p><font face="metro nouveau">The content of this paragraph
will be in the Arial font.</font><p>
```

Figure 3.18. The `face` **Attribute on the** `font` **Element**

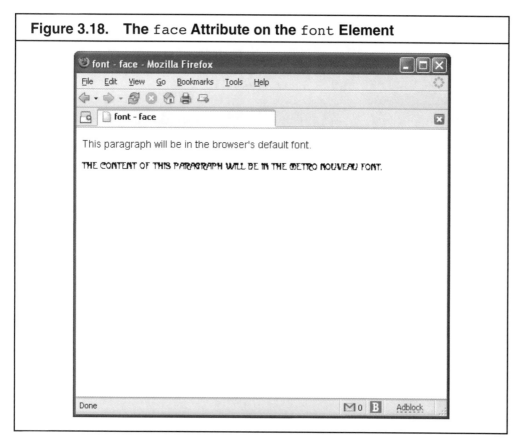

The problem with specifying that a particular font should be used in a document is that the font you specify as the author may not exist on the user's computer.[1] If the font you have specified does not exist on the user's computer, the browser will then default to its own default font. In an attempt to overcome this problem, XHTML allows you to use a comma-delimited list of font names as the value of the face attribute. Keeping in mind that since Macintosh computers do not come with the Arial font, most Web designers also list the Mac equivalent, Helvetica, when specifying the use of the Arial font.

```
<p>This sentence will be in the browser's default font.</p>
<p><font face="arial, helvetica">The content of this sentence
will be in the Arial (or Helvetica) font.</font><p>
```

The space that follows the comma is optional, but standard for most coders. Though not required, if you specify a font name that contains spaces, you should place the name within a pair of single quotes.

```
<p>This sentence will be in the browser's default font.</p>
<p><font face="'comic sans ms', helvetica">The content of this
sentence will be in the Comic Sans MS (or Helvetica) font.</
font><p>
```

```
color="colorname|#hexcode"
```

The color attribute specifies the color of the content of the font element. Color can be specified either by naming the color or by using the hex code for the color, just as I discussed in the bgcolor attribute on <body>.

```
<p>There are <font color="red">a few red words</font> in this
sentence.</p>
```

Figure 3.19.   The color Attribute on the font Element

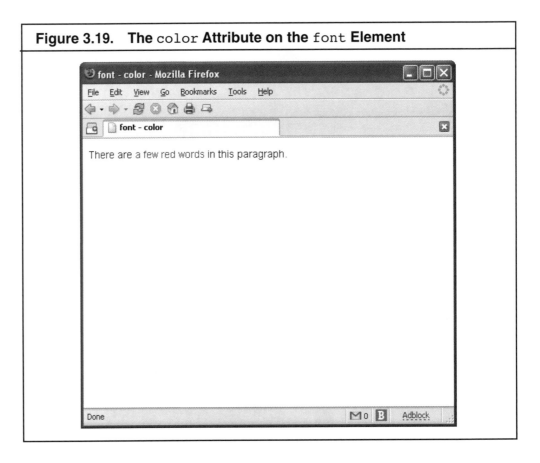

```
size="±n "
```

The size attribute gives the Web author only rudimentary control over the size of the font being used. This is one of the biggest reasons many designers started exploring CSS as a viable option. The ability to control font size is markedly superior in CSS what in markup.)

In order to understand how markup-based font sizes work, you first need to remember that the default font size for your document is considered "size 1." The available size range is from seven to negative two, inclusive but not including zero. Any number you select will then be relative to whatever the font's size was before you specified a value.

```
<p>Most of this paragraph is in the default size. However, some
of the text is set to a <font size="6">size of six</font>, some
is set to a <font size="4">size of four</font>, and some is set
to a <font size="-2">size of negative two</font>.</p>
```

Figure 3.20.   The `size` Attribute on the `font` Element

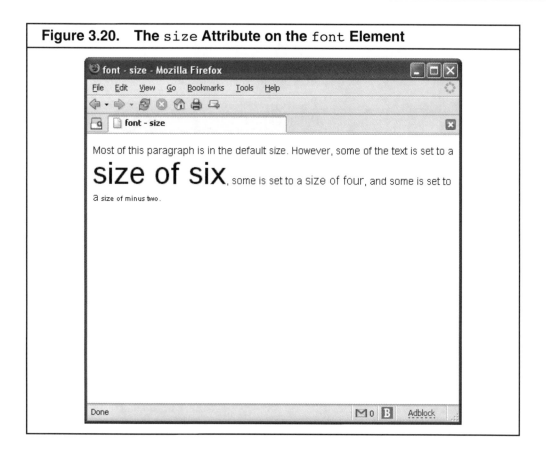

At this point, I will not delve into additional detail on the subject of actual point-size equivalents of the available size values. Instead, I highly encourage you to use CSS to add style to your documents. The following example illustrates why.

```
<p>This paragraph contains some text that has changed <font
color="green">color</font>, <font size="6">size</font>, and <font
face="arial, Helvetica">face</font> individually. It also con-
tains some text that has done <font color="green" size="6"
face="arial, Helvetica"> all three</font>.</p>
```

This is the epitome of tag soup. Just imagine having to repeat any bit of that font code in a document where you have large, green, Arial text a dozen times within a single document. (It could happen.) There has to be a better way. There is—CSS.

HEADINGS

`<h`*n*`>` . . . `<h`*n*`>`
Strict / Transitional / Frameset

Headings are one of the elements that authors have rarely used as they were intended. In most cases, authors have considered how browsers make headings look over what headings are supposed to mean.

Headings are designed to separate your document into sections and to headline those sections. Think of most of the reports that you read. The reports have titles that appear across the title pages of the report. Each major section of the report has a heading that introduces that section. These headings are smaller than the title yet still larger than the main body text.

However, what many longtime Web designers use are headings to generate "big, bold text" and not section headlines. That is exactly what CSS is for.

There are six levels of headings built into XHTML, numbered 1 through 6. This level number replaces the *n* in <h*n*>. In other words, you have available to you six different heading elements: <h1>, <h2>, <h3>, <h4>, <h5>, and <h6>. The catch is that <h1> is, by default, displayed in the largest font, while <h6> is displayed in the smallest font (Figure 3, 21).

```
<h1>Level one heading</h1>
<p>text</p>
<h2>Level two heading</h2>
<p>text</p>
<h3>Level three heading</h3>
<p>text</p>
<h4>Level four heading</h4>
<p>text</p>
<h5>Level five heading</h5>
<p>text</p>
<h6>Level six heading</h6>
<p>text</p>
```

Figure 3.21.   The hn Elements

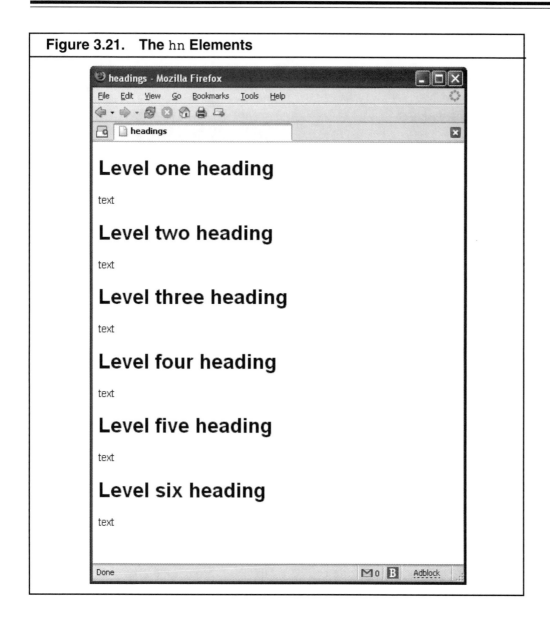

HORIZONTAL RULES

```
<hr />
```
Strict / Transitional / Frameset

The `<hr />` element is used to insert a horizontal rule within a document. `<hr />` is both an empty element (requiring the trailing slash) and a block-level element (always appearing on its own line).

```
<p>This is a sentence.</p>
<hr />
<p>This is another sentence.</p>
```

Figure 3.22.   The hr Element

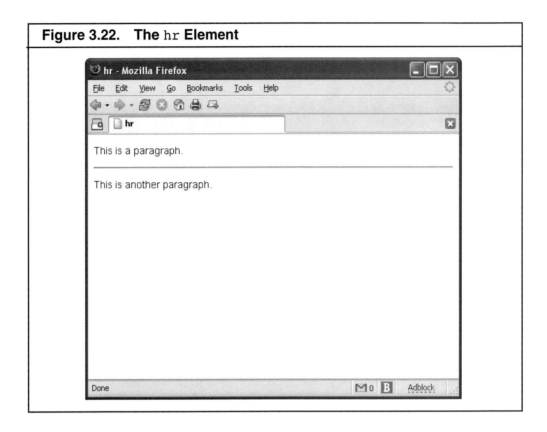

By default, an `<hr />` will take up 100 percent of the line that it is on and will have a 3-D etched effect (Figure 3.22).

The attributes `width, size,` and `align` can be added to the `<hr />` element.

```
width=" . . . "
```

The width of a horizontal rule can be established through the use of the `width=""` attribute. As I have already mentioned, the default value for width is 100 percent. The width can also be set to any other percentage value. For example, if I were to add `width="50%"` to my `<hr />` I would have the following result (Figure 3.23).

```
<p>This is a sentence.</p>
<hr width="50%" />
<p>This is another sentence.</p>
```

Figure 3.23. The `width` Attribute with a Relative Value on the `hr` Element with a Full-Screen Browser Window

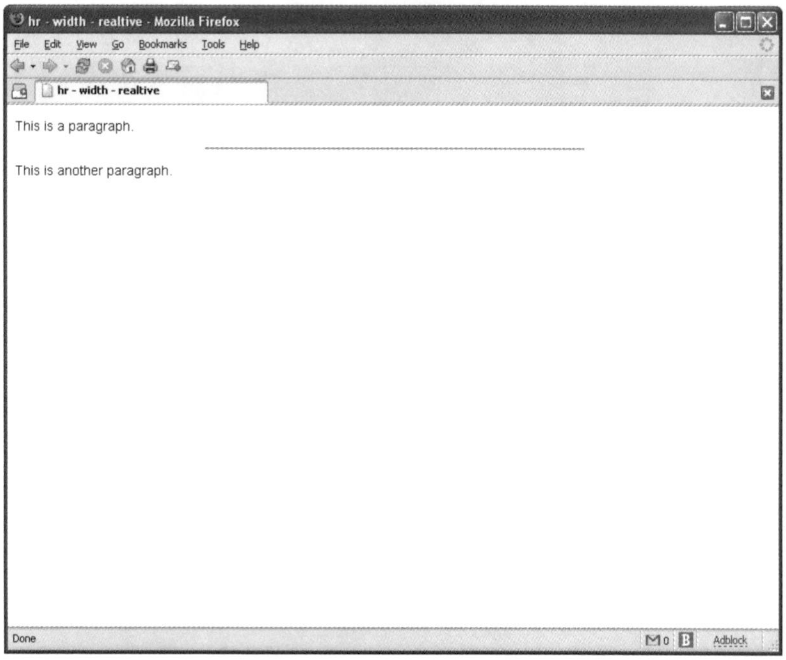

As you can see, the line now takes up the middle 50 percent of the screen. (This assumes that the default value for the align attribute on <hr /> is center.) The use of a percentage as a value is known as a "relative value." This is because, by setting a percentage (in this case 50 percent), the width of the line will be 50 percent of the available space, or relative to the space available. So, if I were to change the width of my browser's window as shown below, the width of the line would adjust accordingly (Figure 3.24).

Figure 3.24.   The `width` Attribute with a Relative Value on the `hr` Element with a Reduced Browser Window

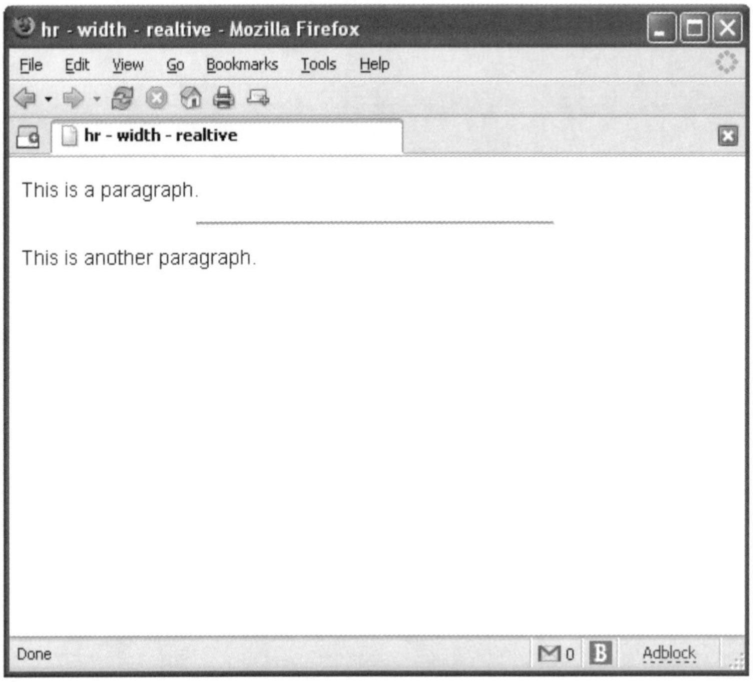

There is another type of value we can use in this case. We can use an absolute value. Let's change the value of width from 50 percent to 600 and see what happens (Figure 3.25).

```
<p>This is a sentence.</p>
<hr width="600" />
<p>This is another sentence.</p>
```

> **Figure 3.25. The `width` Attribute with an Absolute Value on the `hr` Element on a Full-Screen Browser Window**
>

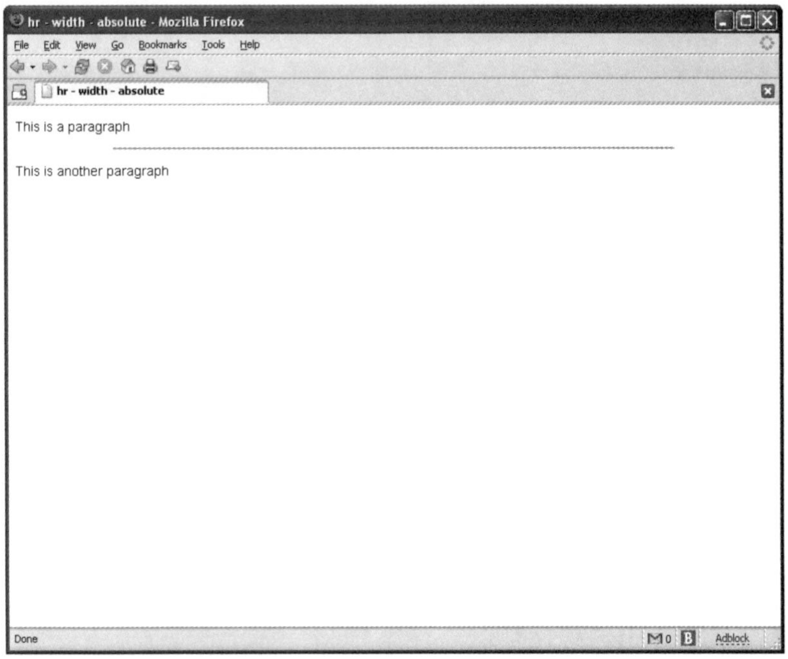

You can see that the line is somewhat longer than it was before. I have specified that the line should be exactly 600 pixels wide. As nice as this may seem, setting an absolute value has some potential negative consequences. Let's shrink the browser window again and see what happens (Figure 3.26).

Figure 3.26. The `width` Attribute with an Absolute Value on the `hr` Element with a Reduced Browser Window

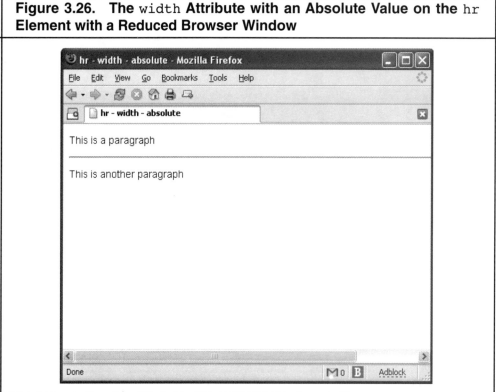

Once the available space shrinks below the size I've set (600 pixels), the line extends past the right edge of the screen and causes horizontal scrolling. This is because since I've set an absolute value, the line cannot adjust as needed.

Rules vs. Reality: Although I'm presenting the absolute/relative issue here, it has applications everywhere you can set a width. Have you ever printed out a Web page and noticed that the page's text and images have been cut off down the right edge of the piece of paper? This is usually because the author of the document has placed the content within a table that has a width greater than 600px (the approximate pixel-width of a piece of paper in portrait mode). Suddenly, the issue of setting an absolute width on something has greater consequence.

The reality of Web page design is that you rarely know what environment your users are in. Do they have high-resolution monitors with more than 1000 pixels to play with horizontally, or are they accessing your document on a cell phone with fewer than 100 pixels horizontally?

I am not saying that you should never use absolute values. There are circumstances in which they are the better choice. Here's how I was taught to approach this decision and how I've taught it for the past ten years. There are reasons to use absolute values. When you think of one, ask yourself if that is the only solution to your problem. If not, stick with a relative value.

ITALICS

```
<i> . . . </i>
```
Transitional / Frameset

This is an inline element that instructs the browser to italicize the text contained within. This element has been deprecated and <em> is the preferred alternative (Figure 3.27).

```
<p>This is a sentence which contains a <i>few words</i> that
are in italics.</p>
```

Figure 3.27.   The i Element

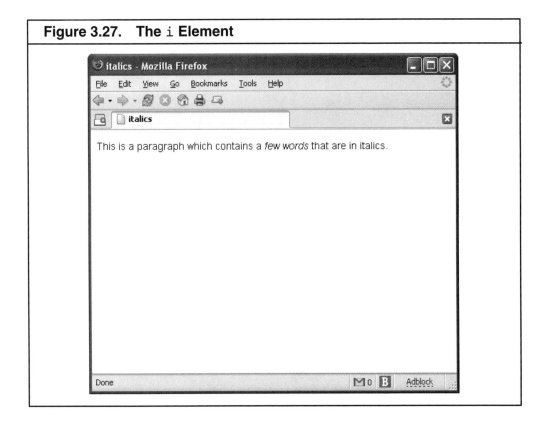

INSERTED TEXT

```
<ins> . . . </ins>
```
Strict / Transitional / Frameset

The <ins> element indicates text that has been inserted into the document, and is usually used in conjunction with the <del> element. Today's browsers will display inserted text as underlined (Figure 3.28).

```
<p>The next meeting of the board is scheduled for <del>Wednesday</
del> <ins>Tuesday<ins>, April 13, 2004.</p>
```

Figure 3.28. The ins Element

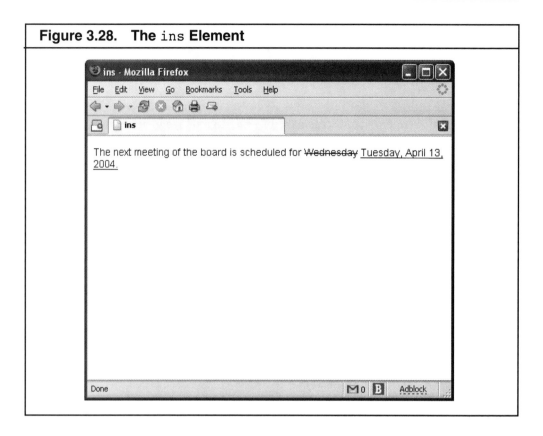

KEYBOARD TEXT

```
<kbd> . . . </kbd>
```
Strict / Transitional / Frameset

The <kbd> element (Figure 3.29) indicates information that should be entered by the user. This element is typically used when giving users instructions involving entering data into a computer. Today's browsers will render this text in a monospaced font and preserve whitespace as with the <pre> element.

```
<p>Enter the following to create a level-one heading:</p>
<kbd>&lt;h1&gt;Hello World!&lt;/h1&gt;</kbd>
```

Figure 3.29.   The kbd **Element**

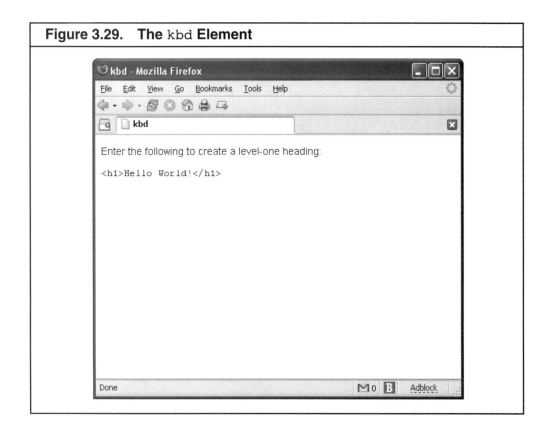

Note: The use of < and > this example is explained at the end of this chapter in the section on character entities.

PARAGRAPHS

<p> . . . </p>
Strict / Transitional / Frameset

The paragraph marker (Figure 3.30) is the most commonly used element in Web design. This is a block-level that contains narrative content.

```
<p>Over the years I've spoken with many librarians concerned
with patron privacy issues when it comes to the library's pub-
lic access PCs. This concern is evident in many library Internet/
computer polices, in which libraries tell patrons that the
privacy of their surfing should not be assumed. While no method
of protecting the privacy of users on the computers is 100%
assured, there are ways to minimize both the amount of informa-
tion and length of time the computer will store information
about your patrons.</p>
<p>The source of the problem is that PCs and browsers are, for
the most part, designed for a one-to-one ratio between the user
and the PC. Granted, Windows does allow you to create multiple
```

```
logins on a computer to separate the different needs of differ-
ent users, but the last thing a library wants to do is to
establish individual user logins and profiles for each of its
patrons. Since no one would ever think this is a feasible
solution, what we end up with is a single login/profile for
hundreds, if not thousands, of users.</p>
<p>This article briefly introduces you to some of the settings
and software hat are available to assist you in protecting your
patrons' privacy when using your public Internet terminals. </p>
```

Figure 3.30.   The p **Element**

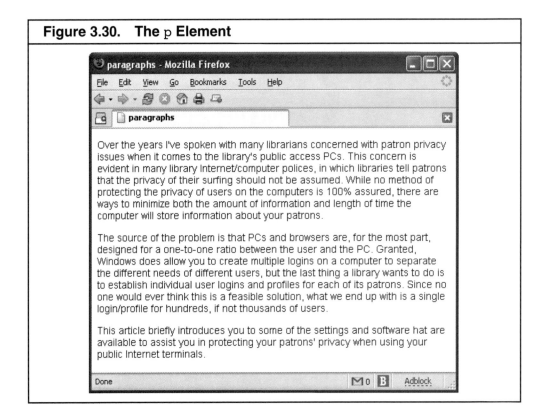

In the past, Web designers have used the paragraph element for two different purposes. The first is to contain narrative content. However, many authors, myself included,
have used it to contain any content, whether narrative or not. In this instance, authors are
using <p> as a generic block-level element, separating its content from other content
with a blank line. (Many a menu has been created in this fashion.) With the advent of the
<div> element, however, this should no longer be necessary. There are two reasons for
this. First, <div> is defined as a generic block-level container. It is designed to contain
content that is not narrative in nature. Secondly, using a paragraph to contain non-narra-
tive content is semantically incorrect. If you cannot describe the content as being a narrative paragraph, then you should not use the paragraph element.

PREFORMATTED TEXT

```
<pre> . . . </pre>
```
Strict / Transitional / Frameset

The `<pre>` element (Figure 3.31) signifies preformatted text. In other words, it contains text whose whitespace must be preserved. Traditionally, preformatted text is used when the whitespace is considered meaningful, as with poetry. However, whitespace may be easily controlled via CSS, so the need for the `<pre>` element has been greatly reduced. By default, browsers will present preformatted text in a monospace font.

```
<pre>
'Twas brillig, and the slithy toves
 Did gyre and gimble in the wabe:
All mimsy were the borogoves,
 And the mome raths outgrabe.
</pre>
```

Figure 3.31.   The pre **Element**

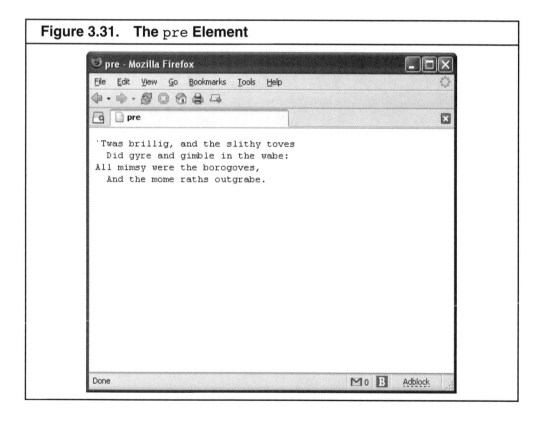

In this example, were the `<pre>` element not used, the additional whitespace at the beginning of the second and fourth lines would not have been displayed. In the past, many authors have resorted to using preformatted text whenever they wanted a monospace font. However, with the use of CSS, this is no longer required nor is it desirable. Additionally, through the application of CSS, preformatted text no longer need be displayed in a monospace font unless that is what you want.

QUOTATIONS

`<q> . . . </q>`
Strict / Transitional / Frameset

The `<q>` element (Figure 3.32) is used to enclose a short quotation. This inline element is not treated differently by today's browsers, so many Web designers have never used it. When used in conjunction with CSS, the `<q>` element enables an author to set all quoted text to be automatically italicized.

The only two attributes commonly used with the `<q>` element (when it is used at all) are `lang` (to specify the language of the quotation) and `cite` (to specify a URL-based source for the quotation).

```
<p>As Han Solo once said <q lang="en-US" cite="http://
www.imdb.com/title/tt0076759/quotes">"Hokey religions and an-
cient weapons are no match for a good blaster at your side,
kid."</q></p>
```

Figure 3.32.   The q Element

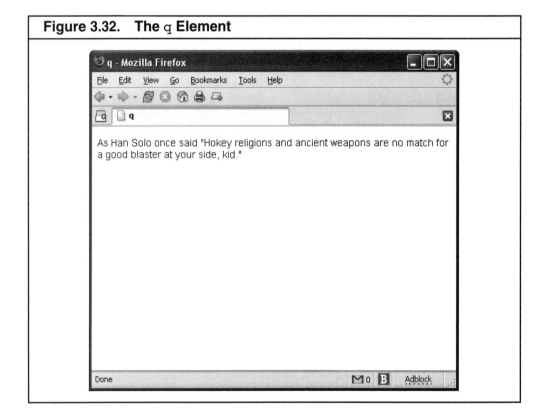

STRIKE-THROUGH TEXT

`<s> . . . </s>`
Transitional / Frameset
See also `<strike>`.

Content of the `<s>` element (Figure 3.33) appears as struck-through text. This element has been deprecated and the preferred method of creating this result is through the use of CSS.

```
<p>This month we had <s>more</s> fewer circs than last month.</p>
```

Figure 3.33.   The s Element

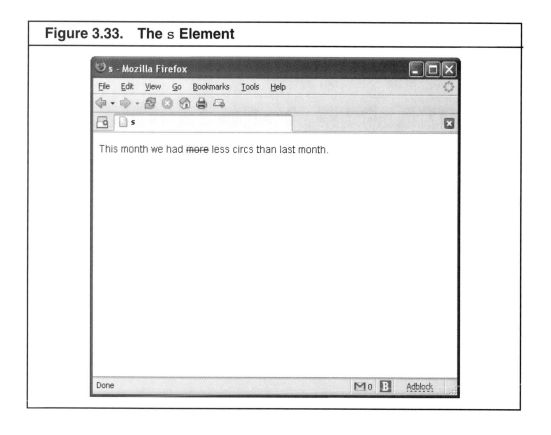

SAMPLE TEXT

```
<samp> . . . </samp>
```
Strict / Transitional / Frameset

Content of the `<samp>` element (Figure 3.34) is considered an example of something, usually computer output. Today's browsers will display sample content in a smaller monospaced font.

```
<p>When attempting to access your library account online, if
you enter an invalid library card number, you will receive the
following warning:<br />
<samp>I can't find that ID. Invalid entry. Please try again.</
samp></p>
```

Figure 3.34.   The `samp` **Element**

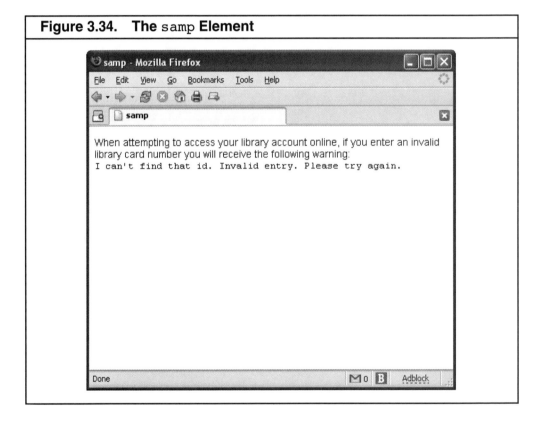

SMALL TEXT

`<small> ... </small>`
Strict / Transitional / Frameset

The `<small>` element changes the size of the enclosed text to appear one size smaller than the text of the parent element. The actual reduction in the size of the text will be relative to the size of the text being used by the browser.

For example, if a user has their browser set to default to a "medium" font, then small text will be displayed in the "smaller" setting. If the browser is set to display the "larger" setting, then `<small>` text will be displayed as "medium."

Figure 3.35.   Firefox's Font-Size Menu

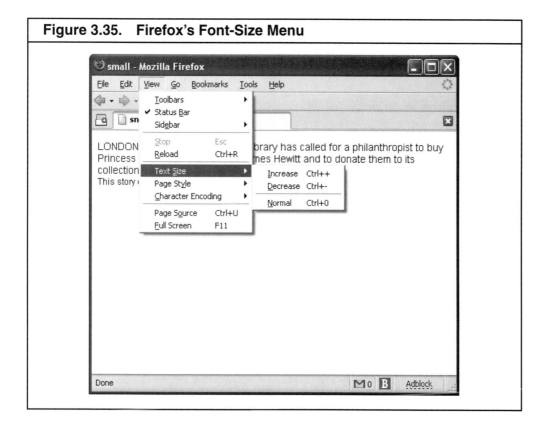

```
<p>LONDON, England — The British Library has called for a phi-
lanthropist to buy Princess Diana's letters to lover James
Hewitt and to donate them to its collection.<br />
<small>This story courtesy of CNN</small></p>
```

Figure 3.36. The small Element

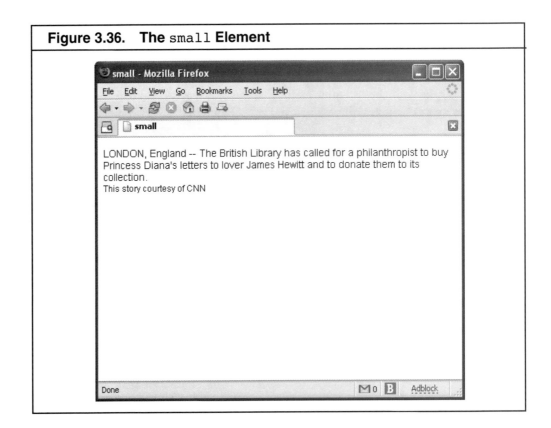

STRIKE-THROUGH TEXT

```
<strike> . . . </strike>
```
Transitional / Frameset
(See also <s>)

As with the <s> element, <strike> displays as struck-through text (Figure 3.37). This element has also been deprecated, and the preferred method of creating this result is through the use of CSS.

```
<p>This month we had <strike>more</strike> fewer circs than
last month.</p>
```

Figure 3.37. The strike Element

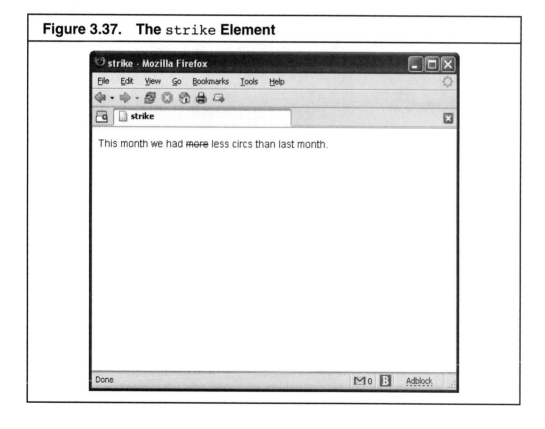

STRONG TEXT

```
<strong> . . . </strong>
```
Strict / Transitional / Frameset

Where the `<em>` element indicates emphasis, the `<strong>` element (Figure 3.38) indicates "strong emphasis." Today's browsers will display `<strong>` text as bold by default.

```
<p>This information is <strong>very important</strong> so please
be sure to read it carefully.</p>
```

Figure 3.38. The `strong` **Element**

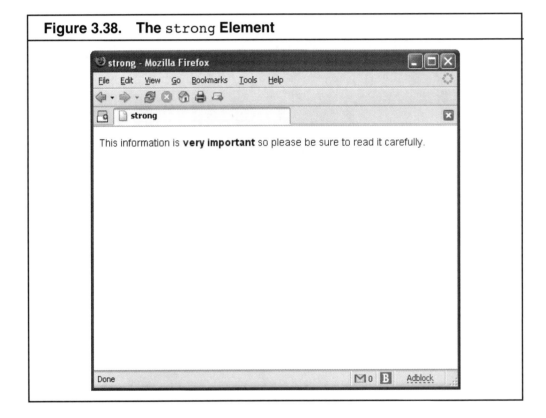

SUBSCRIPT TEXT

```
<sub> . . . </sub>
```
Strict / Transitional / Frameset

The <sub> element (Figure 3.39) indicates subscripted content.

```
<p>Dihydrogen Monoxide is another way of saying H<sub>2</sub>O.
</p>
```

Figure 3.39.   The sub **Element**

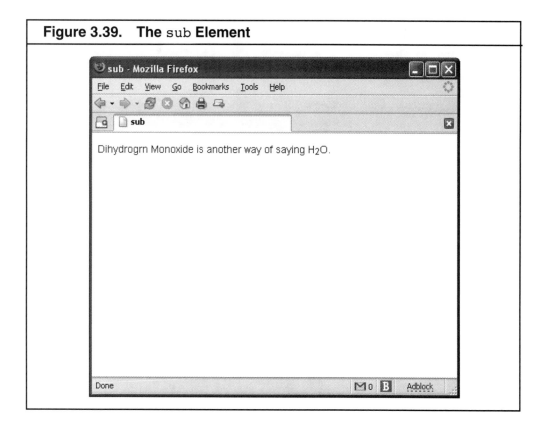

SUPERSCRIPT TEXT

```
<sup> . . . </sup>
```
Strict / Transitional / Frameset

The <sup> element (Figure 3.40) indicates subscripted content.

```
<p>Einstein's famous equation was E=MC<sup>2</sup>.</p>
```

Figure 3.40. The sup **Element**

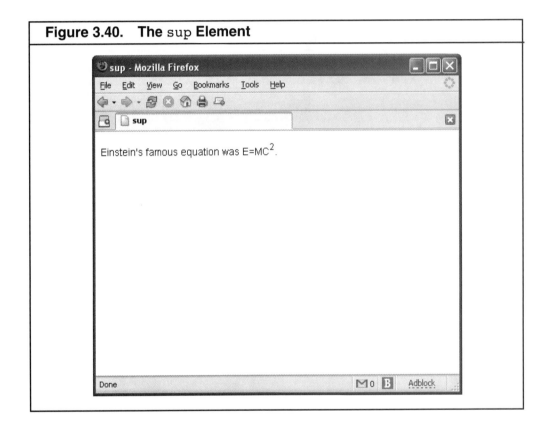

TELETYPE TEXT

```
<tt> . . . </tt>
```
Strict / Transitional / Frameset

The <tt> element (Figure 3.41) presents the contained text in a monospaced font but does not imply any semantic meaning (as with <code> or <kbd>), nor is whitespace preserved (as with <pre>).

```
<p>This sentence contains some <tt>teletype text</tt>.</p>
```

Figure 3.41.   The tt Element

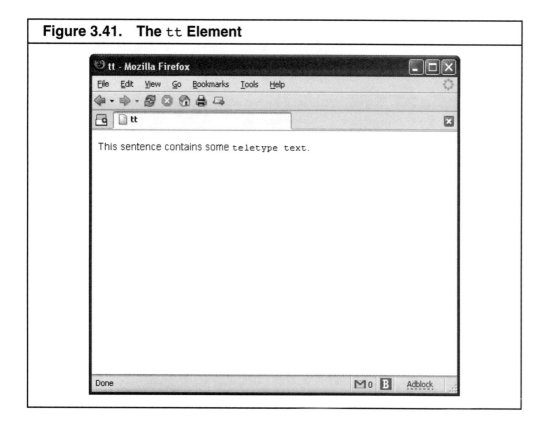

UNDERLINED TEXT

`<u> . . . </u>`
Transitional / Frameset

The `<u>` element (Figure 3.42) indicates underlined content. This element has been deprecated, and it is recommended that underlining be achieved through the use of CSS.

`<p><u>United States v. Nixon</u>, 418 US 683 (1974)</p>`

Figure 3.42.   The u Element

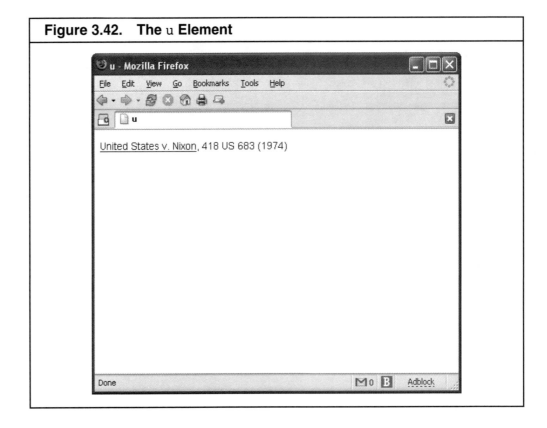

VARIABLE TEXT

```
<var> . . . /<var>
```
Strict / Transitional / Frameset

The `<var>` element (Figure 3.43) is used to indicate that the content represents a variable within the context of the document. Today's browsers will represent `<var>` content as italicized but will not preserve whitespace as they do for the `<pre>` element.

```
<p>The variable <var>n</var> when used in a heading indicates a
number from one to six.</p>
```

Figure 3.43.   The var Element

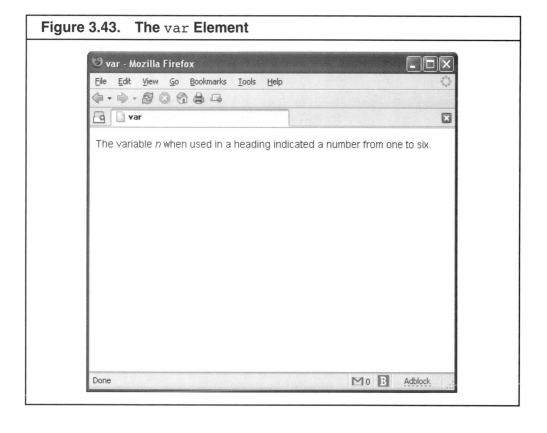

CORE ATTRIBUTES

There are a number of attributes that can be applied to most, if not all, of the elements within an XHTML document. These are known as the core attributes. The following chart gives a brief description of each of them.

Table 3.1
XHTML Core Attributes

class=" *text* "	Used to classify an element as being part of a group. Only used to apply CSS code to the element.
id=" *text* "	Used to identify a particular element within a document. Used for both internal hyperlinks (Chapter 4) and applying CSS (Chapter 13).
lang=" *language-code* "	Used to specify the language of a document. A list of language codes can be found at http://lcweb.loc.gov/standards/iso639–2/langcodes.html
style=" *CSS code* "	Allows for the direct application of CSS code to the element. (Chapter 13)
title=" *text* "	Similar to the alt attribute on images (Chapter 5), this attribute allows the author to provide an additional description of the content of the element. Today's graphical browsers will display the value of this attribute as tip-text.

JAVASCRIPT-RELATED ATTRIBUTES

Beyond the five core attributes there are twelve additional attributes that can be used on almost any element and that activates an associated script. The script is either included as or pointed to as the value for the attribute. The following chart gives a brief description.

Table 3.2
XHTML Javascript-Related Attributes

onclick	Executes the associated script when the element is clicked on (typically used on hyperlinks).
ondblclick	Executes the associated script when the element is double-clicked.
onkeydown	Executes the associated script when a key is pressed down while in a form field.
onkeypress	Executes the associated script when the user presses a key.
onkeyup	Executes the associated script when a key is released while in a form field.
onload	Executes the associated script when the element loads (typically used on the `<body>` element to execute a script when the document is loaded).
onmousedown	Executes the associated script when the primary mouse button is pressed down while over the element.
onmousemove	Executes the associated script when the mouse pointer is moved within the element.
onmouseout	Executes the associated script when the mouse pointer is moved over the element (typically used in conjunction with onmouseover to create rollover effects).
onmouseover	Executes the associated script when the mouse pointer is moved over the element (typically used in conjunction with onmouseout to create rollover effects).
onmouseup	Executes the associated script when the primary mouse button is released while over the element.
onunload	Executes the associated script when the element is 'unloaded' (typically used on the `<body>` element to execute a script when the user leaves a document).

INCLUDING SCRIPTS WITHIN YOUR DOCUMENT

`<script>` . . . `</script>` and `<noscript>` . . . `</noscript>`
Strict / Transitional / Frameset

The `<script>` element is used either to include a script within the document or to specify the location of an external script file to be executed. The most commonly used scripting language in Web pages today is JavaScript but there are others (including Microsoft's VBScript). Since there are multiple scripting languages that can be used, the `type=""` attribute is required to specify which scripting language you're using. The value of the type attribute determines the mime type for the script. If you are linking to an external script file, your code will look like this.

```
<script type="text/javascript" src="script.js"></script>
```

To include script code, specify the type attribute but not a source, and place the code between `<script>` and `</script>`.

```
<script type="text/javascript">
document.write("<h2>This page has been updated: " +
document.lastModified + "</h2>");
</script>
```

The `<script>` element may be placed anywhere within a document. The script will be called and/or executed when the parser encounters the `<script>` element. There is also the `defer="true"` attribute which, when included, will indicate to the parser that the script generates no displayable content (i.e., does not contain any document.write () commands in JavaScript,) and the parser may continue parsing and rendering.

The `language=" . . . "` attribute, which has been deprecated, allowed authors to specify which scripting language was being used. The values for this attribute were never standardized, so the use of the `type` attribute is preferred.

The `<noscript>` element is used to contain alternative content that should be displayed only in cases in which the user's browser does not support scripting or has scripting turned off. Typically, `<noscript>` content provides a message to the user that the document requires scripting support to render the document properly.

```
<noscript>
<p>We're sorry, but our online catalog requires JavaScript to
function properly.</p>
</noscript>
```

INSERTING OBJECTS INTO YOUR DOCUMENT

`<object>` . . . `</object>` and `<param>` . . . `</param>`
Strict / Transitional / Frameset

The `<object>` element (Figure 3.44) is used to include an external file that requires an additional software program to run within your document. Typical examples of embedded objects include Windows and Quicktime videos, MP3 and MIDI audio files, and Java applications. The `<object>` element requires several attributes, including `id`, `classid`, `codebase`, `standby`, and `type` in order to function. The values for these attributes will be determined by the type of object that you are including. Objects will usually include several parameter elements (`<param>`) with which to pass information along to the embedded object.

In the following example I have embedded a Windows Media video file within the document. The included parameters instruct the Windows Media Player to automatically start the video upon loading and allow the user to have access to the user's controls. Of course, the ability for this to work relies on users having the necessary program preinstalled on their computers.

```
<h2>How to use the online catalog</h2>
<object id="mediaPlayer" classid="CLSID:22d6f312-b0f6-11d0-94ab-
0080c74c7e95" codebase="http://activex.microsoft.com/activex/
controls/mplayer/en/nsmp2inf.cab#Version=5,1,52,701"
standby="Loading Microsoft Windows Media Player..."
type="application/x-oleobject">
```

```
<param name="fileName" value="videos/opac.wmv" />
<param name="animationatStart" value="true" />
<param name="transparentatStart" value="true" />
<param name="autoStart" value="true" />
<param name="showControls" value="true" />
</object>
```

Figure 3.44.   The `object` **Element**

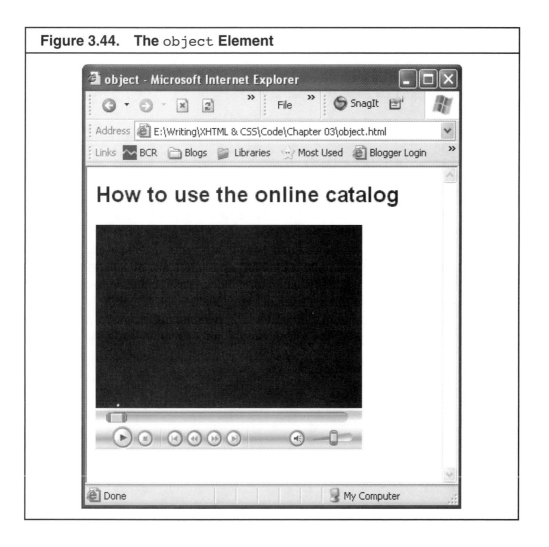

CHARACTER ENTITIES

Character entities, also called special characters, are all the characters you may want to include within your document but that are not available on your keyboard. For example, if you would like to put a copyright statement in your document, how would you type "©"? In a word processor you would access the "insert symbol" command, select the correct symbol, and click the insert button. Unfortunately, in XHTML there is no such button. The method used to specify a character entity is &*value*; where value is either the name of or the numerical value of the character you want to display. Let's look at an actual example (Figure 3.45).

```
<p>&copy; 2004, Michael Sauers</p>
```

or

```
<p>&#169; 2004, Michael Sauers</p>
```

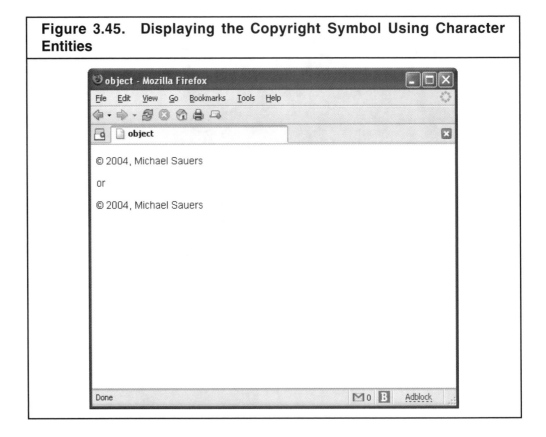

Figure 3.45. Displaying the Copyright Symbol Using Character Entities

Both of these examples give us the same result: a © at the beginning of the paragraph. The first example © uses the name of the character, while the second, ©, uses the numeric value. Notice that we need to precede the value with a '#,' just as we did when using a numeric value to specify a color. All of the possible characters have a numeric value, and most have names. In most cases, using the named value is acceptable and even preferred, since memorizing all of the numbers would be difficult at best. There are, however, a few exceptions. If you want to include an mdash (–) within your document, you might use the name method, `&mdash;`. However, some browsers do not support this, and the numeric value, `&#8212;` should be used instead for better cross-browser support. A reference chart of character entities along with their named and numeric values has been included as Appendix H.

DIACRITICS

If you will be creating any documents in languages such as Spanish or German, you will want to learn the basics of diacritics.

```
&uuml; = ü
&Uuml; = Ü
```

In this example, the first character in the value indicates which letter you're requesting and is followed by the value of the symbol you'd like attached to that letter (in this case an umlaut) Notice also that the first letter is case-sensitive.

OTHER SPECIAL INSTANCES

There are a few additional instances of using character entities that I feel bear mentioning (spaces, greater-than and less-than, and ampersands) due to their built-in quirks.

Spaces

Markup languages collapse extra spaces when they are not necessary. If you still type two spaces after a period out of habit, you may have already noticed that you do not get two spaces when the page is displayed within a browser. (If you didn't notice, don't worry. Most people don't until it's pointed out to them.) If for some reason you feel you *must* have that additional space, you can force the issue through the use of the nonbreaking space character entity.

```
<p>This is an example of forcing additional spacing.  The
trouble is that you need seven additional keystrokes just to
get one additional space.</p>
```

Less-Than and Greater-Than

If you ever need to include a "<" or ">" within your document, it's best to use the matching character entities to display them. The reason for this is to ensure that the browser will not treat the symbols as tags and attempt to interpret their contents as elements. Earlier in this chapter I gave the following code example:

```
<p>The &lt;em&gt; element on the other hand describes the fact
that the content <em>has emphasis</em>.<p>
```

In this case, had I not used < and > it would have started the <em> element instead of displaying "<em>" on the screen.

Ampersands

Browsers today will allow you to get away with a lot of things in your coding that you shouldn't be able to do. Once you start working in XHTML, one of your primary goals should be to write good clean code. Running your code through a validator will force you to do this. One of the most commonly asked questions on XHTML mailing lists these days results from the following validator error:[2]

```
cannot generate system identifier for general entity "something"
```

Here is the code that caused this error:

```
<p>The presenters of the program will be Mr. Smith of the law
firm of Dewey, Cheatam & Howe.</p>
```

What happens here is that the parser/validator sees "&" and expects it to be followed by some text and a semicolon. Because it sees the ampersand, it thinks that we're giving it a character entity even though that is not our intention. The solution: Whenever you need to put an ampersand in your code and are not starting a character entity, replace it with &. Our revised and corrected code now reads:

```
<p>The presenters of the program will be Mr. Smith of the law
firm of Dewey, Cheatam &amp; Howe.</p>
```

NOTES

1. This is a problem no matter which method you use to specify a font's face.
2. We'll be covering XHTML validation in Chapter 11. For now, all you need to understand is that a validator is a program that checks your markup to make sure you're following the rules of the language you're using.

4

Hyperlinks

Hyperlinks are what put the hypertext in the eXtensible Hypertext Markup Language. By placing hyperlinks (also known as 'links') within a document, you make the connections between multiple documents (or between locations within a single document) that allow your users to move from one location to another. There are different types of hyperlinks available to you as an author. The way I like to describe them makes use of the following chart:

A	B
External	Absolute
Internal	Relative

When describing the types of hyperlinks available, you get one descriptor from column A and one descriptor from column B. Although mathematically there are four possibilities, there are actually only three options. They are external absolute, external relative, and internal relative. (We'll discuss Internal Absolute hyperlinks at the end of the chapter.)

ANCHORS

The element used to create a hyperlink is known as an anchor. The code for an anchor element is `<a> . . . </a>`. The content that appears within the anchor is what the user can then click on. In the following example, which words will the user be able to click on?

```
<p>This link will take you to <a>Google</a>.</p>
```

If you said the answer is "Google," you would be right. If you type this code, however, the word will not actually be clickable. We have another piece of code to fill in before it will actually work.

Before I show you that code I'd first like to talk to you about the theory of writing "good" hyperlinks.

WRITING GOOD HYPERLINKS

Compare the previous example with this revision:

```
<p>This <a>link</a> will take you to Google.</p>
```

Assuming that we have included the additional code to make this link work, what is the difference between the two examples?

The answer is that in the first example, "Google" is the hyperlinked word, and in the second, "link" is the hyperlinked word. Assuming that if either link were to be clicked on, we would end up at the Google Web site, the next question is which of the two examples would be preferable.

The correct answer is the first example, the one in which the word "Google" is the content of the anchor. A well-written hyperlink should describe where the user will end up *even if it is taken out of context*. Let's look at another example and then apply this principle.

```
<p>Welcome to the Acme Public Library. If you would like infor-
mation on our hours <a>click here</a>. Information on our
<a>checkout policy</a> is also available.</p>
```

In this example we have two potential hyperlinks. Now, let's look at those two links out of the context of the rest of the paragraph.

click here
checkout policy

Ask yourself the following questions: If I were to click on "click here," where would I end up? If I were to click on "checkout policy," where would I end up?

A user clicking on "checkout policy" might assume that they would arrive at a document that would contain information about the checkout policy of the library. We don't know what a user might assume about what page they'll end up on if they click on "click here."[1]

You may be asking yourself what sort of user would ever see a list of your hyperlinks without their contextual components. The IBM Homepage Reader is a prime example (Figure 4.1). This browser is designed for visually impaired users and reads the content of your page aloud to the user.[2] One of its features is a list of all the hyperlinks in the current document shown down the left side of the screen which the user can navigate with the keyboard. As the cursor moves through the list of hyperlinks, they are read to the user *without context*. (If you think one "click here" is unclear, imagine a user hearing "click here, click here, click here," etc. This renders the page practically useless to the user.)

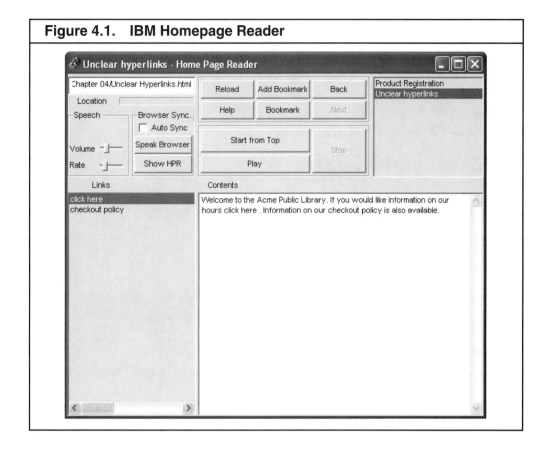

Figure 4.1. IBM Homepage Reader

A problem specific to "click here" is that it's commonly used as a lexical crutch. There is always a better way to write any sentence on a Web page that includes "click here." In the previous example I could have written, "for our circulation policy, click here" but "our circulation policy" is better still.

MAKING A HYPERLINK WORK

Before our hyperlink will work, we need to add an important piece of information—the location of the document we would like to link to. This information will be given in the form of the URL of the linked document and is given as the value of the href attribute.

To link to Google, our revised code is:

```
<p>This link will take you to <a href="http://www.google.com/">
Google</a>.</p>
```

Referring to the hyperlink description chart, let's think about the choices in column A: external or internal.

This is an external hyperlink. Not because we've linked to another remote location on the Internet, but because we have linked from one document to another document. If I linked from one of the documents on my Web site to another document on my Web site, this would still be an external link. In other words, I have linked to a location external to this document (another page). The ownership of the document does not matter. If I have linked from one document to another, I have created an external hyperlink.

The next choice is from column B: absolute or relative? The answer is that this is an absolute hyperlink. In order to explain, I first need to introduce you to how URLs are constructed. Uniform Resource Locators, or URLs (also known as Uniform Resource Indicators, URIs) are comprised of four parts that are relevant to this discussion. Here's a sample URL to work with (Figure 4.2).

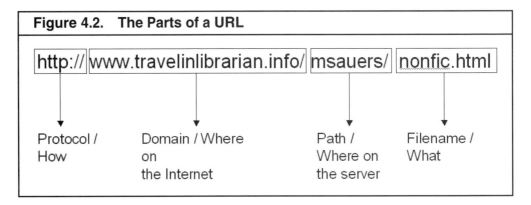

Figure 4.2. The Parts of a URL

As you can see I have labeled the four parts. Here they are in more detail.

- *The protocol (how).*
  This part specifies by which method (protocol) the information should be transferred from the remote computer to the user's computer. If you are linking to another Web page (as you likely will be most of the time), the protocol will be "`http://`" to specify the HyperText Transport Protocol. Other protocols include `gopher://`, `ftp://` (File Transfer Protocol), `wais://` (Wide Area Information Server), `telnet://`, and `https://` (HTTP Secure), each of which should be used only when the situation requires it. The protocol is required in an external hyperlink regardless of the fact that today's browsers will allow you to omit it when typing in a URL.
- *The domain (where on the Internet).*
  This section specifies the name of the computer and in which domain the remote document is located. In this example, we are requesting a document from the computer named "www" in the "travelinlibrarian.info" domain.[3] This information is required in an external hyperlink.
- *The path (where on the computer).*
  This section specifies the directory path within the remote computer on which the requested file is located. The path is optional and is not in all URLs. If a path is not given, the home of "server root" directory is assumed.
- *The filename (what)*
  In this example, we are requesting a particular file "fiction.html." This information is optional. Without it, the remote Web server will send back to the user whatever the default file is set for in the specified (or assumed) path. In most cases this file is named either "index.html" or "default.html."

Taking these explanations into account, our sample URL is external since it specifies both the required parts of a URL – the protocol and the domain. Referring to our Google example, this is an external hyperlink because we've specified the protocol and the domain. (Since we haven't specified a path or a filename, the remote server will assume we want the default file in the root (top) of the site. Try going to http://www.google.com/ and http://www.google.com/index.html and see if you get the same result. You will.[4]

Before you take my word for all this let's look at another one of our types of hyperlinks and you'll start to see things falling into place. To do this you'll need two files to work with. Make a copy of the index.html file off the root of the CD-ROM into a temporary directory. Then create a new XHTML file with the following link in it:

```
<p>Here is a link to the <a href="index.html">home page</a> I
copied from the CD-ROM to my hard drive.</p>
```

Save your new file and open it in your browser. Click on the link and see where you end up. You should now be looking at the page you copied off the CD-ROM.

Is this an external or internal hyperlink? It's external because we've linked from one document (the one we created) to another (the one we copied). Notice that in this example, both of the documents are on the same computer.

Is this an absolute link or a relative link? By process of elimination you've probably guessed that this is indeed a relative link. It is relative because we have *not* specified either the protocol or domain. When you don't, http:// will be assumed. But that leaves us with the question of how the browser knew where to look for the other file. The browser looked for the other file *relative* to the file that contains the anchor. Since the file with the anchor is in the temp directory you created, it will look for the linked file in the same directory.

Let's look at a slight revision to our anchor code. Try to figure out where your browser will look for the index.html now.

```
<p>Here is a link to the <a href="junk/index.html">home page</
a> I copied from the CD-ROM to my hard drive.</p>
```

In this example I have specified both a path and a filename. It's still a relative link, since I haven't specified a protocol or a domain, so it will start where the anchor is, in your temp directory, and then look in the "junk" directory (folder) for the index.html file. (This won't work unless you also created a "junk" folder and moved the index.html file into it.)

Moving between documents within the directory structure of your Web site via relative hyperlinks can get very complicated very quickly. Additional information on "pathing" through your site is included in Resource I on the companion Web site.

HOW TO CHOOSE BETWEEN ABSOLUTE AND RELATIVE HYPERLINKS

For those of you who thought about the ownership of Web pages when you first chose between external and internal hyperlinks, you had the right answer, but to the wrong question. The concept of page ownership is not an issue for external vs. internal hyperlinks. Instead it's an issue for absolute vs. relative hyperlinks. The rule is that, whenever you link to a Web site on a different server (i.e., owned by someone else), you must use an absolute hyperlink. The moment you attempt to link between two different computers, you must specify the domain of the other computer. Once you've specified the domain, you must also specify the protocol. Once you've done both, you have, by default, an absolute hyperlink.

That does not mean that if you're linking between two pages on your own site, you must use a relative hyperlink, but you should anyway. If I link from the BCR homepage to BCR's page about reference databases and used an absolute URL, the link would look like this:

```
<a href="http://www.bcr.org/reference/">Reference Databases</a>
```

Since both of the pages are on the same server I could use a relative hyperlink instead.

```
<a href="reference/">Reference Databases</a>
```

The immediate benefit is less typing and therefore a faster-loading page. The other benefit is much less apparent—you're planning ahead.

To illustrate this, take the two files you have in your temp directory and copy them to a floppy disk. Imagine that the floppy disk is another Web server. If you have another computer you can use, move the file to another computer. Now open your file and click on the link. Provided that both files were moved together (i.e., still both in a single directory), the link will still work. This is the other benefit. If you moved your files, the links within the site will still work. If you had used an absolute hyperlink, specifying the name of the computer (or hard drive) that your pages were on and then moved them to another computer (or floppy disk), the browser would look in the old location for the linked file and fail to find it.

You probably don't expect ever to move your Web site to another computer, but one day you might. Often a site that is undergoing a major redesign will be copied to an alternate server on which the work will be done so that the live site is not interrupted. If you did this with a site full of absolute hyperlinks, none of the links that should have been relative would work on the alternate server. It is better to be prepared for this possibility by using relative hyperlinks than to use absolute hyperlinks now and have to change them all later.

RECONFIGURING RELATIVITY

An additional element placed in the head of your document will directly affect all relative hyperlinks within your document. The element is <base />, and when you place it in your document, all relative hyperlinks will be relative to its value instead of the location of the page. (Base is an empty element and requires the trailing slash to close it.)

Let's say that our current document is located in the "reference" directory (/reference/index.html) and we want to link to the about.html file in the "oed" subdirectory. Our hyperlink would look like this:

```
<!DOCTYPE html PUBLIC "-//W3C//DTD XHTML 1.0 Transitional//EN"
"http://www.w3.org/TR/xhtml/DTD/xhtml1-transitional.dtd">
<html xmlns="http://www.w3.org/TR/xhtml" lang="en">
<head>
<title>Internal Hyperlink Demonstration Document</title>
<meta name="HTTP-Equiv" content="text/html; content="utf-8">
```

```
</head>
<body>
<p>Find out <a href="about/oed.html">more information about the
Online Oxford English Dictionary</a>.</p>
</body>
</html>
```

This is the default behavior for a relative hyperlink. It would start in /reference (since that is where we already are) and then look in /reference/about for the oed.html file. We'd end up at /reference/about/oed.html.

Now, let's add a new line to the head of our document.

```
<!DOCTYPE html PUBLIC "-//W3C//DTD XHTML 1.0 Transitional//EN"
"http://www.w3.org/TR/xhtml/DTD/xhtml1-transitional.dtd">
<html xmlns="http://www.w3.org/TR/xhtml" lang="en">
<head>
<title>Internal Hyperlink Demonstration Document</title>
<meta name="HTTP-Equiv" content="text/html; content="utf-8">
<base href="http://www.bcr.org/" />
</head>
<body>
<p>Find out <a href="about/oed.html">more information about the
Online Oxford English Dictionary</a>.</p>
</body>
</html>
```

The href attribute on the <base> element decrees that all relative hyperlinks within this document must be considered relative to the URL value, *not* to the current location. If we were to click on this link, we could end up at http://www.bcr.org/about/oed.html.

Needless to say, the benefits of doing this are minimal. The only time I've ever seen it used is in documents that were written by certain Web development programs that automatically inserted the URL of the document's location, a useless and redundant use of code.

INTERNAL HYPERLINKS

An internal hyperlink links two locations *within the same document*. If you've ever clicked on a hyperlink at the bottom of a document that sent you back to the top of the document, you've used an internal hyperlink. Setting up an internal link in a document is a two-step process. Step one is to create the anchor that the user will click on. Let's look at a sample document.

```
<!DOCTYPE html PUBLIC "-//W3C//DTD XHTML 1.0 Transitional//EN"
"http://www.w3.org/TR/xhtml/DTD/xhtml1-transitional.dtd">
<html xmlns="http://www.w3.org/TR/xhtml" lang="en">
<head>
<title>Internal Hyperlink Demonstration Document</title>
<meta name="HTTP-Equiv" content="text/html; content="utf-8">
</head>
```

```
<body>
<h1>This document demonstrates the creation of internal
hyperlinks</h1>
<p>There are many paragraphs of information in this document.
I've edited them out for the sake of simplicity.</p>
. . .
<hr />
<p>&copy; 2003, Acme Public Library<br />
Last Updated: 29 November 2003<br />
Back to top</p>
</body>
</html>
```

The last paragraph in the document (essentially the footer) is where we need to create the anchor, so I'll add the code that is included within all types of hyperlinks.

```
<a href="">Back to top</a></p>
```

Now we need to tell the link where to go. By default, browsers assume all hyperlinks are external unless specified otherwise. To specify that a hyperlink is internal we place a "#" as our value.

```
<a href="#">Back to top</a></p>
```

This indicates to the browser that we are looking for a location *within* this document. Without it, and without an "http://", the browser will assume we're looking either for a path or a filename relative to this file—an external link.

We follow the pound sign with the name of the location at which we want to be sent to. Since names are not built into the document, we get to make up whatever we want. However, there are certain guidelines that you should keep in mind when devising a location name.

- Names are case-sensitive. You can use capital letters if you want to, but I recommend using all lower case so you don't have to remember whether you used capital letters.
- Names should be descriptive. You could call our sample internal link #bob but that would hardly be descriptive of where we're linking to.
- Names cannot begin with a number. They must begin with a letter.
- Punctuation should be avoided. Although some punctuation is allowed (hyphens and underscores, for example,) it's just easier to avoid them altogether.

Working with these guidelines, let's call the location we're linking to "#top." Our code now reads:

```
<a href="#top">Back to top</a></p>
```

We have now told the browser that we want to go to a location in this document we know of as "top." The trouble is that the browser doesn't know where "top" is.[5] There are two ways to tell the browser where "top" is. I'll cover both of them and then discuss when you should use one versus the other.

name="top"

The first (and older) way is to name a particular location within your document through the use of another anchor and the `name=""` attribute. To do this we must first decide which line of content we want to have at the top of the browser window after we've clicked on our link. In this case, the level-one heading is the appropriate choice. We need to edit that line of code like this:

```
<a name="top"><h1>This document demonstrates the creation of internal hyperlinks</h1></a>
```

Notice that I have matched the word **"top"** exactly in both locations. However, the *"#"* is not repeated in the **name** attribute. If you put the # here, it won't work.[6] This method will work in all of today's browsers.

Rules vs. Reality: Many "old-time" HTML developers would have left off the </a> in the above code. Although the browsers will allow this, the XHTML will not validate since, if you open an anchor, you must always close it.

id="top"

The other (and newer) way to accomplish the same task is to use the `id=""` attribute on the element you're linking to. Here is how the code would look using this method.

```
<h1 id="top">This document demonstrates the creation of internal hyperlinks</h1>
```

In this case we've *identified* the content of the level-one heading as being the location known as "top." Just as in the `name` attribute method, you must match the name of the location exactly and must not include the pound sign (#). This method will also work in all of today's browsers.

Choosing between `name` and `id`

By looking at the two examples you should notice two benefits to the `id` method.

First, it's more succinct. It uses less typing and therefore leads to a faster-loading document.

Second, it's clearer from a semantic standpoint. Instead of putting an additional anchor around the element and naming the anchor, the `id` method says, "Hey, the content of this element *is* top."

But, there are two small catches. First, older browsers (as recent as early versions of Navigator 4) will not recognize the `id` method and will therefore not follow the hyperlink. Second, the name attribute has been deprecated and is not included in XHTML 1.0 strict.

Taking these issues into account, these days you're probably safe in using the `id` method unless you are aware of a significant percentage of your users that are accessing your site with significantly older browsers. On the projects that I work on today, I use the `id` method and I've yet to have anyone complain that my internal hyperlinks don't work. (However, I don't use them very much, so opportunities for them not to work for certain users are minimal.)

To see a live example of a document that uses internal hyperlinks extensively, look at www.travelinlibrarian.info/recluce/spellsong/characters.html. This is one of my pages that uses internal hyperlinks to allow users to jump from one character's description to another whenever another person's name is mentioned. This page illustrates that internal hyperlinks can move in any direction within a document.

INTERNAL ABSOLUTE

Early in this chapter, I showed you the hyperlink description chart and told you that internal absolute links didn't exist. I also mentioned that some Web authors would argue with me on this point. Let me explain.

If you consider how I've described hyperlinks, then external links link you to another document and internal links link you to another location within the same document. Absolute links include a protocol and a domain, whereas relative ones do not. Taking these facts into account, it seems that a link cannot be both internal and absolute because how can you specify an internal location of a remote document?

Let's look at the following line of code:

```
<p>The character of < a href="http://www.travelinlibrarian.info/
recluce/spellsong/characters.html#Anna">Anna</a> is central to
the books of L. E. Modesitt, Jr.'s Spellsong Cycle.</p>7
```

Before we get into a debate over which type of hyperlink this is, let me explain what happens when a user clicks on it. First it goes out onto the Internet and requests the document "characters.html" from the L.E. Modesitt, Jr. Web site. It then displays the first line of Anna's character description at the top of my window. I can still scroll up or down through the report as needed.

In order for this type of link to work within your document, you would need to retrieve that document and look at the source code, find the listing for Anna, and check to see if the author had named or identified it. If the author had, we'd need to copy that name or id ("Anna" in this case) and append it to the end of the document's URL, including the pound sign. Assuming all of this was done by both them and us, this URL would work. So, what kind of link is this?

The link is external since we're linking to another document, but internal since we're going to a particular location within that document. It's absolute, since we're linking to another server and therefore must include both a protocol and a domain, but internal hyperlinks are relative, since we're looking for a location relative to the start of the document.

What's the answer? There isn't one—not really. This one could be argued forever and everyone would be correct. Ultimately, these links work but aren't used very often. That's what really matters.

A FEW ADDITIONAL WORDS ON INTERNAL HYPERLINKS

The use of internal hyperlinks within documents raises an important issue that I must address—that of document length. How long is too long for a Web page? The real answer to this question is that it depends on your user, and you have no control over the user's preferences. However, there are some things you should keep in mind. To illustrate these points, let's look at the following abbreviated example.

```
<!DOCTYPE html PUBLIC "-//W3C//DTD XHTML 1.0 Transitional//EN"
"http://www.w3.org/TR/xhtml/DTD/xhtml1-transitional.dtd">
<html xmlns="http://www.w3.org/TR/xhtml" lang="en">
<head>
<title>Acme Public Library Annual Report</title>
<meta name="HTTP-Equiv" content="text/html; content="utf-8">
</head>
<body>
<h1>Acme Public Library Annual Report</h1>
<h2 id="toc">Table of Contents</h2>
<ul>
<li><a href="#introduction">Introduction</a></li>
<li><a href="#part1">Part I: Circulation</a></li>
<li><a href="#part2">Part II: Purchasing</a></li>
<li><a href="#part3">Part III: Staff</a></li>
<li><a href="#conclusion">Conclusion</a></li>
<hr />
<h2 id="introduction">Introduction</h2>
. . .
<p><a href="#toc">Table of Contents</a></p>
<hr />
 <h2 id="part1">Part I: Circulation</h2>
. . .
<p><a href="#toc">Table of Contents</a></p>
<hr />
 <h2 id="part2">Part II: Purchasing</h2>
. . .
<p><a href="#toc">Table of Contents</a></p>
<hr />
<h2 id="part3">Part III: Staff</h2>
. . .
<p><a href="#toc">Table of Contents</a></p>
<hr />
<h2 id="conclusion">Conclusion</h2>
. . .
<p><a href="#toc">Table of Contents</a></p>
<hr />

<p>&copy;2004, Acme Public Library<br />
Last Updated: 05 January 2004</p>
</body>
</html>
```

This is our annual report presented as a single long document (about 40 pages) containing more than 600 lines of code. The question is whether or not this document is too long. But, what is the alternative? We could create a directory for the 2004 annual report and divide each of the parts into separate files. The code for our Table of Contents would then read:

```
<!DOCTYPE html PUBLIC "-//W3C//DTD XHTML 1.0 Transitional//EN"
"http://www.w3.org/TR/xhtml/DTD/xhtml1-transitional.dtd">
<html xmlns="http://www.w3.org/TR/xhtml" lang="en">
<head>
<title>Acme Public Library Annual Report</title>
<meta name="HTTP-Equiv" content="text/html; content="utf-8">
</head>
<body>
<h1>Acme Public Library Annual Report</h1>
<h2>Table of Contents</h2>
<ul>
<li><a href="introduction.html">Introduction</a></li>
<li><a href="part1.html">Part I: Circulation</a></li>
<li><a href="part2.html">Part II: Purchasing</a></li>
<li><a href="part3.html">Part III: Staff</a></li>
<li><a href="conclusion.html">Conclusion</a></li>
<hr />
<p>&copy;2004, Acme Public Library<br />
Last Updated: 05 January 2004</p>
</body>
</html>
```

We would need to change the toc link at the bottom of each of our sub-files from `href="#toc"` to `href="toc.html."`

Both methods have benefits and drawbacks. There is no clear answer to which is preferable.

A single file with internal hyperlinks is better if your users intend to print out the document. All they need to do is click the print button once and the whole report will print. However, this is a substantial document and on slower connections, it may take a long enough time to load to frustrate your users.

A multiple file with external hyperlinks will load much more quickly since the files are shorter but will not be as easy to print. In most cases, the user will need to print the Table of Contents document, open part 1, print that, go back, open part 2, etc. Each individual print job will start with page one; thus the whole report will not have contiguous page numbers.

Consider your audience when selecting the best method for you.

E-MAIL LINKS

There is a special type of hyperlink available to you that I did not cover in my chart at the beginning of this chapter. These are the links that, in most cases, generate an outgoing e-mail message when selected by a user. They are known as `mailto:` links.

BUILDING `mailto:` LINKS

Have you ever clicked on someone's name or e-mail address in a Web page and what you got back was a "compose message" window from your e-mail program with the To: field already filled in and, in some cases, the Subject: field filled in? This is the result of a mailto: link.

mailto: links are built similarly to all other types of links from an XHTML perspective. For example, to hyperlink my e-mail address as a mailto: link I would start out by adding the typical anchor code.

```
<a href="">msauers@travelinlibrarian.info</a>
```

The key piece of code that turns this text into a mailto: link is actually the value of the href attribute. If you want to link something to an e-mail address you write your URL in the following format:

```
mailto:address
```

To link this text to my e-mail address, I would write my code to read:

```
<a href="mailto:msauers@travelinlibrarian.info">msauers@travelin
librarian.info</a>
```

When the user clicks on this link (assuming everything is set up properly), a "compose message" window from their e-mail client will appear and the e-mail address in the href value will appear in the To: field. If you want to have the subject line completed automatically as well, you can add that. In the following example, I've set the subject line to be "Web site question".

```
<a href="mailto:msauers@travelinlibrarian.info&subject='Web site
question'">msauers@travelinlibrarian.info</a>
```

I've included single quotation marks around my subject due to the spaces in the text. If your subject text has no spaces, the single quotes are not necessary

CAUTION IS CALLED FOR

mailto: links are used all over the Web and I do not discourage their use, provided you are aware of the downside.

The largest potential problem with mailto: links is that they rely upon the user's computer being set up with an e-mail client, and that client being configured properly to send outgoing e-mail. Though this sounds like a safe assumption, it isn't. The key is that it relies upon a working e-mail *client*. Web-based e-mail systems such as Yahoo! Mail and Gmail will not work with mailto: links. (I have been told that Hotmail will work providing the user is also using Internet Explorer. If they're using another browser, the link will fail.) Also, consider the public access computers in your library. Chances are, for security reasons, that you have disabled or even removed all e-mail clients from those computers. In the case of the computers in your library, mailto: links will not work.

Ultimately, the solution to this problem is to create a Web form into which users can enter information and send it using your server's mail program, but not require the user's computer to be configured in any particular way. I'll be covering this in Chapter 8.

The other problem with mailto: links is spam. One of the ways spam lists are created is through a method known as "scraping" a Web site. In this instance, a program is sent out to check Web pages for e-mail addresses embedded within the markup. If it finds one, it copies it down and adds it to its spam list. Again, a form will help to avoid this problem, but there are solutions if you still wish to have mailto: links. The one I'll demonstrate here is the Automatic Enkoder <http://automaticlabs.com/products/enkoderform> (Figure 4.3).

Figure 4.3.   Enkoder

In the following code example I've completed the form based upon my previous `mailto:` example and clicked `Enkode It >>`. This is the result:

```
<script type="text/javascript">
//<![CDATA[
function hiveware_enkoder(){var i,j,x,y,x=
"x=\"783d2230786c3d3d5c225e7a243f7b243838216536363d3739392b34353b2b34393834" +
"6537342e3738396b6637392a35393974373367776383934756532366438343977363767775 9" +
"3838303b36377a3839382d363b66293938383f326b372a3474397134683521343d382b6533" +
"682e376b382a677436763875386468775e7524305e7a5e3f382d3f7b3b7d7a2b32345e3f24" +
"2d3f6b7a3d386a65763b6938703867376e3330387a383e386b663d3932383f336b342a3874" +
"34713468653d39293729363f667b393d352b3233382a36743876357537643977387534d34" +
"2b396c392a37743a7638753864377732753930347b333f337b3821383d352b6533392e356b" +
"662a34743876347567643a7735753430347a373f342d387b687d382b3834393f382d336b38" +
"3d386a6776346938703967 3b6e3630387a393e676b323d34333624673d357b383f39293329" +
"343d386839713b74372a386b383f3432373d396b393e337a3330386e386734703569397639" +
"6a343d666b382d383f3b386336382b357d656868713874382a676c363f384f39633b76656a" +
"3830326f676b3f70382a6b7a3b302a6e3867747067697176346a682e676b3d2d3838293633" +
"2b293d382f3f2f3b6c7b40383f3d6b343d5e2b247d5e7b5e2d393f647a33303565386a3263" +
"347435433976642a346c352b383d3b213b21347b383d345c22653b3479383d67276727353b" +
"3878333d3b75386e386568736563346138706565372835782729353b2966396f2a72322867" +
"69343d7230343b6369383c6578372e756c3865676e396770743768773b66693f2b352b2d29" +
"367b7b6a393d7d78352e2b633868346137723f43386f2d6463656b4138743d2834696a2938" +
"2d7632373b696939667028356a673c39336e326829306a352b7a3d68393e34383b6b79382b" +
"3d3d385330747a723f697a6e3d672b2e2b6632722a6f766d4343746863616a726543306f7a" +
"642a656e28636a7829677d3f79223b6a3d6576616c28782e636861724174283029293b783d" +
"782e73756273747472283129293b793d27273b666f7228693d303b693c782e6c656e6774683b69" +
"2b3d32297b792b3d782e73756273747228692c31293b7d666f7228693d313b693c782e6c65" +
"6e6774683b692b3d32297b792b3d782e73756273747228692c31293b7d793d792e73756273" +
"7472286a293b\";y='';for(i=0;i<x.length;i+=2){y+=unescape('%'+x.substr(i,2)" +
");}y";
while(x=eval(x));}hiveware_enkoder();
//]]>
</script>
```

This code, when placed in a Web page, will create the exact same result as my previous example. But, if a scraper comes to the page, no e-mail address will be found which can be added to a list.

NOTE: In order for this to work, JavaScript needs to be on in the user's browser. It is not perfect, but it does solve the spam problem.

FORMATTING MAILTO: LINKS

You may have been wondering why I created my `mailto:` hyperlink out of my e-mail address when I just as easily could have written the following:

```
<a href="mailto:msauers@travelinlibrarian.info">Michael Sauers</a>
```

Remember earlier in this chapter I showed you how hyperlinks should be context-neutral? That situation applies here, too. By making an e-mail address, instead of a name, the hyperlinked text, I'm indicating to the user that it is an e-mail link. If I had my name as the hyperlinked text, there's no indication to the user of what will happen when they click on it. Additionally, with the e-mail address displayed on the screen, the user can easily copy it and paste it into a Web-based e-mail program if necessary.

OF URLS AND CHARACTER ENTITIES

There is one last item that I'd like to address in this chapter. Look at the following URL for a search result in Google Images.

```
http://images.google.com/images?q=dean%20koontz&hl=en&lr=&sa=
N&tab=wi
```

If you were to create a hyperlink in your Web page to this URL, you would write it as:

```
<a
href="http://images.google.com/images?q=dean%20koontz&hl=en&lr=
&sa=N&tab=wi">Search for Dean Koontz images</a>
```

In HTML, this would be acceptable code. However, if you were to run this as XHTML through the validator (which checks your code for errors, as covered in Chapter 11), you'll receive the following errors:

> general entity "hl" not defined and no default entity
> general entity "lr" not defined and no default entity
> general entity "sa" not defined and no default entity
> general entity "tab" not defined and no default entity

The problem is that the validator has encountered the three ampersands in the URL, and, assuming that they start a special character, fails to find a terminating semicolon and chokes on the "error."

So, whenever you have an ampersand, *even if it appears within a URL*, code it as &. Your new hyperlink code reads:

```
<a
href="http://images.google.com/images?q=dean%20koontz&amp;hl=en&
amp;lr=&amp;sa=N&amp;tab=wi">Search for Dean Koontz images</a>
```

NOTES

1. I would also argue that since not all Web site users have the ability (for example, patrons with disabilities who cannot use a mouse and must use an alternative device) or the willingness (those who choose to use keyboards, for example) to use a mouse, using the phrase "click here" may alienate some of your users.
2. This browser is the reason you'll always see me write "home page" as two words. The first time it read to me the "BCR hom-a-pudge" I decided that "homepage" no longer worked well for me.

3. Please keep in mind that not all computers are named "www." For example, OCLC's FirstSearch is located at "firstsearch.oclc.org." In this case, the name of the computer is "firstsearch." A "www" is not required. It's just something that most Web sites use for consistency.

4. All URLs should end with either a filename or a "/" as I've shown in my examples. You could change the Google URL in the example to "http://www.google.com" and it will work, but after you click on it, your browser will show you at "http://www.google.com/." What happens is that the remote computer (Google) will send the user's computer back a message saying, "Hey, you left off the trailing slash, please resend your request with the trailing slash," which the user's computer will promptly do. Leaving off a trailing "/" isn't wrong, but it's good form to include it since that's what the computer will do anyway.

5. If you were to try this link without completing the next step, the link will work, but it's purely coincidental. If you link to any internal location without completing the next step, the browser will take you to the top of the document.

6. The following code will also work and validate:

```
<h1><a name="top">This document demonstrates the creation of internal hyperlinks</a></h1>
```

7. This URL does not exist. I've made it up for this example.

5

Images

```
<img />
```
Strict / Transitional / Frameset

Though I remember the days of the Web without graphics—I saw my first copy of Mosaic in 1994 at John Marshall Law School in Chicago—Web pages without images today are few and far between. The `<img />` element is the one that directs the browser to "place an image here." Before I explain this element and all its associated attributes, a brief introduction to graphic file formats for the Web is in order.

WHAT KIND OF GRAPHICS CAN YOU USE?

Today's browsers support three different graphic file formats: .gif, .jpg, and .png. Which you use depends on several factors. Let's take a look at the benefits of each.

.GIF[1]

The Graphics Interchange Format was originally developed for Compuserve back in the 1980s. A longtime standard, it was quickly adopted by the Web design community as the first file format to be used in Web pages. .GIFs had several benefits over other existing formats of the time. Primarily, they were relatively small, and size was a factor when transmitting images over slow connections. .GIF files also had some additional features that Web developers could take advantage of.

- GIFs could be saved in an interlaced format. This is not nearly as important today with the advent of broadband connections in the home, but you've probably seen an interlaced GIF. Like all other image file formats. GIFs load topdown, line by line. An interlaced GIF, however, loads in four passes, looking fuzzy at first and becoming clearer with each pass. This tricks your mind into thinking the image is loading faster even though it's not. It's just an optical illusion, but when people were connecting to the Internet with 14.4 or 28.8 kbps connections, this illusion was very effective.

- .GIFs could be used as imagemaps. An imagemap is a single image with multiple hyperlinked "hotspots." Depending on which hotspot on the graphic you clicked, you received a different result. For example, you've probably visited a site in the past with a map of the United States. You clicked on the appropriate state to view that state's page. (Click on Colorado, you get a Colorado page. Click on Kansas, you get a Kansas page.) We'll be covering the creation of imagemaps later in this chapter.
- .GIFs can be transparent. When I tell my students that all graphics on all Web pages are rectangles (i.e., have four sides), many don't believe me. After all, we've all seen graphics that look like circles. Well, that's the catch: They just look like circles. A transparent .GIF has one of color (usually the background color) that is "transparent." In other words, it automatically matches itself to the background of the page it's on, thus giving the appearance of having more or fewer than four sides.
- .GIFs can be animated. With additional software, you can create a series of .GIFs that, when saved as a single file and played back by the browser appears as a cartoon or a digital flip-book, giving the image the illusion of movement.

.JPG (OR .JPEG)

The Joint Pictures Engineering Group in the mid-1990s devised an alternative to the .GIF format. Though the .JPG format cannot support some of the features that .GIF offers, its smaller file size is a measurable advantage over .GIFs.

The .JPG file format has a built-in method of compressing an image file, resulting in files as much as 50 percent smaller than the same file saved in the .GIF format. With a smaller file, the image will load more quickly. There is, however, a potentially significant drawback to this bandwidth savings.

The .JPG format uses a form of "lossy" compression. In other words, the smaller file size is a result of data being removed ("lost") from the image. In most cases, this lost data is not noticeable to the average user due to limitations both in their monitors and in their own eyes.

Most authors tend to rely on .GIFs for imagemaps since some older browsers did not support JPG-based imagemaps. Today's browser's do support .JPG-based imagemaps.

.PNG

The Portable Network Graphics format was created in the late 1990s as a replacement for both .JPGs and .GIFs. This format advertises itself as a "best-of-both-worlds" solution. .PNGs support all the features contained within .GIFs but have the smaller files sizes of .JPGs with lossless compression (compression without losing any data from the image).

Though all of today's browsers support the display of .PNGs, not all of those browsers support them well. For example, Internet Explorer does display .PNGs but does not support transparency in .PNGs. For this reason, many Web authors have still not started using .PNGs in their pages.

CHOOSING A FILE FORMAT FOR YOUR GRAPHICS

Since .PNGs still have some issues that prevent Web authors from considering them as a serious option, I'll focus this discussion on choosing between the .GIF and .JPG formats.

Potentially, your choice is simple. If you want to use a transparent or interlaced image, .GIF is your format. However, if you don't want either of these features as part of your image, the choice does not automatically become .JPG. The main reason for this is the minor problem of lossy compression. Certain types of images work better and some suffer noticeably from lossy compression. Take a look at the following two graphics saved in both the .GIF (Figures 5.1 and 5.2) and .JPG (Figures 5.3 and 5.4) formats.

Figure 5.1.   .gif photo, 640x480, 159k

Figure 5.2. .jpg photo, 640x480, 38.1k

Figure 5.3. .gif line art, 200x315, 18.6k

Figure 5.4.   .jpg line art, 200x315, 7.4k

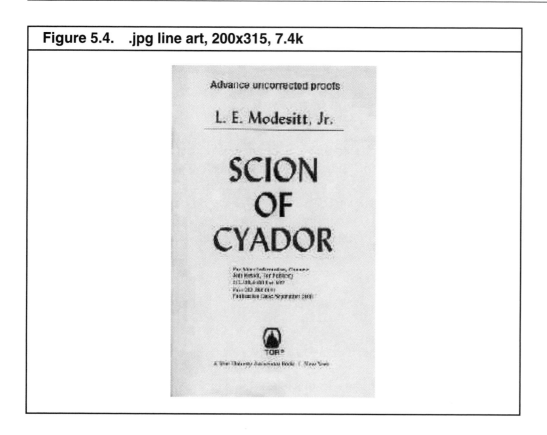

If you examine the photo in both the .GIF and .JPG formats, you shouldn't see much of a difference, if any at all. Complex images such as photographs lend themselves well to .JPG compression because of their level of detail. The more detail you have, the more areas where colors are blended or less distinct, and the more places where the compression process can remove data unnoticed.

On the other hand, looking at the drawing, the .GIF version is crisp where the .JPG version is fuzzy around the edges. In images such as drawings, cartoons, or line art, where there is less detail and color separation is distinct, there are fewer places where data loss can go unnoticed. The result is fuzziness around the edges. You do end up with a faster-loading file, but the image suffers in its quality—a compromise you may not be willing to make.

The decision comes down to the type of image you're placing within your document. If it's a simple image, stick with .GIF. The .JPG format is better suited for photographs and other complex images.

IMAGE ELEMENT BASICS

Images are inline elements. They will be placed exactly where they are specified inline with any surrounding text. To place an image into a document you first need to add the `<img />` element. (Please note that `<img />` is an empty element and therefore requires the trailing slash.)

For example, let's place a library logo at the top of our Web page. Those with previous HTML experience would envision something like the following code.

```
<body>
<img />
<h1>Welcome to the Acme Public Library</h1>
```

As acceptable as this code would be to longtime Web designers, it has a problem that will prevent this code from validating. An image must be placed within something. At the moment, it is a child of <body>, which is an invalid code. For our purposes, we'll place our image within its own <div>. This will have no effect on our layout and will create valid XHTML code. (<div> is similar to <p> in that it's a container for other items. For now, just think of <div> as a different form of <p>. We'll discuss <div>s further in Chapter 13.)

```
<body>
<div>
<img />
<div>
<h1>Welcome to the Mallville Public Library</h1>
```

You're welcome to look at the results of this code in your browser but there's a reason I haven't included a screenshot of the results at this point. As written, our <img /> element accomplishes absolutely nothing beyond putting a place holder for the image in our code. In order for the image to appear we need to specify the name and location of the image we wish to have displayed.

NOTE: For the purposes of this discussion, we'll be assuming that our XHTML and image file are in the same directory on our site. Once your site starts to contain many images, you may want to put all your graphic files in a separate "images" directory and indicate that the images are elsewhere on the service by specifying the path to the appropriate image file. For more information on pathing, see the section on directory structures in Appendix I.

The attribute that we need to add to specify which image we'd like to display is the source attribute, abbreviated as **src="..."** (Figure 5.5).

```
<div>
<img src="library.gif" />
<div>
```

Figure 5.5. Inserting an Image into Your Document

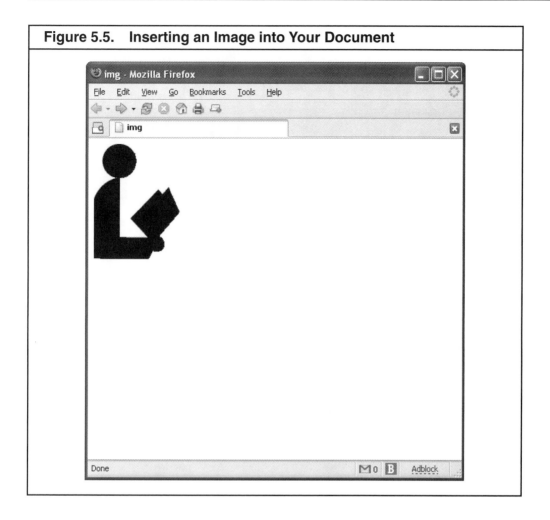

It might go without saying but I like to be specific: in XHTML, `src="..."` is a required attribute. Without the appearance of this attribute on your `<img />` element, the document will not validate.

One more attribute on the `<img />` element is required for your document to validate—the `alt="..."` attribute.

NOTE: The alt attribute is not required in HTML, though all good Web designers were sure to include it for other reasons which I'll be covering shortly.

The alt attribute specifies text that should be displayed when the image, for one reason or another, is not. For example, users with text-only browsers will see, or hear, the alternative text instead of the image (Figure 5.6). Today's graphical browsers will show the alternative text as tip-text (Figure 5.7).

Alternative text should serve one of two purposes: either to say what the picture is, as with a photograph, or explain what the image does, in the case of a "back" button.

```
<div>
<img src="library.gif" alt="Library Logo" />
<div>
```

Figure 5.6.   Alt-text as Displayed in Lynx

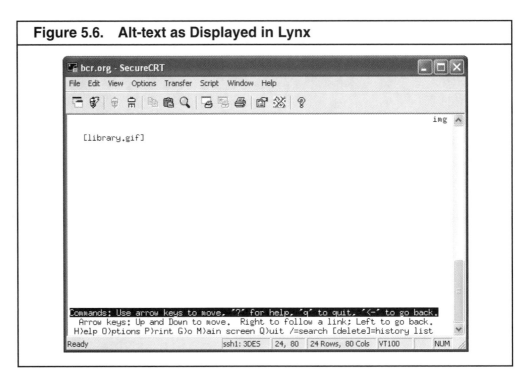

Figure 5.7.   Alt-text as Displayed in IE

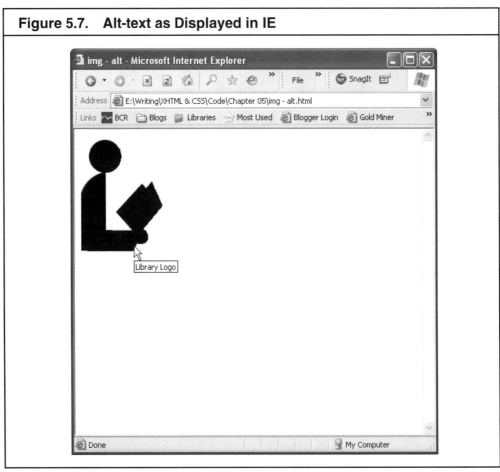

ADDITIONAL IMAGE ATTRIBUTES

All three of the following attributes are in the strict, transitional, and frameset DTDs. However, the first two do have preferred CSS replacements.

height **AND** width

The height and width attributes specify the dimensions of the image in pixels. Though these are not required attributes, they are useful pieces of information to add. The addition of this information does not increase the speed at which the image is loaded or displayed, but it does increase the speed at which the complete page is displayed properly.

When a page is loaded, the text content is loaded first and all of the content that must be retrieved from external files loads next. In this case, the text will load and display, then the images will be loaded. If you do not specify height and width for your images, the text will be displayed and then will move out of the way of the images once they're loaded. If you provide the dimensions of the image in your code, the browser will know how much space to set aside for the image and place the text around that space.

```
<div>
<img src="library.gif" alt="Library Logo" height="100" width="100"
/>
<div>
```

longdesc

The longdesc attribute allows you to specify the URL of a document that provides a narrative description of the image far beyond that which can be displayed within a short bit of alternative text. None of today's browsers that I am aware of actually do anything with this information.

```
<div>
<img src="library.gif" alt="Library Logo" height="100" width="100"
longdesc="http://www.libraryclipart.com/alasymbols.html" />
<div>
```

The next four attributes do not appear in the strict DTD. For each of these, use of the CSS alternative is strongly suggested.

alignment

By default, <img /> is an inline element. As proof, take a look at the following example (Figure 5.8).

```
<p>This is a sentence with an image <img src="bullet.gif" alt=
"bullet" /> in the middle of it.</p>
```

Figure 5.8.   An Image with a Paragraph of Text

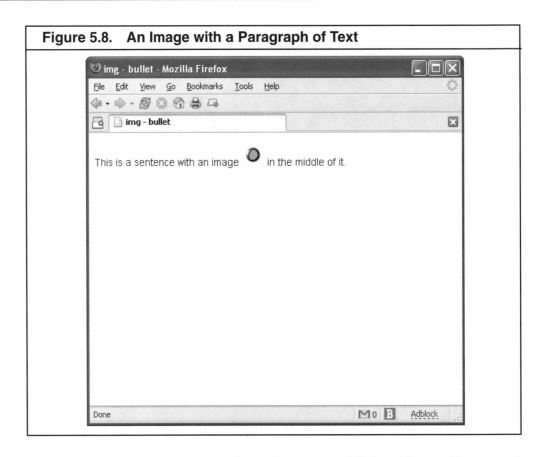

As you can see, the image is placed exactly where specified and the text flows around it as needed. Through the application of the align attribute, we have a minimal amount of control over the placement of our image.

The following table covers the values for the `align` attribute followed by example code and a screenshot of each as displayed in today's browsers.

Table 5.1
`align` **Attributable Values**

left	Sends the image off to the left of the text, forcing the text to wrap around the right side of the image.
right	Sends the image off to the right of the text, forcing the text to wrap around the left side of the image.
top	Aligns the top edge of the image with the adjacent text.
middle	Vertically centers the image with the adjacent text.
bottom	Aligns the bottom edge of the image with the adjacent text. This is the default value.

```
<p><img src="library.gif" alt="Library" align="left" />The image
within this paragraph includes the align attribute with a value of
left. The image within this paragraph includes the align attribute
with a value of left. The image within this paragraph includes the
align attribute with a value of left. The image within this para-
graph includes the align attribute with a value of left. </p>
```

```
<p><img src="library.gif" alt="Library" align="right" />The image
within this paragraph includes the align attribute with a value
of right. The image within this paragraph includes the align
attribute with a value of right. The image within this paragraph
includes the align attribute with a value of right. The image
within this paragraph includes the align attribute with a value
of right. The image within this paragraph includes the align
attribute with a value of right. The image within this paragraph
includes the align attribute with a value of right.</p>
<p>The image in this sentence<img src="library.gif" alt="Library"
align="top" /> has an alignment of top.</p>
<p>The image in this sentence<img src="library.gif" alt="Library"
align="middle" /> has an alignment of middle.</p>
<p>The image in this sentence<img src="library.gif" alt="Library"
align="bottom" /> has an alignment of bottom.</p>
```

Figure 5.9. **The Different Alignment Values for Images**

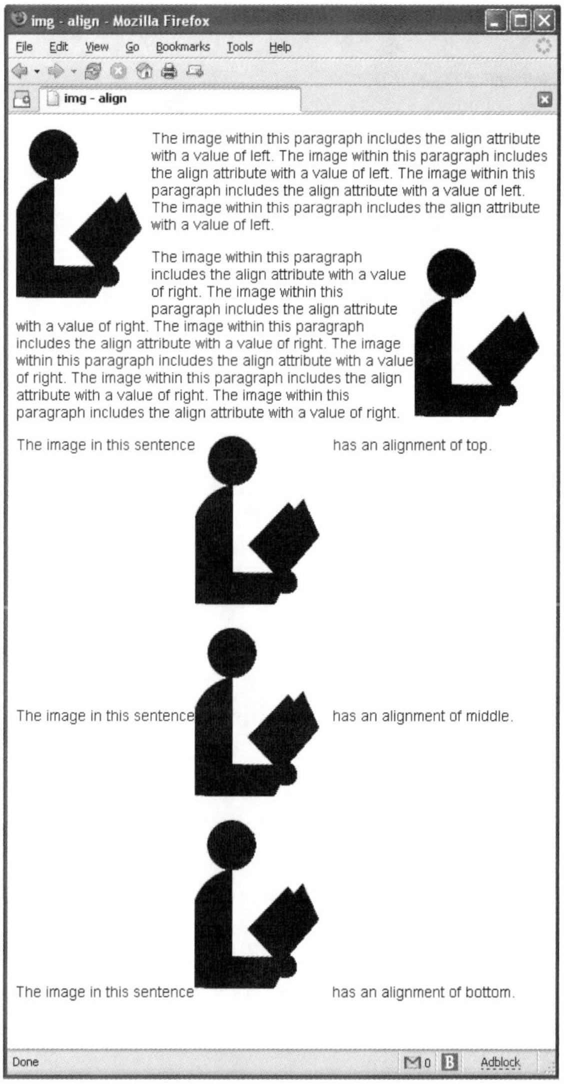

BORDERS

When you add an anchor to text, the text changes color and underlines by default. Let's look at what happens when you add an anchor to an image (Figure 5.10).

```
<p><a href="http://www.google.com"><img src="google.gif"
```

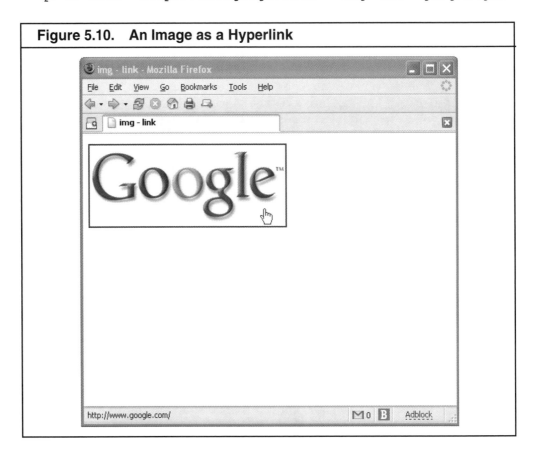

Figure 5.10.   An Image as a Hyperlink

```
alt="Google" /></a></p>
```

As you can see, the image suddenly obtains a colored border. (The color will match whatever colors you've set for your links.) In this example, you can assume that I really don't want that border to appear, especially since this is a transparent image and adding the border ruins that effect.

The odd part about getting rid of this border is that it is done by adding an attribute to the image, despite the fact that the border is caused by the anchor. That attribute is border="*n*," where *n* is the number of pixels thick you would like the border to be. (The default value is "2.") To make the border disappear, set the value of *n* to zero (Figure 5.11).

```
<p><a href="http://www.google.com"><img src="google.gif"
alt="Google" border="0" /></a></p>
```

Figure 5.11. A Hyperlinked Image with No Border

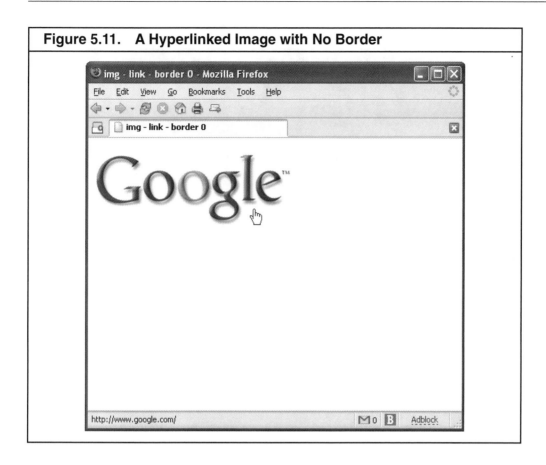

Yes, you can set to any other numerical value. The following example illustrates why this is not recommended (Figure 5.12).

```
<p><a href="http://www.google.com"><img src="google.gif"
alt="Google" border="30" /></a></p>
```

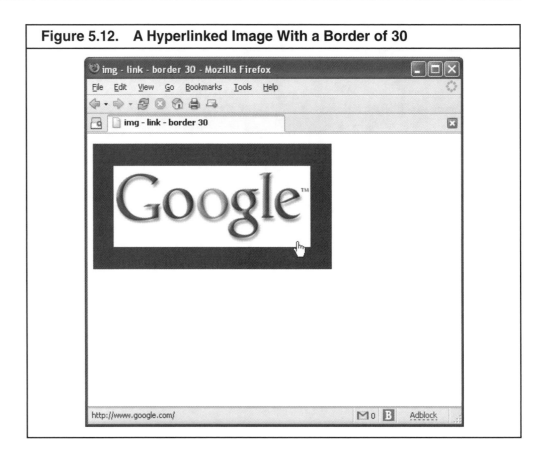

Figure 5.12.   A Hyperlinked Image With a Border of 30

hspace **AND** vspace

As you may have noticed in previous examples, when an image is immediately next to text, the two practically bump up against each other. When you have a transparent .GIF, this may not be much of a problem since you may have a bit of a buffer zone built into the transparent portion of the image. However, if the image proper comes right up to the edge of the image's box (for example, as with a book cover), having your text and image immediately next to each other may not appear as intended. This is where the hspace and vspace attributes come into play. The hspace attribute allows you to specify a buffer zone on the left and right sides of the image into which no other content may encroach. The value for hspace is the number of pixels you wish to set aside. Similarly, the vspace attribute does the same thing as hspace but works above and below the image.

If I wanted to specify a ten-pixel buffer zone around the entire image, I would add the following code (Figure 5.13).

```
<p><img src="library.gif" alt="Library" align="left" hspace="10"
vspace="10" />The image within this paragraph includes the align
attribute with a value of left. The image within this paragraph
includes the align attribute with a value of left. The image
within this paragraph includes the align attribute with a value
of left. The image within this paragraph includes the align
attribute with a value of left. </p>
```

Figure 5.13.   The hspace **and** vspace **Attributes**

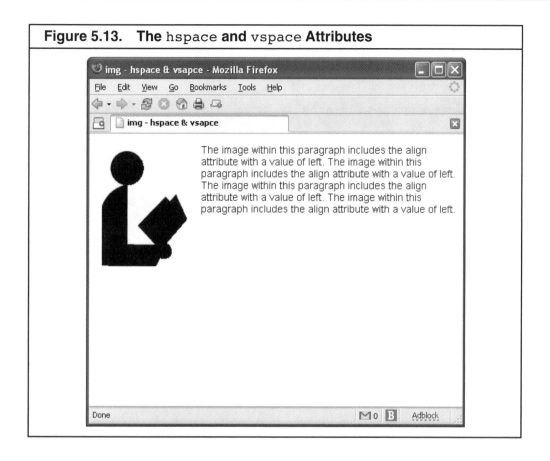

As mentioned previously, these attributes have been replaced with CSS, which provides for far greater control than do hspace and vspace. Because of this, the CSS method for controlling the buffer zone around an image is the preferred method.

IMAGEMAPS

```
<img usemap="" />
<map> . . . </map>
<area />
```
Strict / Transitional / Frameset

As I mentioned at the beginning of this chapter, imagemaps are single images with multiple hotspots (links embedded within the image so that clicking on a different place in the image renders different results).

Traditionally, there have been two types of imagemaps an author could create server-side and client-side. Server-side imagemaps require storing the information on how the imagemap worked in a separate file on the server, forcing a connection back to the server whenever the user clicks on the associated image. Client-side imagemaps have nearly replaced server-side, mainly because they are more efficient, placing all of the imagemap code within the document itself. For this reason I will focus on client-side imagemaps. (Information on how server-side imagemaps work can be found at http://hotwired.lycos.com/webmonkey/96/39/index2a.html.)

To build an imagemap, you first need to place your image into your document. This is done as with any other image through the `<img />` element. (Figure 5.14).

```
<body>
<div>
<img src="shapes.gif" alt="Imagemap sample" />
<div>
</body>
```

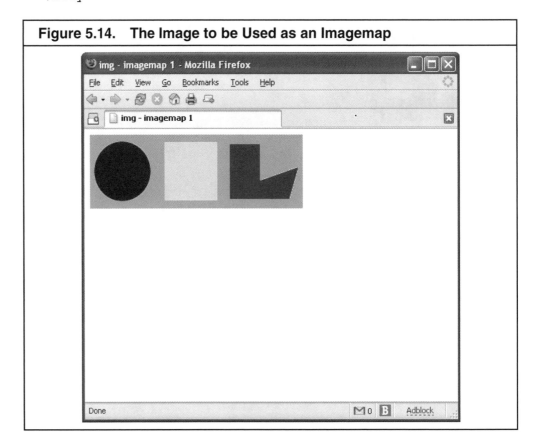

Figure 5.14.   The Image to be Used as an Imagemap

I realize this is not exactly an image you would really use, but it does allow me to illustrate the points of imagemaps well.

Next, you need to identify the image as being associated with a particular set of map coordinates. This is done with the `usemap="`*value*`"` attribute. In this case we'll call it "shapes," since we're associating it with our shapes.gif file.

```
<body>
<div>
<img src="shapes.gif" alt="Imagemap sample" usemap="shapes" />
<div>
</body>
```

The next step is to place the map code within the XHTML document. Map code can be placed anywhere within the body of a document but is traditionally placed at the top, immediately after `<body>`. What we need to do is to indicate the beginning and end of the map code along with the name of the map.

```
<body>
<map id="shapes">
</map>
<div>
<img src="shapes.gif" alt="Imagemap sample" usemap="shapes" />
<div>
</body>
```

Some older browsers will not recognize the id attribute on the map and therefore will not associate the contents of <map> with the image. (This is similar to the name vs. ID issue with internal hyperlinks I discussed in Chapter 4.) To overcome this problem we need to also use the old method of naming the map code.

```
<body>
<map id="shapes" name="shapes">
</map>
<div><img src="shapes.gif" alt="Imagemap sample" usemap="shapes"
/><div>
</body>
```

What now needs to be placed within <map> and </map> is one <area /> element for each hotspot we wish to create. In this case, that will be four, so I'll go ahead and add those elements:

```
<map id="shapes" name="shapes">
<area />
<area />
<area />
<area />
</map>
```

Each <area /> element now needs four attributes; shape, coords, href, and alt. The shape attribute has four possible values.

Table 5.2
area Attributes

circle	Specifies that the hotspot is a circle.
rect	Specifies that the hotspot has four sides.
poly	Specifies that the hotspot has either three sides, or more than four sides, (is a polygon which is not a rectangle).
default	Allows you to specify a hyperlink for any part of the image that is not covered by a hotspot. An area with a shape of default does not require the coords attribute.

Adding the shape attributes to our four areas, we now have:

```
<map id="shapes" name="shapes">
<area shape="circle" />
<area shape="rect" />
<area shape="poly" />
```

```
<area shape="default" />
</map>
```

For each of the three actual shapes (circle, rect, and poly), we need to specify some coordinates. How the set of coordinates are built depends on the type of shape. Here's how they break down:

Table 5.3
shape **Attributes**

circle	Three numbers: the X and Y coordinates of the center of the circle and the value of the radius in pixels.
rect	Four numbers: the X and Y coordinates of the upper-left corner, and the X and Y coordinates of the lower-right corner.
poly	A variable number of pairs of numbers: one X and Y coordinate for each point in the shape. (For example, a triangle would have six numbers.)

Let's take a look at the numbers that would match the image. (The coordinates are based on the upper left corner of the image being 0,0.)

```
<map id="shapes" name="shapes">
<area href="http://www.adobe.com/" shape="circle" coords="47,
48, 41" />
<area href="http://www.google.com/" shape="rect" coords="107,
10, 182, 91" />
<area href="http://www.microsoft.com/" shape="poly" coords="198,
14, 198, 87, 282, 86, 293, 43, 240, 62, 239, 15" />
<area shape="default" />
</map>
```

The big question at this point is how to derive the numbers. What you don't do is guess. (I did have a student admit to this at one point. She was very happy when I gave her a better solution.) In this case you really must rely on one of any number of software programs that will allow you to draw the hotspots and produce the numbers for you. Major Web site creation packages such as Microsoft's FrontPage and Macromedia's Dreamweaver have this function built in. If you don't have access to these programs, there are others out there, such as Life Software's Imagemapper, which will cost you about $15. (http://www.lifesoftplus.com/)

Once you have your hotspots created, it's only a matter of adding the URLs you want them to link to, along with optional alt attributes for each hotspot. You'll also want to turn off the image's border. Here's what my final code looks like (Figure 5.15).

```
<body>
<map id="shapes" name="shapes">
<area href="http://www.adobe.com/" shape="circle" coords="47,
48, 41" href="http://www.google.com" alt="Google" />
<area href="http://www.google.com/" shape="rect" coords="107,
10, 182, 91" href="http://www.microsoft.com" alt="Microsoft"/>
<area href="http://www.microsoft.com/" shape="poly" coords="198,
14, 198, 87, 282, 86, 293, 43, 240, 62, 239, 15" href="http://
```

```
www.adobe.com" alt="Adobe"/>
<area shape="default" href="http://www.bcr.org" alt="BCR" />
</map>
<p><img src="shapes.gif" alt="Imagemap sample" usemap="shapes"
border="0" /><p>
</body>
```

Figure 5.15.   The Finished Imagemap

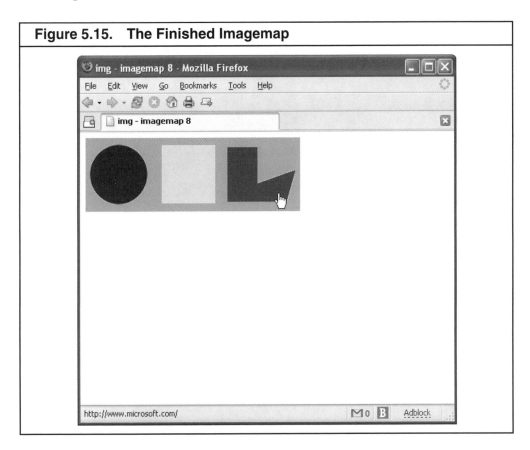

NOTE

1. There is some controversy over how GIF should be pronounced. Some argue that it should be pronounced with a hard G as in gift, while others argue that it should be pronounced with a soft G, as a J is typically pronounced. After years of arguing for the side in favor of the hard pronunciation, I've been convinced that GIF should be pronounced with a soft G; like "jiff." For more details on the controversy and why my mind was changed, read "The GIF Pronunciation page" (www.olsenhome.com/gif/).

6

Lists

WHAT IS A LIST?

In HTML, lists were what you would use when you wanted a group of items to be delineated either by bullets, known as an *unordered* list, or in sequence with either numbers or letters, known as an *ordered* list. (There is a third type of list, a definition list, which we'll discuss later in the chapter.)

In XHTML, lists are for groups of items that are not headings, paragraphs, or blockquotes: i.e., a group of items that belongs in a list. The key difference is that the items may *or may not* need bullets, numbers, or letters. As fine a point as this may be, it is still a valid one. The reason for describing lists as having bullets, numbers, or letters in HTML was that that was the only choice you had. You could change the style of the bullets or the type of numbers or letters, but you couldn't turn them off.

In XHTML, browsers still default to using bullets, letters, or numbers but that is not the fault of your markup; that's the fault of the browser. Once you learn CSS, you can create a list without any markings at all. It's still a list—it just isn't displayed like one HTML coders are used to.

One of the central goals of XHTML is to separate structure from style. If what you're coding is a list, code it as a list. If you then want it to display a certain way, use CSS to adjust it appropriately. (I'll get into this in much more detail, specifically with the CSS code, in Chapter 18.)

TYPES OF LISTS

There are three types of lists available to Web designers: unordered, ordered, and definition. Each is descriptive of what it accomplishes.

- *Unordered*

  An unordered list is a list of items that are not necessarily presented in a particular order, such as alphabetically or by importance.

- *Ordered*

  An ordered list is a list of items that are being presented in a particular order, such as alphabetically or by date. For example, an alphabetical staff list or a list of upcoming events at your library in chronological order is an ordered list.

- *Definition*

  Definition lists are less common. The purpose of a definition list is to present the user with, quite literally, terms and their definitions, as in a glossary. You'll see other ways a definition list can be used later in this chapter.

Since definition lists differ materially from unordered and ordered lists, I'll discuss them at the end of this chapter. First we'll focus more on the common types of lists and their similarities.

UNORDERED LISTS

```
<ul> . . . </ul>
```
Strict / Transitional / Frameset

Unordered lists are used whenever you need to create a list that does not have a specific order. By default, items in unordered lists are displayed in a browser preceded by bullets. Whenever you code a list the first element that you must use is the one that signifies which type of list you're creating. In the case of an unordered list, that element is `<ul>`. To start the list you must first mark the start and end of the list.

```
<ul>
</ul>
```

Within the list is each of the items that belongs in the list. You must also specify the start and end of each item with the element `<li>`. If within this list you wish to include three employees, you would add them each within their own `<li> . . . </li>` (Figure 6.1).

```
<ul>
<li>Joe</li>
<li>Steve</li>
<li>Mary</li>
</ul>
```

Figure 6.1.   An Unordered List

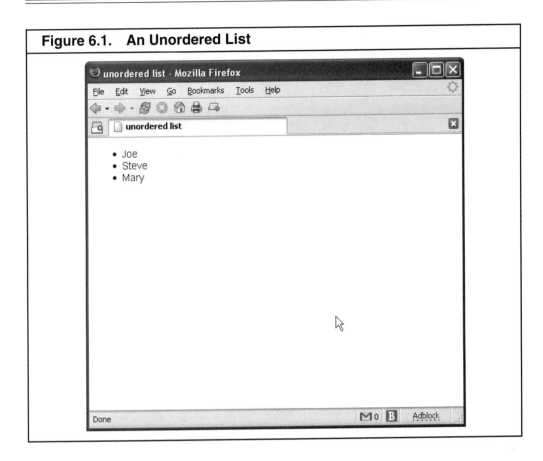

XHTML has three default bullet types built into the language: discs, circles, and squares. These can be controlled by adding the `type=" "` attribute to the `<ul>` element. For example, if you want your bullets to be squares instead of discs you would add the following code (Figure 6.2).

```
<ul type="square">
<li>Joe</li>
<li>Steve</li>
<li>Mary</li>
</ul>
```

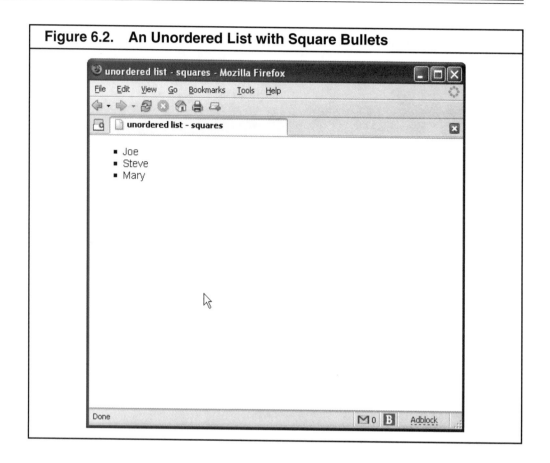

Figure 6.2.　An Unordered List with Square Bullets

Although the type attribute is available to you in the transitional DOCTYPE, it is not available in the strict doctype. It is preferred that you use CSS to control your bullets since this is a style change and CSS gives you many additional options when it comes to bullets. We'll cover applying CSS to lists later in Chapter 18.

ORDERED LISTS

```
<ol> . . . </ol>
```
Strict / Transitional / Frameset

If there is an *implied* order of your items, you should use an ordered list. The order does not need to be readily apparent to the viewer. Structure is the key. The single XHTML difference between unordered and ordered lists is the use of the <ol> rather than <ul> element (Figure 6.3).

```
<ol>
 <li>Joe</li>
 <li>Steve</li>
 <li>Mary</li>
</ol>
```

Figure 6.3.   An Ordered List

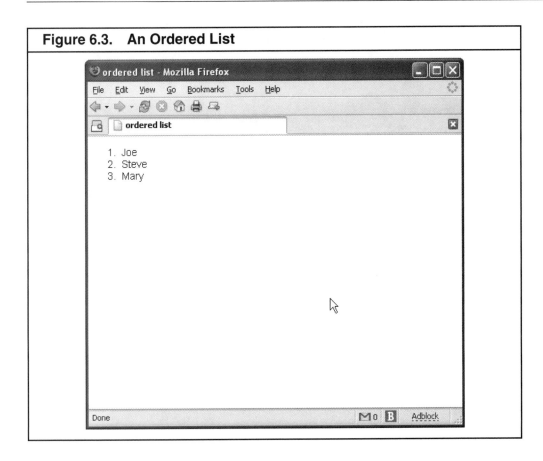

By default, ordered lists use numbers instead of bullets. As in unordered lists, the symbols preceding your list items can be controlled through the `type=""` attribute. However, instead of three options, ordered lists provide you with five:

- `type="1"`
  Numbers, the default setting
- `type="A"`
  Capital letters
- `type="a"`
  Lowercase letters
- `type="I"`
  Uppercase roman numerals
- `type="i"`
  Lowercase roman numerals

If you wanted your list to be the first level in an outline, you might add the appropriate attribute to see uppercase Roman numerals (Figure 6.4).

```
<ol type="I">
 <li>Joe</li>
 <li>Steve</li>
 <li>Mary</li>
</ol>
```

Figure 6.4. An Ordered List with Uppercase Roman Numerals

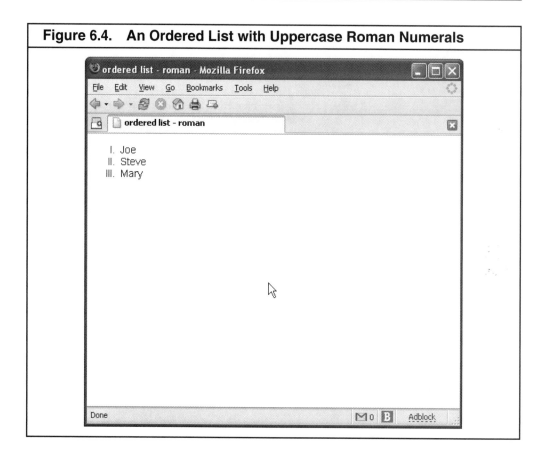

You should notice in this example that the numbers (or letters, as the case may be) are right-justified to the period. This is typically not a problem unless you get into some rather long roman numerals. In that case you may need to adjust your left margin or the numbers may run off the left side of the screen. As with unordered lists, although the type attribute is available to you in the transitional DOCTYPE, it is not available in the strict DOCTYPE. It is recommended that you use CSS to control your bullets since this is a style change and CSS gives you many additional options when it comes to bullets. We'll cover applying CSS to lists in Chapter 18.

NESTING UNORDERED AND ORDERED LISTS

Embedding a list within a list, thus creating a sublist, is known as nesting a list: one list inside of another. This is useful when you need to add an additional level of specificity to your lists. For example, if you were creating a list of employees that included their job responsibilities, you might want it to look something like Figure 6.5.

Figure 6.5.   A Nested List

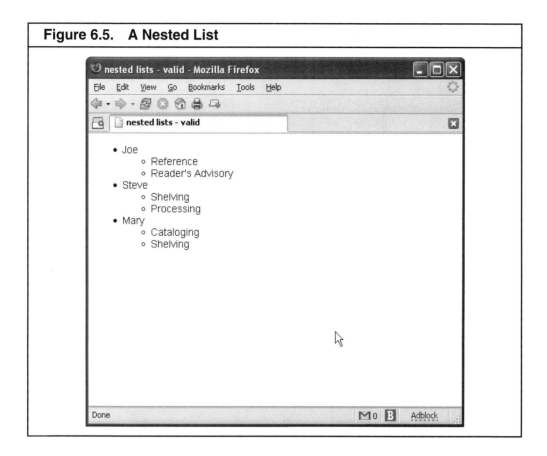

You may notice that when you nest an unordered list, the bullets change to indicate an additional level within the structure of the list. By default, unordered lists have three different bullet types: disc (a filled-in circle), circle (an empty circle), and square (a filled-in square).

These three types will cycle through their order with every level deeper into your list. Thus, on the third level, the bullets will be squares and on the fourth level they'll be discs again. You can control this just by adding the appropriate type attribute to each list.

As I've previously shown, designers using HTML tend to have poor coding habits due to HTML's lax coding rules. There is another situation in which XHTML forces you to pay attention to the rules and code cleanly nested lists.

In HTML, the markup for a nested list would look similar to this:

```
<ul>
<li>Joe</li>
 <ul>
 <li>Reference</li>
 <li>Reader's Advisory</li>
 </ul>
<li>Steve</li>
 <ul>
 <li>Shelving</li>
 <li>Processing</li>
 </ul>
```

```
<li>Mary</li>
 <ul>
 <li>Cataloging</li>
 <li>Shelving</li>
 </ul>
</ul>
```

HTML coders place a nested list between two line items since that is how it will appear on the screen. Though this markup appears as if it would be valid in XHTML, when run through a validator it will point to the nested `<ul>` and give you the following error message:

```
Error: element "ul" not allowed here; assuming missing "li" start-tag
```

Translated into English, you're being told that the nested `<ul>` is in the wrong place. You're probably wondering where should it be located instead. Upon a closer reading of the XHTML DTD[1] you will find the following rule:

```
<!ELEMENT ul (li)+>
```

This means that a `<ul>` element can only contain one, or more, `<li>`s. Looking at the nesting of the code in the previous code example, there is `<ul>` element nested within another `<ul>` element, rendering the markup invalid. However, looking at the rules for `<li>` we find:

```
<!ELEMENT li %Flow;>
```

There is no restriction on what can be contained within an `<li>` element. Therefore an `<li>` element can contain a `<ul>` element. To solve this coding problem, you need to nest the `<ul>` within an `<li>`, waiting to close the primary list only after the secondary list is closed. To accomplish this task, you move the `<li>` from after "Joe" to after the end of the nested list. Here is the revised markup, now valid in XHTML.

```
<ul>
<li>Joe
 <ul>
 <li>Reference</li>
 <li>Reader's Advisory</li>
 </ul></li>
<li>Steve
 <ul>
 <li>Shelving</li>
<li>Processing</li>
 </ul></li>
<li>Mary
 <ul>
 <li>Cataloging</li>
 <li>Shelving</li>
 </ul></li>
</ul>
```

MIXING ORDERED AND UNORDERED LISTS

When you nest lists, you can mix and match ordered and unordered lists. For example, if you want to take the employee list and list the employees' duties in order of importance, using numbers instead of bullets, you would only need to change the nested `<ul>`s to `<ol>`s.

```
<ul>
<li>Joe
 <ol>
 <li>Reference</li>
 <li>Reader's Advisory</li>
 </ol></li>
<li>Steve
 <ol>
 <li>Shelving</li>
<li>Processing</li>
</ol></li>
<li>Mary
 <ol>
 <li>Cataloging</li>
 <li>Shelving</li>
 </ol></li>
</ul>
```

RETHINKING ORDERED AND UNORDERED LISTS

Now that you're familiar with the code involved in creating lists, let's deal with the following question: Which type of list should you use?

At the beginning of this chapter I talked about the difference, not in the coding of lists in HTML vs. XHTML, but in the perceptions of lists in the two languages. In HTML the answer to this question was simple. If you wanted bullets, you used an unordered list. If you wanted numbers or letters, you used an ordered list. If you want indenting, you used a definition list. Why? Because that is what you got when the browser displayed your code.

With XHTML, and more specifically with CSS, the answer is less clear. If the goal is to separate structure from style, you now need to also ask yourself what is dictated by the content of your list. Is it ordered, unordered, or definitions? The answer to this question will tell you which type of list to use.

Let me give you an example. On the BCR home page, they had a menu down the left side of the screen with the following code. (The actual code has been simplified for this example.)

```
<p><a href="sitemap/">Site Map</a></p>
<p><a href="/~shoffhin/about/aboutbcr.html">About BCR</a></p>
<p><a href="/~shoffhin/who/">Contact Us</a></p>
<p>Services<br>
<a href="/~bss/oclcsrvs.html">OCLC</a><br>
<a href="/~ids/Reference/">Reference Databases</a><br>
```

```
<a href="/~randd/internet.html">Internet</a><br>
<a href="/~bss/cat-tech.html">Cataloging</a><br>
<a href="/~randd/Database-menu.html">Database Creation</a><br>
<a href="/~bss/rshar.html">Resource Sharing</a><br>
<a href="/~ids/Hardsoft/">Hardware &amp; Software</a><br>
<a href="library-office.html">Library &amp; Office Supplies</
a><br>
<a href="/~ids/Discounts/">Discounts</a><br>
<a href="/~business/">Accounting</a><br>
<a href="/~shoffhin/consult/">Consulting</a>
</p>
```

What they had created in HTML was four paragraphs with the fourth one including many line breaks in order to have many choices within a particular group. (There was CSS added to this code to increase the left margin for the links under "Services" to treat them as subchoices.) They did this because they didn't want a bullet, number, or letter in front of each menu choice.

When I began to learn XHTML and, as CSS started to gain stronger support from the browsers, I realized that there was a better way to code these menus. The fact that they were lists that browsers, by default, would mark each item with a bullet (or number or letter) was irrelevant to the markup since I could later turn the markers off using CSS. Turning this content into a list was much more accurate. A better way to code this menu would be:

```
<ul>
<li><a href="sitemap/">Site Map</a></li>
<li><a href="/~shoffhin/about/aboutbcr.html">About BCR</a></li>
<li><a href="/~shoffhin/who/">Contact Us</a></li>
<li>Services
 <ul>
 <li><a href="/~bss/oclcsrvs.html">OCLC</a></li>
 <li><a href="/~ids/Reference/">Reference Databases</a></li>
 <li><a href="/~randd/internet.html">Internet</a></li>
 <li><a href="/~bss/cat-tech.html">Cataloging</a></li>
 <li><a href="/~randd/Database-menu.html">Database Creation</
a></li>
 <li><a href="/~bss/rshar.html">Resource Sharing</a></li>
 <li><a href="/~ids/Hardsoft/">Hardware &amp; Software</a></li>
 <li><a href="library-office.html">Library &amp;<br />Office
Supplies</a></li>
 <li><a href="/~ids/Discounts/">Discounts</a></li>
 <li><a href="/~business/">Accounting</a></li>
 <li><a href="/~shoffhin/consult/">Consulting</a></li>
 </ul>
</li>
</ul>
```

I have added an additional four (very short) lines of code but the benefits are twofold. The code now more accurately represents the structure of the content, and we have got built-in left margin increases with the nested list that we will not have to deal with once we start changing the display of your list with CSS.

DEFINITION LISTS

Definition lists are designed to work with sets of terms and their definitions. Based on this description you might think that the only situation in which you would use a definition list is to create a glossary on your site, but the concept of terms and their definitions need not be so literal. The "term" could be the name of a library staff member, and the "definition" could be a short biography. In another example, the "term" could be a date and the "definition" a description of the event taking place on that date. Keeping these examples in mind, the possibilities of the definition list open up immensely.

Unlike unordered and ordered lists which use pairs of elements (<ul> and <li> or <ol> and <li> respectively), a definition list uses sets of three elements: <dl>, <dt>, and <dd>.

<dl>...</dl>

Strict / Transitional / Frameset

<dl> is used to start and end a definition list just as <ul> and <ol> are used.

```
<dl>
</dl>
```

<dt>...</dt>

Strict / Transitional / Frameset

Within a definition list you place one or more "definition terms." We'll use this list to create a simple events calendar for the library. Our "terms" will be event titles and their dates (Figure 6.6).

```
<dl>
<dt>Story Time - Every Thursday</dt>
<dt>The Art of Book Collecting For Beginners - February 21st</dt>
<dt>Introduction to the Internet - March 1st</dt>
</dl>
```

Figure 6.6. A Definition List with Three Terms

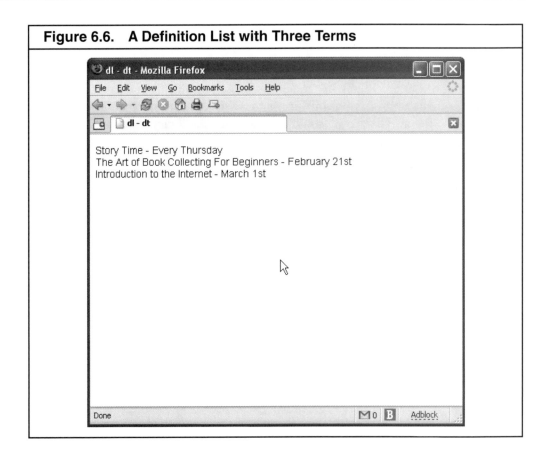

At this stage, our list looks like one of our earlier lists but without either bullets or numbers. (Don't look at this as an easy way to create a list without bullets. If you're writing an unordered or ordered list and don't want the bullets or numbers, use CSS to turn them off.)

`<dd>...</dd>`

Strict / Transitional / Frameset

Within each term you need to then place one or more pieces of "definition data" or the information related to your term. In this example, each of these titles and dates has an associated description (Figure 6.7).

```
<dl>
 <dt>Story Time — Every Thursday</dt>
  <dd>Miss Gwynneth, our children's librarian, will read a few new
  selections from our children's collection each week beginning
  at 6:30pm. Storytime usually lasts for about 30 minutes.</dd>
 <dt>The Art of Book Collecting For Beginners — February 21st</dt>
  <dd>Local author Michael Sauers will be in our community room
  to present on the art of collecting "modern first editions."
  He'll be bringing plenty of books from his personal collec-
  tion to show to the attendees.</dd>
```

```
<dt>Introduction to the Internet — March 1st</dt>
    <dd>Young Adult librarian Laura will present a one-hour in-
    troduction to the Internet so you can keep up with your
    teens. This session will be hands-on, so space is limited.
    Please sign up ASAP.</dd>
</dl>
```

Figure 6.7.   A Definition List with Terms and Data

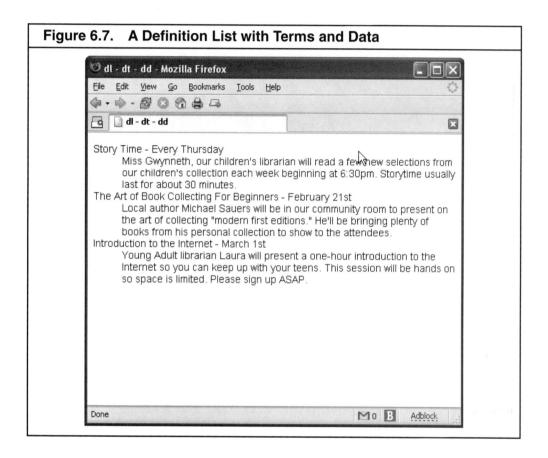

As you can see in the screenshot, the terms will be along the left margin of the page but their associated definitions will have an increased left margin. (The right margin is not moved by default. Both margins can be changed through the use of CSS.)

Note also that I said each term can have "one or more" items of data. Let me add a new line of code to show you how this can be done (Figure 6.8).

```
<dt>The Art of Book Collecting For Beginners — February 21st</dt>
    <dd>Local author Michael Sauers will be in our community room
    to present on the art of collecting "modern first editions."
    He'll be bringing plenty of books from his personal collection
    to show to the attendees.</dd>
    <dd>Michael will not be able to appraise books as part of his
    presentation.</dd>
```

Figure 6.8.   One Term with Two Items of Data

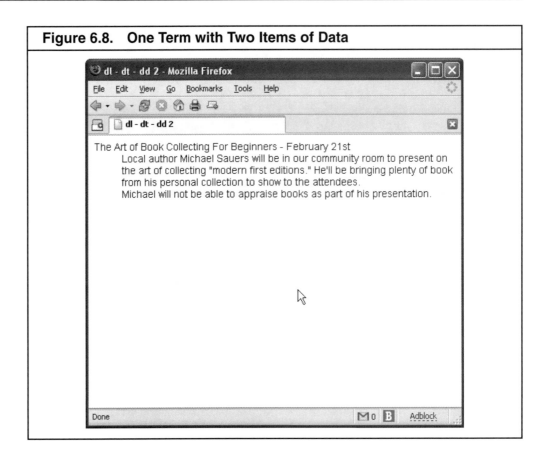

As shown in the screenshot, each new item of data will be started on its own line and will wrap accordingly. But, since we're attempting to write not only valid code (which this is) but also semantically clean code, let's look at another way to do the same thing (Figure 6.9).

```
<dt>The Art of Book Collecting For Beginners — February 21st</dt>
   <dd>Local author Michael Sauers will be in our community room
   to present on the art of collecting "modern first editions."
   He'll be bringing plenty of books from his personal collection
   to show to the attendees.<br />
   Michael will not be able to appraise books as part of his
presentation.</dd>
```

Figure 6.9. One Term with Reformatted Data

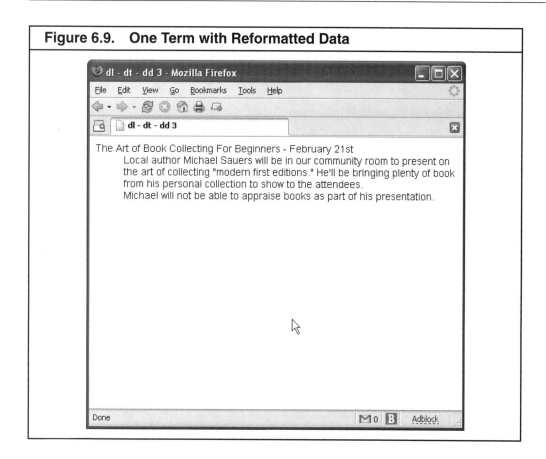

Although the result of this code is not visually different from the previous example, it is semantically different. Since both of the original data items are both part of the same description of the single presentation on the single date, it is semantically more accurate to include them in a single item of data. For the visual presentation, we've used a single line break to divide the idea into two parts.

Multiple data items are better used when there are multiple items associated with a particular "term." Here's a better example of the use of multiple data items for the same term, still using a calendar as the example (Figure 6.10).

```
<dl>
  <dt>Saturday, Feburary 21, 2004</dt>
  <dd>The Art of Book Collecting For Beginners — 2pm<br />
Local author Michael Sauers will be in our community room to
present on the art of collecting "modern first editions."
He'll be bringing plenty of books from his personal collection
to show to the attendees.<br />
Michael will not be able to appraise books as part of his
presentation.</dd>
  <dd>Book Signing with Michael Sauers - 7pm<br />
In the evening, Mr. Sauers will be back again to sign his
newest book "The Collector's Guide to Dean Koontz".<br />
Books will be available for purchase at the event.</dd>
</dl>
```

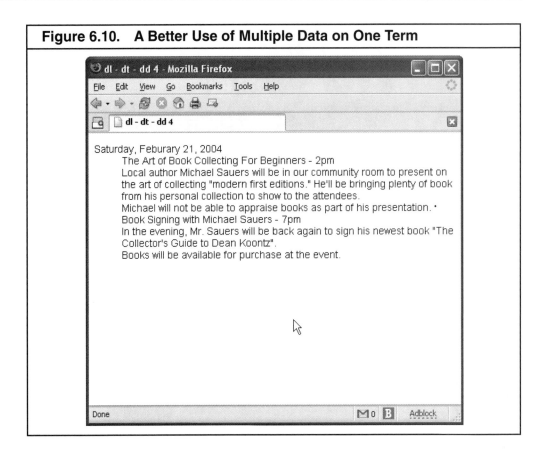

Figure 6.10.   A Better Use of Multiple Data on One Term

In this example, we have two events (data items) happening on the same date (term). This is a more appropriate use of multiple data items within the same term.

NOTE

1. DTD is an abbreviation for Document Type Definition. DTDs are one type of file that lays out the rules for a markup language. (Schemas are the other type and are not dealt with in this book.) The DTDs for XHTML 1.0 Strict, Transitional, and Frameset are reprinted in Appendices D, E, and F for those interested in delving a little deeper into the rules of XHTML.

7

Tables

WHAT ARE TABLES AND WHAT ARE THEY FOR?

Tables have been around since HTML 2.0. When tables were first created, the intent was to lend structure to tabular data—data that must be presented in rows and columns. (Anything that you would place in a spreadsheet is tabular data.)[1] Web authors quickly discovered that since any content can be placed within a table, the rows and columns of a table could be easily converted into a gridlike system to be used for layout. Tables are not, however, intended for the purpose of layout and should not be used in this manner.

For those of you with any substantial HTML experience, this may be a troubling concept. If you can't use tables for layout, how can you create the complex layouts we're used to? We'll be dealing with the alternatives of table-based layouts in Chapter 20, CSS Positioning. All of the examples I'll be presenting to you in this chapter will use tables for their intended purpose, to give structure to tabular data.

BUILDING YOUR TABLE

We're going to prepare a basic table showing our library's circulation statistics for the past month by week. Figure 7.1 shows what we'll be developing.

Figure 7.1.   The Finished Table

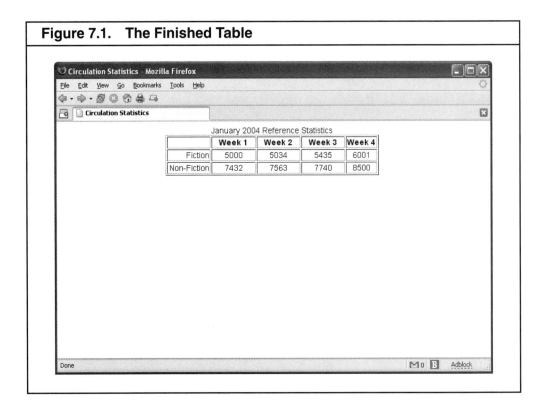

Remember, XHTML is designed to give structure to our content. We could continue to modify the appearance of the table using CSS.

`<table>...</table>`

Strict / Transitional / Frameset

First, we need to establish the beginning and ending of our table. To do this we use the `<table> ... </table>` element.

```
<!DOCTYPE html PUBLIC "-//W3C//DTD XHTML 1.0 Transitional//EN"
"http://www.w3.org/TR/xhtml/DTD/xhtml1-transitional.dtd">
<html xmlns="http://www.w3.org/TR/xhtml" lang="en">
<head>
<title>Circulation Statistics</title>
<meta name="HTTP-Equiv" content="text/html; content="utf-8">
</head>
<body>
<table>
</table>
</body>
</html>
```

```
<tr>...</tr>
```

Strict / Transitional / Frameset

Next, we establish the number of rows in our table. Looking at Figure 7.1, we see that we need three rows. Each row within a table is indicated by the element `<tr> . . . </tr>`.

```
<body>
<table>
 <tr>
 </tr>
 <tr>
 </tr>
 <tr>
 </tr>
</table>
</body>
```

```
<td>...</td>
```

Strict / Transitional / Frameset

The next step in establishing our table's structure is to specify the number of cells within each row. Until you start using CSS you should think in terms of cells rather than columns when you're working with tables. (I'll introduce you to columns at the end of the chapter.) Referring again to Figure 7.1, we need five cells per row. Table cells are marked with the `<td> . . . </td>` element. Cells are also known as "table data." The code to markup a simple table can get very long very quickly.

```
<table>
 <tr>
  <td></td>
  <td></td>
  <td></td>
  <td></td>
  <td></td>
 </tr>
 <tr>
  <td></td>
  <td></td>
  <td></td>
  <td></td>
  <td></td>
 <tr>
  <td></td>
  <td></td>
  <td></td>
  <td></td>
  <td></td>
 </tr>
</table>
```

Cells are known as "table data" because it is within the cells that the content will appear. Content (data) can only appear within a cell. Only a `<td>` can be the child of a row, so rows cannot contain any content. Also, the table element is not allowed to directly contain content; it may only contain other elements (such as `<tr>`) as children.

We now need to place the content within the cells. Our revised code will be:

```
<table>
 <tr>
  <td></td>
  <td>Week 1</td>
  <td>Week 2</td>
  <td>Week 3</td>
  <td>Week 4</td>
 </tr>
  <td>Fiction</td>
  <td>5000</td>
  <td>5034</td>
  <td>5435</td>
  <td>6001</td>
 <tr>
  <td>Non-Fiction</td>
  <td>7432</td>
  <td>7563</td>
  <td>7740</td>
  <td>8500</td>
 </tr>
</table>
```

Let me take a moment to point out to you a few items about this code. The first is that, since we want the first cell in the first row to be empty, we have not given it any content. The second is that since tables are two-dimensional (visually) but markup is one-dimensional (the code is linear written top down), one of the two dimensions of the table needed to go. The creators of HTML and XHTML decided to lose columns. This is why you should think in terms of cells rather than columns.

Let's take a look at the results of our code so far (Figure 7.2).

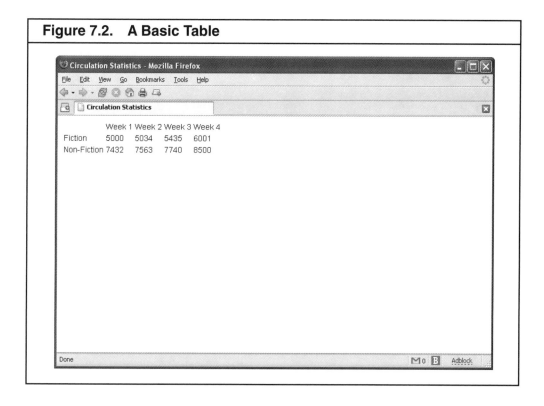

Figure 7.2.   A Basic Table

As you can see, we have the basic table but it's still not exactly what we want. Here's what we still need to address:

- The content of our first row is not bolded.
- The empty cell has no inside border.
- The table doesn't have a caption yet.
- The table is not centered on the page.
- The alignment of our cell content is incorrect.
- The column widths are not equal.

See the difference

border=" _n_ "

The border property established both the appearance of lines in a table along with the thickness (in pixels) of the outside edge of the table. In FireFox, the default value is "0," meaning no border or lines, while IE's default is "1," telling the lines to appear and the outside edge to be two pixels thick.

Although our final result has no lines, border="0," I always recommend turning the lines on while you're working and then turning them off when everything's done. (This makes it much easier to troubleshoot any coding problems during development.)

So, to make sure that our lines appear since we're working in FireFox, I'm going to add the border attribute to the table element (Figure 7.3).

```
<table border="1">
```

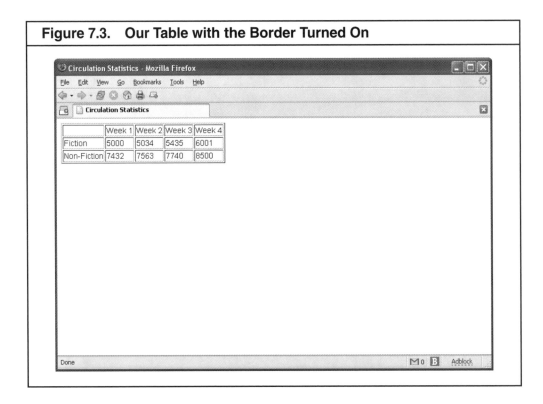

Figure 7.3.   Our Table with the Border Turned On

<th>...</th>

Strict / Transitional / Frameset

Let's take care of the first row before anything else. In Figure 7.1 we saw that the contents of the first row are bolded and centered. You might do something like this:

```
<tr>
 <td></td>
 <td align="center"><b>Week 1</b></td>
 <td align="center"><b>Week 2</b></td>
 <td align="center"><b>Week 3</b></td>
 <td align="center"><b>Week 4</b></td>
</tr>
```

This will work, but a few problems may arise. First, as previously discussed, the use of <b> is something that should be avoided and replaced with CSS. Secondly, this seems like tag soup—too much code to accomplish just two small changes. Lastly, if you have some experience with tables already, you may realize that we can move the alignment attributes from each cell onto the single row. (If you're not familiar with this, we'll be covering it a little later in this chapter.)

This is one of the few times that I am going to say that CSS is not necessarily the solution. Yes, you can replace the code with a few small lines of CSS, but since we're working with tables, there is a built-in solution that will not only achieve the look we want but will also be structurally and semantically accurate. That solution is to use table headers.

Imagine that you were entering this data into a spreadsheet. You might use the first row to hold information about what is contained in each column. These are known as header cells. By changing the relevant cells from table data to table header, you have labeled the content of the first row as being "headers."

Additionally, today's browsers will, by default, center and bold that content (Figure 7.4).

```
<tr>
 <th></th>
 <th>Week 1</th>
 <th>Week 2</th>
 <th>Week 3</th>
 <th>Week 4</th>
</tr>
```

Figure 7.4.   Our Table with Headers

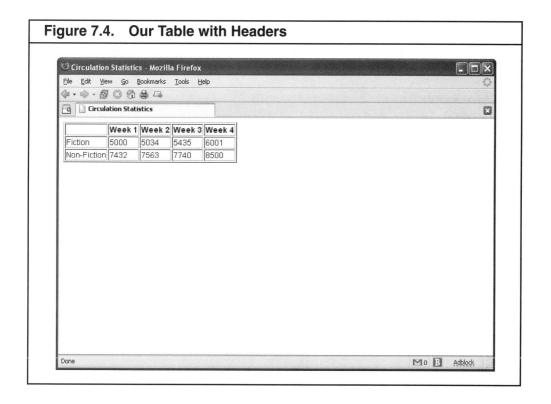

Don't forget to change both the starting and ending elements.

The fact that our header content is both centered and bolded has been decided by the browser. There is nothing built into XHTML that says this is how table header content should look. Remember, the markup is describing what the content is, not what it looks like. If you want your table header content to appear differently, you can always change it using CSS.

You may also have noticed that I changed the first cell, our empty cell, from table data to table header. Since this cell has no content, there was no technical reason for me to do this. However, for consistency's sake it makes little sense to have some cells in a row be data while others are headers. Regardless of the fact that there is no content, the empty cell is still part of our first row, which contains header information. (Logically, it would make more sense to have a table header row element available to us, one that would replace `<tr>` instead of `<td>` but alas, no such element exists.)

CREATING AN "EMPTY" CELL

Let's address the empty cell in the upper left corner of the table. The issue we have here is the fact that the inside borders of a cell will not appear unless there is content. Since our cell has no content, and we want this cell to have an inside border, we have a problem. How do we give a cell content to turn on an inside border without actually displaying any content to the user?

NOTE: From a design perspective, some of you may argue that the cell looks fine as it is, since the empty cell is in the upper left corner. However, if this empty cell were somewhere in the middle of the table, indicating that data was missing by the fact that the cell contained no content, it would look out of place without inside borders.

A common suggested solution is to use a space. Let's try inserting a space in the correct cell and take a look at the results (Figure 7.5).

```
<tr>
 <th> </th>
 <th>Week 1</th>
 <th>Week 2</th>
 <th>Week 3</th>
 <th>Week 4</th>
</tr>
```

Figure 7.5. An Empty Cell With a Space that Works in Firefox but not in IE (shown)

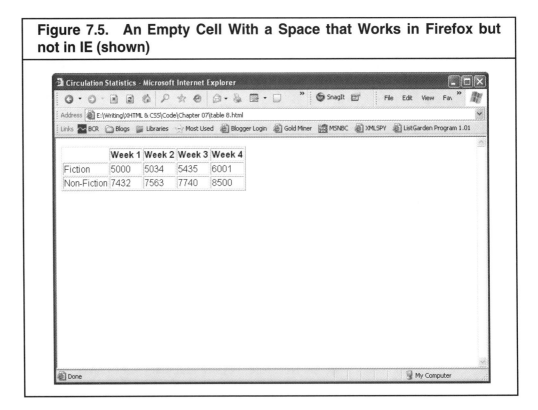

Unfortunately, IE does not recognize a single space that has no other content surrounding it. This is the same problem as when we discussed putting multiple spaces after punctuation. We force the browser to pay attention to a space by using a nonbreaking space (Figure 7.6).

```
<tr>
 <th> </th>
 <th>Week 1</th>
 <th>Week 2</th>
 <th>Week 3</th>
 <th>Week 4</th>
</tr>
```

Figure 7.6.   Our Table With an Empty Cell that Works in Both IE and Firefox (shown)

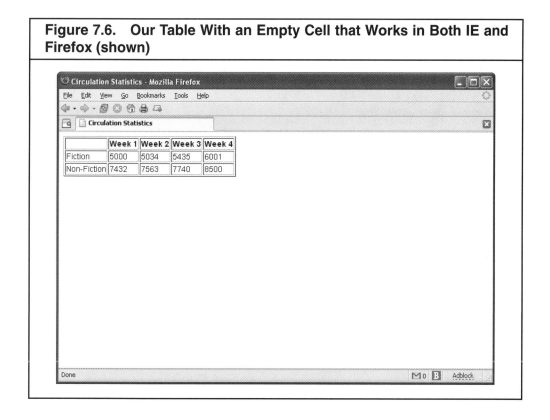

This solves our problem with the least amount of hassle.

In the interests of full disclosure, there is another solution, albeit one I do not recommend: the use of a "spacer .gif." Over the years, many designers have created small 1×1-pixel transparent .GIFs and then placed them within table cells. The idea is to create a graphical "shim" that can be used to manipulate table cells. This has three inherent problems that lead me not to recommend this as a solution. First, it creates more code, thereby leading to tag soup. Second, text is faster than graphics. A 1×1-pixel image is very small and loads very quickly, but text is still faster.

```
<caption>...</caption>
```

Strict / Transitional / Frameset

The `<caption>` element allows you to give your table a short title to your table. Traditionally, the `<caption>` element is placed on the line immediately following the `<table>` element (Figure 7.7).

```
<table>
<caption>January 2004 Reference Statistics</caption>
 <tr>
```

Figure 7.7. Our Table with a Caption

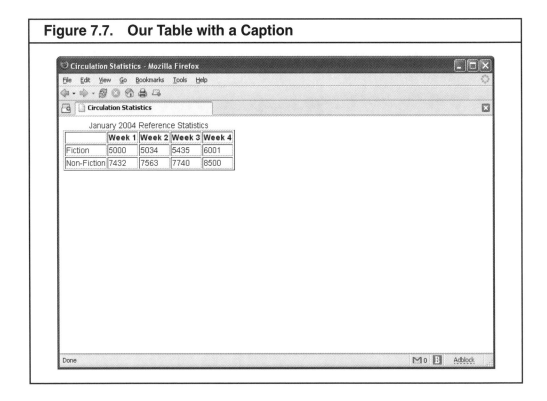

As you can see in the screenshot, by default a table's caption appears above vertically and centered horizontally. You have a limited ability to move the caption through the use of the `align=""` attribute. The available values for the align attribute in this case are `top` (the default), `bottom` (moves the caption below the table), `left`, and `right` (Figures 7.8 through 7.10).

Figure 7.8.   The Caption with `align="bottom"`

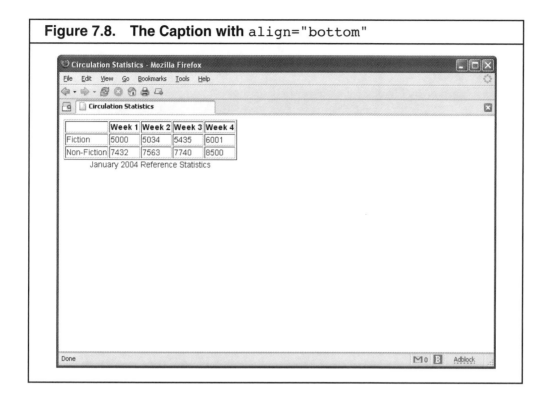

Figure 7.9.   The Caption with `align="left"`

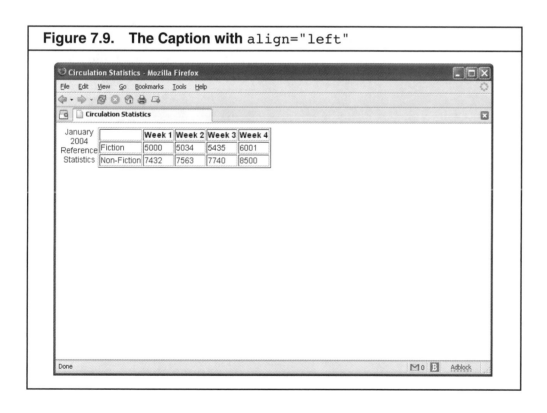

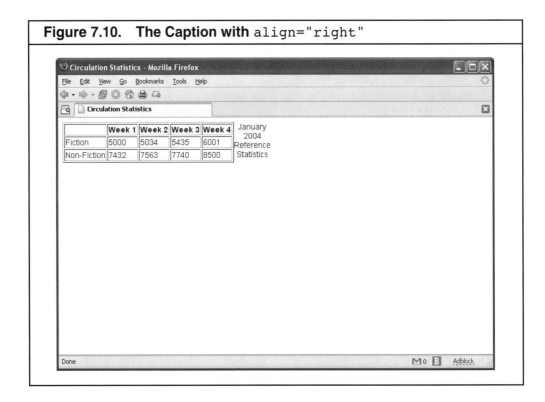

Figure 7.10. The Caption with `align="right"`

The benefit of `<caption>` is that we have attached this information to the table it-self. Were we to make changes to the table the caption would also be affected. (We'll be doing this next.) By making the caption text part of the table we have also achieved a more semantically correct result.

`width=""`

Transitional / Frameset

The table still looks somewhat compressed. By default, the size of the table is based upon the table's content. We can override that default and establish the size of the table ourselves through use of the `width=""` attribute.

We'll start by changing the width of the whole table. As we did when we changed the width of the `<hr/>` element, we can set the width of a table either via an absolute (pixel) or relative (percentage) value. We'll use a relative value to modify the table so it fills 50% of the page. To do this, we need to add `width="50%"` to the `<table>` element (Figure 7.11).

```
<table border="1" width="50%">
```

Figure 7.11.   Our Table With a 50 Percent Width

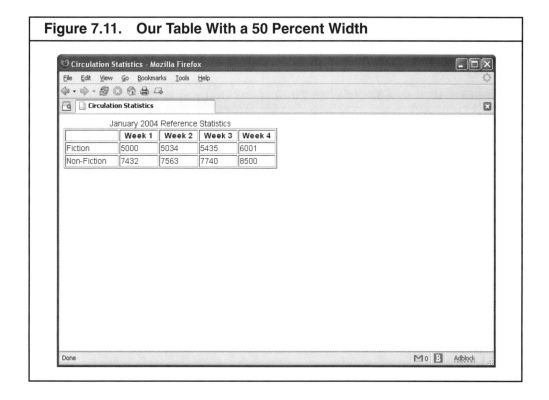

As you can see, the table now fills the middle 50 percent of our page, but the first column is still wider than the other columns. This is because the width of a column will be based upon its content unless we say otherwise. The browser has figured out what percentage of the entire table each column used before we changed the width of the table and adjusted the column width accordingly for our larger table. If the width of the first column, based on the contents of the cells in that column, were 37 percent of the width of the whole table before we modified that width, then that column would continue to fill 37 percent of the table after we adjusted the table's width. We can, however, also control column width through the use of the width attribute.

According to Figure 7.1, each of our columns should be of equal width. Since we have five columns, the math works out to 20 percent per column. The question is where in our code to add width attributes that affect the columns. We could set the width of every cell individually within the table. In this case, it wouldn't take too long, since we only have 15 cells, but what if we had a table with hundreds or even thousands of cells? This method would be highly inefficient.

Rather than set each cell individually, we can accomplish the same task with a minimal amount of code by setting the width of just one cell within each column. Which cell doesn't matter. For our purposes, we'll add the width attribute to the first cell in each row (Figure 7.12).

```
<tr>
 <th width="20%"> </th>
 <th width="20%">Week 1</th>
 <th width="20%">Week 2</th>
```

```
<th width="20%">Week 3</th>
<th>Week 4</th>
</tr>
```

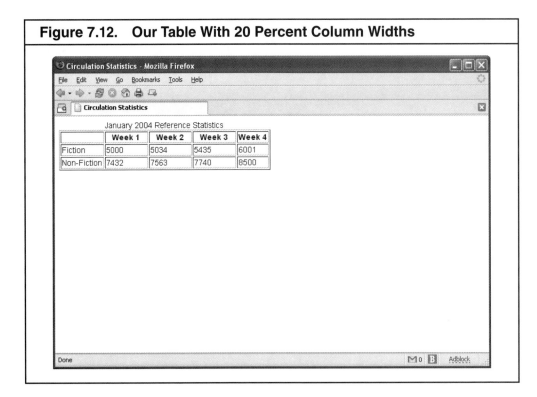

Figure 7.12.   Our Table With 20 Percent Column Widths

It may appear that I left out some code from the last cell in the row. This was intentional. I could have added the width attribute to the last cell, but since each of our first four columns fills 20 percent of the whole table, the last one must automatically take up whatever space is left to total 100 percent of our table. In this case, the "missing" amount is 20 percent, which is automatically applied to our fifth column.

`align=""`

Strict / Transitional / Frameset

Aligning the table

We also wanted to center the table on the page. This can be done through the addition of the `align=""` attribute to the `<table>` element. In this case, we only need to make one little change to the code. There are two things you should notice about the result (Figure 7.13).

```
<table align="center" width="50%">
```

Figure 7.13.   Centering our Table

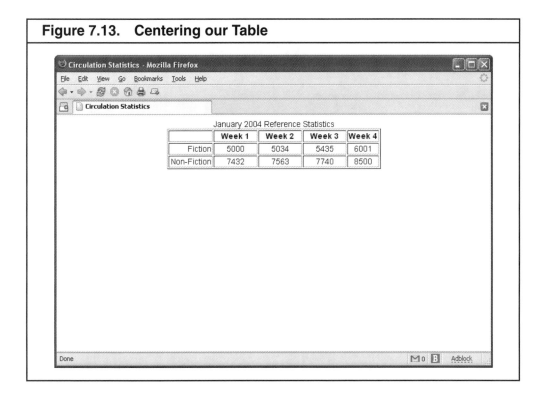

First, now that the table has moved to the center of our page, the caption has moved along with it. Second, the `align` attribute, when set on the table as a whole, is not inherited by the table cells. In other words, this use of the `align` attribute centered the table, but not any of the content within the table's cells. This change can be made with the `align` attribute, but in a different location. Let's look at that now.

Aligning table content

The `align=""` attribute can also be placed on any row or cell within the table. There are four values available to us: `left` (the default,) `right`, `center`, and `justify` (full justification.)

This is what we'd like to end up with (Figure 7.14).

Figure 7.14.   Aligning your Table's Content

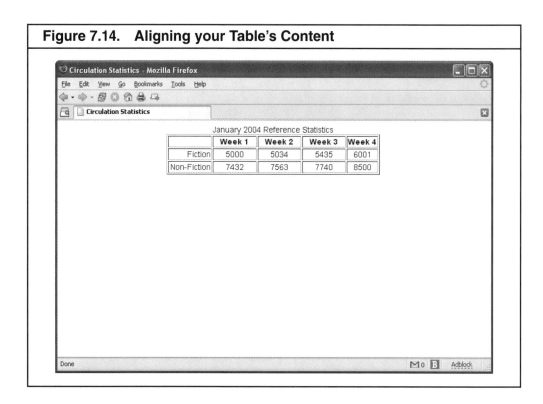

We want to center the numbers but, right-justify the content of the first column. There are several ways we can go about achieving this result, but the key is to look for the path of least code.

The following code is technically correct and would achieve the desired result.

```
<tr>
 <td align="right">Fiction</td>
 <td align="center">5000</td>
 <td align="center">5034</td>
 <td align="center">5435</td>
 <td align="center">6001</td>
</tr>
<tr>
 <td align="right">Non-Fiction</td>
 <td align="center">7432</td>
 <td align="center">7563</td>
 <td align="center">7740</td>
 <td align="center">8500</td>
</tr>
</table>
```

Though this does work, there is far more code than we need.

Here's another way to accomplish the same thing. For the purpose of clarity, we'll break it down into two steps.

The first step is to put the align="right" on the table rows instead of the table cells (Figure 7.15).

```
<tr align="center">
 <td>Fiction</td>
 <td>5000</td>
 <td>5034</td>
 <td>5435</td>
 <td>6001</td>
</tr>
<tr align="center">
 <td>Non-Fiction</td>
 <td>7432</td>
 <td>7563</td>
 <td>7740</td>
 <td>8500</td>
</tr>
</table>
```

Figure 7.15.   Centering all of our Content

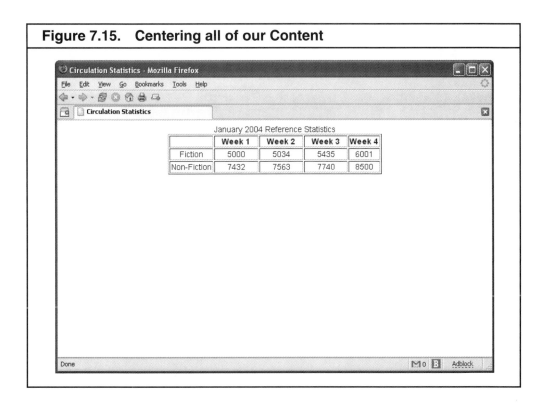

In this case, the alignment is inherited by the children of the rows, and all of the content is centered. However, we do not want the content of the first column to be centered. We want that content to be right-justified. To do this, we add `align="right"` to the appropriate cells (Figure 7.16).

```
<tr align="center">
 <td align="right">Fiction</td>
 <td>5000</td>
 <td>5034</td>
 <td>5435</td>
 <td>6001</td>
</tr>
<tr align="center">
 <td align="right">Non-Fiction</td>
 <td>7432</td>
 <td>7563</td>
 <td>7740</td>
 <td>8500</td>
</tr>
</table>
```

Figure 7.16.   Right-justifying our First Column

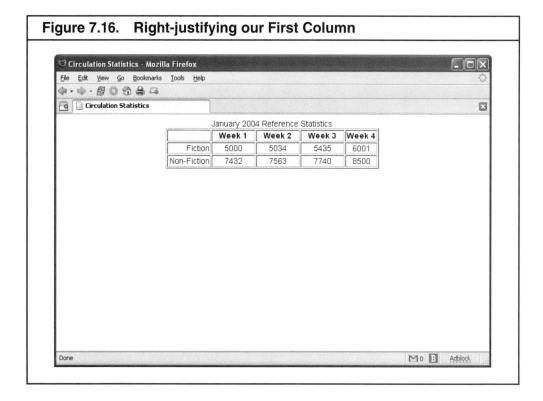

This accomplishes the same goal without nearly as much code. (We can also tackle this job through the use of the `<col>` element. We'll cover that later in this chapter.)

NOTE: Both the align and width attributes have been deprecated. Both of these attributes have CSS equivalents and that method is preferred.

WIDE CELLS AND TALL CELLS

The sample table has the same number of cells in each row, but this may always be your goal. Let's add a fourth row to our table with only one cell (Figure 7.17).

```
  </tr>
  <tr>
   <td>Good news. Circ number are going up.</td>
  </tr>
 </table>
```

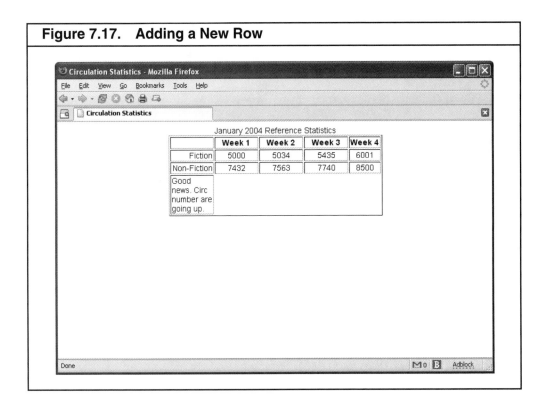

Figure 7.17.   Adding a New Row

The browser assumes that, since we had five cells in every other row, that we must also have five cells in this row and have only bothered to put content into the first one. It treats the other four cells and empty cells. What I'd like to do is to make this row contain one cell that stretches across all five columns. To do this I need to add a `colspan="5"` to the appropriate `<td>` element (Figure 7.18).

```
 <tr>
  <td colspan="5">Good news. Circ number are going
  up.</td>
 </tr>
```

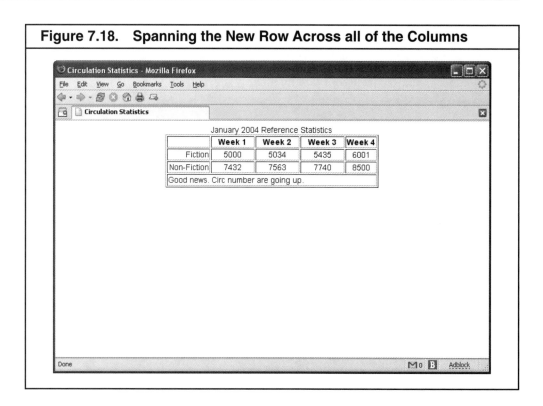

Figure 7.18.   Spanning the New Row Across all of the Columns

The rowspan attribute is similar to the colspan attribute but works in a vertically. Let's add a new first column to our table that contains only one cell (Figure 7.19).

```
<table border="1" width="75%" align="center">
<caption>January 2004 Circulation Statistics</caption>
<tr>
 <th> </th>
 <th>Week 1</th>
 <th>Week 2</th>
 <th>Week 3</th>
 <th>Week 4</th>
 <td>Created on 02.16.04</td>
</tr>
```

Figure 7.19.   Adding a New Column

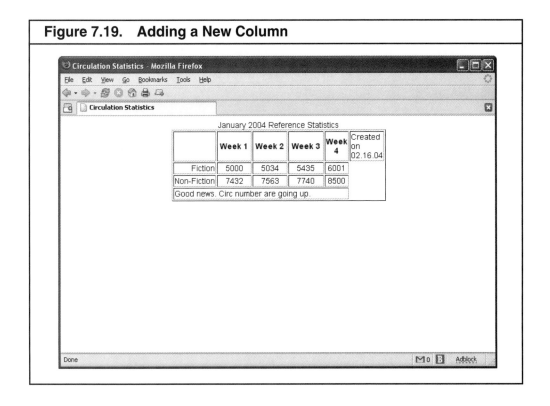

This time, the browser has assumed that since we now have six columns in our first row, we should have six columns in every row. To make the cell extend to the bottom of the table we add `rowspan="4"` (Figure 7.20).

```
<th>Week 4</th>
<td rowspan="4">Created on 02.16.04</td>
</tr>
```

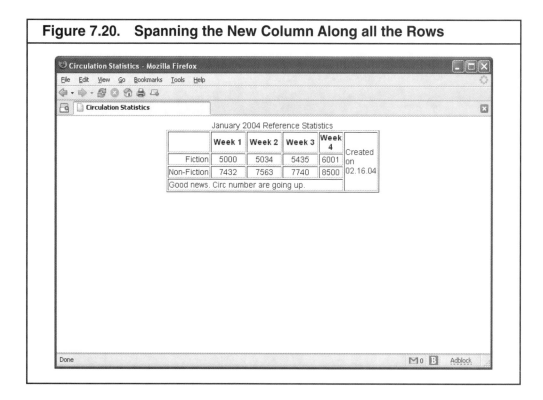

Figure 7.20.   Spanning the New Column Along all the Rows

The use of rowspan adds one additional issue to be addressed—the concept of vertical alignment. This is handled through the use of the valign="" attribute. The three values for valign are top, middle (the default,) and bottom. If we wanted to have the text centered horizontally at the top of this cell we add:

```
<td rowspan="4" align="center" valign="top">Created on 02.16.04
</td>
```

You may have noticed that the addition of a sixth column misaligned all the column widths we set earlier. This is why you want to plan out your table first. At this point we should go back and readjust our column widths to match the new design. I'll leave that to you.

The remaining adjustments will be based upon the 3x5 table in Figure 7.1. We will not include the additional row and column we've just added.

FINE-TUNING THE APPEARANCE OF THE TABLE

There are a few additional attributes you can add to your table that will affect the appearance of your table. As with the width and align attributes, these attributes have been deprecated and CSS methods are preferred.

background="..."

Transitional / Frameset

The background element allows you to set a colored background for the entire table or for individual rows or cells as you require.

cellspacing="n"

Transitional / Frameset

The cellspacing attribute is added to the <table> element. This sets the number of pixels of space between cells. For example, if you were to add cellspacing="10," Figure 7.21 shows your result.

Figure 7.21.   Adding the cellspacing **Attribute**

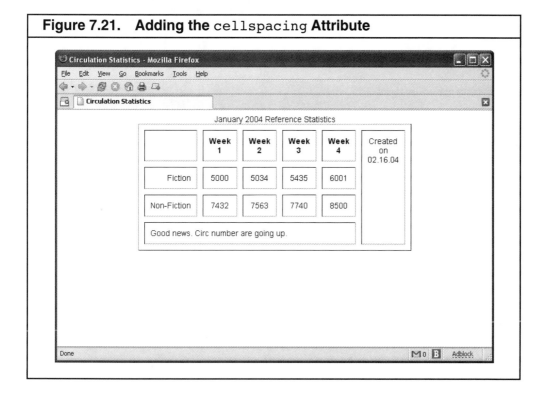

The setting of `cellspacing` in XHTML is an all-or-nothing proposition. This attribute sets the same spacing on all cells. Through CSS you can control the spacing between cells individually.

cellpadding="n"

Transitional / Frameset

The `cellpadding` attribute, also placed on `<table>` sets, in pixels, the amount of space between the inside border of a cell and the cell's content. `cellpadding="10"` would result in what's shown in Figure 7.22.

Figure 7.22.   Adding the `cellpadding` Attribute

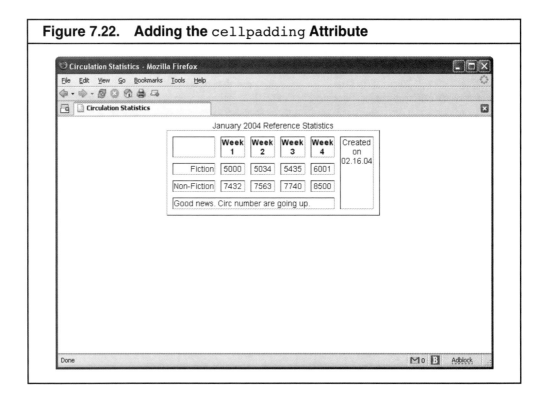

As with `cellspacing` this is an all-or-nothing proposition. With CSS you can control this setting on cells individually.

TURNING OFF THE LINES

Now that we've got our table all filled in and looking about right, let's go back and turn off those lines (Figure 7.23).

```
<table border="0">
```

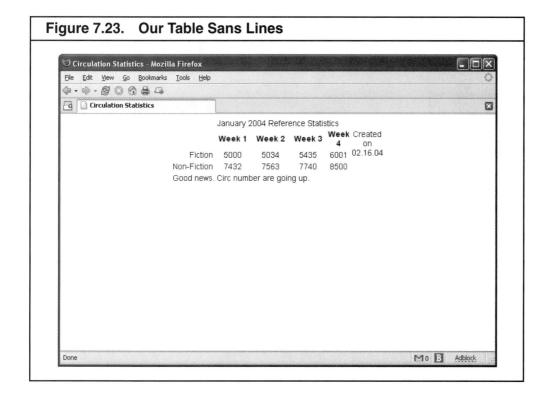

Figure 7.23. Our Table Sans Lines

ADDING ADDITIONAL STRUCTURE TO TABLES

There are additional elements and attributes that, when added to your table, can give additional levels of structural and/or semantic clarity. In some cases the use of the elements themselves doesn't do anything visually to the table as most users will see it. In other cases, these elements and attributes have the potential to give your table an additional level of accessibility, though most browsers do not yet take advantage of those features. (For that reason, I will not go into all of these elements in depth but will only introduce their basic uses.)

summary="..."

Transitional / Frameset

The summary attribute allows you to add a narrative summary of the data that the table is presenting to the user. The intention here is that a voice-based browser would read the summary by default and give the user the option of hearing all of the data.

```
<table border="0" align="center" width="50%" summary="This table
shows an increasing number of circs throughout the month of
January 2004.">
```

Heads, feet, and bodies

`<thead>`, `<tfoot>`, and `<tbody>`
Strict / Transitional / Frameset

This is another set of table code that is not widely used. These elements have great potential, but since no browser that I'm aware of makes any use of the code, no one bothers to use them.

The elements `<thead>`, `<tfoot>`, and `<tbody>` allow you to break your document down into separate sections that the browser can then interpret differently. For example, if we edited our table to include these elements (and removed the extra left-column and bottom row) it would look like this:

```
<table border="0" align="center" width="50%" summary="This table
shows an increasing number of circs throughout the month of
January 2004.">
<caption>January 2004 Circulation Statistics</caption>
<thead>
 <tr>
  <th width="20%"> </th>
  <th width="20%">Week 1</th>
  <th width="20%">Week 2</th>
  <th width="20%">Week 3</th>
  <th>Week 4</th>
 </tr>
</thead>
<tfoot>
 <tr>
  <th width="20%"> </th>
  <th width="20%">Week 1</th>
  <th width="20%">Week 2</th>
  <th width="20%">Week 3</th>
  <th>Week 4</th>
 </tr>
</tfoot>
<tbody>
 <tr align="center">
  <td align="right">Fiction</td>
  <td>5000</td>
  <td>5034</td>
  <td>5435</td>
  <td>6001</td>
 </tr>
 <tr align="center">
  <td align="right">Non-Fiction</td>
  <td>7432</td>
  <td>7563</td>
<td>7740</td>
  <td>8500</td>
 </tr>
</tbody>
</table>
```

Before we look at the screenshots there's one important thing I need to point out. Notice that first comes `<thead>`, then `<tfoot>`, then `<tbody>`. Despite the order you might think you should code them in, this is the proper order.

In browsers that have minimal support for this code, the `<tfoot>` region will be automatically displayed as the last row of the table, despite the fact that it is coded second. Unfortunately, browsers that don't understand this code will display the `<tfoot>` section as the second row of the table, just as if the table head, foot, and body elements didn't exist (Figure 7.24).

Figure 7.24. Table Head, Foot, and Body

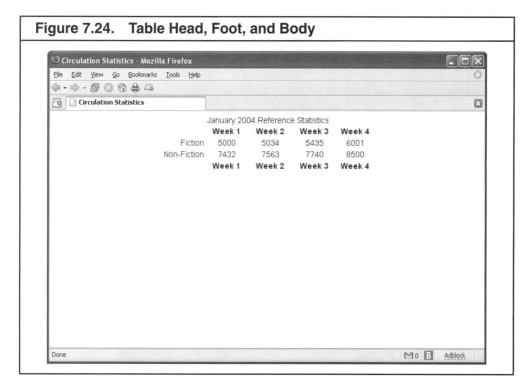

The potential of these elements is compelling should the browsers implement them. For example, picture a table with hundreds of rows, which obviously causes page scrolling. Through the use of these elements, a browser could display the row within `<thead>` every dozen or so rows depending on the screen size or, place the `<thead>` row at the top of the screen and the `<tfoot>` row at the bottom and place a scrollbar within the `<tbody>` area of the table, thus keeping the header and footer rows on the screen at all times.

Column Control

```
<col /> and <colgroup>
```
Strict / Transitional / Frameset

I spent most of this chapter directing you not to think in columns when designing an XHTML table. You can use columns in certain situations, however, I maintain that you should only think in columns as an afterthought. Do your main table design as I've previously suggested and then come back to this column code when you're finished to see if you can tighten your code up a little bit.

XHTML includes two column-based elements, `<col />` and `<colgroup>`. Both of these elements sit within the table but outside (before) the rows. The `<col />` element specifies columns within a table. If I were to add this element to our table it would look like this:

```
<table border="0" align="center" width="50%" summary="This table
shows an increasing number of circs throughout the month of
January 2004.">
<caption>January 2004 Circulation Statistics</caption>
<col />
<col />
<col />
<col />
<col />
<thead>
```

All I have done by adding this code is to tell the browser that my table has five columns. This by itself does nothing. However, I can now move my width attributes from my cells to my columns.

```
<table border="0" align="center" width="50%" summary="This table
shows an increasing number of circs throughout the month of
January 2004.">
<caption>January 2004 Circulation Statistics</caption>
<col width="20%" />
<col width="20%" />
<col width="20%" />
<col width="20%" />
<col width="20%" />
<thead>
  <tr>
   <th> </th>
   <th>Week 1</th>
   <th>Week 2</th>
   <th>Week 3</th>
   <th>Week 4</th>
  </tr>
</thead>
```

Admittedly, this is not less code than our original but it is semantically more correct.

The `<colgroup>` element allows you to gather multiple columns into a single group that can be manipulated as one. In this case I'll use colgroup to give the first and last two columns yellow backgrounds. I realize that I'm jumping ahead of myself in this case as I'm using CSS to set the backgrounds, but that's the only way this will work (Figure 7.25).

```
<table border="0" align="center" width="50%" summary="This table
shows an increasing number of circs throughout the month of
January 2004.">
<caption>January 2004 Circulation Statistics</caption>
<colgroup style="background: yellow">
 <col width="20%" />
 <col width="20%" />
```

```
</colgroup>
<col width="20%" />
<colgroup style="background: yellow">
 <col width="20%" />
 <col width="20%" />
<colgroup>
```

Ultimately, the use of <col /> and <colgroup> are the most useful in conjunction with CSS.

Figure 7.25. Setting the Column Background Colors with the col **Element**

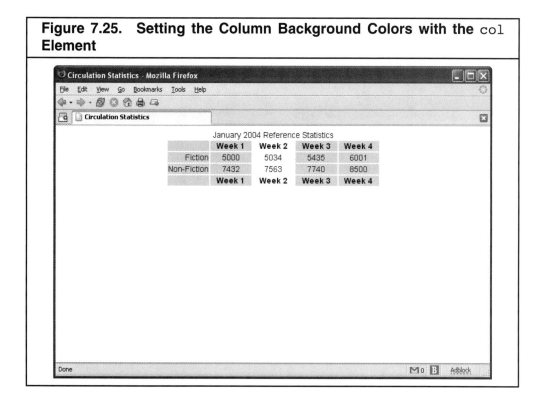

TABLES AND NONVISUAL BROWSERS

```
id=" . . . " and headers=" . . . "
```
Strict / Transitional / Frameset

The W3C included two additional attributes that can be used in tables and are designed to purely assist nonvisual browsers in the presentation of tabular data. Unfortunately, I am unaware of any browser today that supports any of these attributes and I have never seen them used in a live Web site. In the interest of completeness I will provide brief examples of each of them here.

In conjunction with the id attribute, the headers attribute can be used to associate data cells with header cells.

```
<tr>
 <th> </th>
 <th id="w1">Week 1</th>
 <th id="w2">Week 2</th>
```

```
<th id="w3">Week 3</th>
<th id="w4">Week 4</th>
</tr>
<tr align="center">
<td align="right">Fiction</td>
<td headers="w1">5000</td>
<td headers="w2">5034</td>
<td headers="w3">5435</td>
<td headers="w4">6001</td>
</tr>
<tr align="center">
<td align="right">Non-Fiction</td>
<td headers="w1">7432</td>
<td headers="w1">7563</td>
<td headers="w1">7740</td>
<td headers="w1">8500</td>
</tr>
```

A nonvisual browser could render this result by speaking the content of the identified cell before the content of each associated data cell.

This can also be accomplished through the use of the scope attribute. In this example, the col value for scope represents "all data in this column."

```
<table border="1" width="75%" align="center">
<caption>January 2004 Circulation Statistics</caption>
<tr>
<th> </th>
<th scope="col">Week 1</th>
<th scope="col">Week 2</th>
<th scope="col">Week 3</th>
<th scope="col">Week 4</th>
</tr>
<tr align="center">
<td align="right">Fiction</td>
<td>5000</td>
<td>5034</td>
<td>5435</td>
<td>6001</td>
</tr>
```

Additional information regarding the potential uses of the headers, scope, and axis attributes can be found in section 11.4.1 of the HTML 4.01 recommendation (www.w3.org/TR/html401/struct/tables.html#h–11.4).

NOTE

1. When attempting to decide whether or not to put your data into a table, ask yourself whether or not you would put it into a Word document or an Excel file. Statistics are perfect for a spreadsheet. If you were writing a document that needed columns you wouldn't suddenly decide to use Excel instead of Word.

8

Web Forms

WHAT IS A WEB FORM?

Forms are a way for a Web page to gather information from a user, process that information, and send a result back to that user. If you've ever used a search engine, you've used a form. If you look at Google's home page, you'll see a single text box and two buttons. You enter keywords into the text box, click one of the two buttons, wait just a moment or two, and receive a list of matching results. That text box and those buttons make up a form (Figure 8.1).

Figure 8.1.   The Form on Google's Home Page

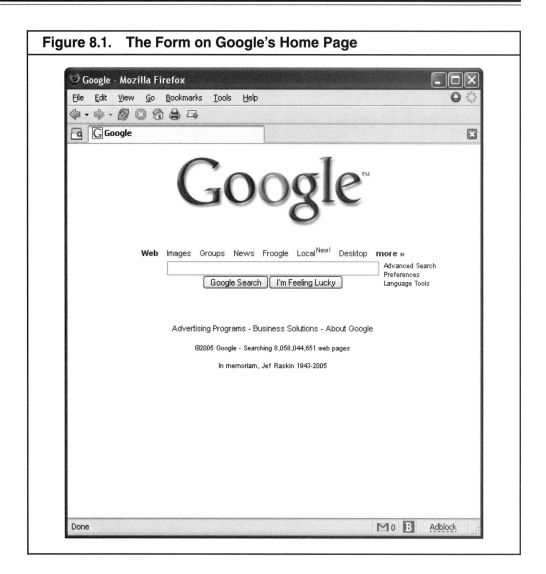

If you've ever made a purchase at an online store such as Amazon.com, you've filled out a form that included your billing information and shipping address. In this case you're completing a more complicated, multipage, form which is gathering your information, processing your credit card information, and instructing the seller at the other end to process your items for shipping (Figure 8.2).

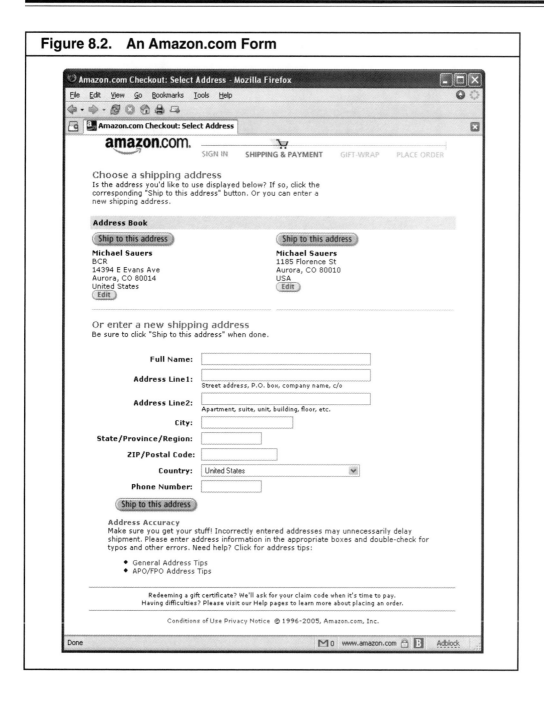

Figure 8.2. An Amazon.com Form

On the BCR Web site (www.bcr.org), there are forms to allow libraries to order products and to sign up for our workshops. In the case of a workshop registration, we collect information about the workshop attendees, the workshops they wish to attend, and billing information. Once this information has been collected, an e-mail message is sent to the BCR staff member who handles workshop registrations, an e-mail message is sent back to the registrant, and the information is automatically appended to a database on BCR's server (Figure 8.3).

Figure 8.3. BCR's Workshop Registration Form

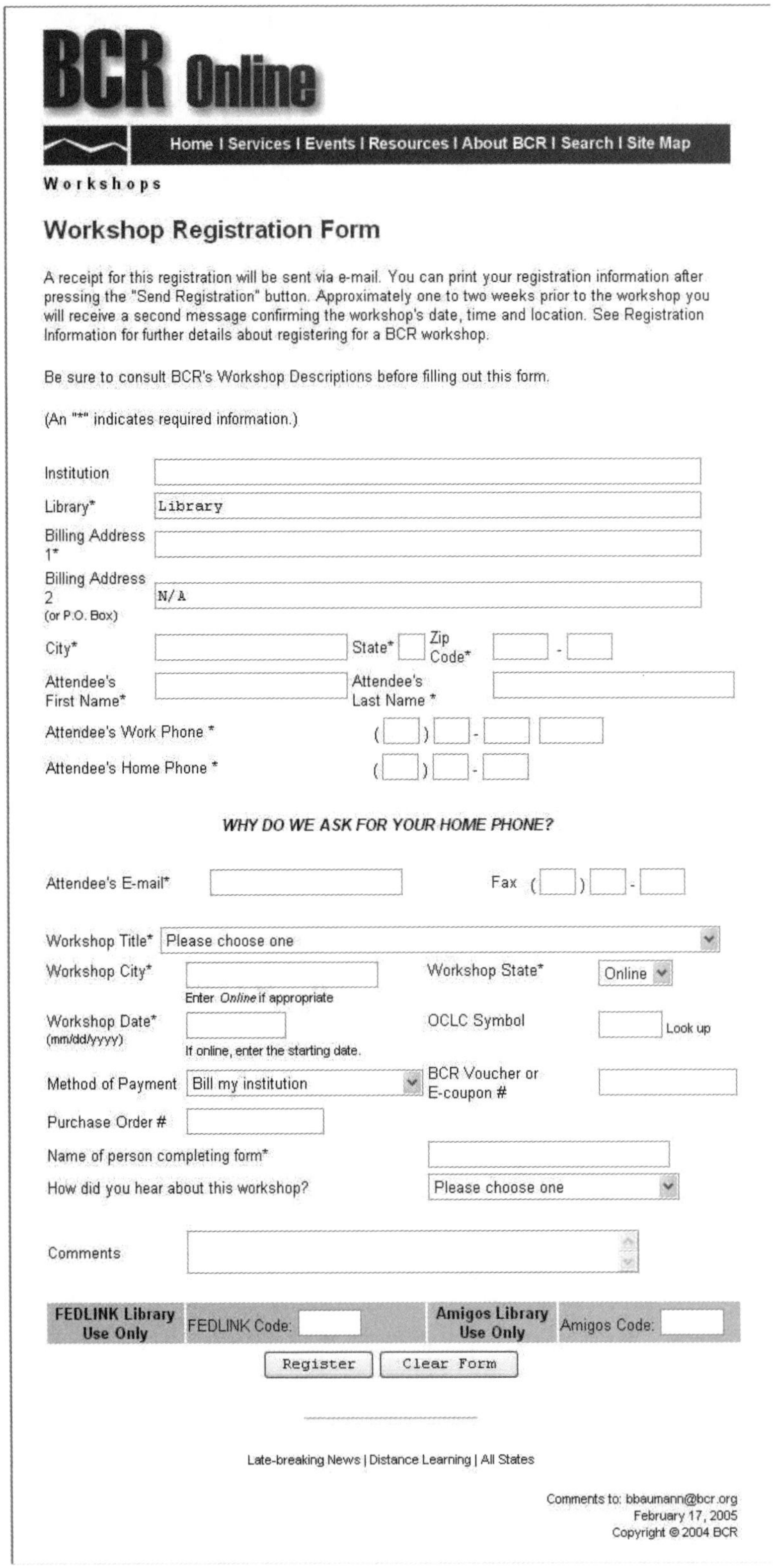

BCR Online

Home | Services | Events | Resources | About BCR | Search | Site Map

Workshops

Workshop Registration Form

A receipt for this registration will be sent via e-mail. You can print your registration information after pressing the "Send Registration" button. Approximately one to two weeks prior to the workshop you will receive a second message confirming the workshop's date, time and location. See Registration Information for further details about registering for a BCR workshop.

Be sure to consult BCR's Workshop Descriptions before filling out this form.

(An "*" indicates required information.)

Institution

Library* Library

Billing Address 1*

Billing Address 2 (or P.O. Box) N/A

City* State* Zip Code* -

Attendee's First Name* Attendee's Last Name *

Attendee's Work Phone * ( ) -

Attendee's Home Phone * ( ) -

WHY DO WE ASK FOR YOUR HOME PHONE?

Attendee's E-mail* Fax ( ) -

Workshop Title* Please choose one

Workshop City* Enter *Online* if appropriate Workshop State* Online

Workshop Date* (mm/dd/yyyy) If online, enter the starting date. OCLC Symbol Look up

Method of Payment Bill my institution BCR Voucher or E-coupon #

Purchase Order #

Name of person completing form*

How did you hear about this workshop? Please choose one

Comments

FEDLINK Library Use Only FEDLINK Code: Amigos Library Use Only Amigos Code:

Register Clear Form

Late-breaking News | Distance Learning | All States

Comments to: bbaumann@bcr.org
February 17, 2005
Copyright © 2004 BCR

Another example is a feedback form on a Web site. Maybe it's a form you can fill out to make an online interlibrary loan (ILL) request. In this case, your information is collected and most likely then e-mailed to the library's ILL department for further processing. This last example, an ILL request form, is the example that we'll be using throughout this chapter.

A FEW IMPORTANT NOTES ABOUT WEB FORMS

Designing a form involves deciding what questions to ask and how to ask them. The next step is typically laying out the form so that it fits into the design of the intended site. We will not be doing layout in this chapter. We are only concerned with getting the form on the page and making it work. We'll deal with making it look good in Chapter 19.

Once the form is on the screen, the next step is to make the form work; to instruct the form in what to do with the data that the user has given it. I will be discussing all of these issues in the second half of this chapter, but I can only go so far. The problem is that once the form has gathered the data, it must then pass that data along to a program known as a script. The script is the program that does the actual processing of the data. Which script you use depends on what you would want to do with the data. Unfortunately, creating a script is well beyond the scope of this book. There are prewritten scripts freely available on the Web, which you can download and use.

Additionally, form-processing scripts must be placed within a certain directory on your Web server. (Usually the directory named "cgi-bin.") Unless you are the Web server administrator, chances are you don't have access to this directory.

For these reasons I will walk you through the process of creating a form and show you what you would need to do next for one particular scenario only. Ultimately, you will need to either study your Web server documentation or speak with your Web server administrator in order to get everything working.

By the end of this chapter, you will not have a working form, but you will have the knowledge necessary to determine which questions to ask and/or which instructions to look for in your library.

FORM ELEMENTS

Strict / Transitional / Frameset

The following is a quick run-through of the elements that we'll be using in this chapter. There aren't many but some of them have multiple uses based on the type of data you're attempting to gather from your users.

- `<form> . . . </form>`
  This is the element that indicates the start and end of your form. All other form elements are children of `<form>`.
- `<input />`
  This is the most commonly used form element. This element is used to collect several different types of data from your users. The type of data collected is set by the type attribute.

- `<textarea>` . . . `</textarea>`
  This element also collects data from the user but creates a large multiline box into which a user can enter text.
- `<select>` . . . `</select>` and `<option>` . . . `</option>`
  These elements are used in combination to create a list of choices that a user may select from. The construction of these lists is similar to lists created with `<ul>` or `<ol>` and `<li>`.
- `<fieldset>` . . . `</fieldset>` and `<legend>` . . . `</legend>`
  The `<fieldset>` element is used to create logical groupings of form fields. The `<legend>` element is used to label a fieldset.

WRITING THE FORM

As I've already mentioned, a form must be contained within `<form>` and `</form>`. A Web page may contain multiple forms but a form may not contain another form. For an example of a page with multiple forms, look at Soople (www.soople.com/). Each of the 13 cells that contains a search button is an individual form (Figure 8.4).

Figure 8.4.   Thirteen Forms on One Page

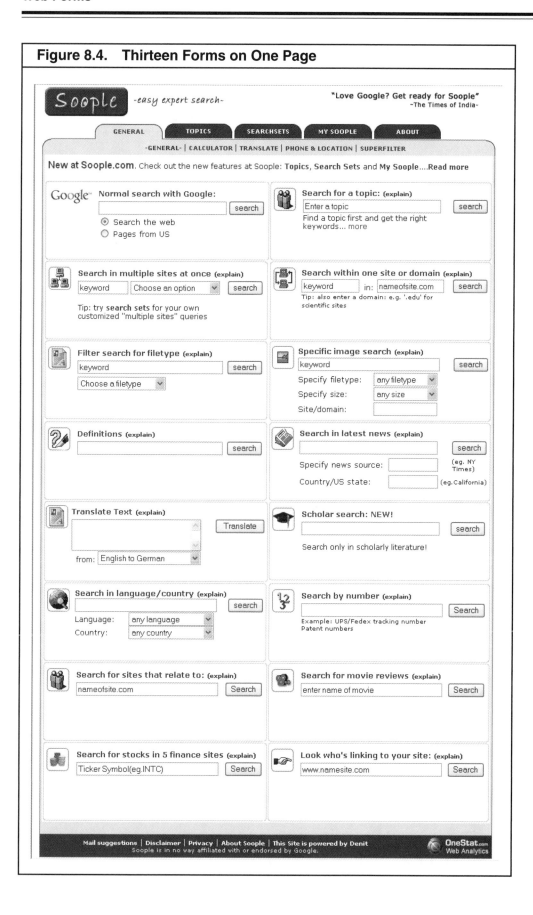

To create a page with a single form, we need to start a basic XHTML document and add our `<form>` and `</form>` elements, leaving a blank in which to work.

```
<!DOCTYPE html PUBLIC "-//W3C//DTD XHTML 1.0 Transitional//EN"
"http://www.w3.org/TR/xhtml/DTD/xhtml1-transitional.dtd">
<html xmlns="http://www.w3.org/TR/xhtml" lang="en">
<head>
<title>Acme Public Library ILL Request Form</title>
<meta name="HTTP-Equiv" content="text/html; content="utf-8">
</head>
<body>
<form>
</form>
</body>
</html>
```

The `<form>` element does nothing by itself. If you were to take a look at our page thus far in any browser, you would just see a blank document. `<form>` is just used as a container for the rest of our form elements.

The `<form>` element has two required attributes that must be present for our form to work: `method` and `action`. Since at this stage we're just concerned with getting our form onto the page, we'll leave these out for now and come back to them later.

Before we go any further in the creation of our form, let's add a heading on the page, before `<form>` so we're sure that our users understand what this form is supposed to do for them. Since this will be our one and only heading on the form, we should use a level-one heading. If you think the display of the heading is too large or should be centered, we can change that with the application of CSS.

```
<body>
<h1>ILL Request Form</h1>
<form>
</form>
```

DECIDING WHAT TO ASK THE USER

Before we dive into putting a bunch of questions or requests for information on our form, we should do a little planning. Let's consider what questions we'd like to ask of our users.

Since this is an ILL form, there is some basic information that we need about the user making the request. Here's the list I've come up with:

· Name
· Telephone Number
· E-mail address
· Library Card Number

Next, we'll need to ask for some information about the item the user is requesting. I suggest the following items:

- Title
- Author
- Type (book, article, A/V)
- Citation information
- Relationship to the library (faculty, staff, student)
- Amount willing to pay for the item
- Date needed by
- Additional comments from the user
- Would you like to receive the library's electronic newsletter?

Though the last two items are not necessary, at least the first one (in one form or another) should be included at the bottom of most forms.

BUILDING OUR FORM

Looking at our list, the first piece of information we need from our user is a name. We need to determine what type of input we're asking for. The first question we need to ask ourselves is, "Are we giving the user a choice?" Asking the user for his or her name, we are clearly not offering a choice.

So, the next question is whether this request requires the user to enter one or more lines to give us the information we need. In the case of a name, we need only one line. Since we're not giving the user a choice and require only one line of input, we will use the `<input>` element.

```
<form>
<div>
Name: <input />
</div>
</form>
```

The `<input>` element by itself does nothing. We need to add a few attributes to complete our code.

The first attribute is `type=""`. The type attribute tells the browser what type of box to put on the screen. In the case of a single-line text box, the value for type needs to be `"text."`

```
<form>
<div>
Name: <input type="text" />
</div>
</form>
```

The second attribute is `name=""`. Whenever you collect input from the user, you must give that input a name that can be referenced. Taking the code one step further, we now have:

```
<form>
<div>
Name: <input type="text" name="" />
</div>
</form>
```

A name for any input within a form must be unique, must start with a letter or an underscore, may contain numbers, and is case-sensitive. These are the technical requirements. To these I add that the name of an input should also be descriptive of that input. For example, if you have three boxes in a form, naming them box1, box2, and box3, although technically correct, would not be descriptive and would cause you problems in the long run.

When naming input, in some cases, the script you will use to process this data will have certain naming requirements. This is one of those cases. The requirement here is to name this input: "name" (Figure 8.5). (I''ll explain more about naming requirements later in this chapter.)

```
<form>
<div>
Name: <input type="text" name="name" />
</div>
</form>
```

Figure 8.5.   Asking for the User's Name

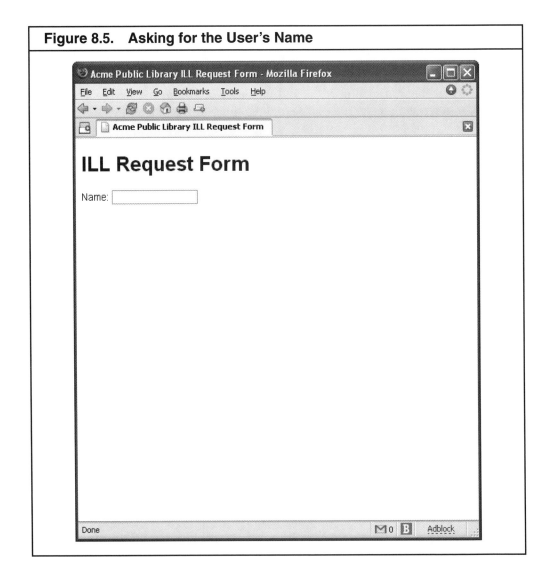

Now that we can actually look in a browser and see this form start to take shape, let's cover some questions you might have. First, why didn't we ask for the user's first and last names in separate fields? For the sake of simplicity, we are not using more fields in this form than are necessary. Of course, should you choose to break up a field into multiple fields in future forms, you can do so.

Second, what exactly is done with the name attribute? Whenever a form collects data from a user, it puts all of the collected data into a two-column chart. The first column is for the name of the data and the second is for the data itself. If I were to fill out the form as it is now it would look like Figure 8.6.

Figure 8.6.   Starting to Fill out the Form

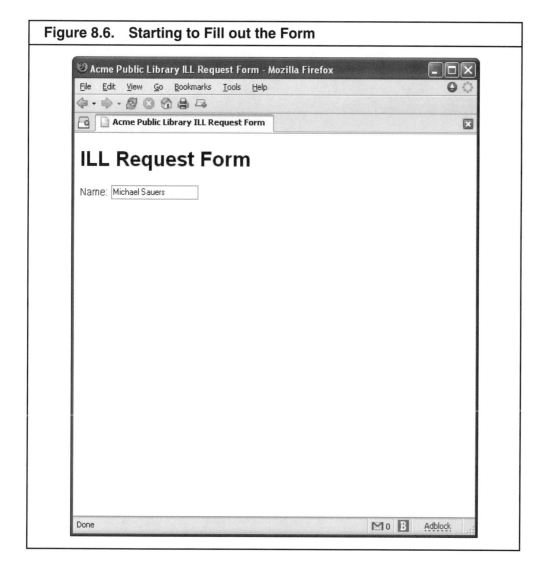

The resulting table would look like this:

name	Michael Sauers

As we continue to build our form and collect data from the user, additional rows will be added as this information is collected. I'll continue to add these rows in the table too so you can visualize the progress.

NOTE: It is a good idea when writing a form to keep a list of all of your field names on a piece of notepaper. Later, when you turn on the form, you'll need to remember all the names of the fields you've created. Though you may have a memory good enough to remember a dozen or so field names, forms tend to grow to have scores of fields and remembering all of them can be difficult.

Moving on to the next field, let's add a line break so the next request for information is on the next line. The next line requests the user to enter a telephone number, so is it a choice-based option? It is clearly not, so we now decide if we need one or more lines. A phone number requires one line of input, and we can go ahead and name this field "phone." Our code now looks like Figure 8.7.

```
<div>
Name: <input type="text" name="name" /><br />
Phone Number: <input type="text" name="phone" />
</div>
```

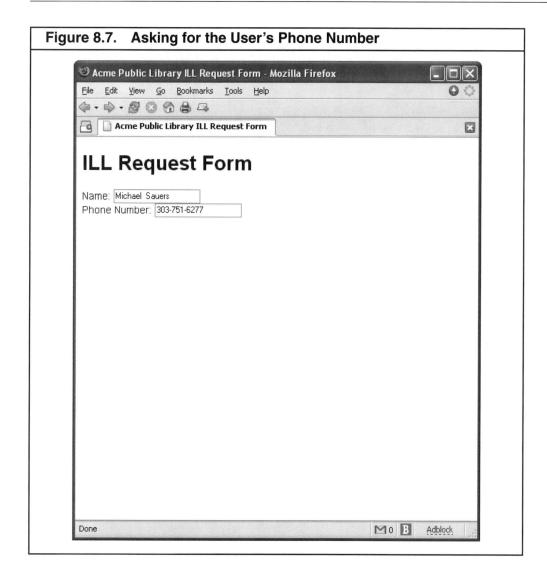

Figure 8.7. Asking for the User's Phone Number

Updating the data, the table would now look like this:

name	Michael Sauers
phone	303–751–6277

The next two items of input we need to request are the patron's e-mail address and their library card number. Neither of these are choice-based requests nor would either require more than one line of input. Therefore, we'll just update both items in one step (Figure 8.8).

```
<div>
Name: <input type="text" name="name" /><br />
Phone Number: <input type="text" name="phone" /><br />
E-mail Address: <input type="text" name="email" /><br />
Library Card Number: <input type="text" name="card" />
</div>
```

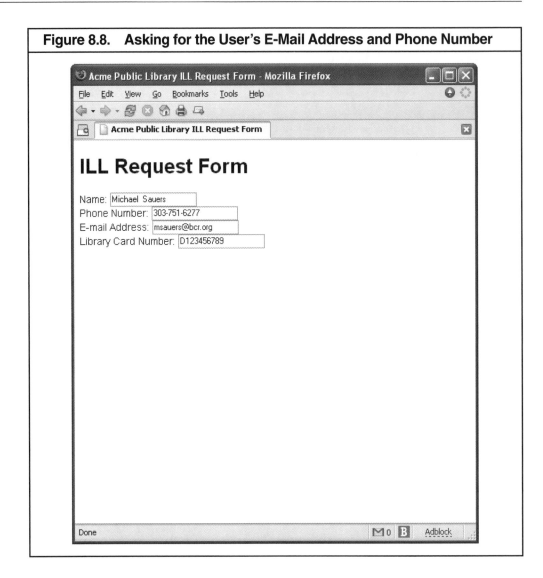

Figure 8.8.   Asking for the User's E-Mail Address and Phone Number

The e-mail address input is another field for which the script we're using requires a certain name. The name for the card number input was my choice. When choosing field names, try to keep them short and simple.

Based on the screenshot of the results and some sample data, here is the updated results table.

name	Michael Sauers
phone	303–751–6277
email	msauers@bcr.org
card	D123456789

Before we go any further in the design of our form, let's take a moment to manipulate our text boxes.

Text input boxes, by default, are approximately 20 characters wide and have no limit on the number of characters that you can enter into them. By default, they are also blank.

To change the width of a text input box, we add the `size="`*n*`"` attribute. The value for size must be a numeric value representing the number of characters wide you intend the box to be.

Forms also have the built-in ability to set the maximum number of characters that a text input box will accept. This is set via the `maxlength="`*n*`"` attribute, the value of which is the number of characters you wish to limit the box to.

Lastly, you can put default text into a text input box by adding the `value=""` attribute. (Remember, text input boxes derive their values from the data given by the user. By adding a value attribute, we are giving the box a default value of our choosing.)

Taking these options into account, what changes might we make to the work we've done so far?

- Twenty characters for a full name might be a bit short for some of our patrons. Although they can enter more than 20 characters, they'd probably like to be able to see what they've entered. Let's extend that box to 35 characters.
- To standardize the input of the phone number, let's limit entry to eleven characters. We should now shrink the box to 11 characters so that users don't think that they can add more. (If we're requiring users to input data in a certain format, we should also indicate that somehow on the screen.)
- For this form, we will assume that all library card numbers are ten digits long and therefore change and limit the input box accordingly. We will also assume that all library card numbers in the system start with "D1," so we'll go ahead and put those characters in the box for our users.

Here's a look at our adjusted code along with the results displayed in the browser (Figure 8.9).

```
<div>
Name: <input type="text" name="name" size="35" /><br />
Phone Number: <input type="text" name="phone" size="11"
maxlength="11" /> (xxx-xxx-xxxx)<br />
E-mail Address: <input type="text" name="email" /><br />
Library Card Number: <input type="text" name="card" size="10"
maxlength="10" value="D1" />
</div>
```

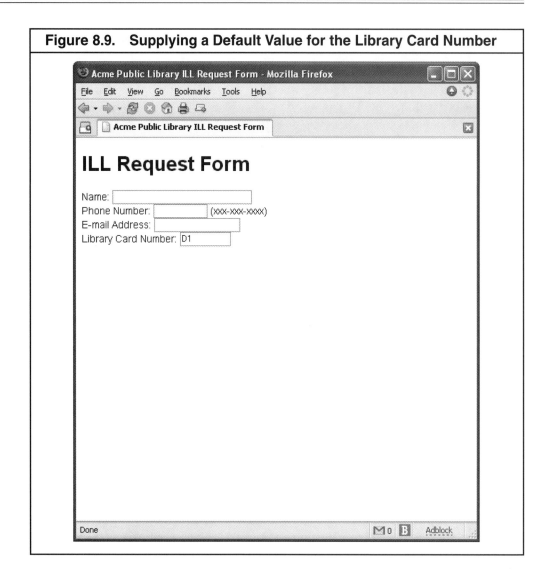

Figure 8.9.   Supplying a Default Value for the Library Card Number

As is now the case with our "card" text box, default text that you, the form's author, put into the box through the value method is entirely editable by the user. They can ignore this text or change it as they choose.

Later on, we'll be setting up some code to require that certain fields be filled in. If we place default text into the box ourselves, we have given that field data and it would therefore pass any requirement testing we might perform on it later, regardless of whether the user entered any additional data.

Neither of these is a reason not to enter default text, but you should keep this in mind when deciding whether to use this option.

There is one additional option available that you may wish to use in the case of requesting the user's library card number. This is the password input type, which works like a text box but with one significant difference: it hides the user's input on the screen. I'll make this change in the code, then discuss it in more detail.

```
Library Card Number: <input type="password" name="card" size="10"
maxlength="10" />
```

I have made two changes to this line of code. The first was to change the type attribute to password. This causes the box to display asterisks instead of the user's actual typed input.

The second change was to remove the `value` attribute, thus giving the box no default content. Changing this field to a password box will obscure all of the box's content, and a preset value of `"D1"` would appear to the user as `"**"`. Some users might misconstrue this and think the password field had already been filled in.

Although it is a good idea to use a password box when asking the user for sensitive information, it is not a feature that should be relied on for security purposes. All a password field does is prevent someone from "shoulder-surfing" your user. The password field does not encrypt your user's input in any way and will send you that input in an unsecured manner along with all of the rest of their data.

Let's move on to the next set of questions that we want to present to our users. These questions involve requests for information about the item they're asking for. Since these questions are logically separate from the previous set, we'll put them in their own <div>.

```
</div>
<div>
</div>
</form>
```

The first two requests we need to make in this section of our form are for the item's title and author. These are clearly not choice-based questions, nor should they need more than one line each for the user's input. I'll put in those lines of code now, then point out a few particulars (Figure 8.10).

```
<div>
Title: <input type="text" name="itemTitle" size="40" /><br />
Author: <input type="text" name="author" size="30" /><br />
</div>
```

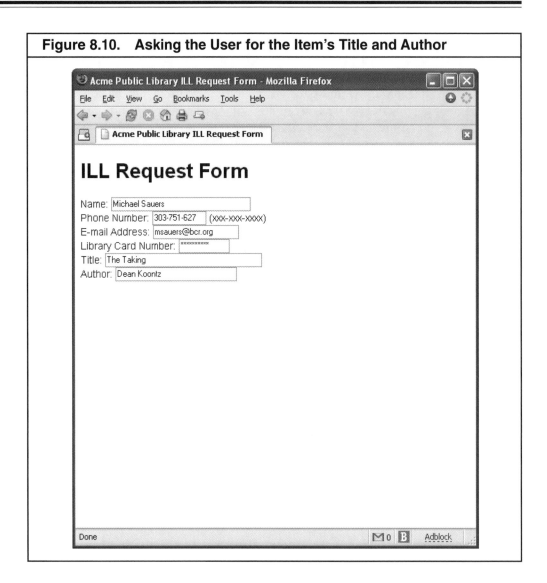

Figure 8.10.   Asking the User for the Item's Title and Author

Here's the updated table of results based on Figure 8.10.

Name	Michael Sauers
Phone	303–751–6277
Email	msauers@bcr.org
Card	D123456789
itemTitle	The Taking
author	Dean Koontz

We can safely assume that 20 characters may not be sufficient space for either a title or an author's name, so we can extend both text boxes. I had assigned the title box a value of 40 characters and the author box a value of 30 characters.

You should also have noticed that I named the input box "itemTitle." On principle, I agree that "title" would be a more appropriate name, but the script has reserved the name "title" for another purpose and using it here would not generate the desired result. I have chosen to name the box "itemTitle" rather than "itemtitle" to preserve the design convention of capitalizing the second word in a two-word string. This practice is not required, but if you choose to do otherwise, you should be consistent. At any rate, all references to this box must be exactly the same.

The next piece of input we're asking our user to provide is what type of media the requested item is. Again, we need to ask ourselves if this is a choice-based question. Let's say that this library will only process requests for certain types of media—books, articles, journals, and audio/video items. We can establish that this is a choice-based question, so our follow-up question needs to be whether these choices are mutually exclusive (i.e., should we allow the user to be able to choose more than one from the list?) In this case, the answer is yes, these choices are mutually exclusive. (Some students have asked whether books on tape wouldn't be considered to be both books and A/V items. They would be A/V items only.)

When you ask a user to select from a list of mutually exclusive choices, one of your options is to use radio buttons. Radio buttons allow you to display all your choices on the screen, each associated with a button that the user can select. If they choose one button and then change their mind and choose another, the first button will turn off when the second one turns on. (In case you're wondering, yes, this all harkens back to those old manual buttons on car radios.)

Radio buttons are still created using the input element, but we need to set the type attribute to "radio" rather than "text." We also need to name the buttons. Let's start building our code (Figure 8.11).

```
<div>
Title: <input type="text" name="itemTitle" size="40" /><br />
Author: <input type="text" name="author" size="30" /><br />
Type: <input type="radio" name="type" />Book
</div>
```

Figure 8.11.   Radio Button for Item Type

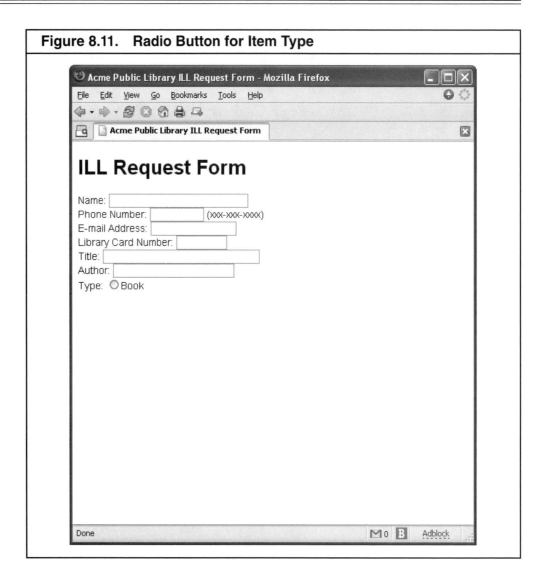

Looking at the new code, you can see that the `<input>` element has placed a radio button in front of the word "Book," indicating to the user that selecting this button tells us that the type of the item is "book." However, from the forms standpoint, clicking on that particular button will not give "type" any value. In all our previous examples, the value of the named box came from what the user typed in. In the case of radio buttons, since the user isn't typing anything in, we instead we need to supply the value of the button. To do this we add the `value` attribute.

```
<div>
Title: <input type="text" name="itemTitle" size="40" /><br />
Author: <input type="text" name="author" size="30" /><br />
Type: <input type="radio" name="type" value="book" />Book
</div>
```

With this update to the code, if the user selects the radio button for "book," our table will update to include "`type=book.`" Before we look at our updated table, let's put in our other three choices. (figure 8.12)

```
Type: <input type="radio" name="type" value="book" />Book
<input type="radio" name="type" value="article" />Article
<input type="radio" name="type" value="Journal" />Journal
<input type="radio" name="type" value="a/v" />Audio/Video
</div>
```

Figure 8.12.   Adding More Radio Buttons for Item Type

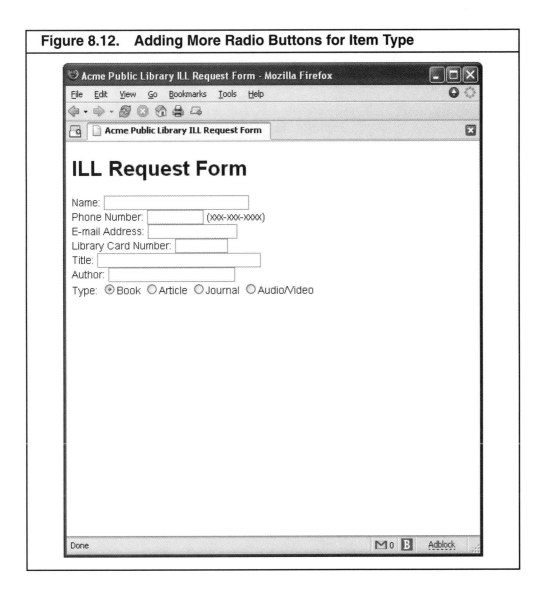

You should notice that I coded the "A/V" choice differently from the rest of the radio buttons. In the case of radio buttons, the form's author sets the value for each button, so the value we set ("a/v") does not need to be the same as what the user sees on the screen as the choice ("Audio/Video"). This way, we can generate exactly the data we want and reword or abbreviate the results as needed.

But why do all of our radio buttons have the same value for the name attribute? I already told you that every input must have a unique name. To be more accurate, and redefining the requirement to include radio buttons, each *group* of buttons must have a unique name. The fact that all of the buttons in this group have the same name is what makes them mutually exclusive. If we were to add another question to our form that involved radio buttons, those buttons would all need to have the same name, yet have a name unique to their group. This allows you to have multiple inputs that use radio buttons without those buttons interfering with each other.

Our resulting table based upon the previous screenshot is now:

name	Michael Sauers
phone	303–751–6277
email	msauers@bcr.org
card	D123456789
itemTitle	The Taking
author	Dean Koontz
type	book

Radio buttons have one additional feature that you should be aware of. You may have noticed that when the form is loaded in a browser, none of the radio buttons are selected by default. If, however, you were asking a question for which you would like one of the choices of response to be selected by default, you could add the attribute checked="checked" to make a particular option the default selection.

RULES vs. REALITY: In HTML, this attribute would be written as checked without it equaling anything. However, since we're in an XML environment when writing XHTML, all attributes must equal a value. The correct value is checked.

Next, we'll ask for any citation information the user may have about the item. We'll use another text box to gather this information (Figure 8.13).

```
<input type="radio" name="type" value="a/v" />Audio/Video<br />
Citation: <input type="text" name="citation" size="30" />
</div>
```

Figure 8.13. Asking the User for an Item Citation

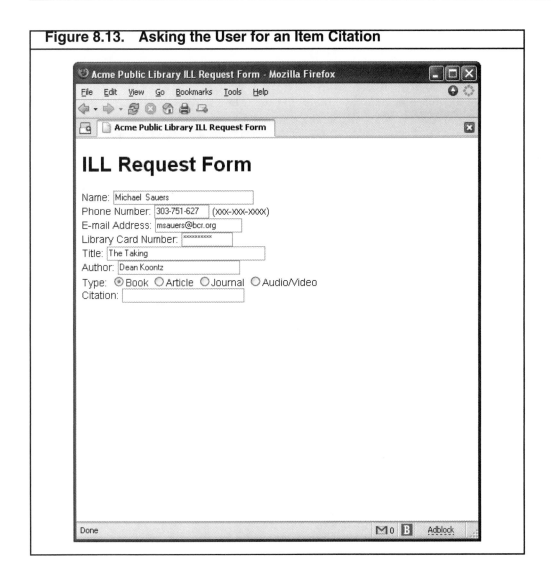

In this instance, since the request is for a book, the user has intentionally left the citation field blank. We are currently allowing any fields on this form to be left blank. Later, I'll show you a method for requiring that a field have user-supplied data. Updating our results table accordingly, we now have:

Name	Michael Sauers
phone	303–751–6277
Email	msauers@bcr.org
Card	D123456789
itemTitle	The Taking
author	Dean Koontz
Type	book
citation	

The next question gets a little more interesting. We are assuming that this ILL form is being used within an academic library. Therefore we should ask what is the relationship between the requestor and the institution. We need to do this because in an academic library there may be different ILL policies that apply to different types of borrowers. This is another case in which we are giving the user a mutually exclusive choice. However, in this case I am not going to suggest that we use radio buttons. The alternate option is to use a drop-down menu. If you've used Windows, macros, or the Web for more than about five minutes you have used a drop-down menu. Drop-down menus allow you to offer a list of choices to a user while taking up a minimal amount of screen space.

Drop-down menus are not coded using the `<input>` element, but with markup that is similar in structure to ordered and unordered lists. With lists, you use one element (`<ul>` or `<ol>`) to specify that there is a list, and another (`<li>`) to specify each item within the list. With drop-downs, the elements are `<select>` and `<option>` respectively (i.e., we need to allow the user to select from a list of options).

To do this, we add a line break to the end of the previous line of code and then add the start and end `<select>` elements along with a name for the list.

```
Citation: <input type="text" name="citation" size="30" /><br />
Borrower type:
<select name="borrower">
</select>
</div>
```

From here we add one line for each `<option>` we want to offer the users (Figure 8.14).

```
<select name="borrower">
<option>Adjunct Faculty</option>
<option>Faculty</option>
<option>Staff</option>
<option>Student</option>
<option>Public</option>
</select>
```

Figure 8.14. A Drop-down List for Borrower Type

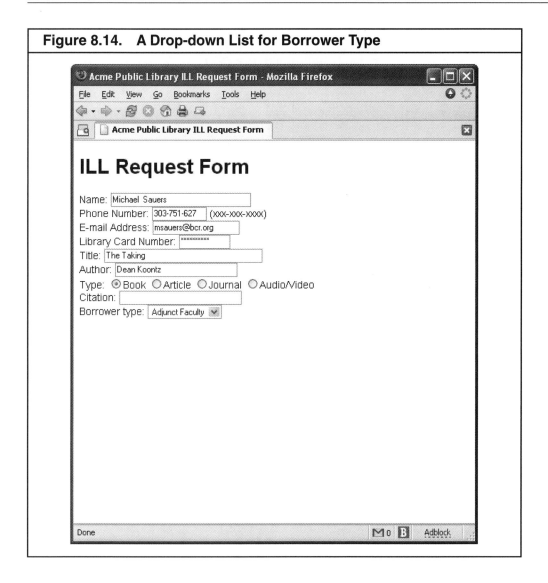

The screenshot shows how the form looks when loaded before any input has been added by the user. The default selection in the drop-down is "Adjunct Faculty" because this is the first item in the list. The item that is selected when the form is submitted is the value that will be submitted to the script. Without any further changes and based on the previously entered data, our table now reads:

name	Michael Sauers
phone	303–751–6277
email	msauers@bcr.org
card	D123456789
itemTitle	The Taking
author	Dean Koontz
type	book
citation	
borrower	Adjunct Faculty

The width of the longest option (in this case, "Adjunct Faculty") determines the width of the drop-down menu. You can adjust this using CSS.

Suppose you do not want the first option in the list to be the default choice. You may prefer to have "Student" be the default choice, since the majority of the ILL's in the library are requested by students. The simple solution is to change the order of the options and make "Student" first on the list, but this is not necessarily the best solution.

You may have noticed that I listed these options in alphabetical order. Changing the order of these options will not make that much of a difference, but what if you were asking for a day of the week and wanted Wednesday to be the default option? Or if you were asking for a month and you wanted September to be the default option? In either instance, changing the order of the options to have the default at the top would be illogical. The method for setting a default option without changing the order of the listed options is the selected attribute. Let's the code to make "Student" the default choice (Figure 8.15).

```
<select name="borrower">
<option>Adjunct Faculty</option>
<option>Faculty</option>
<option>Staff</option>
<option selected="selected">Student</option>
<option>Public</option>
</select>
```

Figure 8.15.   Setting the Default Option on Borrower Type

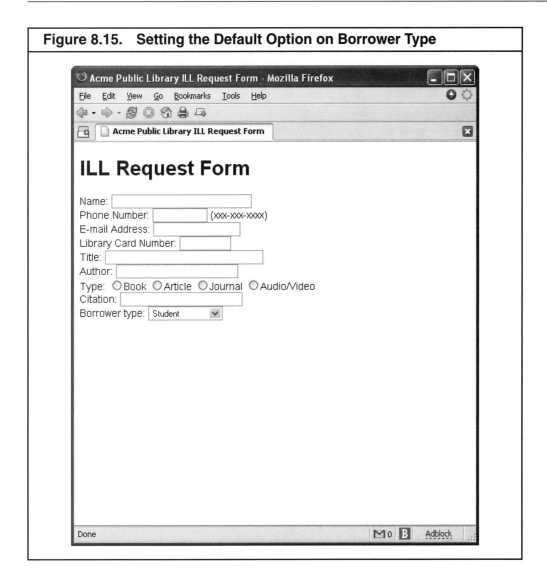

Unlike radio buttons, drop-down menus do not have to offer mutually exclusive choices. With a minor adjustment to the code, a drop-down list can allow a user to select more than one of the options presented. This code is the multiple attribute, applied to the <select> element (Figure 8.16).

```
<select name="borrower" multiple="multiple">
<option>Adjunct Faculty</option>
<option>Faculty</option>
<option>Staff</option>
<option selected="selected">Student</option>
<option>Public</option>
</select>
```

Figure 8.16.   Allowing for Multiple Selections

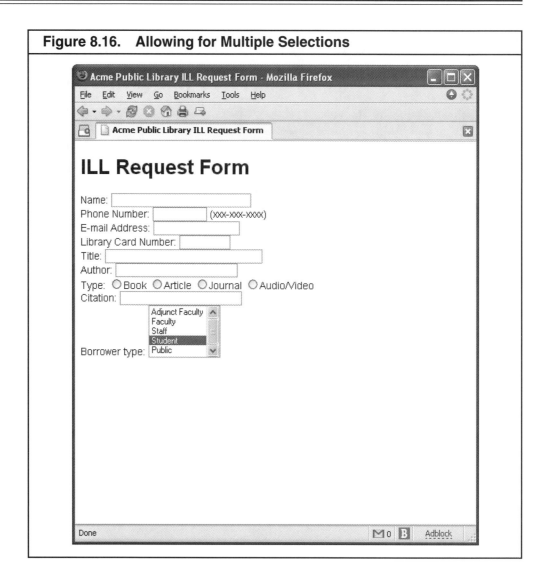

The drop-down list is now a scrollable box that shows three options at a time. The open box indicates to users that they may select more than one of the available options. (Multiple options can be selected through either the shift-click or ctrl-click methods.)

By default, most of today's browsers show three options at a time. Older browsers, such as Netscape Navigator 4.x, showed five items at a time by default. As the form's author, you have control over the number of items shown at one time, and can modify the default through the use of the size attribute on the `<select>` element. In this example, I will specify that four items be shown at a time (Figure 8.17).

```
<select name="borrower" multiple="multiple" size="4">
<option>Adjunct Faculty</option>
<option>Faculty</option>
<option>Staff</option>
<option selected="true">Student</option>
<option>Public</option>
</select>
```

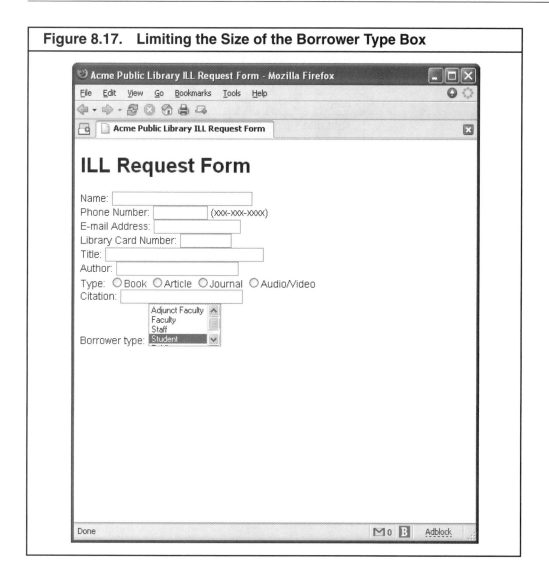

Figure 8.17.   Limiting the Size of the Borrower Type Box

Although you can set the size attribute to a value of two or one, I do not recommend that you do so. With either choice the height of the scroll bar is so minimal as to render it practically useless, and with only one choice showing at a time, users may be unaware that they can select multiple options.

If you do allow for multiple selections, and the user selects more than one option, your results table will contain a row for each of the options selected. For example, if we were to add a question that asked for the color of the book and the user chose both the "red" and "green" options, your results table would read:

name	Michael Sauers
phone	303–751–6277
email	msauers@bcr.org
card	D123456789
itemTitle	The Taking
author	Dean Koontz
type	book
citation	
borrower	Adjunct Faculty
color	red
color	green

The next two items are the amount the user is willing to pay for the item and the date they need the item by. We'll go ahead and add them now with a set of text boxes (Figure 8.18).

```
</select>
<br />
Amount willing to pay: $<input type="text" name="amount" size="5"
maxlength="5" /><small>##.##</small><br />
Date needed by: <input type="text" name="date" size="10"
maxlength="10" /><small>mm-dd-yyyy</small>
</div>
```

Figure 8.18.   Asking the User for Amount Willing to Pay and Date Needed by and Supplying On-screen Instructions

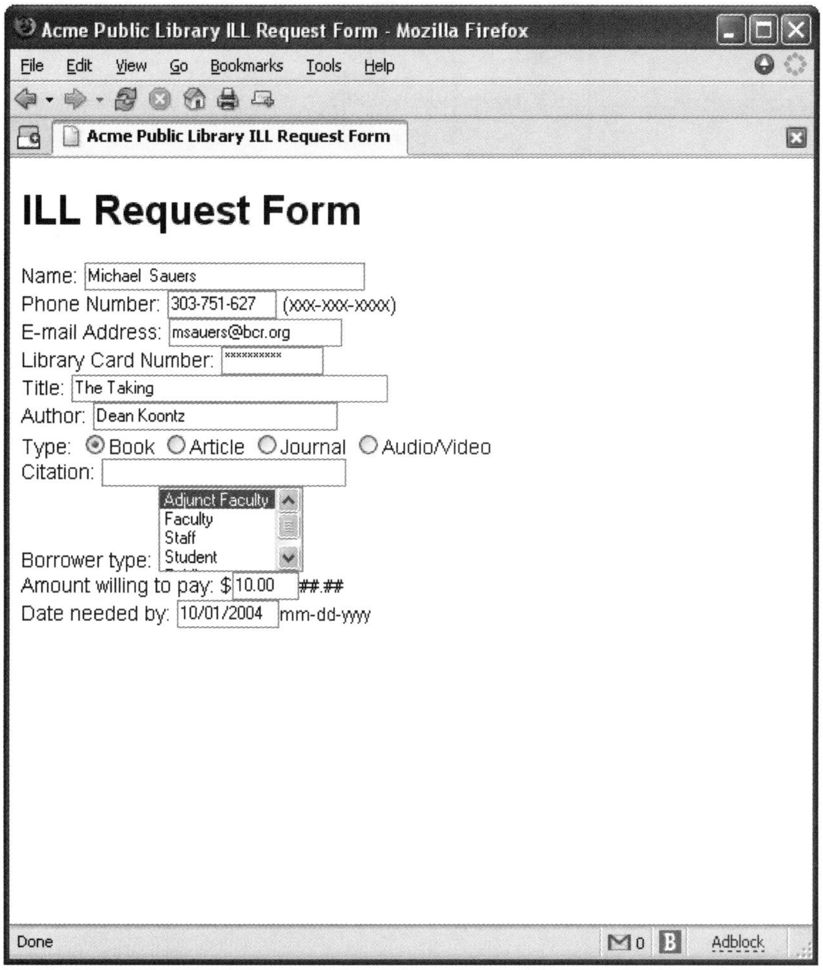

I have added additional text around the boxes to indicate how I want to receive the user's input. For the dollar amount question, I've specified that I would like four numbers, including a decimal point. For the date question I'd like a two-digit month, two-digit day, and four-digit year, separated by hyphens. None of this actually prevents the user from giving their input in a different format, but it does discourage this.

NOTE: Through the use of JavaScript there are ways to be more specific in restricting types of data input. For more information, read "Restrict keyboard input with this quick-and-easy JavaScript" by Edmond Woychowsky. (http://builder.com.com/5100–6371–1044655.html)

With the additional user input as shown in the previous screenshot, our results table now reads:

name	Michael Sauers
phone	303–751–6277
email	msauers@bcr.org
card	D123456789
itemTitle	The Taking
author	Dean Koontz
type	book
citation	
borrower	Adjunct Faculty
amount	10.00
date	10/01/2004

Next, we want to ask the user to supply us with any additional information or comments they may have. This time, we are not offering the user a choice. We also should not restrict the user to only one line on input. Although a text box will technically allow an unlimited amount of input, a single line is visually restrictive. This case requires a multiline text box. These are created using the `<textarea>` element. I'll put the code into the form, then explain how it works (Figure 8.19).

```
Date needed by: <input type="text" name="date" size="10"
maxlength="10" /><small>mm-dd-yyyy</small><br />
Please add any additional information that may assist us in
processing your request:<br />
<textarea name="comments" cols="40" rows="5"></textarea>
</div>
```

Figure 8.19. Adding a `textarea` **for User Comments**

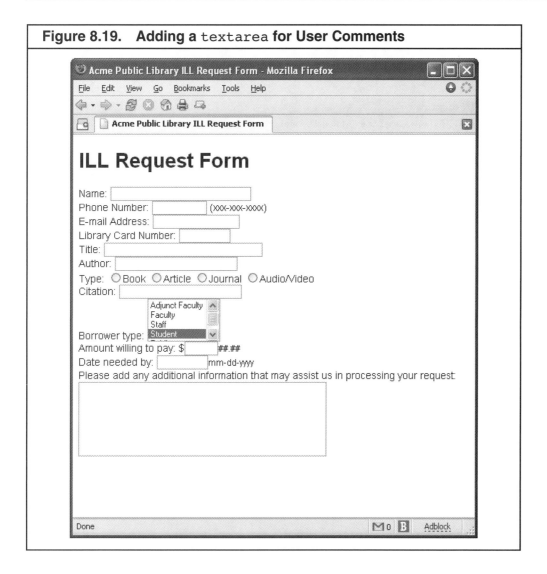

By default `<textarea>` will be 20 characters wide and two lines high. By adding the `cols` and `rows` attributes, I have extended the size of the box to be 40 characters wide and five lines high.

The fact that I opened and closed the `<textarea>` element without giving it any content, does not mean that it is an empty element that can be written as `<textarea />`. This element can have content, but I left it blank because I didn't want to have any content by default. If I were to modify the element to include content, this would be the result (Figure 8.20).

```
<textarea name="comments" cols="40" rows="5">This is some de-
fault content.</textarea>
```

Figure 8.20.   Adding Default Content to Our `textarea`

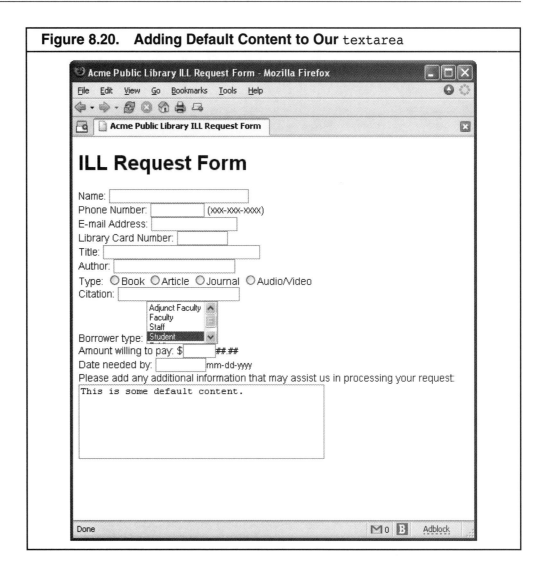

You should always start and end a `<textarea>` on the same line. If I were to start my `<textarea>` on one line of code and then end it on another line, by placing a hard return in my code like this . . .

```
<textarea name="comments" cols="40" rows="5">
</textarea>
```

. . . some browsers would interpret the hard return as five spaces. When the cursor was placed within the box, it would not be in the upper left corner, but five spaces in on the first line.

Lastly, the value of a `<textarea>` when submitted will be whatever the user has entered into the box (Figure 8.21).

Figure 8.21. Our Table With the Default Comment Text Replaced by the User

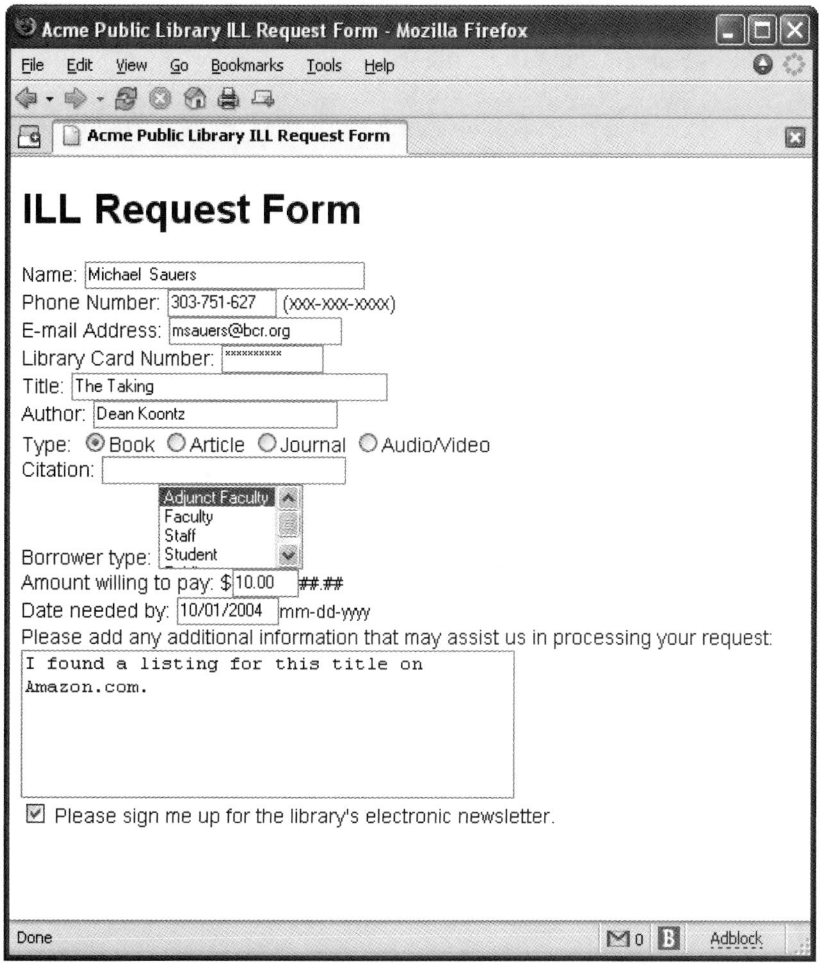

Based upon Figure 8.21, our result table now reads:

Name	Michael Sauers
Phone	303–751–6277
Email	msauers@bcr.org
Card	D123456789
itemTitle	The Taking
author	Dean Koontz
Type	book
citation	
borrower	Adjunct Faculty
amount	10.00
Date	10/01/2004
comments	I found a listing for this title on Amazon.com.

The last question we want to ask is whether the user would like to sign up for the library's electronic newsletter. In this case we are asking the user a choice-based question, and the answers are mutually exclusive: yes or no. However, instead of radio buttons there is one other option we have: a checkbox. Try rephrasing the question as a statement: "Please sign me up for the library's electronic newsletter." Now we can offer the user a single box which they can check or leave unchecked to signal agreement or disagreement. To create a checkbox we use the <input> element (Figure 8.22).

```
<textarea name="comments" cols="40" rows="5"></textarea><br />
<input type="checkbox" name="newsletter" />
Please sign me up for the library's electronic newsletter.
</div>
```

Figure 8.22.   Adding a Checkbox

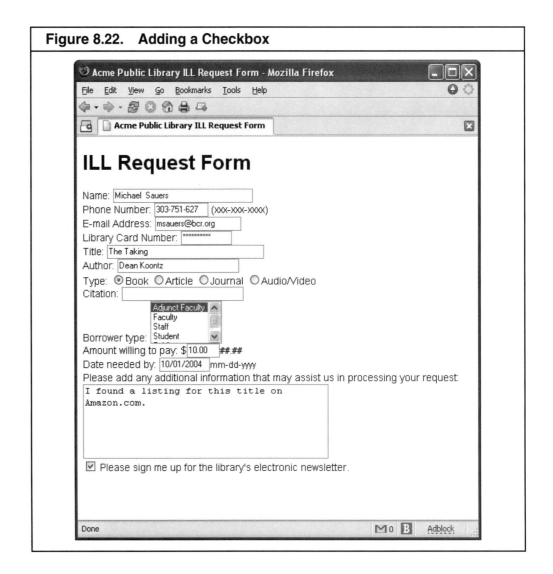

In the case of a checkbox, there is no value that the user can type in (as in a text box), nor is there one supplied by us (as in a radio button), nor is there one implied (as in a drop-down list). If checked, the value of "newsletter" will be relayed to the table as "on." If the box is checked our results table will now read:

name	Michael Sauers
phone	303–751–6277
email	msauers@bcr.org
Card	D123456789
itemTitle	The Taking
author	Dean Koontz
Type	book
citation	
borrower	Adjunct Faculty
amount	10.00
Date	10/01/2004
comments	I found a listing for this title on Amazon.com.
newsletter	on

If the box is not checked, however, the value for newsletter will not be "off." If a checkbox is not checked, the name/value combination will not be reported at all. If the user does not wish to receive the newsletter, there will be no newsletter line in our results table. The item is treated as if it had been ignored completely.

Figure 8.23. The BCR Print Request Form

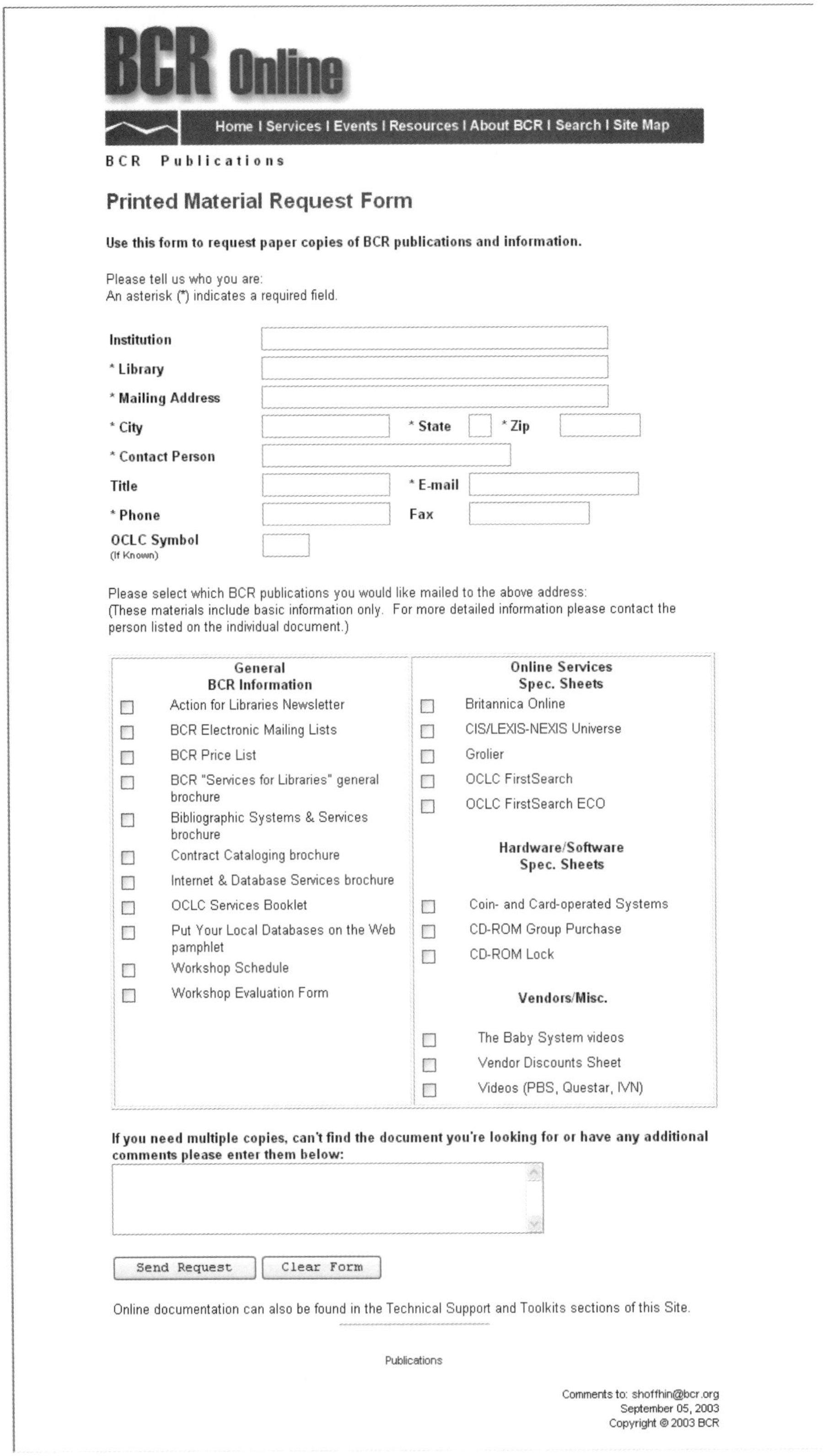

BCR Online

Home | Services | Events | Resources | About BCR | Search | Site Map

BCR Publications

Printed Material Request Form

Use this form to request paper copies of BCR publications and information.

Please tell us who you are:
An asterisk (*) indicates a required field.

Institution
* Library
* Mailing Address
* City * State * Zip
* Contact Person
Title * E-mail
* Phone Fax
OCLC Symbol (If Known)

Please select which BCR publications you would like mailed to the above address:
(These materials include basic information only. For more detailed information please contact the person listed on the individual document.)

General BCR Information	Online Services Spec. Sheets
Action for Libraries Newsletter	Britannica Online
BCR Electronic Mailing Lists	CIS/LEXIS-NEXIS Universe
BCR Price List	Grolier
BCR "Services for Libraries" general brochure	OCLC FirstSearch
Bibliographic Systems & Services brochure	OCLC FirstSearch ECO
Contract Cataloging brochure	**Hardware/Software Spec. Sheets**
Internet & Database Services brochure	Coin- and Card-operated Systems
OCLC Services Booklet	CD-ROM Group Purchase
Put Your Local Databases on the Web pamphlet	CD-ROM Lock
Workshop Schedule	**Vendors/Misc.**
Workshop Evaluation Form	The Baby System videos
	Vendor Discounts Sheet
	Videos (PBS, Questar, IVN)

If you need multiple copies, can't find the document you're looking for or have any additional comments please enter them below:

Send Request Clear Form

Online documentation can also be found in the Technical Support and Toolkits sections of this Site.

Publications

Comments to: shoffhin@bcr.org
September 05, 2003
Copyright © 2003 BCR

In this form, BCR is asking users which print materials they would like to receive. They've used checkboxes here because they only need to know which ones they want (the ones they've checked). If they have not checked a particular one, BCR does not need that information, since a list of publications a user does not want would be useless.

If you decide that you don't want to receive the value "on," you can change the output via the value attribute. For example, if you wanted your results table to have "subscribe" for the value of "newsletter" when the box is checked, you would change your code to read:

```
<input type="checkbox" name="newsletter" value="subscribe" />
```

BUTTONS

Strict / Transitional / Frameset

Now that we have asked for all the information we need, we should add two buttons— one that submits the form and one that resets the form. Buttons are added via the <input> element. I have set the type attribute to "submit" and "reset" respectively (Figure 8.24).

```
</div>
<div>
<input type="submit" />
<input type="reset" />
</div>
```

Figure 8.24.   Default Buttons

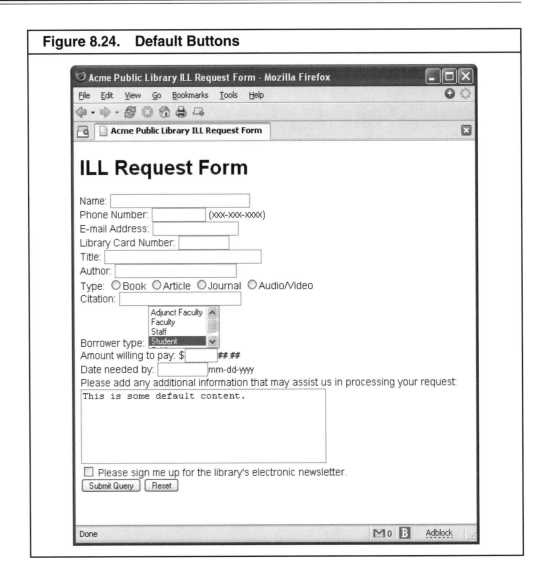

These lines of code generate the buttons we're looking for, but they don't exactly say what we need them to say. By default, the way in which "submit" and "reset" buttons are labeled are set by the browser. In this case, we have "Submit Query" and "Reset." Though the "Reset" button could be considered appropriate, a button labeled "Submit Query" is not exactly what we need. You can change the way a button is labeled by adding a value attribute to each button. The value for the value attribute is how the button will be labeled. Let's modify the buttons to better suit the form (Figure 8.25).

```
</div>
<div>
<input type="submit" value="Send Request" />
<input type="reset" value="Clear Form" />
</div>
```

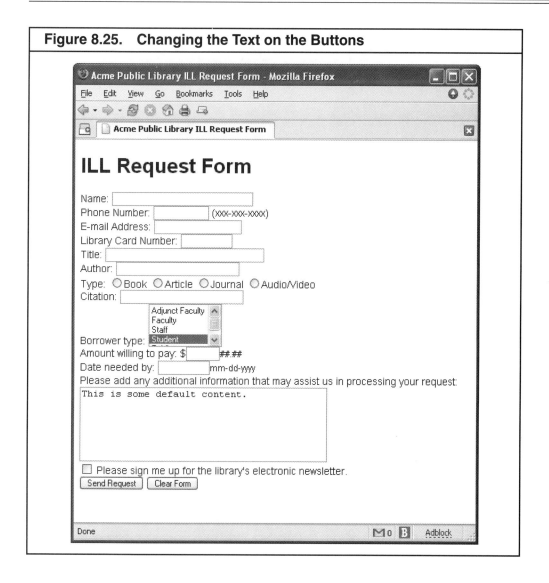

Figure 8.25. Changing the Text on the Buttons

A button with `type="submit"` when clicked will send the results to the script attached to the form. Since we have not yet linked a script to this form, nothing will happen if the submit button is clicked. (We'll be doing this in the next section.)

The reset button, when clicked, will change the form fields back to their default state. If a field was empty when the form was loaded, it will be empty again. In the case of the relationship question, if the value had been changed to Faculty, it would be set back to Student.

You can create generic buttons by setting the value attribute to "button." In this case the button does not include a default label, and you must therefore set one using the value attribute (Figure 8.26).

```
<input type="button" value="Print" />
```

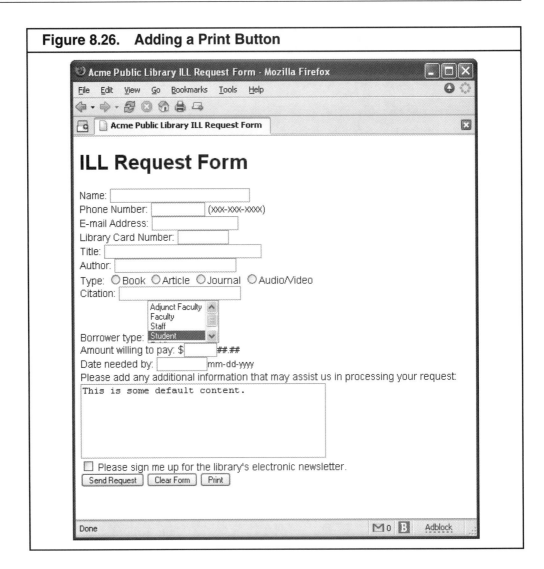

Figure 8.26.   Adding a Print Button

Generic buttons do nothing on their own. As the author you must assign them a function, which is usually accomplished through the application of JavaScript. If you did want to turn this into a print button, you would add:

```
<input type="button" value="Print" onlick="window.print();" />
```

The result of clicking this button would be the same as if the user selected File|Print from the browser's menu.

There is one additional input type that we have not used on this form. A `type="upload"` field is probably the rarest input type used in forms. This creates a box into which a filename and/or path may be typed along with a browse button, giving the user the ability to browse their computer for a particular file. The file listed in the box when submitted will be attached to the submitted results table. Unless you need to receive a file from your user, there is no reason to use this input type.

A live example of a form that uses `type="upload"` is the W3C validator at validator.w3.org.

TURNING ON THE FORM

Now that we have completed the front-end of our form—the part that the user interacts with—we need to add code to the form that provides the instructions on how to process the data the user will supply.

The first stage in this process is to add two key pieces of information to our form: how we want the data submitted to the script and the location of the script we want to receive the data. Both of these are specified via attributes on the `<form>` element.

DATA SUBMISSION METHODS

Strict / Transitional / Frameset

The first attribute to add is the `method=""` attribute. This attribute specifies by which of two methods we wish to submit our data to the script. Our two choices are `"get"` and `"post."`

The `get` method collects all the names and values from the form and appends them to the URL of the script. This is mainly used in situations when you are passing information along to a search engine. For example, if you do a search in Google and look at the URL of the results page, you'll see an array of "*this=that*" separated by plus signs. One of those pairs will be something like "q=keyword+nextkeyword." In this example "q" is the name of the text input box and "keyword nextkeyword" is what I searched on. Google's form is using the `get` method.

The `get` method has some limitations and issues that you need to be aware of. First off, URLs cannot be more than 1024 characters in length. Therefore, the address of your script, all of your field names, all of the user's input, plus all of the additional characters cannot total more than 1024 characters. In our form, there is the distinct possibility that we'll go over that amount, so the `get` method is not for us in this case.

The other reason that we won't be using the `get` method for this form is related to patron privacy. Every time a computer either enters a URL or a Web server receives a request for a URL, that information is stored in a log file. If we were to use the `get` method, every ILL request that came through our form would be logged somewhere on the server. In respect of patron privacy, this is information we should neither want nor keep.

Our other option, the one we'll use here, is `"put."` The `put` method collects the results table and places it into a temporary file that is in turn passed along to the script. Unlike the `get` method, there is no size limitation, nor are there patron privacy issues. The generated file can be of any length (including attached files if you used an upload input type) and is not permanently stored on either the user's or server's system.

Our updated code now reads:

```
<form method="post">
```

GIVING THE FORM AN "ACTION"

Strict / Transitional / Frameset

Once you've added the method attribute, the other attribute you need to add is `action=""`. The value for this attribute typically points to the script that you wish to have process the submitted data. However, it doesn't have to point to a script. There is another option available to you. That option is a `mailto: link.`

E-MAILING YOUR RESULTS

Strict / Transitional / Frameset

I mentioned at the beginning of this chapter that what we want our form to do is to collect the information from our users and e-mail it to a recipient at the library. Go ahead and add a `mailto:` link, filling in your own e-mail address for now.

```
<form method="post" action="mailto:msauers@travelinlibrarian.info">
```

At this point you can reload your form, fill in all the fields, and submit the form. Depending upon the setup of your computer there are a few different things that can happen.

For many of you, the form my seem to reload itself. If this happens, chances are the submission was successful and you'll have the e-mail in your inbox within a few minutes. However, there was no actual indication to you (the user) that the submission was successful.

Some of you may have been notified that an e-mail program was attempting to send a message and been prompted to approve it. (This is a security feature in some mail programs to prevent them from being hijacked by worms.) Provided that you approved the sending, the e-mail was sent and the form reloaded itself.

The third possibility is that you received some sort of error message that indicated you aren't set up to send outgoing e-mail. Usually this error message contains something to the effect of "no default e-mail client"—not exactly the most descriptive of error messages. As I discussed earlier in Chapter 4, `mailto:` links rely on the user's browser being configured to use an e-mail program also installed on the user's computer. If there is an e-mail client installed and properly configured to work with the browser, then everything should work as planned, but it may still be unclear to the user whether anything was sent at all. If this connection between the user's browser and e-mail program has not been made for any reason, a `mailto:` will fail. Since your library's public access computers most likely do not include local e-mail clients, your form when set up in this manner, will fail for users sending the input from within your library.

For now let's continue with the example and assume that it did work. You should have received your e-mail by now. Open it and take a look. Here's the one I received (Figure 8.27).

Figure 8.27. The E-mailed Result via `mailto:`

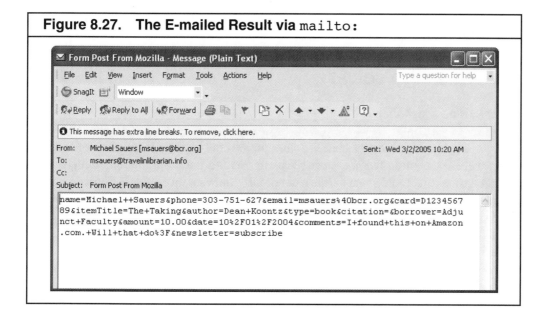

If you read it carefully, all the data from the results table based upon the data you entered into the form is there. In fact, it's in the same format that a `get` method would have generated, just in an attached file instead of as part of a URL. All of your names and values are connected by equal signs, all of the spaces have been replaced with plus signs, and if you included any punctuation, some of those characters have been replaced by their hexadecimal equivalents. For example, the question mark I entered at the end of my comment has been sent as `%3F`.

So, even when the mailto: action works, we still have considerable problems. Here's a list of the more pressing ones.

- `mailto:` actions are inherently unreliable since they rely on the user's computer, and we have little or no control over that.
- The resulting e-mail has no subject line. (We can resolve this by changing our action to read `"mailto:address?subject=text"` but that doesn't solve the reliability problem.)
- Even an e-mail message that does reach the intended recipient successfully is not in a format convenient for processing, or even for reading.

In addition to addressing the most obvious issues, we may want to ask ourselves the following questions.

- What do we do if we want the resulting e-mail to be sent to multiple e-mail recipients?
- Wouldn't it be better for the user to see an onscreen confirmation or be sent an e-mail confirmation the information has been sent?
- Should the user be sent a message thanking them for submitting their information and providing other additional information?
- What do we do if we want the gathered data stored in a comma-delimited file on our server for later importing into a database or spreadsheet?

All of these issues can be dealt with easily through the use of a script. For this example, I'll be using the script "Yform."

E-MAILING VIA A SCRIPT

Strict / Transitional /Frameset

YForm is a free script that has been around for several years and suits the needs for this form well. It has more features than I'll be discussing here, but the remaining features do not have a direct relevance to this example. If you want more detailed instructions on the use of YForm, you can find excellent documentation at the U.S. Naval Academy Web site (www.usna.edu/Masters/questions/quest–008.htm). The script itself can be downloaded from Domino Computing Services (www.dominocs.com/Freeware/).

NOTE: As I mentioned earlier, a script must be installed in a particular directory on the server, usually "cgi-bin," and will need to be configured to work with your mail server. Please consult your server documentation or server administrator regarding the installation of any scripts on your system. Before you do that, ask your server administrator if a suitable script is already installed.

You will need to begin by setting the appropriate value for the action attribute. I'll assume that the script has been placed in the cgi-bin directory off of server root. Based on this assumption, my code now reads:

```
<form method="post" action="/cgi-bin/Yform.cgi">
```

What this does is tell the form to send the collected data as a temp file to the YForm script located in the server's cgi-bin directory.

One requirement is specifying to whom the resulting e-mail message should be sent. The questions are where do we do this and how do we do this. Let's think about the where question first. The first reaction from many of my students is to suggest that we put this information into the script. Although this is technically possible it is not exactly a good solution. The first problem is that you would need to learn at least some of the programming language that the script is written in. (That language is usually Perl but can be one of several other languages.) This would hardly be an efficient use of your time just to set the to: field in an e-mail message.

The other problem with this solution is that it locks the script into sending all the data it processes to a single e-mail address. What if your site has three forms on it, all asking for different user input, all needing to be sent to a different staff members? If we coded the recipient's address into the script, we would now need to have three scripts on our server, one for each form, with only a single line of code that differed in each script. Again, this is hardly an efficient use of our time or server storage space.

The answer to where is in the form itself. By using this method we can customize each form to send to whomever it needs to yet still allow multiple forms to use a single script.

Now that we know where to place the recipient's address, we need a way to send information to the script that the script can process accordingly. All of those names and values that the form collects are just pieces of information that are sent to the script to be processed. What we need is a method to create additional names and values that the script is looking for. In most cases there is no reason that this information needs to be visible to the user as part of the on-screen form.

ENTER THE HIDDEN FIELD

Strict / Transitional / Frameset

Through the use of hidden fields, we can manually create names and values that will be sent to the script along with all the data entered by the user. Hidden fields may be placed anywhere within the form, but are usually placed immediately after the `<form>` element. Let's look at an example.

```
<form method="post" action="/cgi-bin/Yform.cgi">
<input type="hidden" name="recipient"
value="msauers@bcr.org" />
```

Hidden fields are created using the `<input>` element with a type of `"hidden."` Setting an `<input>` element to a hidden type keeps those fields from displaying to the user. In this case, the script will look for `"recipient=address"` in the submitted data. When the script sees that combination, it will place the value for recipient in the To: field of the outgoing e-mail message. (If you want to send the e-mail to multiple recipients, you can set the value of the recipient field to a comma-delimited list of addresses.)

The next hidden field gives the e-mail message a subject.

```
<input type="hidden" name="subject" value="ILL Request" />
```

We need to make sure that the e-mail message our recipient receives has a valid From: field so that we may respond to the user if we need to. The YForm script will look for the contents of the "email" field and places its value in the From: field. This is YForm's assigned use of the field named "email." In this case, we've used a feature of the script but did not put it in a hidden field.

YForm also has an assigned meaning for the "name" field. The script will take the value of the name field as entered by the user and attach it to the e-mail address. Instead of seeing "From: msauers@travelinlibrarian.info" you would see "From: Michael Sauers [msauers@travelinlibrarian.info]." (Actual results will vary among e-mail clients.)

Next we should deal with the order in which the data is sent to us. Some browsers will return the information in the order in which the questions were originally asked. Others will send the data back in an apparently random order. However, we may want to send the information to be displayed to the recipient in a different order entirely, perhaps with the data about the requested item displaying before the personal information. The YForm script manages this with the field "sort," which we can use to reorder our data.

By setting a value of "sort" to `"alphabetic"` the data will be sorted alphabetically by field name. In most cases, this is not particularly useful. We can also specify the sort order through the use of `"order:field1,field2 . . . "` as the value.

So, even though in this case we want to receive the data in the order in which we asked for it, to be sure we get what we want, we'll add this line of markup:

```
<input type="hidden" name="sort"
value="order:name,phone,email,card,itemTitle,author,type,citation,borrower,amount,
date,comments,newsletter" />
```

Consider now what happens if the user neglects to supply important information without which we cannot process the ILL request. Which fields in our firm should be required? We absolutely must have values for name, phone, card, itemTitle, author, and amount. Try to resist the temptation to require values for fields which are not absolutely necessary.

Requiring fields is similar to sorting them. The field name is `"required"` and the value must be a comma-delimited list of the fields you want to require.

```
<input type="hidden" name="required"
value="name,phone,card,itemTitle,author,amount" />
```

If the user submits the form without completing one or more of these fields they will automatically see a page indicating which fields have not been completed and requiring them to return to the form to complete those fields. The e-mail will not be sent unless all required fields have been completed.

Before we move on to the next hidden field, I'd like to take this opportunity to point out a design issue. Whenever you require that a certain field in a form must be completed, you should always indicate to the user the fact that the field is required. Something as simple as putting an asterisk before the field's label will suffice. What you should never do, however, is use a colored (or even bold-faced) font. This could cause a significant accessibility problem. If your user is accessing your form via a text-only or speech-based browser, neither color nor other visual styles will be presented to them, and they will not perceive a required field as anything different from the other ones.

You should now review your code and add an asterisk in front of each of your required field labels.

Whenever you connect to a Web page, certain information about your environment is announced to the Web server. This information includes your computer's IP address and the name of the browser you're using, along with a few other items. The YForm script gives us the ability to "trap" and report this information in the e-mail the script sends out. To do this we use a field named `"env_report"` (for environmental report) with a value of the names of the items we wish reported. The following line of code will report back to us the user's IP address and the name of the browser they're using.

```
<input type="hidden" name="env_report"
value="REMOTE_ADDR,HHTP_USER_AGENT" />
```

Please note that the values in this case are in all caps. Typing them in lower case will prevent the information from being reported.

This "trapped" information isn't something everyone will want reported and is hardly necessary, but we can glean some useful information in regard to our users for statistical purposes. From the IP address we can tell whether the person filled out the form from within the library, from a computer on campus, or from offsite. (This is assuming you know the IP addresses or ranges for the machines in your library and/or campus.) Though the ILL request won't be treated any differently based on this information it is a potentially useful statistic.

Additionally, the name of the browser can provide a rough idea as to which browsers are being used by your patrons. This information could be useful when considering how to design your site.

All the hidden fields we've added so far deal with the e-mail message we'll be receiving at the end of this process. We also need to deal with what the user sees after submitting the form. At a minimum, the user should get some sort of on-screen confirmation that their data has been sent. We might also send them a courtesy copy of the resulting e-mail and offer them a link back to the library's site.

Provided the form was filled in and submitted successfully, the user will automatically be presented with a screen confirming the submission. This screen will also "echo back" to the user the information that they submitted. (I'll show you a screenshot of this when we're through with this section.) Through the use of hidden fields, we can control the appearance and handling of this page.

The first thing we can do is add a "thank you" message to this screen. This is accomplished via the form's "title" field. The value we give the title field will appear as the XHTML `<title>` of the confirmation page and as a heading at the top of the confirmation page.

```
<input type="hidden" name="title" value="Thank you for submit-
ting your request" />
```

This is YForm's assigned use of the field named `"title"` and the reason we named the field holding the title of the item being requested `"itemTitle"` rather than `"title."`

We can also give the user a link on this page to take them to another page in the site. This link gives the user the ability to navigate away from the confirmation page without having to back out through the form. There are two fields you need to use to accomplish this. `return_link_title` is the text of the link and `return_link_url` is the address of the page to which you would like the link to send the user.

```
<input type="hidden" name="return_link_title" value="Back to the
library home page" />
<input type="hidden" name="return_link_url"
value="http://www.travelinlibrarian.info/" />
```

(There are additional fields available in the YForm script that allow you to manipulate the appearance of this page. Refer to the documentation cited earlier for further details.)

Using the `"sendcourtesy"` field we can have the script automatically send the user an e-mail copy of the e-mail that we'll be receiving. We can use various additional fields to add text to the e-mail sent to the user that will not appear in the e-mail we receive.

- `courtext1`
  The value of this field will appear at the beginning of the e-mail as a greeting and/or introductory text.
- `courfieldlist`
  Specifies whether or not the user's e-mail should include the data they entered. Including this information is considered good form as it allows the user to verify the information they submitted.
- `courtext2`
  This value will appear after the user's data allowing you to complete the body of the e-mail.
- `courclose`
  Inserts a closing after the courtext2 value such as "sincerely."

- myname, myemail, and mywebsite
  You can use these fields to create a signature file that will appear at the end of the message.

Adding all of these fields looks like this:

```
<input type="hidden" name="courtext1" value="Your request has
been sent to the ILL department for processing. Here is the
information you sent us." />
<input type="hidden" name="courfieldlist" value="yes" />
<input type="hidden" name="courtext2" value="If any of this
information is incorrect please contact the ILL department as
soon as possible so that we may correct the information." />
<input type="hidden" name="courclose" value="Sincerely," />
<input type="hidden" name="myname" value="Michael Sauers, ILL
Department Head" />
<input type="hidden" name="myemail" value="msauers@bcr.org" />
<input type="hidden" name="mywebsite" value="http://www.bcr.org/
" />
```

Lastly, we can not only e-mail this data but automatically store it in a data file for later importing into a database or spreadsheet. This is accomplished through the use of the "database" and "delimiter" fields.

The value for the database field is the path and filename for the data file you wish to append all incoming data to. The value for the delimiter field is the character you wish to use to separate one field from another.

```
<input type="hidden" name="database" value="illdata.txt" />
<input type="hidden" name="delimiter" value="~" />
```

When this data is saved to a data file, the file will be a text file, the data from each submitted form will be appended on a single line, and the character you specified as the delimiter will separate each submitted value. You should not use a comma as your delimiter unless you are sure that your users will never enter a comma as data. If just one user enters the character that you've specified as the delimiter, your data file will become corrupted. It is best to pick an obscure character such as a tilde (as I have done) or a back tick (') since these characters are unlikely to be entered by a user.

As our table now stands, a line in the data file would look like this:

```
Michael Sauers~303-751-6277~msauers@bcr.org~D123456789~The
Taking~Dean Koontz~book~Adjunct Faculty~10.00~10/01/2004~I found
a listing for this title on Amazon.com.~on
```

TESTING YOUR FORM

With the exception of adding some code to make our form more accessible, the form is now complete. You should now open the form in your browser, fill it out, submit it, and check your inbox for the appropriate results.

Try experimenting with the submission process. If you have multiple e-mail addresses, try filling out the form as a user from one address sending to another address. If you don't have multiple e-mail addresses, ask a co-worker if you can user their e-mail address as the user. This way, you can see both the resulting and confirming e-mails arrive in different accounts.

Also, try filling out the form incorrectly a few times so you can see the results. Try skipping over one or more of the required fields so you can see what the user would see if they did the same thing.

THE CODE AND THE RESULTS

Here is the complete code for our form as it stands right now. Use this to double-check your code if you're having any problems. I have also included screenshots of the form (Figure 8.28), an error page (Figure 8.29), a confirmation page, (Figure 8.30), the confirmation e-mail (Figure 8.31), and the results e-mail (Figure 8.32) so you can compare them to your own.

```
<!DOCTYPE html PUBLIC "-//W3C//DTD XHTML
1.0 Transitional//EN" "http://www.w3.org/TR/xhtml/DTD/xhtml1-
transitional.dtd">
<html xmlns="http://www.w3.org/TR/xhtml" lang="en">
<head>
<title>Acme Public Library ILL Request Form</title>
<meta name="HTTP-Equiv" content="text/html; content="utf-8">
</head>
<body>
<h1>ILL Request Form</h1>
<form method="post" action="/cgi-bin/Yform.cgi">
<input type="hidden" name="recipient"
value="msauers@bcr.org" />
<input type="hidden" name="sort"
value="order:name,phone,email,card,itemTitle,author,type,
citation,borrower,amount,date,comments,newsletter" />
<input type="hidden" name="required"
value="name,phone,card,itemTitle,author,amount" />
<input type="hidden" name="env_report"
value="REMOTE_ADDR,HHTP_USER_AGENT" />
<input type="hidden" name="title" value="Thank you for submit-
ting your request" />
<input type="hidden" name="return_link_title" value="Back to
the library home page" />
<input type="hidden" name="return_link_url"
value="http://www.travelinlibrarian.info/" />
<input type="hidden" name="courtext1" value="Your request has
been sent to the ILL department for processing. Here is the
information you sent us." />
<input type="hidden" name="courfieldlist" value="yes" />
<input type="hidden" name="courtext2" value="If any of this
information is incorrect please contact the ILL department as
soon as possible so that we may correct the information." />
<input type="hidden" name="courclose" value="Sincerely," />
```

```
<input type="hidden" name="myname" value="Michael Sauers, ILL
Department Head" />
<input type="hidden" name="myemail" value="msauers@bcr.org" />
<input type="hidden" name="mywebsite" value="http://www.bcr.org/" />
<input type="hidden" name="database" value="illdata.txt" />
<input type="hidden" name="delimiter" value="|" />
<div>
Name: <input type="text" name="name" size="35" /><br />
Phone Number: <input type="text" name="phone" size="11"
maxlength="11" /> (xxx-xxx-xxxx)<br />
E-mail Address: <input type="text" name="email" /><br />
Library Card Number: <input type="password" name="card" size="10"
maxlength="10" />
</div>
<div>
Title: <input type="text" name="itemTitle" size="40" /><br />
Author: <input type="text" name="author" size="30" /><br />
Type: <input type="radio" name="type" value="book" />Book
<input type="radio" name="type" value="article" />Article
<input type="radio" name="type" value="Journal" />Journal
<input type="radio" name="type" value="a/v" />Audio/Video<br />
Citation: <input type="text" name="citation" size="30" /><br />
Borrower type:
<select name="borrower" multiple="multiple" size="4">
<option>Adjunct Faculty</option>
<option>Faculty</option>
<option>Staff</option>
<option selected="selected">Student</option>
<option>Public</option>
</select>
<br />
Amount willing to pay: $<input type="text" name="amount" size="5"
maxlength="5" /><small>##.##</small><br />
Date needed by: <input type="text" name="date" size="10"
maxlength="10" /><small>mm-dd-yyyy</small><br />
Please add any additional information that may assist us in
processing your request:<br />
<textarea name="comments" cols="40" rows="5">This is some de-
fault content.</textarea><br />
<input type="checkbox" name="newsletter" value="subscribe" />
Please sign me up for the library's electronic newsletter.
</div>
<div>
<input type="submit" value="Send Request" />
<input type="reset" value="Clear Form" />
<input type="button" value="Print" onlick="window.print(/);" />
</div>
</form>
</body>
</html>
```

Figure 8.28.   Our Completed and Filled-in Form

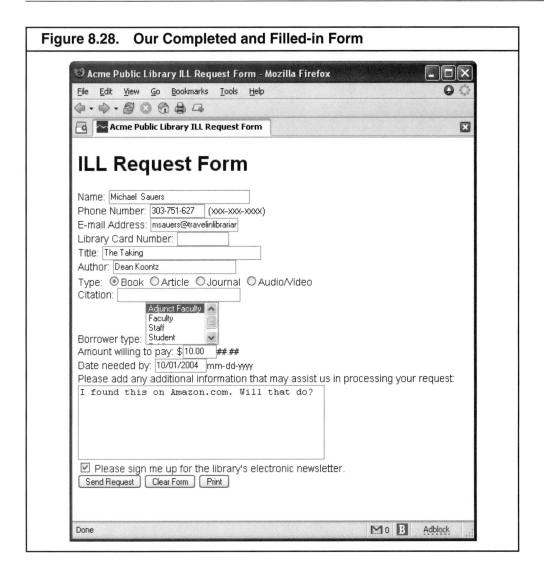

Figure 8.29.   The Error Page

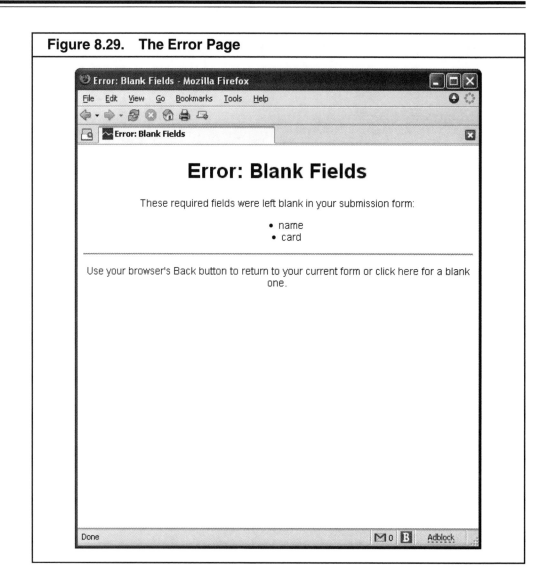

Figure 8.30.   The Confirmation Page

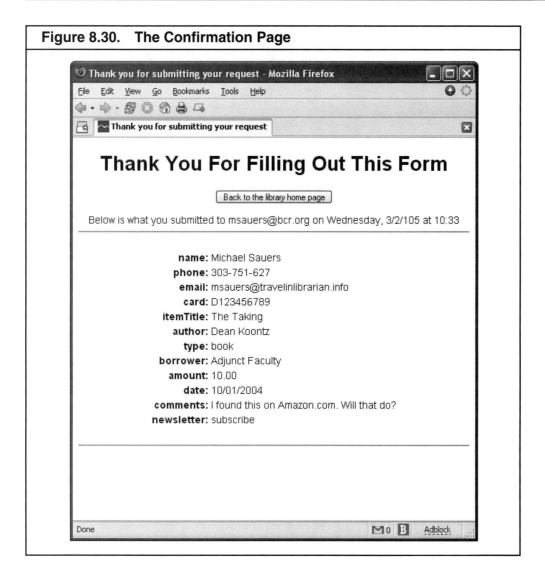

Figure 8.31.   The Confirmation E-mail

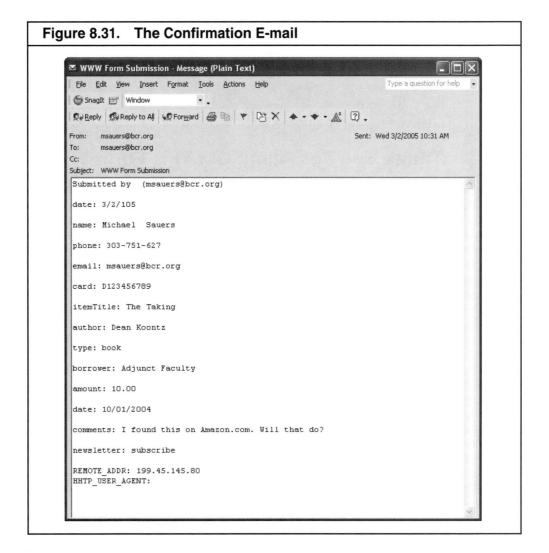

Figure 8.32. The Form Results as E-mailed to the Recipient

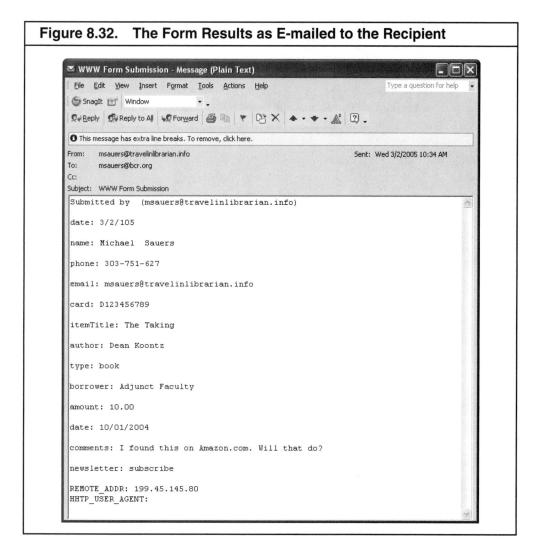

MAKING YOUR FORMS MORE ACCESSIBLE

Strict / Transitional / Frameset

Some additional markup elements and attributes when added to your form not only give it more visual appeal but may also assist users with accessibility issues. These elements are `<fieldset>` and `<legend>`, along with the `<label>` element in conjunction with the `for=""` and `id=""` attributes.

ORGANIZING YOUR FIELDS

So far, we have organized our fields into three distinct groupings: patron information, item information, and buttons via `<div>` elements. From a structural standpoint the `<div>`s do the job, but the `<fieldset>` element can be used to create more logical groupings of fields named `<fieldset>`. The `<fieldset>` element is more structurally and semantically sound within a form than is a `<div>` and in today's browsers will cause a border to appear around the enclosed content. When used in conjunction with CSS, the `<fieldset>` element provides greater flexibility in the layout of a form.

Replace the `<div>` elements around the first two groupings of fields with `<fieldset>` elements. Do not replace the `<div>` elements around the buttons, since we don't want the border to appear here.

RULES vs. REALITY: A careful reading of the XHTML DTD shows that fieldsets (and legends, which we'll cover next) can be used anywhere within a document—i.e., they are not children of `<field>` but children of `<body>`. However, from the documentation out of the W3C, it is clear that the intention of the authors was that `<fieldset>` only be used as a child of `<form>`.

Don't worry about things like spacing issues between and with the fieldsets. We'll take care of those issues in Chapter 19.

Once the form has been grouped into `<fieldset>`s, we can label each of these areas with the `<legend>` element. This element must appear as a child of `<fieldset>` and traditionally appears immediately following start `<fieldset>`. The content of the `<legend>` element is what you would like to name each grouping. If we add the following code you'll see the result.

```
<fieldset>
<legend>Patron Information</legend>
 . . .
</fieldset>
<fieldset>
<legend>Item Information</legend>
```

Figure 8.33.   Organizing your Form with `fieldset` **and** `legend`

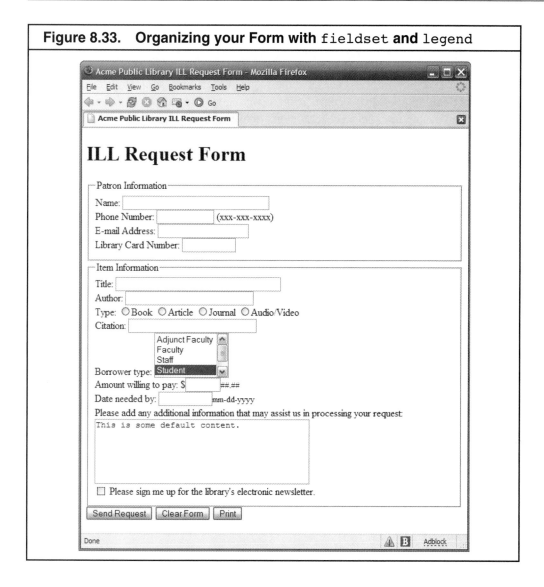

Today's browsers will place the content of the `<legend>` element on the top line of the `<fieldset>` box. This can be manipulated with CSS.

LABELING FIELDS

The `<label>` element was developed in 1998 but didn't really catch on because browsers were slow to implement its features. Through the use of the `<label>` element and its associated `for` and `id` attributes, we can increase the accessibility of the form, give it additional functionality, and increase the code's semantic accuracy.

Here is our Name: field as it is now:

```
Name: <input type="text" name="name" size="35" /><br />
```

Let's look at it again with the addition of the `<label>` element along with the `for` and `id` attributes.

```
<label for="name">Name: </label>
<input id="name" type="text" name="name" size="35" /><br />
```

This has no effect on how users see the form in their browsers. However, use of the `<label>` element gives us two significant advantages. The first is that now that we have placed "Name:" within the `<label>` element we can effect `<label>`'s content CSS. The other benefit of `<label>` is that now that these two items have been associated with each other (via `for="name"` and `id="name"`), if the user clicks on "Name:" the cursor will automatically appear in the name input box. (Moving the cursor into a box is known as giving that box "Focus.")

Consider doing this with a set of radio buttons. Those buttons make small targets for many users. By putting their related text into a `<label>` element and then associating the label with the buttons via the `for` and `id` attributes, we have enabled the user to click not only on the buttons themselves, but also to click on the associated words, which should make larger targets.

Instead of walking you through each element one at a time, I have revised the code to incorporate the `<label>` element.

```
<fieldset>
<legend>Patron Information</legend>
<div>
<label for="name">Name: </label>
<input id="name" type="text" name="name" size="35" /><br />
<label for="phone">Phone Number: </label>
<input id="phone" type="text" name="phone" size="11"
maxlength="11" /> (xxx-xxx-xxxx)<br />
<label for="email">E-mail Address: </label>
<input id="email" type="text" name="email" /><br />
<label for="card">Library Card Number: </label>
<input id="card" type="password" name="card" size="10"
maxlength="10" />
</div>
</fieldset>
<fieldset>
<legend>Item Information</legend>
<div>
<label for="itemTitle">Title: </label>
<input id="itemTitle" type="text" name="itemTitle" size="40" />
<br />
<label for="author">Author: </label>
<input id="author" type="text" name="author" size="30" /><br />
Type:
<input id="book" type="radio" name="type" value="book" />
<label for="book">Book</label>
<input id="article" type="radio" name="type" value="article" />
<label for="article">Article</label>
<input id="journal" type="radio" name="type" value="Journal" />
<label for="journal">Journal</label>
<input id="av" type="radio" name="type" value="a/v" />
<label for="av">Audio/Video</label>
<br />
```

```
<label for="citation">Citation: </label>
<input id="citation" type="text" name="citation" size="30" /><br />
<label for="borrower">Borrower type: </label>
<select id="borrower" name="borrower">
<option>Adjunct Faculty</option>
<option>Faculty</option>
<option>Staff</option>
<option selected="true">Student</option>
<option>Public</option>
</select>
<br />
<label for="amount">Amount willing to pay: </label>
$<input id="amount" type="text" name="amount" size="5"
maxlength="5" /><small>##.##</small><br />
<label for="date">Date needed by: </label>
<input id="date" type="text" name="date" size="10" maxlength="10"
/><small>mm-dd-yyyy</small><br />
<label for="comments">Please add any additional information that
may assist us in processing your request:</label><br />
<textarea id="comments" name="comments" cols="40" rows="5"></
textarea><br />
<input id="newsletter" type="checkbox" name="newsletter" />
<label for="newsletter">Please sign me up for the library's
electronic newsletter.</label>
</div>
</fieldset>
```

9

Frames

Frames are the division of a browser window into multiple independent documents, commonly resulting in the appearance of multiple scrollbars. Frames have been part of Web design for years. They were first introduced by Netscape in the mid 1990s and were added to HTML 3.2. Their intention was to give authors flexibility over displaying multiple documents.

Frames came with their own set of design problems. The back button in early browsers did not support frames, causing a single click of the back button to send the user back to the page they had been viewing before they entered the frames-based site. This sometimes issued the equivalent of three or more back steps.

Beyond the early technical problems, designers wreaked havoc when they got their hands on frames. I remember one particular U.S. senator's Web site that divided the screen into no fewer then eight sections. One of the smallest areas was used to display press releases, a fact that due to the size of the frame, forced users to read the press releases ten words at a time. Other authors who probably did not have a good understanding of navigational concepts caused users to become lost within their frames, not knowing where to click or which frame would change. Lastly, authors would lock you into their site by placing their banner across the top in one frame while presenting content from another unrelated site in a lower frame. This gave the user the impression that the content was coming from one site, when in fact it was coming from another. Because of all these problems, many users today avoid sites that use frames. Additionally, most authors avoid the use of them altogether.

I consider myself one of the last holdouts on the subject of frames. I believe that, with a little knowledge of how frames work and with a dab of common sense, frames can be used as a legitimate design choice. That said, I ultimately do not recommend that any author use frames unless they have a solid grasp on the mechanics, design implications, and user views. If you feel you have all of these qualifications and still want to use frames, go ahead.

CREATING A FRAMESET DOCUMENT

When you use frames in your site, you must first create what is known as a frameset document. This is the XHTML file that tells the browser how to divide the browser window and which documents to display within each frame.

If you are to create a document that contains two frames, you must create three documents—the two displayed documents and the frameset document. To create four frames, you must create five documents, and so on. A frameset document is started the same way that any other XHTML document is started but you must specify the frameset doctype. (This is done only for the frameset document, not the documents that will be displayed for the user.)

```
<!DOCTYPE html PUBLIC "-//W3C//DTD XHTML 1.0 Frameset//EN" "http:/
/www.w3.org/TR/xhtml/DTD/xhtml1-frameset.dtd">
<html xmlns="http://www.w3.org/TR/xhtml" lang="en">
<head>
<title>Acme Public Library</title>
<meta name="HTTP-Equiv" content="text/html; content="utf-8">
</head>
</html>
```

A frameset document does not necessarily contain a <body>. Frameset documents contain a <frameset> instead.

```
<!DOCTYPE html PUBLIC "-//W3C//DTD XHTML 1.0 Frameset//EN" "http:/
/www.w3.org/TR/xhtml/DTD/xhtml1-frameset.dtd">
<html xmlns="http://www.w3.org/TR/xhtml" lang="en">
<head>
<title> Acme Public Library</title>
<meta name="HTTP-Equiv" content="text/html; content="utf-8">
</head>
<frameset>
</frameset>
</html>
```

NOTE: A frameset document will contain a <body> within the <noframes> area. We'll cover this later in the chapter.

All your work setting up the individual frames of your document will be done between start and end <frameset>.

SPECIFYING INDIVIDUAL FRAMES

The first example is a document with only two frames. We will specify that we want two frames, and what documents are to be displayed within those frames. We will start by creating documents that we'll be displaying. Here is the code for toc.html and intro.html.

```
toc.html
<!DOCTYPE html PUBLIC "-//W3C//DTD XHTML 1.0
```

```
Transitional//EN"  "http://www.w3.org/TR/xhtml/DTD/xhtml1-
transitional.dtd">
<html xmlns="http://www.w3.org/TR/xhtml" lang="en">
<head>
<title>Main Menu</title>
<meta name="HTTP-Equiv" content="text/html; content="utf-8">
</head>
<body>
<h1>Main Menu</h1>
<ul>
<li>Hours</li>
<li>Catalog</li>
<li>Google</li>
</ul>
</body>
</html>
```

intro.html

```
<!DOCTYPE html PUBLIC "-//W3C//DTD XHTML 1.0 Transitional//EN"
"http://www.w3.org/TR/xhtml/DTD/xhtml1-transitional.dtd">
<html xmlns="http://www.w3.org/TR/xhtml" lang="en">
<head>
<title>Intro Page</title>
<meta name="HTTP-Equiv" content="text/html; content="utf-8">
</head>
<body>
<h1>Welcome to the Acme Public Library</h1>
<p>Please select your choice from the menu on the left.</p>
</body>
</html>
```

NOTE: In a real-life scenario, my introductory page would include much more than just a welcome and a one-sentence paragraph. I'm just trying to keep things simple for the examples.

Now that we have our individual documents, we need to tell our frameset document that we would like these documents included as part of the frameset. To do this we use the <frame> element.

```
</head>
<frameset>
 <frame src="toc.html" />
 <frame src="intro.html" />
</frameset>
</html>
```

If you look at this code in your browser, you won't see much. This is because we have not specified how we want the frames themselves to appear. Until we do this, our documents will not display. To accomplish this we need to look back to the <frameset> element. On this element we need to add one of two attributes; rows="" or cols="". Since we have implied in our text that we want the menu to appear to the left, we should use the cols attribute. (If we were to use the rows attribute we would end up with one frame on top of the other.)

```
</head>
<frameset cols="">
 <frame src="toc.html" />
 <frame src="intro.html" />
</frameset>
</html>
```

The next step is to specify the size of the columns. Let's suppose that we want the left column to take up 20 percent of the browser window and the right column to take up 80 percent. Our code would look like this:

```
</head>
<frameset cols="20%, 80%">
 <frame src="toc.html" />
 <frame src="intro.html" />
</frameset>
</html>
```

We now see what the results look like in the browser (Figure 9.1).

Figure 9.1.   Our Column-based Frames

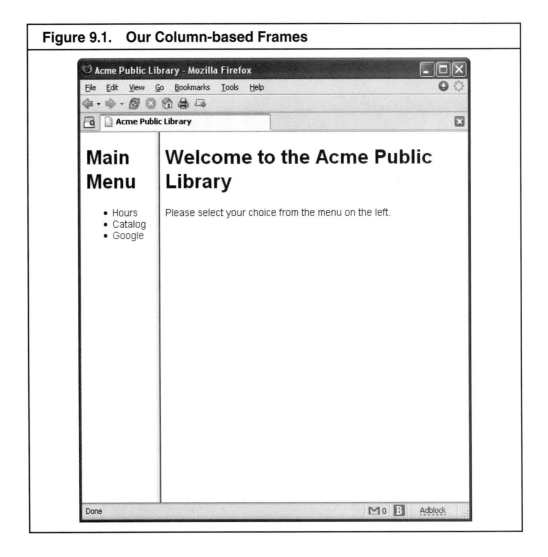

As with any other items for which you set a width and/or height, you can also set these parameters as absolute values. For example, if I wanted the left column to take up 200 pixels I would change the code to read `cols="200,*"`. In this case, since we don't know the size of the user's window and can't put in a second value, you can use `"*"` to specify "whatever's available."

Just to see it, although admittedly it doesn't fit with the text we've written, try changing `cols` to `rows` and see what happens (Figure 9.2).

Figure 9.2.   Our Frames as Rows

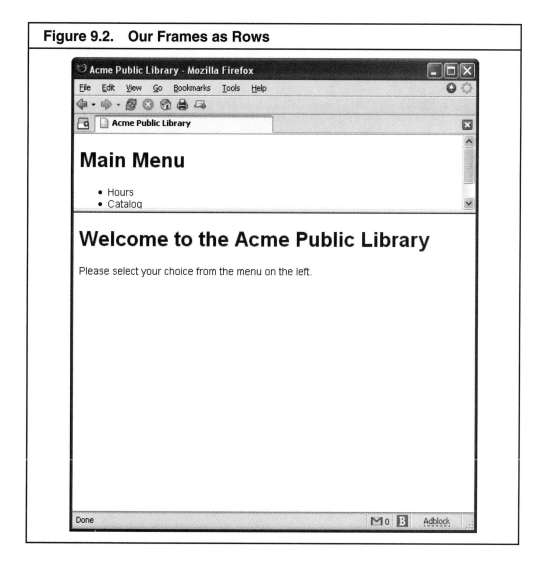

We can give our frameset as many columns or rows as we'd like. Just remember that when using `cols` you're working left to right, and when using `rows` your're working top-down.

MIXING ROWS AND COLS

What if you wanted to have one row across the top of the page (like a banner), then have the lower part of the screen divided into two columns? (This is where many authors started getting into trouble—mixing rows and columns.) Your code would look like this (Figure 9.3):

```
<frameset rows="20%, 80%">
 <frame src="banner.html" />
 <frameset cols="25%, 75%">
  <frame src="toc.html" />
  <frame src="intro.html" />
 </frameset>
</frameset>
```

Figure 9.3.   Mixing Rows and Columns

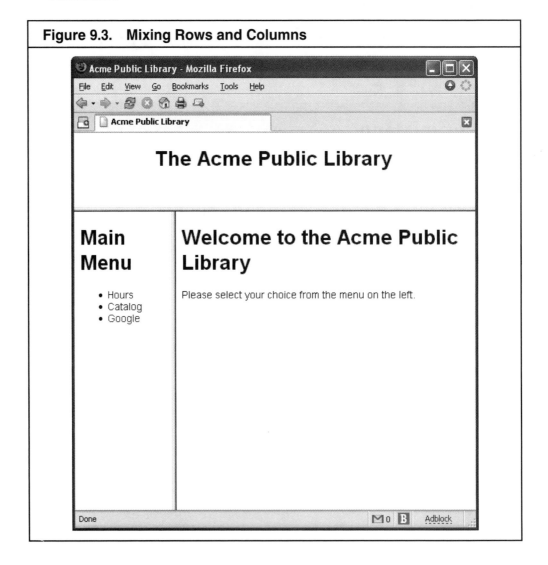

In this example, the window will first be divided into two rows, the first taking up the top 20 percent of the window and displaying the contents of the banner.html file. The second row will then be divided into two columns of 25 percent and 75 percent respectively, displaying toc.html and intro.html. We'll use our original two-column layout for the remainder of the chapter.

CONTROLLING THE APPEARANCE OF YOUR FRAMES

There are six additional attributes that you can add to your `<frame>` elements to control the appearance of your frames. These are `scrolling`, `frameborder`, `noresize`, `marginheight`, `marginwidth`, and `longdesc`.

scrolling=""

Frameset

The scrolling attribute controls if and when scrollbars appear on a particular frame. There are three values for this attribute:

- `auto`
  This is the default value. Scrollbars appear if they are needed.
- `no`
  Scrollbars will not appear even if they are needed.
- `yes`
  Scrollbars will appear whether they are needed or not.

frameborder="*n*"

Frameset

The `frameborder` attribute is assigned a value in pixels, specifying the size of the border between the current frame and any adjacent frames. A `frameborder` value of zero will turn off the borders enitrely. If adjacent frames have different values for `frameborder` set, the higher value will take precedence.

noresize="noresize"

Frameset

By default, a user can resize the frames as presented. (Take this opportunity to move your mouse cursor over the border between the two frames and drag the border to the left or right.) By adding the `noresize` attribute, we can lock the borders in place. As with other attributes such as `noshade`, the value for `noresize` is `noresize`.

marginheight="*n*" and marginwidth="*n*"

Frameset

These attributes allow you to specify in pixels the size of the margin between adjacent frames. `marginheight` specifies the top and bottom margins while `marginwidth` specifies the left and right margins. CSS, however, is a better tool for controlling margins.

```
longdesc="..."
```

Frameset

This attribute is designed to allow the author to provide a URL that points to a description of the frame's content (or to alternative content for nonvisual browsers). Unfortunately, no current browser supports this attribute in this context.

GETTING YOUR HYPERLINKS TO WORK PROPERLY

Let's go ahead and add some hyperlinks to our toc.html file. Here is the revised toc.html code along with the code for the files we're linking to.

toc.html
```
<!DOCTYPE html PUBLIC "-//W3C//DTD XHTML 1.0 Transitional//EN"
"http://www.w3.org/TR/xhtml/DTD/xhtml1-transitional.dtd">
<html xmlns="http://www.w3.org/TR/xhtml" lang="en">
<head>
<title>Main Menu</title>
<meta name="HTTP-Equiv" content="text/html; content="utf-8">
</head>
<body>
<h1>Main Menu</h1>
<ul>
<li><a href="hours.html">Hours</a></li>
<li><a href="opac.html">Catalog</a></li>
<li><a href="http://www.google.com/">Google</a></li>
</ul>
</body>
</html>
```

hours.html
```
<!DOCTYPE html PUBLIC "-//W3C//DTD XHTML 1.0 Transitional//EN"
"http://www.w3.org/TR/xhtml/DTD/xhtml1-transitional.dtd">
<html xmlns="http://www.w3.org/TR/xhtml" lang="en">
<head>
<title>Hours</title>
<meta name="HTTP-Equiv" content="text/html; content="utf-8">
</head>
<body>
<h1>Hours</h1>
<ul>
<li>Monday — Friday: 9am—5pm</li>
<li>Saturday: Closed</li>
<li>Sunday: Noon—4pm</li>
</ul>
</body>
</html>
```

opac.html
```
<!DOCTYPE html PUBLIC "-//W3C//DTD XHTML 1.0 Transitional//EN"
"http://www.w3.org/TR/xhtml/DTD/xhtml1-transitional.dtd">
<html xmlns="http://www.w3.org/TR/xhtml" lang="en">
<head>
<title>Online Catalog</title>
<meta name="HTTP-Equiv" content="text/html; content="utf-8">
</head>
<body>
<h1>Online Catalog</h1>
<p>We're sorry but the online catalog is currently down. Please
try again later.</p>
</body>
</html>
```

Once you have created the two additional files and made the changes to toc.html, test the hyperlinks by clicking on the hours link (Figures 9.4 and 9.5).

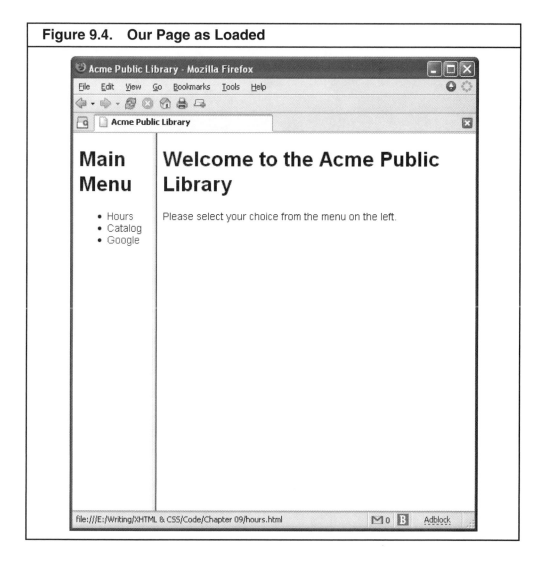

Figure 9.4.   Our Page as Loaded

Figure 9.5.   Our Page After Clicking on the Hours Link

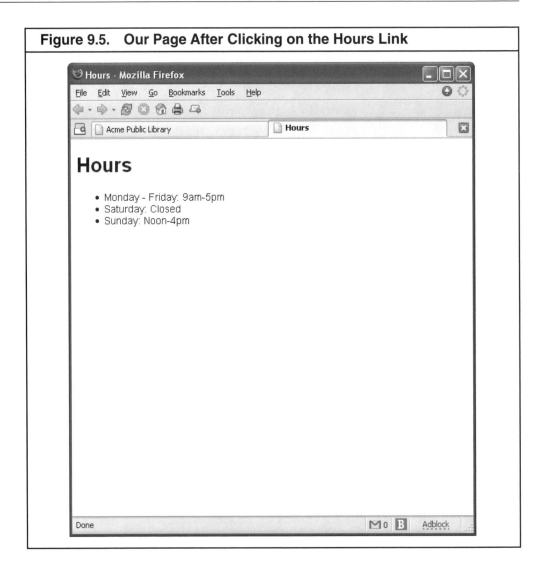

What should have happened is that the left frame would change, replacing toc.html with hours.html. Unfortunately, this is not the results we received. What we want to happen instead is for the right frame to change when a link is clicked in the left frame. To this effect, we need to add some additional code to our frameset document.

First, we need to identify each of our frames. To do this we add the id=" " attribute to each of our <frame> elements.

```
</head>
<frameset cols="20%, 80%">
 <frame src="toc.html" id="toc" />
 <frame src="intro.html" id="content" />
</frameset>
</html>
```

Once we have identified the frames, we can now give our hyperlinks a target—the frame in which we would like the linked documents to appear. We can specify the same target for each individual link in the document, but since the majority of them will have the same target, we can simply add a "base target" to the entire document.

```
toc.html
<meta name="HTTP-Equiv" content="text/html; content="utf—8">
<base target="content" />
</head>
```

The results of selecting any of the links in toc.html will now appear in the content frame (Figure 9.6).

Figure 9.6. hours.html Displayed in the Correct Frame

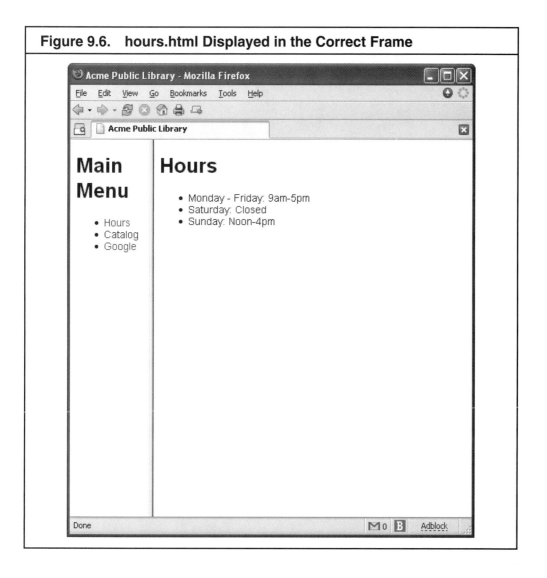

However, this is a problem when it comes to the Google link in our table of contents. It is poor form, unethical, and in some cases, a potential legal issue to present someone else's content in one of your frames. Unless you have made it abundantly clear through text on the screen that the content you are displaying is not yours you should never display someone else's content within your frameset. Even if you do make it clear, I still recommend you avoid it if at all possible.

That said, in the case of our Google link, clicking on the link should cause the Google page to appear, taking up the entire browser window and making our frames disappear altogether. We can make this happen by using one of four built-in targets. Those targets are:

- `_self`
  Loads the resulting page into the frame that contains the hyperlink. This is the default—what happened before we added our base target.
- `_top`
  Loads the resulting page on top of all other content, essentially replacing the frameset document with the new document.
- `_blank`
  Loads the resulting document into a new, unnamed window (a pop-up).
- `_parent`
  Loads the resulting document one level up within a frameset. This is designed to support documents using nested frames. Nested frames are not recommended and will not be discussed here.

To solve the problem with the Google link, we will add the `target="_top"` attribute to the individual hyperlink. Since we're adding this attribute to an individual link, it will override our base target.

```
toc.html
<ul>
<li><a href="hours.html">Hours</a></li>
<li><a href="opac.html">Catalog</a></li>
<li><a href="http://www.google.com/" target="_top">Google</a></li>
</ul>
```

FRAMES AND ACCESSIBILITY ISSUES FRAMESET

When it comes to accessibility, there are few things in XHTML that will cause more potential problems than frames.

First, search engines don't like frames and will therefore not index any content within a frames-based site. This is a serious potential problem, since many users will use a search engine to find your site.

Secondly, some browsers do not support frames. Many of these browsers are those specifically designed for users with disabilities, such as text-only browsers. Other browsers such as Blazer, the browser on my Trēo600 smartphone, do not support frames as well as the standard browsers.

Figures 9.7 though 9.9 show the frames-based HyperHistory site (www.hyperhistory.com/online_n2/History_n2/a.html) in three different browsers, each of which handle frames differently.

Figure 9.7.   HyperHistory as Displayed in Firefox

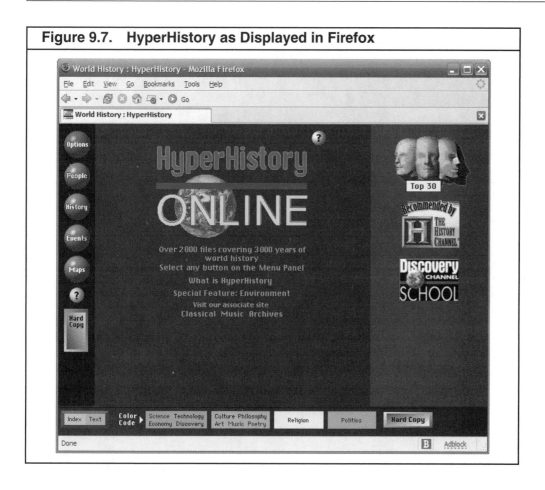

Figure 9.8.   HyperHistory as Displayed in Lynx

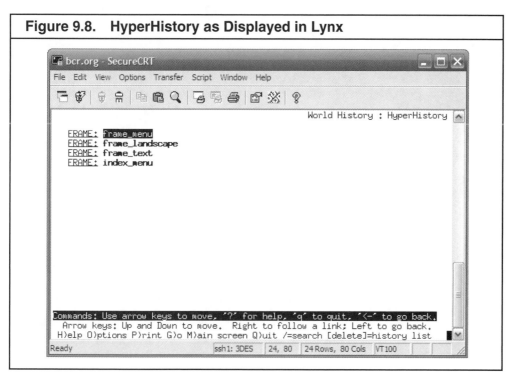

Figure 9.9.   HyperHistory as Displayed in Blazer (on a Trēo600)

Both of these problems can be addressed through the use of the `<noframes>` element.

Search engines are not set up to access the linked documents listed in the `<frame>` elements. If you take another look at our example as it stands, there is no content beyond the content of the `<title>` element for a search engine to index.

For browsers that do not support frames, at worst the user will see nothing. At best the user will see links to the included documents, toc.html and intro.html. Though this does give them access to the content of those documents, the user may be unsure which document to access because of the filename as presented. (This is yet another reason to pick good filenames.)

Once a `<noframes>` element is applied the content of the `<noframes>` element will be both indexed by search engines and displayed for users whose browsers do not support frames.

In our frames-based page, we should include in the `<noframes>` area the content of both our intro page (with modified text to fit our "new" design) and our menu. This is what the revised code looks like (Figure 9.10).

```
<!DOCTYPE html PUBLIC "-//W3C//DTD XHTML 1.0 Frameset//EN" "http:/
/www.w3.org/TR/xhtml/DTD/xhtml1-frameset.dtd">
<html xmlns="http://www.w3.org/TR/xhtml" lang="en">
<head>
<title> Acme Public Library</title>
<meta name="HTTP-Equiv" content="text/html; content="utf—8">
</head>
<frameset cols="20%, 80%">
 <frame src="toc.html" id="toc" />
 <frame src="intro.html" id="content" />
</frameset>
<noframes>
<body>
<h1>Welcome to the Acme Public Library<h1>
<p>Please select your choice from the menu below.</p>
<h1>Main Menu</h1>
<ul>
<li><a href="hours.html">Hours</a></li>
<li><a href="opac.html">Catalog</a></li>
<li><a href="http://www.google.com/"></a></li>
</ul>
</body>
</noframes>
</html>
```

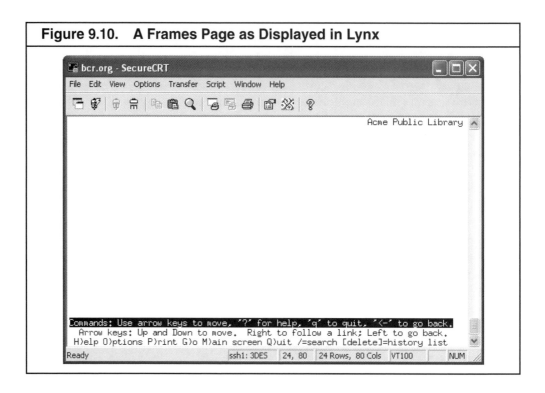

Figure 9.10.   A Frames Page as Displayed in Lynx

Notice that we do need to include a <body> element within a frameset document. Without the <body> element as shown in the headings, paragraphs and lists will not validate, since they must appear within a <body> element.

INLINE FRAMES

<iframe>
Frameset

Inline frames are used often, but in a manner completely transparent to most users. What inline frames allow an author to do is to pull one document into another document. For example, let's take a look at the following code (Figure 9.11).

```
<!DOCTYPE html PUBLIC "-//W3C//DTD XHTML 1.0 Transitional//EN"
"http://www.w3.org/TR/xhtml/DTD/xhtml1-transitional.dtd">
<html xmlns="http://www.w3.org/TR/xhtml" lang="en">
<head>
<title>iframe example</title>
<meta name="HTTP-Equiv" content="text/html; content="utf-8">
</head>
<body>
<p>In this document I've created an iframe and am using it to
display the content of the GoogleNews page.</p>
<iframe src="http://news.google.com/" id="window" width="100%"
height="500">
<p><a href="http://news.google.com/">Proceed to GoogleNews</a></p>
</iframe>
```

```
<p>Notice that since the content of the iframe is larger than
the size that I set, it has it's own scrollbar.</p>
</body>
</html>
```

Figure 9.11.   Displaying GoogleNews in an Inline Frame

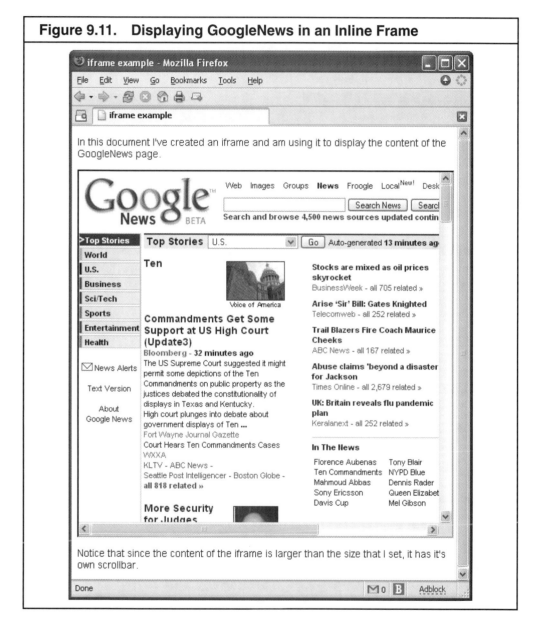

This `<iframe>` specifies that an inline frame should appear with the content of the news.html file inside it. The width of 100 percent tells the iframe to use all of the available space, and the height attribute specifies a height of 500 pixels.

In this case, I have also identified the `<iframe>` as "window." If I include hyperlinks in my content with `target="window,"` the results of those links will be displayed within the `<iframe>`.

Additionally I could put some text in between start and end `<iframe>` which would be displayed in browsers that do not support the `<iframe>` element (Figure 9.12).

Figure 9.12.   Our `iframe` Document as Displayed in Lynx, which Doesn't Support the `iframe` Element.

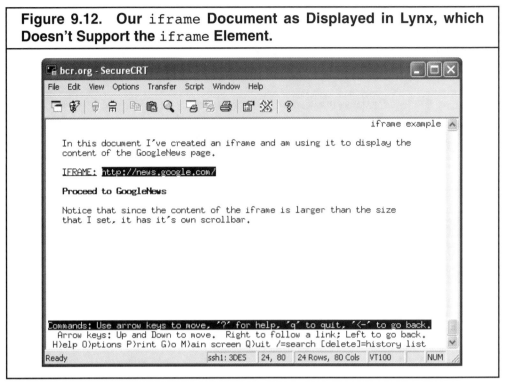

Why most users don't notice inline frames is because they're rarely used as obviously as this example. In many cases commercial sites use inline frames to place banner advertisements within their pages, allowing the advertisements to be supplied by a third party's server. In those cases, the inline frames and the images are the exact same size and therefore display no scroll bars to indicate the fact that the `<iframe>` element is being used (Figure 9.13).

Figure 9.13.   An Ad Placed via an `<iframe>` on the User Friendly Site

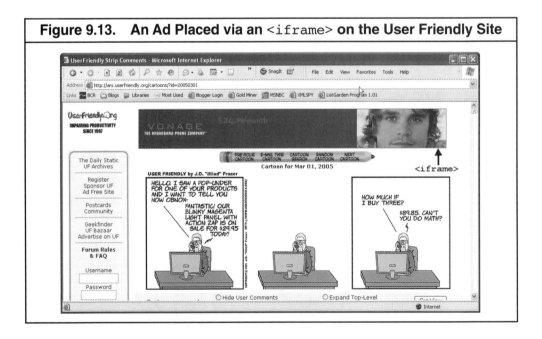

10

Metadata

WHAT IS METADATA?

Metadata has one of those definitions that you would be scolded for giving as an answer to your teacher back in grade school. Simply put, metadata is "data about data."

Remember how I defined XML as a metalanguage? A language for creating languages? This is the same concept. Metadata is information about other information.

When it comes to Web pages, metadata generally refers to extra descriptive information about the content of your document; additional keywords, or an overall description of the document as a whole. Metadata can be used to pass information about your document along to the Web server or parser for processing purposes. In Chapter 2, I had you put some metadata into your document that did this exact thing. Refer back to the discussion of your document's encoding scheme. In that example, we used a single line of metadata to tell the server and/or browser which encoding scheme the document was using. That is, data describing an aspect of our document: data about data.

In this chapter, we will examine the two different uses of metadata and some of the different metadata schemes available to you. First we'll discuss the type of metadata that can improve the indexability of your documents. Then we'll discuss the metadata for passing information along to the server and/or browser.

METADATA AND INDEXING

One of the purposes of metadata is to give your document additional information beyond the actual displayable content of your document that can be indexed by a search engine or other processing software. Through the use of keywords and descriptions, many Web authors seek to give their documents a higher ranking in search engines.

RULES vs. REALITY: Due to a significant amount of metadata manipulation on the part of unscrupulous Web authors, almost all of the major search engines today do not take metadata into consideration when ranking, or even indexing, a Web page. However, if you have installed any indexing software so that your users can search your site from within your site, this metadata can still be of significant use to you.

The element used to add metadata to a document is <meta />. Notice that this is an empty element and therefore needs the trailing slash. Since we're providing information about the document as a whole, the <meta /> element must appear within the <head> of the document.

```
<head>
<title>Metadata example</title>
<meta />
</head>
```

The <meta /> element has two required attributes: name="..." and content="...". The name attribute specifies the kind of metadata you are supplying, and the content attribute specifies the data itself. Here is a simple example.

```
<head>
<title>Metadata example</title>
<meta name="description" content="This page is designed to explain
the use of metadata in XHTML." />
</head>
```

In this example, I have provided a narrative description of the content of my document. Previously, many Web search engines would not only index the content of this line but also give the content significant weight in ranking the page, as well as using the content of description metadata as the short description displayed along with the document's title in the results list. As I stated previously, most search engines today don't do this anymore.

The other traditional name for metadata is "keywords." Here's the same document with some keyword metadata added.

```
<head>
<title>Metadata example</title>
<meta name="description" content="This page is designed to ex-
plain the use of metadata in XHTML." />
<meta name="keywords" content="metadata, markup, semantic web,
rdf, resource description framework, dublin core" />
</head>
```

Keyword metadata allows you to add a comma-delimited list of keywords and keyphrases that could be indexed by the search engine. There is no requirement that these keywords appear anywhere else in your document. Since metadata is not displayed to the user as document content, this can cause some confusion for your users when they do a search and find your document.

For example, here is the metadata from the BCR homepage. (www.bcr.org)

```
<meta name="description" content ="The Bibliographical Center
for Research (BCR) is organized as a nonprofit corporation to
assist in the effective and economical delivery of high-quality
library and information services.">
<meta name="keywords" content="BCR,libraryservices,OCLC,
netLibrary,FirstSearch,SilverPlatter,reference,training,
cataloging,Internet,Web">
<meta name="author" content="Sharon Hoffhines, Michael Sauers,
Lisa Holmberg">
<meta http-equiv="Content-Type" content="text/html; charset=utf-8">
<meta http-equiv="no-cache">
```

(We'll be covering the "no-cache" line later in this chapter.)

As you can see, we have a short narrative description of the document and a list of keywords. One of the keywords is `"silverplatter"` (one of the companies we partner with). Back when search engines paid significant attention to metadata keywords, if a user searched for "silverplatter," there was a good chance the BCR home page would appear as a result. However, when the user got to that page, it was highly likely that "silverplatter" didn't actually appear in the document as they saw it.

There are other potential problems with metadata keywords that you'll need to keep in mind. The first is the exact problem that led most search engines to abandon using metadata as a ranking tool. Reliance upon metadata for ranking depends upon the Web author writing metadata honestly and accurately. There is no authority control, and as librarians, we understand what chaos can result from that situation.

The other big problem is the potential for legal issues. In one famous case, a retailer that sold inline skates used the term "rollerblades" in their Web site's metadata. Unfortunately for them, that is a trademarked term and they didn't have permission to use it. They were sued and lost.

OTHER METADATA EXAMPLES

If you look back at BCR's metadata you'll see that they also have an "author" metadata line. Metadata in XHTML is flexible enough to allow you to place just about anything in the name field. In BCR's case, we decided to add author metadata to all of our pages, not for indexing purposes (although our site search engine can index this information if we'd like it to), but more for internal tracking purposes.

Another use of metadata that you might see is something like this:

```
<meta http-equiv="PICS-Label" content='(PICS-1.1 "http://
www.icra.org/ratingsv02.html" l gen true for "http://
www.webpan.com/msauers/libdir/" r (cz 1 lz 1 nz 1 oz 1 vz 1)
"http://www.rsac.org/ratingsv01.html" l gen true for "http://
www.webpan.com/msauers/libdir/" r (n 0 s 0 v 0 1 0))' />
```

This is metadata under the Platform for Internet Content Selection standard. This was a standard developed several years ago by Microsoft and other companies in an attempt to give a rating system to Web pages. The content of this metadata indicates the level of the document's content in such areas as adult content and violence. Unfortunately, examples of this are rare since the standard never truly caught on.

ENTER RDF

RDF or Resource Description Framework, is an XML standard for metadata. Since entire books have been written on this topic alone, I will give you an overview of it here. RDF allows you to create a separate XML file of just the metadata for a document or group of documents that you can then link to. RDF is what you would use if you needed to add a significant amount of metadata to an item (such as in a digital photographical archive) in which the metadata is the only indexable content.

Here is an example of an RDF document describing a CD collection from the W3 Schools site <www.w3schools.com/rdf/rdf_example.asp>. Take a look and I believe you'll be able to understand the basics. If you would like to read more about RDF, visit www.w3.org/RDF/.

```
<?xml version="1.0"?>
<rdf:RDF
xmlns:rdf="http://www.w3.org/1999/02/22-rdf-syntax-ns#"
xmlns:cd="http://www.recshop.fake/cd#">
<rdf:Description
 rdf:about="http://www.recshop.fake/cd/Empire Burlesque">
 <cd:artist>Bob Dylan</cd:artist>
 <cd:country>USA</cd:country>
 <cd:company>Columbia</cd:company>
 <cd:price>10.90</cd:price>
 <cd:year>1985</cd:year>
</rdf:Description>
<rdf:Description
 rdf:about="http://www.recshop.fake/cd/Hide your heart">
 <cd:artist>Bonnie Tyler</cd:artist>
 <cd:country>UK</cd:country>
 <cd:company>CBS Records</cd:company>
 <cd:price>9.90</cd:price>
 <cd:year>1988</cd:year>
</rdf:Description>
</rdf:RDF>
```

DUBLIN CORE

Although there are minimal standards for metadata within XHTML and more stringent standards within RDF those standards are not enough to meet the needs of librarians. They cover the inclusion of metadata within or the linking of metadata to a document, but neither of these offers taxonomy for the type of data to be included. This is where Dublin Core comes in.

The Dublin Core (named after Dublin, Ohio, home of OCLC, not Dublin, Ireland) was created by OCLC, the Library of Congress, and other organizations to set up a taxonomy for the type of metadata that should be included with a document. This taxonomy specifically considers the needs of librarians. It is not designed to take the place of a full MARC record for an item but it is significantly more detailed than XHTML-based keywords and description metadata.

A list of all of the Dublin Core elements along with descriptions can be found at dublincore.org/documents/dces/.

Here's an example of RDF metadata (http://archive.dstc.edu.au/RDU/PICS/dc-in-rdf-ex.html).

```
<?xml:namespace href="http://www.w3c.org/RDF/" as="RDF"?>
<?xml:namespace href="http://purl.org/RDF/DC/" as="DC"?>
<RDF:RDF>
  <RDF:Description  RDF:HREF="http://purl.org/metadata/
dublin_core_elements">
 <DC:Title>Dublin Core Metadata Element Set: Reference Descrip-
tion</DC:Title>
 <DC:Creator>Stuart Weibel</DC:Creator>
 <DC:Creator>Eric Miller</DC:Creator>
 <DC:Subject>Metadata, Dublin Core element, resource descrip-
tion</DC:Subject>
 <DC:Description>This document is the reference description of
the Dublin Core Metadata Element Set designed to facilitate
resource discovery.</DC:Description>
  <DC:Publisher>OCLC Online Computer Library Center, Inc.</
DC:Publisher>
 <DC:Format>text/html</DC:Format>
 <DC:Type>Technical Report</DC:Type>
 <DC:Language>en</DC:Language>
 <DC:Date>1997—11—02</DC:Date>
 </RDF:Description>
</RDF:RDF>
```

METADATA AS SERVER INSTRUCTIONS

Although metadata is most commonly associated with enhancing the description and indexing of a document, it can serve another purpose. Metadata can be used to pass instructions along to the processing agent. When it comes to Web pages, the processing agent is the browser.

CHARACTER ENCODING

As discussed earlier in this book, since the XML prolog can cause problems with several of today's browsers, we need to rely upon the use of metadata to send information about which character set we're using to the browser. To review, here's what that line of code looked like.

```
<meta http-equiv="Content-Type" content="text/html; charset=utf—
8" />
```

This line of code emulated an HTTP header, sending to the browser the fact that the document it was receiving was of the "text/html" MIME type and the character set being used was "utf—8."

In this case, what the browser does with that information is completely transparent to the user since we're working in English. If you were to change `"utf-8"` to another character set, say `"euc-jp,"` you would see the difference.

Some other uses of metadata we'll be discussing will have a much more visible result when the browser loads the document.

REDIRECTS

Have you ever gone to a Web site and seen a message that "this page has moved"? Usually those pages will also include information about updating your bookmark along with a note that if you wait a few seconds, you'll automatically be sent to the new location. The part that sends you to the new location is done through a metadata redirect. Here's what the code looks like.

```
<meta http-equiv="refresh"
content="10;url=http://www.travelinlibrarian.info/">
```

By placing this line of code in the head of your document, the browser will display the page, then wait ten seconds. After ten seconds, the browser will be automatically redirected to the given URL (www.travelinlibrarian.info in this example).

Here is a full example of a document using this feature (Figure 10.1).

```
<!DOCTYPE html PUBLIC "-//W3C//DTD XHTML 1.0 Transitional//EN"
"http://www.w3.org/TR/xhtml/DTD/xhtml1-transitional.dtd">
<html xmlns="http://www.w3.org/TR/xhtml" lang="en">
<head>
<title>My First XHTML Document</title>
<meta name="HTTP-Equiv" content="text/html; content="utf-8">
<meta http-equiv="refresh" content="10;url=http://www.bcr.org/">
</head>
<body>
<h1>We've moved</h1>
<p>We're sorry. The page you are attempting to access has moved
to http://www.bcr.org/. Please update any links and bookmarks
you may have to this page. For your convenience, after ten
seconds you will automatically be sent to the new location.</p>
</body>
</html>
```

Figure 10.1.   The Redirect Page

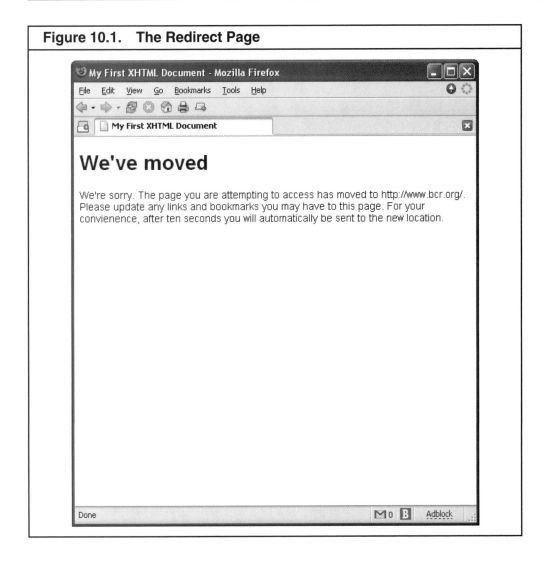

A few important notes about using refresh metadata

You may be thinking that it might be more efficient to set a zero time limit on the refresh. This way, when a user accesses the old URL, they are automatically sent along to the new page without having to read all of that information. Though this may seem like a good idea at first, setting an automatic redirect on a document can cause a number of problems for your user, the least of which is confusion when they attempt to use the back button to move away from the page they've been redirected to. Once they've reached that page, if they use the back button, they'll go back to the page with the refresh command, which will instantaneously send them forward once again. In this scenario, the user is stuck in a loop and unless they know how to get out of it, they will only become confused and frustrated. You should also set a long enough time to be sure that the user can read all of the information you've given them on the redirected page. Nothing would be more frustrating for a user than to see a screen of text only to be sent along to the next document before they've had the chance to read all of the text.

Lastly, be sure to include a link to the document you're sending them to, preferably as a URL (especially if you're sending them to another domain). Some older browsers do not support this feature and may not redirect the user as you've intended. By giving them a link to the document, you allow them to move themselves along should their browser not do it for them, or if they do not wish to wait the full length of the time you've set.

ROBOT CONTROL

The `robots` metadata allows you to have some control over whether or not a page is indexed by search engines. For this, you are given four options:

- `index`
  Tells the robot to index this page (default)
- `follow`
  Tells the robot to follow links to other pages found in this page (default)
- `noindex`
  Tells the robot to not index this page.
- `nofollow`
  Tells the robot not to follow any links to other pages in this page.

Each of these options may be set independently or in combination to fit your needs. Here are some examples:

```
<meta name="robots" content="noindex,nofollow" />
```

Do not index this page or follow any links within this page.

```
<meta name="robots" content="index,nofollow" />
```

Index the contents of this page but do not follow any links within this page.

```
<meta name="robots" content="noindex" />
```

Do not index the contents of this page but follow links found within this page.

CACHE CONTROL

Lastly, you can use metadata to control how a browser caches your document. In review, whenever you view a document in your browser, a copy of that document is stored on your hard drive in what is known as the cache. This allows the browser to quickly display the document the next time you view it, eliminating the need to retrieve a fresh copy from the Web every time you bring it up. However, your site may have certain documents that are updated often, and you would like to ensure that your users are always viewing the current version (your home page, for example).

The easiest way to control how a browser caches your document is to prevent caching altogether. The code to do this is as follows.

```
<meta http-equiv="pragma" content="no-cache" />
```

This will instruct most browsers to not cache the document. However, some older browsers that are still in use today (Internet Explorer 5, in particular) do not recognize this command. In order to account for those browsers you need to use the following:

```
<meta http-equiv="expires" content="-1" />
```

This leads us directly to the other method of cache control—setting an expiration date on a document. By setting an expiration date, you are allowing the document to be cached but are also telling the browser to not use the cached version if it is beyond the expiration date. In the previous example, we've told the browser that the document expired yesterday. Since we are always a day past yesterday, this will have the same effect as preventing the document from being cached in the first place.

A more complete setting of an expiration date would look like this:

```
<meta http-equiv="expires" content="Mon, 05 Apr 2004 10:35:00
GMT" />
```

NOTE: If you give a fully qualified date and time you must put it in the format (shown) as specified in RFC1123. (www.faqs.org/rfcs/rfc1123.html)

11

Validating Markup

As I've mentioned throughout this book, the central goal of marking up your documents with XHTML is to enforce the rules of good, clean, solid structure to your document. As you have already learned, XHTML has a significant number of rules governing which elements can be placed within other elements, as well as rules for required elements and required attributes. Although you will eventually remember the more common rules and apply them easily when you code a document, it is virtually impossible to remember them all. This is where the W3C markup validator comes into play.

The W3C markup validator ("the validator") is a Web-based validating parser that will read your document and identify any errors contained within your document based upon the rules of the language you're using as declared in the DOCTYPE statement. By availing yourself of the validator you'll not only end up with error-free markup, but you will also internalize the rules of XHTML.

The validator is located at http://validator.w3.org/ (Figure 11.1).

Figure 11.1.   The W3C Validator

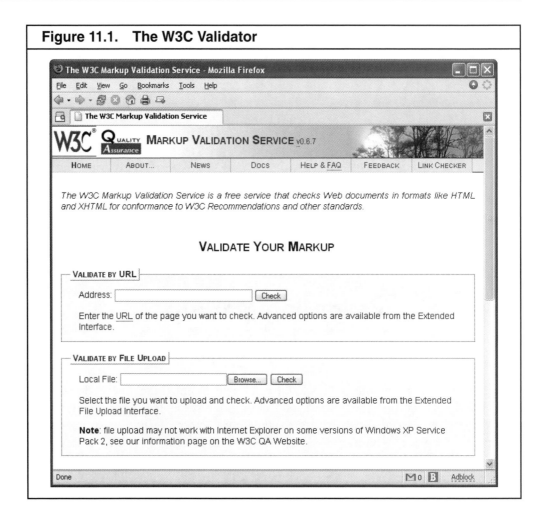

Validating your document is as simple as pointing the service to your document and clicking "Check." Interpreting the results, however, takes a little getting used to. Before we take a look at some results, let's first talk about the two methods available for submitting your document to the validator.

VALIDATION METHODS

The validator offers two methods for submitting your document. These are known as "Validate by URI" and "Validate by File Upload." Which method you use depends on the location of the document you wish to submit.

- Validate by URI
  The URI method is used when your document is located on a live Web server. (URI, or Uniform Resource Indicator, is just another term for the more commonly used URL, or Uniform Resource Locator.) To use this method, you need only type the URL of the file into the available text box and then click the "Check" button.

- Validate by File Upload
  The file upload method is used when your document is stored on a local, non-server, resource such as your hard drive or a floppy disc. In this case, you click the "Browse" button, find the file on your local system, select it and click OK, and then click the "Check" button.

NOTE: There is a third method which many Web developers use. By creating a bookmark of the following piece of JavaScript, you will have a bookmark which, when clicked, will submit the document you are currently looking at in your browser to the validator. Here is the code to do this:

```
javascript:window.open("http://validator.w3.org/check/referer?"+
document.location.href);self.load(location.href);
```

(This method acts as a "by URI" validation so the page you're validating does needs to be live on a server.)

VALIDATOR OPTIONS

Both options for submitting your document have links to what is known as the "extended interface." Both of these links provide access to the same set of options. The only difference is the submission method. The options available are the same so I am showing only one of the two possible screenshots (Figure 11.2).

Figure 11.2.   Upload Extended Interface

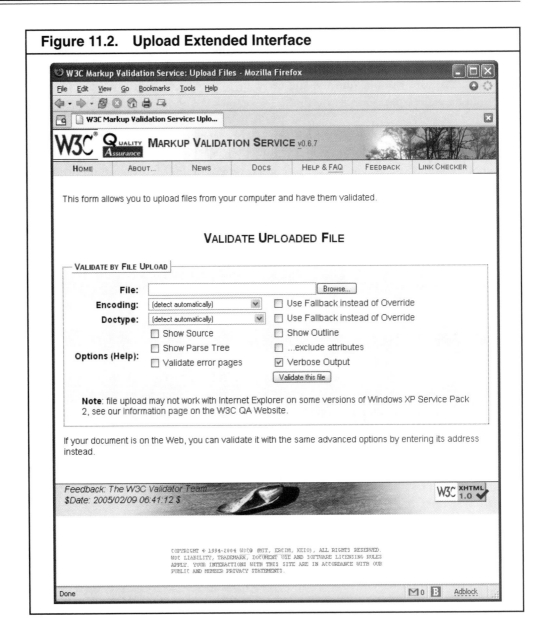

Here are the details on each of the available options.

- *Encoding*
  This option allows you to override the character encoding scheme your document is using. By default, the validator will use the encoding scheme specified in your document. You may choose another encoding scheme for testing purposes.

  By selecting the "use fallback instead of override" option, you're instructing the validator to use the encoding scheme specified by the validator *only if* your document does not specify an encoding scheme in the code.

- *Doctype*
  The Doctype option works similarly to the encoding option, allowing you to override the document's specified doctype for testing purposes. By selecting the "use

fallback instead of override" option, you instruct the validator to use the specified encoding scheme *only if* your document does not specify a doctype.

- *Show Source*
  This option directs the validator to reprint the source of the document in addition to any errors found.
- *Show ParseTree*
  This option will show you how the parser read your document.
- *Validate Error Pages*
  If for some reason the validator encounters an error page instead of the document you've indicated, using this option will instruct the validator to validate the markup of error page.
- *Show Outline*
  This option instructs the validator to generate an outline based on the document's <h1> through <h6> elements (provided they are present). This allows you to test for proper organization of your headings.
- *. . . exclude attributes*
  This option suppresses attributes from the validator. If checked, attributes will not be validated.
- *Verbose Output*
  This option instructs the validator to include additional information with the resulting report (such as helpful explanations of the error messages). This is a useful option for authors new to the validator.

VALIDATOR ERRORS

Once you have submitted a document to the validator, assuming there are errors to report, you will see a report similar to this (Figure 11.3).

Figure 11.3.   Sample Validator Errors

W3C® Quality Assurance MARKUP VALIDATION SERVICEv0.6.7

| HOME | ABOUT... | NEWS | DOCS | HELP & FAQ | FEEDBACK | LINK CHECKER |

Jump To:
Results

Address: http://www.travelinlibrarian.info/recluce/
Encoding: utf-8   (detect automatically)
Doctype: XHTML 1.0 Transitional (detect automatically)
Errors: 5

REVALIDATE WITH OPTIONS

[Revalidate] :   ☐ Show Source   ☐ Outline
                   ☐ Parse Tree   ☐ ...no attributes
                   ☐ Validate error pages ☐ Verbose Output

Help on the options is available.

NOTE: The Validator XML support has some limitations.

THIS PAGE IS NOT VALID   **TRANSITIONAL!**

Below are the results of attempting to parse this document with an SGML parser.

1.   *Line 46, column 2:* **"DOCTYPE" declaration not allowed in instance**

     `<! D OCTYPE html PUBLIC "-//W3C//DTD XHTML 1.0 Transitional//EN"`

2.   *Line 48, column 66:* **document type does not allow element "html" here**

     `...tp://www.w3.org/1999/xhtml" lang="en" xml:lang="en">`

     The element named above was found in a context where it is not allowed. This could mean that you have incorrectly nested elements -- such as a "style" element in the "body" section instead of inside "head" -- or two elements that overlap (which is not allowed).

     One common cause for this error is the use of XHTML syntax in HTML documents. Due to HTML's rules of implicitly closed elements, this error can create cascading effects. For instance, using XHTML's "self-closing" tags for "meta" and "link" in the "head" section of a HTML document may cause the parser to infer the end of the "head" section and the beginning of the "body" section (where "link" and "meta" are not allowed; hence the reported error).

3.   *Line 50, column 6:* **end tag for "head" which is not finished**

     `</head>`

     Most likely, You nested tags and closed them in the wrong order. For example <p><em>...</p> is not acceptable, as <em> must be closed before <p>. Acceptable nesting is: <p><em>...</em></p>

     Another possibility is that you used an element (e.g. 'ul') which requires a child element (e.g. 'li') that you did not include. Hence the parent element is "not finished", not complete.

4.   *Line 78, column 23:* **end tag for "hr" omitted, but OMITTAG NO was specified**

     `<hr style="width: 50%">`

     You may have neglected to close a tag, or perhaps you meant to "self-close" a tag; that is, ending it with "/>" instead of ">".

5.   *Line 78, column 0:* **start tag was here**

     `<hr style="width: 50%">`

Feedback: The W3C Validator Team
Date: 2004/07/21 10:24:06

W3C XHTML 1.0 ✓

Following is a list of the most common errors you may be presented with and what these errors mean to your code.[1]

- *Element "FOO" undefined*
  There is an element in your document that does not exist in the DOCTYPE specified. The most common two reasons for this error are either that you have misspelled an element or that you are using the strict DOCTYPE yet specified an element that exists only in the transitional DOCTYPE

- *Document type does not allow element "FOO" here*
  You have placed something as a child of an element that does not allow that child. For example, in a strict document you have placed an anchor as a direct child of a blockquote.

- *Document type does not allow element "FOO" here; assuming missing "BAR" start-tag*
  This is similar to the previous error but a bit more more specific. For example, if you improperly nest a list within another list it will yell at you for placing a `<ul>` without first starting an `<li>`.

- There is no attribute *"FOO"* for this element (in this HTML version)
  You have specifyied an attribute on a particular element that the DOCTYPE does not allow. For example, you have misspelled an attribute or you have placed the `alink` attribute on the body element, yet have specifyied the strict DOCTYPE.

- *Required attribute "FOO" not specified*
  A required attribute on a particular element has not been specified. For example, you have specified and `<img>` but have not included the alt attribute.

- *End tag for "FOO" omitted, but its declaration does not permit this*
  In most cases, this error is not exactly what it seems. This error is usually triggered by starting an element without properly closing a previous element, rendering the started element an improper child of the previously started element. The validator attempts to point to the source of the problem by indicating the next error.

- *Start tag was here*
  This message shows where the validator believes the source of the previous error is to be found. It is not actually an error message—it's more of an informative tip to help you troubleshoot the preceding error.

- *End tag for element "FOO" which is not open*
  You have closed an element without opening it. For example, your document contains three `<p>`s but four `</p>`s.

- *Value of attribute "FOO" cannot be "BAR"; must be one of "FOO," "BAR," "BAZ"*
  You have given an attribute a value that does not exist within the attributes predefined list of available values. In most cases you have misspelled the value.

When validating a document, do not assume that you should take the first report and attempt to fix all of the listed problems before rerunning the report. In many cases, a single structural error (such as forgetting to close a paragraph) may cause a cascade of additional errors throughout your document. Fix one or two errors at a time, then rerun the report. I have seen cases in my classes where a first run reports dozens of errors, and after the first error is fixed and the report rerun, the number is reduced to only two or three errors.

THE END RESULT

Once you have fixed all of the errors the validator has found, you should see the following (Figure 11.4).

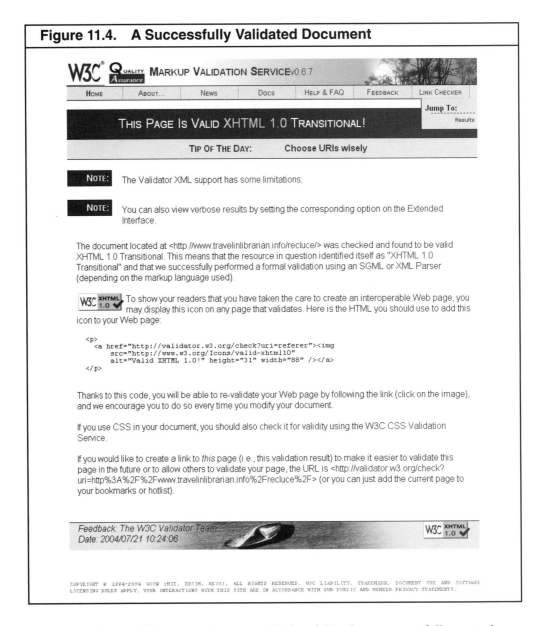

Figure 11.4.   A Successfully Validated Document

Once you've see this screen, give yourself a hand. You have successfully created your first valid XHTML document.

NOTE

1. A complete list of the error messages and their meanings can be found at http://validator.w3.org/docs/errors.html

PART II
CSS ESSENTIALS

12

Introduction
to CSS

Now that you've got a firm grasp on XHTML, it's time to move on to Cascading Style Sheets (CSS). Now that you have written your content and added your markup to give it structure, you need to decide how you want the document to appear to your users. (I will assume that the browser defaults are not enough to make you happy.) This is where CSS becomes useful. CSS allows you to give *style* to your document.

WHY USE CSS?

Cascading Style Sheets (CSS) were introduced to solve a growing problem in the realm of Web design: the integration of structure and style. In other words, the purpose of CSS is to separate structure from style.

HTML was intended to give structure to documents. In its original incarnation, it didn't even have the ability to include images in documents. There was no need for this, since the original browsers were text-only. As browsers became graphical and developed further, the need to control how the document looked on the screen became more important—so important, in fact, that the development of markup was briefly hijacked by the browser makers, resulting in what we now recall as the "browser wars."

The browser wars were the result of the browser makers (mainly Netscape and Microsoft) deciding that the HTML standards did not support all that they felt they should and started to add their own elements and attributes. These additions were, of course, only supported in the makers' own browser and not the others, thus causing design confusion and "best viewed in . . ." messages on Web pages. Once the W3C regained control of HTML from the browser makers, a standardized method was necessary.

CSS was the first of the technologies that rose from the rubble of that war. Its purpose was to create a new language dedicated solely to the appearance of documents, leaving the structure of the documents to the markup language—HTML (and now XHTML).

CSS BENEFITS

Using CSS has a few significant benefits for today's Web designer, but don't let the small number fool you. These benefits are *significant*. They are the ability to control the appearance of your entire Web site from a single file and the ability to create different styles for different platforms. Let's take a look at these in more detail.

- When you separate your structure (markup) from your style, you have the ability to create a single file containing all your style code. This code can then be applied to multiple documents.

  If you are not using CSS and you set your document's font in the markup of 1000 pages and then decide you want to change fonts, you'll need to make that change in a minimum of 1000 locations. (This assumes you don't have the tag-soup habit of using <font> over and over again within a document. This could increase the number of changes needed exponentially.)

  Conversely, when you have put your font control within a single CSS file and then directed each of your 1000 documents to follow the rules of the CSS file, you would need to make this change only once and in only one location. This advantage alone is obvious and evidence of the benefit of using CSS.

- Within the CSS specifications is a technology known as "media types," The rules of CSS consider that you may wish to display your document not only on a computer monitor but also on a cell phone and/or printed on paper. Each of these different display media have considerable differences. Paper has page breaks while screens do not, and computer monitors can display significantly more information at once than a cell phone screen can.

  By taking advantage of CSS media types you can prepare the same information to be presented in different ways depending on the media being used by the user.[1]

I would hope that reading about these two benefits has you excited about using CSS, but before we get into writing CSS, I want to point out a few things you should always keep in mind.

- *Older browsers don't support CSS.*
  Markup has been around longer than CSS. Early browsers will not support CSS since it didn't exist when they were written. The first version of Netscape Navigator to support CSS was 4.5. The first version of Microsoft's Internet Explorer to support CSS was 5. Anything earlier than this will not have support for CSS. Additionally, "support" doesn't mean "supported well or completely." All of today's current browsers versions have CSS solid support.[2] The higher the version number, the better the support. I will focus on current browsers in this book, but will address significant issues with older browsers (or between current browsers).

- *Not all of today's browsers support all features or versions of CSS.*
  Just as HTML and XHTML have different versions, CSS has different levels. Current browsers support most of CSS Level 1. Most current browsers most of CSS Level 2. Very few support any items in CSS Level 3, as it was still in development at the time of this publication. The real concern, though, is not into which level a certain CSS feature falls, but rather whether that feature works in today's browsers. (This is because, unlike markup languages, CSS does not require us to specify which version we're using.) Due to browser support, my examples will mostly include CSS Level 1 code. Some will include CSS Level 2, but none will include CSS level 3. I will focus on CSS code that is supported in the majority of current browsers (focusing mainly on FireFox, Mozilla, Opera, Navigator, and IE), but when a browser support issue arises, I will mention it.

Let's move on to writing CSS code.

NOTES

1. I will examine the basic mechanics of CSS media types in Chapter 21, including some of the properties used in printing. However, support for media types these days is minimal. I will provide the basics that will allow you to be prepared for the time when this aspect of CSS gains more support.
2. By "today's browsers" I mean IE6 (and higher), Navigator 7.x (and higher), Opera 7.x (and higher), FireFox (all versions), and Mozilla (all versions).

13

CSS Mechanics

This chapter will focus on the mechanics of writing CSS code. If you are new to CSS, the contents of most of the examples in this chapter will be new to you, and the brief explanations I've attached to them may not be sufficient. This is because this chapter focuses on the mechanics of writing the code and the different options you have available to you in creating the code. In most cases, what the code does (i.e., the results that will be presented to the user) will be explained in the following chapters.

THE LOOK OF CSS

CSS code is noticeably different from that of markup (XHTML) code. In XHTML you use tags, elements, attributes, and values. CSS uses selectors, declarations, properties, and values.

When building CSS code you always begin with a selector. Often, a CSS selector will have a matching markup element, but not always. Let's write some CSS code that will change the background color of our document. If you have HTML experience the `bgcolor` attribute may come to mind. This attribute was placed on the `<body>` element. When you change the background color of the document you are actually changing the background color of the document's body. So, in this case our selector is body.

`body`

Just as in markup where the element must always come first, in CSS the selector must come first. You should think of the selector as the item you wish to affect. In this example we want to have an effect on the body of the document.

What follows the selector is the declaration. The declaration is always enclosed in a pair of braces (also known as "squirrelly brackets") as shown below.

```
body { }
```

This is the first material difference between markup and CSS. In markup, all the code is enclosed in a pair of tags. In CSS, some of the code is outside a pair of braces while other parts are within the braces.

It is important to have at least one space separating the selector and braces. You can have additional space if you'd like (I'll show you why you might want them later in this chapter).

Inside the braces appears one or more declarations. The declaration is made up of a property/value pair. Think of the property as the part of the selector you want to affect. If we wish to change the background color of the document's body, our property will be `background-color`.

```
body {background-color}
```

Many properties consist of multiple words such as in our example, `background-color`. Whenever this happens, the words will always be separated by a hyphen instead of a space. A space will never appear within the name of a property.

The property must then be followed by a colon. A space after the colon is good coding form but is not required. I will include this space.

```
body {background-color: }
```

Following the colon is the value. The value is what we want to set the property to. If we want to set the background color of the document's body to blue, our value is `blue`. Unlike in HTML, where there are two different ways to specify color, there are five different ways available to us in CSS, though not all of them are supported. I've covered specifying color in Chapter 3.

```
body {background-color: blue}
```

This is our final code. In English, we have set the background color of the document's body to blue.

TYPES OF SELECTORS

Before we move on to further examples, let's discuss selectors. There are seven different types of selectors. Let's look at each of them briefly.

TYPE SELECTORS

Type selectors are the most common selectors. The example we've been working with uses a type selector. Here are few more examples:

```
p  {text-indent: 5%}
h1 {color: yellow}
h2 {text-align: center}
```

In these examples we've indented our paragraphs 5 percent of the available space, set our level-one headings to have yellow text, and centered our level-two headings.

You may have noticed that I used more than one space after each of my selectors. By lining up the code vertically your CSS becomes easier to read and later edit. This many CSS authors use the tab key after typing in a selector.

Type selectors can become more complex. Suppose you want to center both your Level 1 and Level 2 headings. You might suggest writing the following code:

```
h1 {text-align: center}
h2 {text-align: center}
```

Though this code is technically accurate, it is redundant. The following is a more compact and efficient code:

```
h1, h2    {text-align: center}
```

In this case we have specified two different selectors, separated by a comma. The comma works as a conjunction ("and"), so we have specified that our Level 1 *and* Level 2 headings should be centered. Be sure not to forget the comma. Two selectors without a comma between them have a completely different meaning. (The space following the comma is not required but is good form.)

You can string together as many selectors as you'd like. For example, if you want all of your headings, regardless of their level, to be centered, you can change your code to read:

```
h1, h2, h3, h4, h5, h6        {text-align: center}
```

Whenever you want to affect multiple selectors the same way, string your selectors together and use a single declaration. Type selectors are supported by all browsers with CSS support.

Inheritance, or, the Parent/Child Relationship

Before I go any further in introducing you to the other types of selectors, I need to introduce you to the concept of inheritance, also known as the "parent/child relationship" as it comes to CSS selectors and your markup.

Before I describe this concept to you, let's take a look at a simple XHTML document we can use as an example:

```
<!DOCTYPE html PUBLIC "-//W3C//DTD XHTML 1.0 Transitional//EN"
"http://www.w3.org/TR/xhtml1/DTD/xhtml1-transitional.dtd">
<html xmlns="http://www.w3.org/TR/xhtml" lang="en">
<head>
<title>Acme Public Library</title>
<meta name="HTTP-Equiv" content="text/html; content="utf-8">
</head>
<body>
<h1>Welcome to the Acme Public Library</h1>
```

```
<p>Please select from the following choices</p>
<ul>
<li><a href="hours.html">Hours</a></li>
<li><a href="branches.html">Branch Locations</a></li>
<li><a href="circ.html">Circulation Policies</a></li>
</body>
</html>
```

If you look at this document as having a hierarchical structure, you can verbally describe the "relationships" between the elements as if the document were a family tree.

For example, both the `<title>` and `<meta />` elements are considered "children" of the `<head>` element because they occur between/within `<head>` and `</head>`. `<head>` is considered the "parent" of both `<title>` and `<meta />`.

`<h1>`, `<p>`, and `<ul>` are all considered "children" of `<body>` in this example. However, `<li>` is considered a "child" of `<ul>` and therefore a "grandchild" of `<body>`. All three `<li>`s are considered "siblings" since they all have the same parent; `<ul>`.

Why is any of this important? Well, in CSS, elements "inherit" the properties of the parent. If you were to set the color of text to be red on a body selector, all the text will have the same color (red), since all the text is considered a descendant of the `<body>` element.

Once you have a firm grasp of the parent/child relationship, you can start to manipulate it to your advantage.

DESCENDANT SELECTORS

Here is what a descendant selector looks like:

```
ul li {color: green}
```

The lack of a comma between our two selectors creates a descendant selector. Descendant selectors allow for style selection based on the context of the element. In this example we've set the color of list items that are children on unordered lists. In this CSS code, list items that are children of ordered lists will not be affected. Only those within unordered lists will be affected by the color change.

Like type selectors, descendant selectors can be expanded as far as you like. Here is a more complex example:

```
ul li em  {font-weight: bold}
ol li em  {font-style: italic}
```

By adding the additional space and em as a third selector in line one, I have written rules which indicate that all emphasized text within list items that are part of unordered lists should be bolded, and emphasized text in list items that are part of ordered lists should be italicized. If you want to have an effect on a portion of your document only when it is a child of something else, you use a descendant selector. Descendant selectors work in all current browsers.

ADJACENT SIBLING

Adjacent sibling selectors are also contextual selectors. But rather than specifying when an item is a child of another, these selectors allow you to specify when one item immediately follows another.

```
p       {text-indent: .25in}
h1 + p  {text-indent: 0in}
```

On the first line I have specified that paragraphs should be indented one quarter inch. (Indenting something only affects the first line of that item.) The second line states that paragraphs that immediately follow Level 1 headings should not be indented (i.e., should be indented zero inches).

Figure 13.1.   Manipulating Indents with CSS

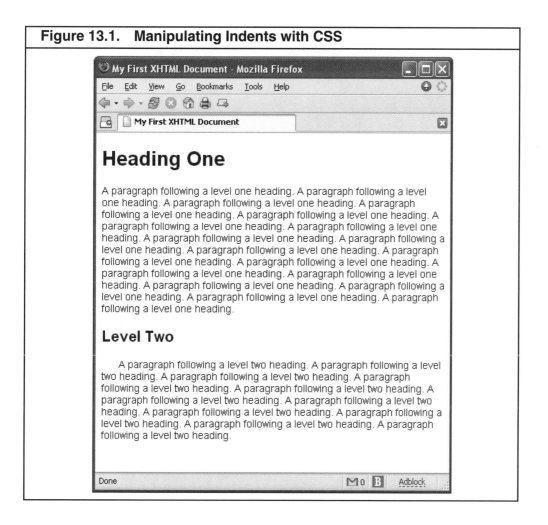

In the Figure 13.1 screenshot, I've illustrated this effect. "Chapter One" is a Level 1 heading. All of the paragraphs in my document are indented with the exception of the first one (a layout feature in many modern novels). Adjacent sibling selectors are supported in most current browsers.

ATTRIBUTE SELECTORS

Attribute selectors allow you to specify styles that are applied only when certain attributes appear on a particular element. Attributes can be matched in any of four ways:

[attribute]

```
q[cite] {background: yellow}
```

In this example, quotes that have a citation will have a yellow background.

[attribute=value]

```
table[width="50%"] {color: red}
```

Tables that have a width of exactly 50 percent will have red text.

[attribute~=value]

```
table[summary~="library"] {font-family: fantasy}
```

Tables that have a summary attribute in which the word library occurs will use a fantasy font.

[attribute|=value]

```
*[lang|=fr] {font-style: italic}
```

Any element that is in French will be italicized. (An asterisk can be used in place of an selector to specify any/all selectors.)

The | = (pipe equals) specifies a value list separated by hyphens. This is mainly used in language attributes since that is the one place where the hyphen is required as part of the value (i.e., "en-US").

Attribute selector support is spotty in current browsers.

PSEUDO SELECTORS

Pseudo selectors receive influence from outside factors or are predetermined parts of larger items. Here are two examples of pseudo selectors:

```
p:first-letter  {font-size: 200%}
p:first-line    {font-weight: bold}
```

In this example, :first-letter and :first-line are the pseudo selectors which have been applied to paragraphs. (They could have been applied to anything else, hence blockquote:first-letter would affect the first letter of a blockquote.) I have made the first letter of my paragraphs twice as large as normal and bolded all text on the first line of the paragraph.

Since this code as written would affect all paragraphs in my text, I might want to modify it to merge with my adjacent sibling example to ensure that this only happens to the first paragraph within a chapter. The revised code would read:

```
p                     {text-indent: .25in}
h1 + p                {text-indent: 0in}
h1 + p:first-letter   {font-size: 200%}
h1 + p:first-line     {font-weight: bold}
```

This shows how you can mix and match your selectors as needed. My result is that I've doubled the size of the first letter and bolded the text of the first line of only paragraphs that immediately follow level-one headings, as shown in the following screenshot (Figure 13.2).

Figure 13.2.   Changing First Letters and First Lines with CSS

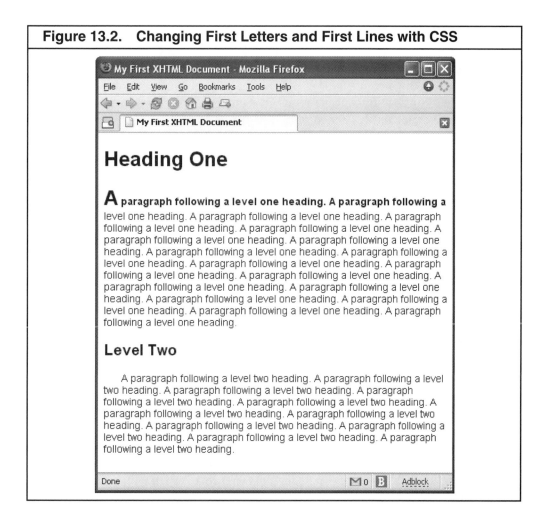

Let's switch gears now and take a further look at declarations before examining classes and IDs.

SOME MORE ABOUT DECLARATIONS

In all of the examples so far, I've shown you how to change a single property on one or more selectors. Suppose we want to change both the background color and the text color for the document's body. We might try something like this:

```
body {background-color: black}
body {color: white}
```

This would display as white text on a black background and, as with the example in which we did the same thing to both Level 1 and Level 2 headings, this is technically accurate but not very efficient. When you have a single selector on which you would like to make multiple changes, you can compress your code into a single statement. Here is the revised, more efficient and compact code:

```
body {background-color: black; color: white}
```

The key to setting multiple declarations on a single selector is to separate your declarations with a semicolon. Like a comma, which acts as an "and" between selectors, a semicolon acts as an "and" between declarations. What I've told the browser here is to change the body's background color to black *and* change the body's text color to white.

You can also write it like this:

```
body {background-color: black;
    color: white}
```

Writing your code this way will render the exact same results as writing it on the same line. However, we have continued the vertical stacking of our code, thus making it easier to read and edit in the future.

CLASSES AND IDS

Classes and IDs take the basic functionality of selectors and extend them. At the beginning of the chapter I said that selectors usually, but not always, match up with a markup element. In all the examples I've supplied so far, the selectors have lined up perfectly with XHTML elements. We have modified headings, paragraphs, blockquotes, and list items, all of which are identified by markup elements. In each of these cases (with the exception of the descendant and adjacent sibling examples), I have modified the entirety of a particular item. Take as an example the following code, which will change all Level 1 headings to be red and centered.

```
h1 {color: red;
    text-align: center}
```

Suppose I want one of my Level 1 headings to be right-justified instead. We might consider using either a descendant or an adjacent sibling selector, but let's think about that for a minute.

A descendent selector requires the level-one heading we want to change to be the child of something else. Since a heading can only be the child of body and there can only be one body in a document, we can not use body to create a unique instance of a heading.

An adjacent sibling selector requires us to specify which element our Level 1 heading followed. It might follow a paragraph, but then again it might follow a list—we really just don't know. Suppose we want all our Level 1 headings to be centered except for two of them and one of those follows a paragraph and the other follows a list.

We can create generic rules and exceptions to existing rules that can be applied as needed. Both can be accomplished through the use of either a class or an ID.

ID

An ID selector allows the author to create a generic selector to uniquely identify a particular element within a document. In my CSS code I will create two IDs, one called "large" and one called "small". I'll them apply them using the ID attribute in my markup.

```
CSS:
#large {font-size: 150%}
#small {font-size: 50%}


XHTML:
<p>This is normal sized text.</p>
<p id="large">This text is larger than normal.</p>
<p id="small">This text smaller than normal.</p>
<p id="large">This text should be normal size.</p>
<p id="small">This text should also be normal size.</p>
```

When you create an ID, you must precede it with a "#" in your CSS code. Then you create a matching ID attribute in your markup.

A few notes about naming IDs:

- ID names are case-sensitive. If you create an ID named #Bob, you must use id="Bob" in your markup.
- The names you give IDs should be descriptive of what they identify or what they do. In the above example, #large and #small are logical choices since that's what they do to the text.
- As with titles and filenames, short is more efficient than long.
- Avoid all punctuation. Although some characters are allowed (hyphens and underscores, for instance) it's easier to avoid them altogether.
- ID names can not start with a number. They must start with a letter. Therefore, #a1 will work but #1a will not.

Figure 13.3 Shows the Result of this Code.

Figure 13.3.   Incorrect Display of our Use of the id Attribute

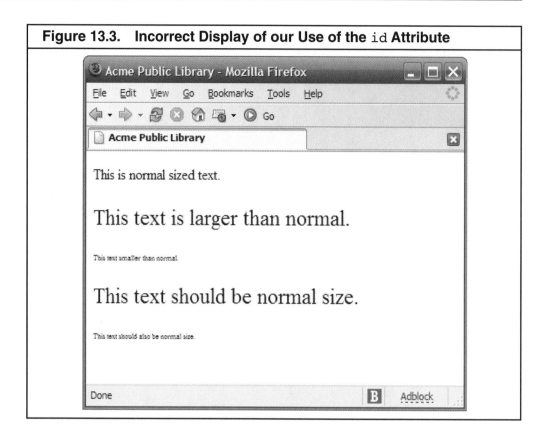

RULES vs. REALITY: You should notice that both of my `id="large"` lines have larger text and both of the `id="small"` lines have smaller text. This is actually an incorrect implementation of the rules. In fact, all of today's browsers incorrectly implement IDs. However, if you were to run this code through the validator you would see the following error message:

```
Line 15, column 7: ID "large" already defined
<p id="large">This text should be normal size.</p>
An "id" is a unique identifier. Each time this attribute is
used in a document it must have a different value. If you are
using this attribute as a hock for style sheets it may be more
appropriate to use classes (which group elements) than id (which
are used to identify exactly one element).
```

Remember that we used the `id` attribute for internal hyperlinks. You couldn't have, nor would you want to have, two different items in your document with the same id. Use ID when you are *identifying a unique* instance.

CLASS

At first glance, class will look very similar to ID. Let's look at some code.

```
CSS:
.business {font-weight: bold}
.personal {font-style: italic}
```

XHTML:
```
<p>People I know.</p>
<ul>
<li class="business">Rosario</li>
<li class="personal">Laura</li>
<li class="business">Susan</li>
<li class="personal">Gwynneth</li>
</ul>
```

In this example, I have made a list of people I know and classified each of them as to whether they're a business or a personal acquaintance. According to CSS, list items classified as business will be bolded and list items classified as personal will be italicized (Figure 13.4).

Figure 13.4.   Display of our Use of Classes

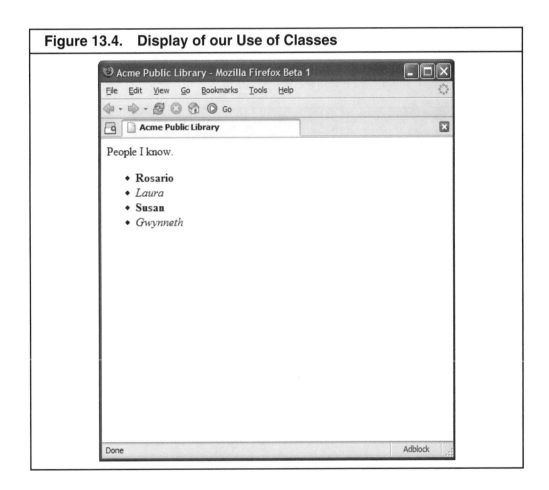

Here's where classes have much more flexibility than IDs. Unlike IDs, classes are not unique, since multiple items can be classified the same way. Therefore, classes can be used one or more times as the need arises.

Having created these classes this way, not only can I use them as often as I want but I can also use them on any element I want. If for some reason later in my document I have a definition term whose text is the name of a personal acquaintance, I can add the personal class to that <dt> element as shown below.

```
<dl>
<dt class="personal">Laura</dt>
 <dd>She's a really amazing editor.</dd>
</dt>
</dl>
```

Now Laura's name will be italicized (Figure 13.5).

Figure 13.5.   Our `personal` Class as Applied to the Contents of a `dt` Element

LIMITING CLASSES AND IDS TO PARTICULAR ELEMENTS

Suppose you want to change the alignment of very important headings. You might consider creating a class named .important. However, you want important level-one headings to be centered but important level-two headings to be right-justified. Take a look at the following code (Figure 13.6).

CSS:
```
h1.important     {text-align: center}
h2.important     {text-align: right}
```

XHTML:
```
<h1>Left Justified</h1>
<h1 class="important">Centered</h1>
<h2>Left Justified</h2>
<h2 class="important">Right Justified</h2>
<p class="important">This text will not be effected and will be
left justified.</p>
```

Figure 13.6.   Applying a Class to a Particular Element

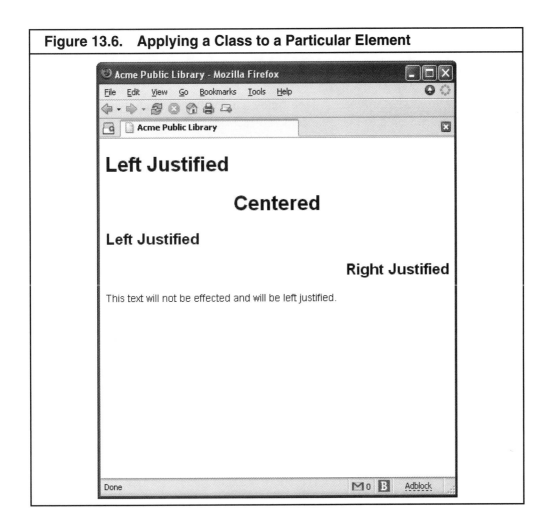

By coding a type selector and immediately following it with a class name, we've specified the declaration that should be applied *only* when the class appears on a particular element. Since we did not specify a non-element specific declaration for .important or have an .important class specifically for paragraphs, the paragraph on line five will not be affected.

Technically, you can also use this trick with IDs. Though it will work in some browsers, we run into a technical problem.

First, we change .important to #important. The next step is to change class="important" to id="important." We end up with the following code:

CSS:
```
h1#important  {text-align: center}
h2#important  {text-align: right}
```

XHTML:
```
<h1>Left Justified</h1>
<h1 id="important">Centered</h1>
<h2>Left Justified</h2>
<h2 id="important">Right Justified</h2>
<p id="important">This text will not be affected and will be
left-justified.</p>
```

Can you spot the problem? I'll give you a hint. Look at the second and fifth lines of the XHTML code. What's wrong?

We have now used a *unique* ID three times. This will work only when the browser incorrectly implements the rules. We could correct this by making sure we only use ID once, but then we have redundant code in our CSS.

CHOOSING BETWEEN CLASSES AND IDS

The question I usually hear from students at this point in my CSS workshop is "Why bother using IDs at all since classes are more flexible?"

The difference between IDs and classes is mostly semantic, so if you wanted to forget that IDs even existed and only use classes, you'd have no problems from a technical standpoint. From a semantic standpoint, however, you'd be writing poorly thought-out code.

You can't classify a single item until there are other items to classify along with it. (It's like when you're taught to write an outline in grade school. You're not supposed to have an "A" unless there's also a "B.") When you single something out, you've identified it; you've made it unique.

Let's say that you want to create a page with two columns and *not* use tables to do it. To accomplish this, you need to create two boxes into which you place your content and then move one box to the left of the screen and the other to the right, placing them next to each other. In this example you can identify one of the boxes as #left and the other as #right. If one is a menu and the other is news you could call them #menu and #news. You have two unique items that will not be repeated again on the page. This is the time to use IDs instead of classes.

HOW TO AFFECT LARGE PORTIONS OF A DOCUMENT

All the examples we have seen so far have affected one or more elements individually. The key word here is "individually." Suppose I wanted to affect multiple elements as if they were a single item? For example, take a look at the following code. The results are shown in Figure 13.7.

CSS:
```
p {background-color: red}
```

XHTML:
```
<p>This is a paragraph.</p>
<p>This is another paragraph.</p>
<p>This is a third paragraph.</p>
```

Figure 13.7.   Three Paragraphs with Individual Red Backgrounds

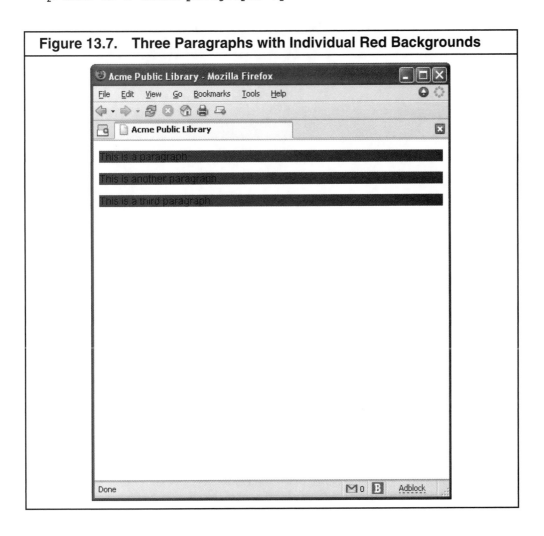

As you should have been able to predict, all my paragraphs have a yellow background. Another way to look at it is that *each* of my paragraphs has a yellow background—i.e., the spaces in between my paragraphs are not affected.

Suppose I want a red background on all three paragraphs *including* the space in-between, as shown in the screenshot in Figure 13.8?

Figure 13.8: Three Paragraphs with a Single Red Background

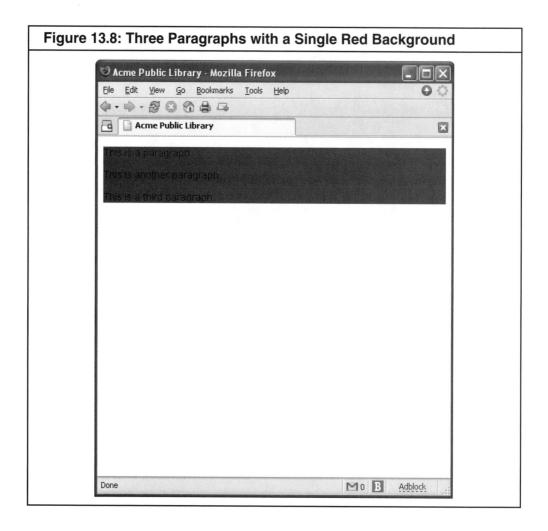

First, I would need to devise a way to enclose all three of my paragraphs within something on which I can change the background-color property. This is where the XHTML element `<div>` comes into play. If you have considerable prior HTML experience, you may already be familiar with this element. In XHTML, since the attributes dealing with style have either been removed or are discouraged, there really isn't much use for `<div>` until you start applying CSS to it.

The `<div>` . . . `</div>` element doesn't mean anything by itself. It allows you to create a "division" of your document or a block, the contents of which are affected by any and all properties placed on the `<div>`. Another way to look at it is that it creates a new parent from which the `<div>`'s children can inherit properties.

To accomplish our goal of creating a single background on all three paragraphs, we first need to place a division around our three paragraphs. To do this we change our code to the following:

CSS:
```
p {background-color: yellow}
```

XHTML:
```
<div>
<p>This is a paragraph.</p>
<p>This is another paragraph.</p>
<p>This is a third paragraph.</p>
</div>
```

By adding the `<div>` to contain our paragraphs, we have put an invisible box around them. (Remember this "box" concept. We'll be delving into it more deeply in Chapter 16.) Then we need to change the appropriate property of the box—the `background-color`.

What we do not want to do is change our p selector to a div selector. In this simple example, that would technically create the same result, but in the long run we'd be painting ourselves into a corner. Chances are, in a document of any substantial size, you will have multiple divisions. If we used div as our selector we will be putting a red background on all of our divisions and we may not want to do that. Instead, I suggest we create a class to do the job. This way we can use the class on this `<div>` and not others.

Here's the next step to revising our code.

CSS:
```
.red {background-color: red}
```

XHTML:
```
<div>
<p>This is a paragraph.</p>
<p>This is another paragraph.</p>
<p>This is a third paragraph.</p>
</div>
```

Lastly, we need to apply the class to our `<div>`. To do that we add the class attribute to line one as shown.

CSS:
```
.red {background-color: red}
```

XHTML:
```
<div class="red">
<p>This is a paragraph.</p>
<p>This is another paragraph.</p>
<p>This is a third paragraph.</p>
</div>
```

With this final adjustment to our code, we've created a section of our document with a red background that includes all three paragraphs.

The `<div> . . . </div>` element is used to create generic sections of a document. Through the application of the `<div>` element you can apply CSS to whole sections of your document that contain other elements.

HOW TO AFFECT SMALL PORTIONS OF A DOCUMENT

Let's take another look at the code we used to classify my personal and business acquaintances.

```
CSS:
.business {font-weight: bold}
.personal {font-style: italic}

XHTML:
<p>People I know.</p>
<ul>
<li class="business">Rosario Garza</li>
<li class="personal">Laura Prakel-George</li>
<li class="business">Susan Johns-Smith</li>
<li class="personal">Gwynneth Gunnels</li>
</ul>
```

After I presented you with this, I then went on to show that we could apply my `personal` class to a definition term that contained a personal name. Suppose we want to have that class apply to someone's name in the middle of a paragraph? For example, how would we apply the class to Laura's name in the following paragraph?

```
<p>My best friend is Laura Prakel-George. I've known her since
we met in high school when we were fifteen.</p>
```

We can't place the class attribute on the paragraph element since that would both classify the *whole* paragraph as a personal acquaintance and result in italicizing *all* of the text in the paragraph. What we want to do is classify and therefore bold Laura's name.

The XHTML element `<span> . . . </span>` allows you to subdivide the contents of an element into a smaller section. First we can place a `<span>` around the item we want to affect. Since we want to affect Laura's name we'll place a `<span>` around just Laura's name.

```
<p>My best friend is <span>Laura Prakel-George</span>. I've
known her since we met in high school when we were fifteen.</p>
```

Notice that we did not include the period or the space before Laura's name. Next, we apply the class to the spanned text like this (Figure 13.9).

```
<p>My best friend is <span class="personal">Laura Prakel-George</
span>. I've known her since we met in high school when we were
fifteen.</p>
```

Figure 13.9.   Applying a Class Using the span Element

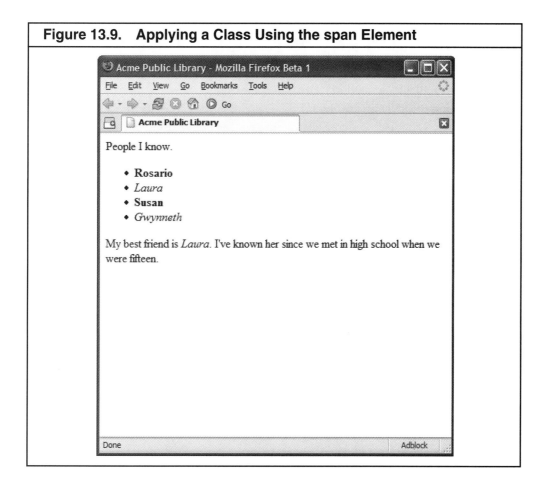

A `<span>` is used as a child of another element. It can contain as much or as little content as needed but should not contain other elements. For example, if we had a class that increased the text size by 10 percent and wanted to apply this increase to the last three words of one paragraph and the first three words of the next paragraph, we would *not* do the following:

```
...this is the end <span class="bold">of one paragraph</p>
<p>This is the</span> beginning of the next paragraph...
```

This may work in some browsers but it uses improper nesting. We have both ended and started paragraph elements as children of a span. This code will not validate. To solve this problem, we must revise the code to read:

```
...this is the end <span class="bold">of one paragraph</span></p>
<p><span class="bold">This is the</span> beginning of the next
paragraph...
```

GETTING YOUR MARKUP AND CSS TO WORK TOGETHER

There are four methods for getting your markup to pay attention to your CSS. The four methods are embedding, linking, inline, and importing. Each of the four methods has advantages and disadvantages which I'll cover in the next four sections. (The concepts of "importance" and user style sheets will be covered toward the end of the chapter in "The Cascade.")

EMBEDDING CSS

Embedding your CSS means placing your CSS code within the `<head>` of your XHTML document. (Remember, the document's `<head>` contains information about the document as a whole. Since we're dictating the appearance of the entire document, the code belongs in the head.) In order to embed your CSS within your document's `<head>` you must first add a few lines of markup. To review, here's the beginning of our XHTML document.

```
<!DOCTYPE html PUBLIC "-//W3C//DTD XHTML 1.0 Transitional//EN"
"http://www.w3.org/TR/xhtml/DTD/xhtml1-transitional.dtd">
<html xmlns="http://www.w3.org/TR/xhtml" lang="en">
<head>
<title>My First XHTML Document</title>
<meta name="HTTP-Equiv" content="text/html; content="utf-8">
</head>
```

Though style information can be placed anywhere between `<head>` and `</head>`, when embedded, it is typically placed after the title and the metadata. `<style>` . . . `</style>` indicates that the contained code is style code is.

```
<head>
<title>My First XHTML Document</title>
<meta name="HTTP-Equiv" content="text/html; content="utf-8">
<style>
</style>
</head>
```

Now we need to add the code that tells the browser what style language we're using. This is done by adding the type attribute to our open style element.

```
<head>
<title>My First XHTML Document</title>
<meta name="HTTP-Equiv" content="text/html; content="utf-8">
<style type="text/css">
</style>
```

NOTE: In the past it was common practice to enclose any CSS code within markup comments to hide CSS code from older browsers that would display the CSS as part of the document instead of interpreting the code as style information. Since browsers that old (Netscape 2.x, for example,) are hardly in use any more, common practice no longer includes these comment markers.

As a simple example, if we had a short bit of CSS code to change just a few items on our document it might look like this:

```
<head>
<title>My First XHTML Document</title>
<meta name="HTTP-Equiv" content="text/html; content="utf-8">
<style type="text/css">
body {background-color: black;
      color: white}
p {text-indent: 5%}
</style>
</head>
<body>
<p>Here is the text of our first sample document that is formatted
using CSS. The text should be white on a black background. This
paragraph should also be indented 5% of the available width.</p>
</body>
</html>
```

The advantage of embedding your CSS code in the head of a document is that you only have one document with which to work while you are developing a style for your site. This allows you to edit both your CSS and markup without having to switch between multiple files.

The disadvantage is that any CSS embedded in the document will only apply to the document in which it is embedded. At the beginning of this Chapter I explained that one of the greatest benefits to CSS is the ability to create a single style file and apply it to all of the documents on your site. Embedding your CSS does not accomplish that goal. We have created a style for this document and no other. In order to apply this style code to multiple documents, we must move it out of our document, save it as its own document, then link the documents.

LINKING CSS

The ability to create links between markup documents and CSS files is where the real power and flexibility of CSS is demonstrated. Through linking, you have the ability to create CSS styles and link them to as many or as few documents within your site as you choose.

If you plan to link a CSS file to your document, you must create the markup document and CSS file separately. (I covered the issues involving the creation and saving of the markup document in the first part of this book.) Your CSS file is created in the same general manner. You can use notepad or HTML-Kit or any other program that allows you to save your files in ASCII (text-only) format. The CSS file must contain only CSS code and nothing else. If you first created your CSS code through embedding and then wanted to move it to a separate file, you would move only the CSS code, not `<style>` or `</style>`.

Lastly, you must save the newly created file with a .css extension. Without this extension many browsers will fail to read or implement your CSS file correctly. (All the other rules for choosing good filenames that I discussed in naming XHTML files, such as case-sensitivity, descriptiveness, and punctuation, also apply to CSS files.) I have named this CSS file "style.css."

Now that we have created and saved the separate CSS file, we need to change the code in the XHTML document. Since the CSS affects the appearance of the document as a whole, this linking code belongs in the `<head>` of the document. The XHTML element is `<link />`. (Link is an empty element, just like `<meta />` and `<img />` so you will need the trailing "/".)

Here's our revised code:

```
<head>
<title>My First XHTML Document</title>
<meta name="HTTP-Equiv" content="text/html; content="utf-8">
<link />
</head>
```

Just as with `<style>`, `<link />` can appear anywhere between open and close head. Traditionally it is placed last within the document's head.

The `<link />` element by itself doesn't do anything. There are three required attributes that we must include in order to make `<link />` work. These are `rel`, `type`, and `href`.

The `rel` attribute establishes the relationship between the linked document and the document containing the link. Since the linked document is a stylesheet document `"stylesheet"` is the value of the `rel` attribute.

```
<link rel="stylesheet" />
```

The next attribute type is the same attribute we used on `<style>` when we embedded our CSS. This attribute tells the browser which language our style code is written in. Since the language hasn't changed, we'll still use `"text/css"` as the value.

```
<link rel="stylesheet" type="text/css" />
```

Lastly, the `href` attribute, as when used on an anchor, points the browser to the location of the linked file. Since with very few exceptions the CSS file will be stored on the same server as the markup document, the value for href should be a relative path to the file. (We'll assume that both the CSS and XHTML files are on the same server and in the same directory. If they are in different directories, the rules of relative pathing as discussed in Appendix Source I apply.)[1]

```
<link rel="stylesheet" type="text/css" href="style.css" />
```

If you set this up exactly as written, you should see the results of your CSS code applied to your XHTML document just as if you had embedded the code. You can now take this same line of code and place it in the head of every document in your site. If you were to then decide to change the size of the paragraph indents you could change the code in one location (the CSS file) and have each document automatically update accordingly.

Sometimes you may want to create more than one CSS file. On the BCR site there are two files, major.css and minor.css. The major.css file has all the style information for the pages with green menus on the left side and the minor.css file has the style code for all the pages that don't include the green menus. When they write a new document with a menu down the left, they link to major.css. When they write a new document that doesn't include a menu down the left, they link to minor.css. Once the appropriate CSS files are written, all you have to do is link to them. This saves time in coding new pages and removes the need for all the site's authors to learn how the site should look.

There is one temporary drawback to linking your CSS. When I discussed embedding CSS I recommended that, while you're developing your site you should embed, rather than link. By embedding your CSS during the development process you eliminate the need to work with multiple files at the same time. Even if you're comfortable manipulating multiple documents at the same time, I still recommend that you work with one page and embed the CSS within that page. Once you have the style code set, place it in a separate file and start linking it to your other files. I've found that this is the best way to work with CSS even after you feel you're comfortable with it.

INLINE CSS

Inline CSS is a technically valid yet rarely used method of applying your CSS to your markup. Here is a simple example of inline CSS.

```
<p style="text-align: justify; background: red">This is a fully
justified paragraph with a red background.</p>
```

What I've done here is add CSS code to a particular element (`<p>`) using the style attribute.

The advantage of this method is the ability to apply a style to a particular element within another particular element.

The disadvantages are a lack of flexibility and an apparent mixing of technologies, both of which contribute to the rarity of this method. If you wanted another element in your document to be fully justified and to have a red background, you would have to add the same style attribute and value to that other element. Since this is an inefficient way to write code, I advise creating a class to have available when you need it.

The issue of mixing technologies issue is more nebulous. Although this mixing is technically correct, many authors think it *just looks wrong*. One of the reasons to have CSS in the first place is to separate structure and style. Though we do have to add some structure to make our styles work (`<div>` and `<span>`, for example) this blurs the boundaries too much for some. Unless you feel that you must inline your CSS, I recommend that you avoid it.

IMPORTING CSS

Importing CSS allows you to pull in a CSS file when you need it. Though this sounds similar to what happens when you link to a CSS file, it does have a significant difference that adds an additional level of flexibility. By importing, you can pull in another CSS into either embedded CSS or into a linked CSS file.

Let's look at an import command when used within embedded CSS. We can modify the embedded CSS we used in a previous example.

```
<style type="text/css">
body    {background-color: black;
 color: white}
p       {text-indent: 5%}
@import (url: "/style2.css");
</style>
```

We have included some embedded CSS in our document but directed the browser to also refer to the CSS code in the style2.css file. We could produce the same result as if we had done the following:

```
<link rel="stylesheet" type="text/css" href="/style.css" />
<style type="text/css">
body    {background-color: black;
 color: white}
p       {text-indent: 5%}
</style>
```

In this example we've linked the contents of the style2.css file and applied the contents of the embedded CSS. The only difference is the *order* in which the rules are applied. The @import command allows greater flexibility in the order in which your CSS rules must be applied. (We'll go into more detail in the next section.)

The other benefit to importing your CSS file instead of linking it is accidental. Netscape Navigator 4, with its poor CSS support, does not support the @import command and will therefore ignore any CSS you include in an imported CSS file. The result is that you can hide CSS code from Netscape Navigator 4. Why would you want to do this? Well, Netscape Navigator 4's poor CSS support is well documented. The more basic properties and values are supported, but not sufficiently to make NN4 a viable CSS development platform. To circumvent this problem designers have set up basic CSS styles (fonts, alignments, colors, etc.) in linked style sheets, then placed more advanced CSS properties (mostly positioning) in separate style files and imported the style sheets. This way, browsers that support CSS get some basic styles but only more advanced browsers (read "not Netscape Navigator 4") get a more advanced layout.

In a more extreme approach, some designers go as far as putting all of their CSS into a single style sheet and then importing it. In this case, all CSS-supporting browsers get the style-based layout while Netscape Navigator 4 users get no styles at all. For these users, the page will appear as plain black-on-white and left-justified. Although I describe this as an extreme use of the technology, it does give users with a particularly older browser a functional page, just one not that's very pretty.[2]

THE CASCADE

Earlier in this chapter I introduced you to the concept of inheritance, the fact that elements will, by default, inherit the properties of the parent element. The reason setting the background color of the body automatically sets the background color of all of the paragraphs in the document is that the paragraphs are children of body. Inheritance, however, is only half the picture. The other half is the cascade—the order in which CSS rules are read and implemented.

CASCADE ORDER

The cascade order is the order in which all CSS rules are applied to the document. The basic order is as follows:

$$\text{Linked} \rightarrow \text{Embedded} \rightarrow \text{Inline}$$

This means that any CSS brought into a document through the linked method will apply first, followed by any embedded CSS, followed by any inline CSS.

Let's look at some code:

```
style.css:
body    {background-color: red;
 color:  navy}
p       {text-indent: 5%;
  text-align: justify}


XHTML:
<!DOCTYPE html PUBLIC "-//W3C//DTD XHTML 1.0 Transitional//EN"
"http://www.w3.org/TR/xhtml/DTD/xhtml1-transitional.dtd">
<html xmlns="http://www.w3.org/TR/xhtml" lang="en">
<head>
<title>My First XHTML Document</title>
<meta name="HTTP-Equiv" content="text/html; content="utf-8">
<link rel="stylesheet" type="text/css" href="style.css" />
<style type="text/css">
body {background-color: green}
</style>
</head>
<body style="background-color: yellow">
<p>This is a paragraph.</p>
</body>
</html>
```

What color will the document's background be? Due to the cascade, the answer is "yellow." First, the document will read the instructions in the linked style sheet, which on line one say to make the background color red. It will then read the instructions in the embedded style sheet, which say to make the background color green. Lastly, the browser will read the inline style instructions which say to make the background color yellow.

The order in which CSS rules are written within each level also matters. Let's look at a modified example.

```
<!DOCTYPE html PUBLIC "-//W3C//DTD XHTML 1.0 Transitional//EN"
"http://www.w3.org/TR/xhtml/DTD/xhtml1-transitional.dtd">
<html xmlns="http://www.w3.org/TR/xhtml" lang="en">
<head>
<title>My First XHTML Document</title>
<meta name="HTTP-Equiv" content="text/html; content="utf-8">
<link rel="stylesheet" type="text/css" href="style.css" />
<style type="text/css">
body {background-color: green}
```

```
body {background-color: yellow}
</style>
</head>
<body>
<p>This is a paragraph.</p>
</body>
</html>
```

I have removed the inline style and added another line to my embedded CSS. The background color of my document will still end up being yellow, but in this case it is because of the last CSS rule the browser read within the embedded style sheet. (Had there been an inline style included, the inline style would have had the final word.)

You may have noticed that I did not place imported style sheets into the cascade order. Where an imported style sheet falls in the cascade order depends on where you put it in your code. If I take the content of my style.css file used in the previous example and add a new line one, like this . . .

```
@import url(style2.css)
body    {background-color: red;
 color:  navy}
p       {text-indent: 5%;
  text-align: justify}
```

. . . then the cascade order will look like this:

Imported → Linked → Embedded → Inline

If, however, I move the import command out of the CSS file and into my embedded CSS . . .

```
<style type="text/css">
@import url(style2.css)
body {background-color: green}
</style>
```

. . . then my cascade order becomes:

Linked → Imported → Embedded → Inline

If I move it again so my embedded style sheet reads . . .

```
<style type="text/css">
body {background-color: green}
@import url(style2.css)
</style>
```

. . . then my cascade order becomes:

Linked → Embedded → Imported → Inline

Suppose I add an additional CSS rule after my import command in my embedded style sheet.

```
<style type="text/css">
body        {background-color: green}
@import url (style2.css)
p           {text-align: justify}
</style>
```

My cascade order has just become:

Linked → Embedded (body) → Imported → Embedded (p) → Inline

In other words, if my imported style sheet tells the document to right-justify paragraphs, the embedded rule to fully justify my paragraphs would override, since it is the last rule to be read regarding paragraphs.

USER STYLE SHEETS

Suppose that you and your library's Web site committee of a dozen employees, including the library director and a board member, have spent six months putting together the best-designed Web site of the year. You've developed the content and the layout. You've written perfectly validated code for your markup and the cleanest and most efficient CSS anyone has ever seen. Not only does it look exactly the same in all the current browsers, but it also degrades nicely and looks pretty good in non-CSS-supporting browsers. Your job is done and everyone is happy.

You, not whoever does the coding, not anyone else on your committee, have the final say as to how your library's pages appear on the user's screen. The users have final control over how your page looks on their screens. This may sound frustrating and somewhat of a disappointment, but, in today's browsers, this is by design. Before I explain just what gives the user final say, let me revise our cascade just a bit.

Linked → Embedded → Inline → User

The reason that the user has final say is to account for accessibility issues; to overcome designs that can cause users with disabilities to have dificulties reading your document. For example, you may choose a certain-size font that is too small for users with significant visual impairments, or you may put red text on a green background causing problems for people with red-green color blindness. Although you can minimize or even prevent some of these potential issues, no single design can be expected to account for all possible disabilities that any of its users may have. To account for this, many of today's browsers allow users to turn off style sheets and, in some cases, allow users to specify their own style sheets. We'll take a look at these features in Microsoft's Internet Explorer 6, since this is currently the most commonly used browser.

In Internet Explorer 6, select the "**Tools|Internet Options . . .**" (Figure 13.10) menu and then by selecting the "**Accessibility . . .**" button in the lower right corner of the "**General**" tab (Figure 13.13).

Figure 13.10. Finding IE's Internet Options Menu

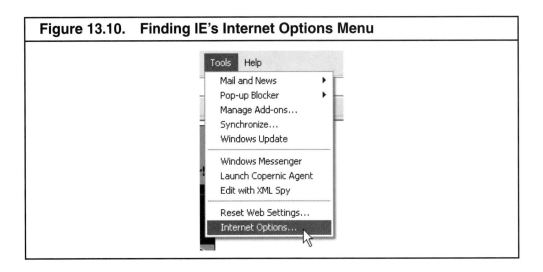

Figure 13.11. IE's Options

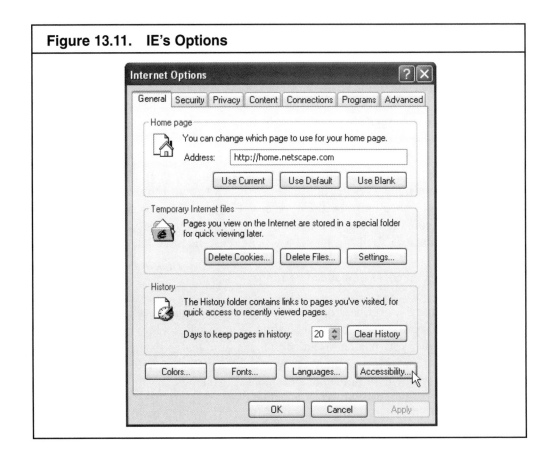

The three options in the "**Formatting**" section allow the user to ignore all colors, font styles, and font sizes (regardless of whether you have specified them in either your markup or your CSS though CSS.)

The single option under "**User style sheet**" when checked allows the user to browse the hard drive for a CSS file they have already written and saved. When selected, that style sheet will automatically be applied to any page the user views on that computer (Figure 13.12).

Figure 13.12.   IE's Accessibility Options

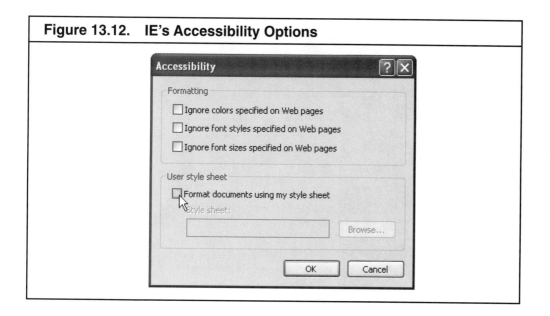

Let's look at my home page as it appears to most users (Figure 13.14).

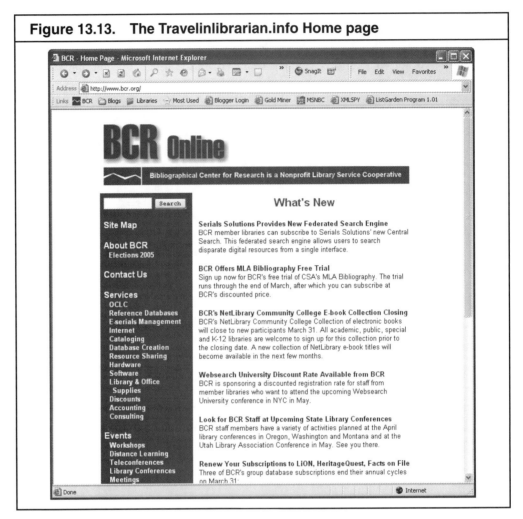

Figure 13.13.   The Travelinlibrarian.info Home page

I will now direct my browser to ignore all site-specified colors and font settings. I will then select a CSS file located on my hard drive, mystyle.css.

```
mycss.css
body {font-size: 200%;
      font-family: verdana;
      font-weight: bold}
```

In creating this CSS file I acted as if I was a user with significant visual impairments that require my text to be very large and in high contrast in order for me to read it (Figure 13.15).

Figure 13.14. The Travelinlibrarian.info Home page with user CSS Applied

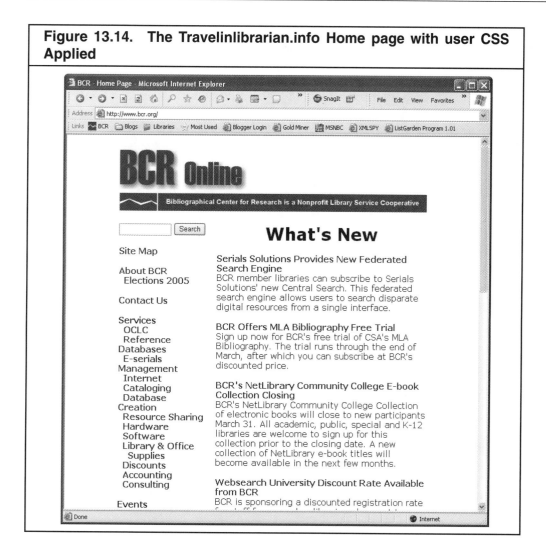

The layout of the page itself hasn't changed but the visual display is noticeably different.

The greater proportion of your users will never apply their own CSS to your documents. The important part to remember is that, whenever you design a Web site, the *user*, not you, makes the final decision about how the page looks on their screen.

IMPORTANT

First let me show you where ! `important` fits into the cascase:

$$\text{Linked} \rightarrow \text{Embedded} \rightarrow \text{Inline} \rightarrow \text{User} \rightarrow \text{!important}$$

Importance may be applied to any CSS declaration no matter where that declaration appears. Let's add importance to the paragraph-indent declaration in the following CSS code.

```
p {text-align: justify;
   text-indent: 5% ! important;³
   font-size: 1.1em}⁴
```

In adding the importance command, I have specified that this rule is to be followed, regardless of any other rule further down in the cascade. In other words, if this CSS appears in my linked CSS file, but later on in a page's embedded CSS it says that paragraphs should be indented 10 percent, my "important" 5 percent indent has precedence. This means that any rule given importance overrides the cascade.

By adding ! important, you have the potential of overriding a user's style sheet. This is what the CSS2 specification has to say on the matter:

> "CSS attempts to create a balance of power between author and user style sheets. By default, rules in an author's style sheet override those in a user's style sheet (see Cascade rule 3).
>
> However, for balance, an "!important" declaration (the keywords "!" and "important" follow the declaration) takes precedence over a normal declaration. Both author and user style sheets may contain "!important" declarations, and user "!important" rules override author "!important" rules. This CSS feature improves accessibility of documents by giving users with special requirements (large fonts, color combinations, etc.) control over presentation.
> *Note. This is a semantic change since CSS1. In CSS1, author "!important" rules took precedence over user "!important" rules."*

If the user's browser supports CSS1, then your ! important rule will override theirs. If it supports CSS2, then their ! important rule will override yours. The problem is that you don't know which version of CSS your user's browser supports. Taking away the user's ability to control their environment is not a practice I encourage.

COMMENTS

You have the ability to put comments that will be ignored by the browser into your CSS code, just as <!-- and --> allow you to do in XHTML. Within CSS the comment markers are /* and */.

```
/* whole page */
body  {background-color: white; color: black;
    margin: 10%}
/* menu */
.menu {background-color: green; color: white}
a    {color: white}
a:hover {font-size: 105%; color: yellow}
/* news */
p    {text-align: justify}
```

As with markup comments, many Web authors refrain from including comments within code. You might want to use comments when you're writing longer CSS code in which certain sections of the code affect certain sections of the page. In the above example, I have included comments labeling sections of my CSS code to show which parts affect the whole page, which sections affect the menu on the page, and which parts affect the news section of the page.

Also as with markup comments, CSS comments can span multiple lines.

```
/* This is a comment that spans multiple lines.
 This is how I would write the type of comment
 that does much more explaining of my code than
 labeling my code as in the previous example. The
 spacing at the beginning of the lines is not
 required, but is more visually appealing.
*/
```

A PLAN FOR WRITING CSS

In the next several chapters, I'll be explaining many of the options that are available to you in CSS. However, even once you have the mechanics down cold and know all the options that are available to you, you still need a plan for writing your CSS.

1. *Write your content first.*
   Many authors try to come up with a design first and then try to fit the content into the design. It is easier if you create your content first, and then worry about how that content should appear. If you've moving an existing site to CSS this has already been done.

2. *Write clean and concise markup.*
   Try to avoid any markup the goal of which can be accomplished with CSS. Also, keep your markup semantically clear. If it's a list, code it as a list. If you want big, bold text and the content is not a heading, code it as a paragraph. You can later use CSS to make the text big and bold. If you move a site to CSS, make a copy of several pages, strip out all of the attributes pertaining to style and clean out your semantically incorrect markup. (You should be left with black text on a white background and everything left-justified.) Then rebuild the pages CSS.

3. *Design before you code.*
   This is the most important one. Get some colored pencils and sketch out your design. When you go to create your CSS code, have that picture next to you and aim for that result. You may need to modify the design along the way. Without a goal in mind, you'll be wasting too much time just playing around.

4. *Embed, then link.*
   When you put your design together, work on a single document and embed your CSS. This allows you to focus on a single file and not have to worry about multiple files or directory structures on your site. Once you've finalized your design and code, move the CSS to a linked file and start applying it to your other documents.

NOTES

1. I recommend that you place all your CSS files either in server root (so that the relative path is always "/filename.css" or, as with images, if you have more than a few, place all CSS files in a "css" directory off of server root (so that the relative path is always "/css/filename.css").

2. Some authors will even take this one step further by including a line in the page that encourages users of older browsers to upgrade. In the imported CSS file they instruct that text to not appear on the screen through the use of `{display: none}`. If the browser is reading the imported CSS, then the user does not get the message, but users of Netscape Navigator 4 will get the message. Since some users do not have control over which browser they use, or have older equipment that may not handle a newer browser, this is not a practice I recommend.

3. Note that there must be a space both before and after the exclamation point.

4. Many of you may not be familiar with the "em" unit of measurement. I'll be covering this in the chapter on text formatting.

14

Colors, Measurements, and URLs

Colors, measurements, and URLs are all items that are specific to CSS values. In other words, in all three cases these values may be applied to different properties. For example, color may be applied to a background or text, and measurements may be applied to widths or margins. URLs are reserved for specifying images, but this can be done for both backgrounds and bullets in lists.

SPECIFYING COLOR IN CSS

In Chapter 4, I discussed the two different ways in which color can be represented in XHTML—by name and by hexadecimal notation. Both of these methods are available in CSS. If you want to set the color of your text as red you can use either of the following lines of code:

```
body {color: red}
body {color: #ff0000}
```

Officially, the CSS specification only supports 16 named colors—aqua, black, blue, fuchsia, gray, green, lime, maroon, navy, olive, purple, red, silver, teal, white, and yellow. Although other named colors will work in most browsers, if you are not specifying one of these sixteen colors you should use one of the other methods. CSS provides three additional methods for specifying color. These methods are unique to CSS.

ABBREVIATED HEXADECIMAL

The CSS specification allows for six-character hexadecimal notations to be abbreviated to three characters in a particular circumstance. As long as the color you're specifying has three matched pairs of values, you may abbreviate the notation. For example, the hexadecimal notation . . .

```
body {color: #ff0000}
```

. . . may be abbreviated . . .

```
body {color: #f00}
```

This abbreviation would not work on the following:

```
body {color: #7fffd4}
```

There is no abbreviation for this color (aquamarine) since the only matching pair is the middle pair, the value for green.

RGB RANGE

If you find either of the hexadecimal notation methods too confusing to use, CSS does offer a method for specification of color using RGB values. Here is our "red" example again using this method:

```
body {color: rgb(255,0,0)}
```

In this case, each of the three values (red, green, and blue) are given a value from zero (none) to 255 (all). This method may be easier but it is less efficient since it does require more characters to complete than the hexadecimal or abbreviated hexadecimal methods.

RGB PERCENTAGES

The final method for specifying color in CSS is similar to the RGB range method in which you specify RGB values without using hexadecimal values, but instead of a range you specify a percentage of that range. Continuing with the "red" example, we would write the RGB percentage as:

```
body {color: rgb(100%,0%,0%)}
```

Although this is supported by today's browsers, as are the other methods, I have never seen this used in a live Web page.

UNITS OF MEASUREMENT IN CSS

When you want to specify the size of something in CSS, whether it be the size of the font, the width of an item, or the size of a margin, you have nine different values to choose from. Three of these values are relative while the other six are absolute (dependent on no other factors). I will review each one, then examine further when certain values are appropriate and when certain ones are not.

RELATIVE UNITS

- *Percentage.*
  Use of a percentage value will set the size of the item a percentage above or below the current setting. The first example will reduce the font size of blockquotes by 20 percent, while the second example will increase them by 20 percent.

  ```
  blockquote {font-size: 80%}
  blockquote {font-size: 120%}
  ```

- *Pixels (px).*
  Despite the fact that pixels are generally considered an absolute value, when used to specify font sizes, they are relative to the resolution of the device used to display the document. For example, 100 pixels is 100 pixels regardless of the device being used, but on a PC screen with a resolution of 1024×768 pixels, the physical length of a 100-pixel line will be different than on a Treo600 screen with a resolution of 160×160 pixels. This example sets a 600-pixel width on anything identified as "wrapper."

  ```
  #wrapper {width: 600px}
  ```

- *Element font-height (em).*
  An em is based on the size of a lower-case letter "m" in the font being used. Because the size of letters vary from font to font, 1em is different in different fonts. 1em is equivalent to the default size of the font being used by the browser. The following example will set the font to be 25 percent larger than the default.

  ```
  p {font-size: 1.25em}
  ```

The important thing to remember about using ems is that sizing of the item will be relative to its parent. Take a look at this example:

```
<style type="text/css">
body         {font-size: .9em}
blockquote   {font-size: .8em}
</style>
</head>
<body>
<p>This text will be at .9em.</p>
<blockquote>This text will actually be displayed at .72em.</
blockuote>
</body>
```

The blockquote is a child of body. If body text is set at .9em, setting blockquote text to be .8em will make the text size 80 percent of its parent. Eighty percent of .9em is .72em. If you're not careful, an inheritance problem can occur and you can end up with miniscule text.

- *Element x-height (ex).*
  According to the W3C The 'ex' unit is defined by the font's 'x-height.' The x-height is so called because it is often equal to the height of the lowercase "x." However, an "ex" is defined even for fonts that don't contain an "x." I have never seen this unit of measurement used in a live Web page.

ABSOLUTE UNITS

- *Points (pt).*
  Most people are familiar with points from using word-processing software. You probably already knew that 12pt is larger than 10pt. But what is a point? Points used by CSS are equal to 1/72 of an inch.

  ```
  body {font-size: 12pt}
  ```

- *Picas (pc).*
  Picas are probably the least-used unit of measurement in CSS. One pica is equal to 12 points, 12pt is the equivalent of 1pc and 24pt is the equivalent of 24pt.

  ```
  body {font-size: .9pc}
  ```

- *Inches (in), centimeters (cm), and millimeters (mm).*
  These are standard units of English and metric measurement and should not require explanation.

  ```
  #container   {width: 7in}
  body         {margin: 5mm 3cm}
  ```

WHICH MEASUREMENT IS BEST?

The issue of which unit of measurement is best is hotly contested in CSS discussion groups today. However, current convention says the following:

- If you're working on-screen and accessibility is your primary goal, use ems. They are flexible and allow the user to change the browser's default font size while still scaling the text accordingly.
- If you're working on-screen and control is your primary goal, use pixels. The pixel measurement allows you to specify a particular size. However, it will not scale for the user.
- If you're working in a print environment, use points since they were specifically designed for print. Using points in a screen environment, although tempting, will create too many variations in your display. For example, when using points, a Mac will display the identical text up to 25 percent smaller than will a Windows system.

SPECIFYING URLS IN CSS

The main reason you'll need to use a URL within CSS is to specify the location of an image that you want to designate as the background for a document (or a particular item) or to use an image as a bullet in a list. Here's what that code will look like using an absolute URL:

```
body {background: url(http://www.foo.bar/images/clouds.gif)}
```

As you can see, the format `url()` is similar to the use of `rgb()` when specifying color using the rgb method.

Alternatively you can also use a relative URL:

```
body {background: url(images/clouds.gif)}
```

There is an important item about the processing of relative URLs that you must be aware of before using them. Relative URLs are pathed based upon the location of the CSS code, not the XHTML code. For example, if you embed your CSS in your XHTML document, and that document is in server root, then the path to the .gif file in the previous example is `/images/clouds.gif`.

However, if you link to a CSS file and that CSS file is in a 'css' directory off of server root (`/css/style.css`) then the path to your .gif file is `/css/images/clouds.gif`.

Unfortunately, Netscape Navigator 4.x has a bug in it that causes relative pathing to be based on the XHTML file regardless of the location of the CSS. If a significant number of your users are still using this browser you may want to consider avoiding relative URLs altogether.

Lastly, if your URL contains any parentheses, commas, spaces, single quotes, or double quotes, you must "escape" them by preceding those characters with a `"\"`.

```
body {background: url(\"cloud\ background.gif\")}
```

15

Formatting Text with CSS

Once you have a grasp of the mechanics of CSS—how to write and place your CSS code in relation to your markup—it then becomes a question of deciding just how you want your document to appear. In this chapter, we'll cover the properties and values that are available for text formatting. These include alignment, color, size, and spacing. (Throughout the rest of this book we'll be discussing special topics in CSS, all of which require a basic understanding of the text formatting properties.)

NOTE: All the code samples in this chapter do not represent complete minimal XHTML documents. I've left out certain lines such as the DOCTYPE and titles to save space. All the files on the CD, are complete documents.

FONT-FAMILY

The font-family property specifies the actual font to be used. As with specifying a font using the `<font>` element, if you specify a font that the user's computer does not have installed, the next font in a comma-delimited list should be used. Failing all choices in the list, the default font should be used.

One powerful feature that the font-family property has over the `<font>` element is the ability to specify one of five generic font families. These families are:

Value	Definition
sans-serif	Fonts without serifs. The default is usually Arial.
cursive	Fonts that look as if they were hand written. The default is usually Comic Sans MS.
fantasy	Fonts that are more creative or non-traditional. The default is usually **Impact**.
monospace	Fonts in which each letter takes up the same amount of space. The default is usually Courier or Courier New.

This feature allows you to specify a few specific fonts within a family but allow for a graceful default so that you can assume your users, if nothing else, will at least see the right kind of font.

In the following code sample I've directed the `.tahoma` class to look for Tahoma first. Failing that, it will look for Albany. Failing both of those, it will use the browser's default san-serif font. The other classes will follow their declarations appropriately (Figure 15.1).

```
<head>
<style type="text/css">
.tahoma {font-family: tahoma, albany, sans-serif}
.albany {font-family: albany, sans-serif}
.sans   {font-family: sans-serif}
</style>
</head>
<body>
<p class="tahoma">This text will be in the Tahoma font.</p>
<p class="albany">This text will be in the Albany font.</p>
<p class="sans">This text will be in the Arial font since that
is the default sans-serif font in my browser.</p>
</body>
```

Figure 15.1. The `font-family` Property

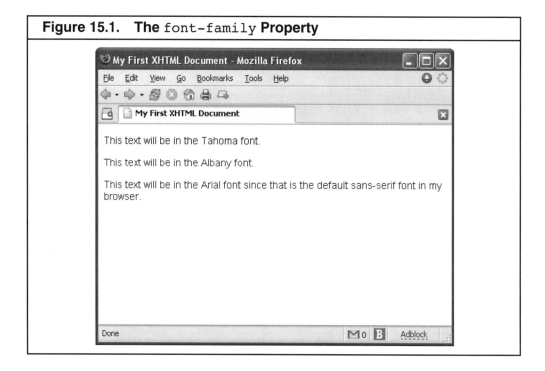

FONT-STYLE

The font-style property allows you to change the appearance, or style of the font. The three available values are:

Value	Definition
oblique	Slant the enclosed text. Browsers that support this value typically slant the normal version of the font.
italic	Switch to the italic version of the font. All graphical browsers support this.
normal	Set the enclosed text to a normal font. Used to undo either of the other two choices.

The following code example shows the use of all three properties (Figure 15.2).

```
<head>
<style type="text/css">
.italic  {font-style: italic}
.oblique {font-style: oblique}
.normal  {font-style: normal}
</style>
</head>
<body>
<p class="italic">This text will be italicized.</p>
<p class="oblique">This text will be oblique.</p>
<p class="italic">This text will be italicized except for a few
<span class="normal">non-italic words</span> in the middle of
the sentence.</p>
</body>
```

Figure 15.2. The font-style **Property**

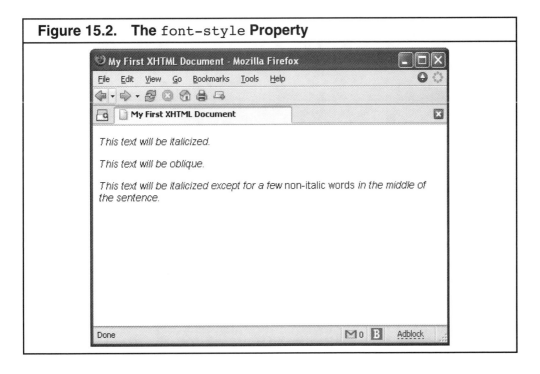

FONT-WEIGHT

The font-weight property is the CSS equivalent of the <b> element. As with most other CSS properties it is more flexible than its XHTML counterpart. The values are:

Value	Definition
normal	Resets the font back to its default weight.
bold	Creates "thick" characters.
bolder	Sets the enclosed text as being one step "thicker" than the current setting.
lighter	Sets the enclosed text as being one step "thinner" than the current setting.
100, 200, 300, 400, 500, 600, 700	Sets the definitions of thin to thick characters. 400=normal. 700=bold.

The following code sample shows the results of all of the possible font-weight values (Figure 15.3).

```
<head>
<style type="text/css">
.bold    {font-weight: bold}
.bolder  {font-weight: bolder}
.lighter {font-weight: lighter}
.normal  {font-weight: normal}
.one     {font-weight: 100}
.two     {font-weight: 200}
.three   {font-weight: 300}
.four    {font-weight: 400}
.five    {font-weight: 500}
.six     {font-weight: 600}
.seven   {font-weight: 700}
</style>
<body>
<p>This text contains words with many different weights. <span
class="bold">This sentence is bolded with one <span
class="bolder">bolder</span>, one <span class="lighter">lighter</
span>, and one <span class="normal">normal</span> word</span>.
The numeric values for font-weight are <span class="one">100</
span>, <span class="two">200</span>, <span class="three">300</
span>, <span class="four">400</span>, <span class="five">500</
span>,<span class="six">600</span>, and <span class="seven">700</
span>.
</body>
```

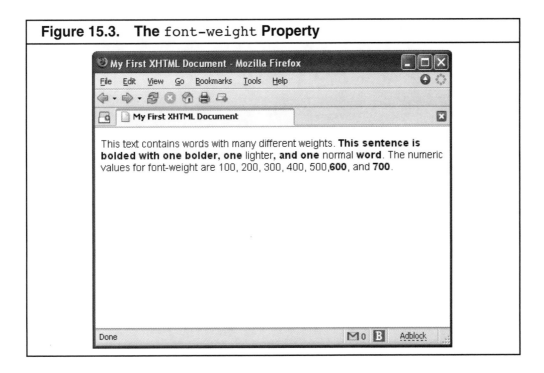

Figure 15.3. The `font-weight` **Property**

FONT-VARIANT

There are currently only two possible values for the `font-variant` property: small-caps and normal. small-caps creates capital letters the height of lowercase letters and normal undoes this command (Figure 15.4).

```
<head>
<style type="text/css">
.smallCaps        {font-variant: small-caps}
</style>
</head>
<body>
<p>This paragraph contains some <span class="smallCaps">text
in small-caps</span>.</p>
</body>
```

Figure 15.4.   The `font-variant` **Property**

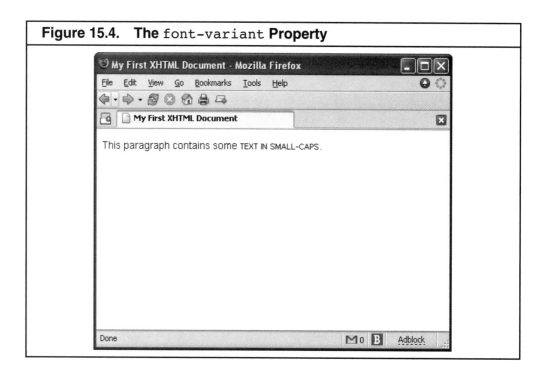

FONT-SIZE

Unlike `<font size="`*n*`">` the font-size property finally gives Web designers complete mastery of the size of the text. Any of the CSS units of measurement may be used, including points. However, when dealing with font-size there are a few things to consider.

- Units such as mm, cm, in, px, and pt are designed for a print universe in which paper size varies very little, if any at all. Using any of these units in a screen-based environment will render inconsistent results based upon the resolution and dpi of the user's monitor.
- If you choose to use one of these units, some browsers will lock the user into that size and will not allow them to adjust the font to a larger or small size as needed. This creates a significant accessibility problem.

Using a relative unit of measurement (em, ex, percentage) allows the user to adjust their font sizes to fit their needs (Figure 15.5).

NOTE: I have included examples of using absolute sizes below but I do not recommend doing this in a non-print environment.

```
<head>
<style type="text/css">
h1          {font-size: 200%}
p           {font-size: 1em}
blockquote  {font-size: .8em}
.big        {font-size: 16pt}
</style>
```

```
</head>
<body>
<h1>Examples of the font-size property</h1>
<p>This paragraph has been set to a 1em size, the default, to
give you something to compare the rest of the text to. Remember
it is <span class="big">not</span> recommended that you use
absolute units of measurement for non-print environments. Re-
member this advice from Accessible Information:</p>
<blockquote
cite="http://www.rnib.org.uk/xpedio/groups/public/documents/
publicwebsite/public_fontsizes.hcsp"><p>Using relative values
in your coding gives control to the people using your site. It
allows them to view the same version that everyone else sees,
but they can choose to have bigger fonts for example. Most
importantly this option gives the necessary flexibility, but
preserves your styling and branding.</p></blockquote>
</body>
```

Figure 15.5.   The `font-size` **Property**

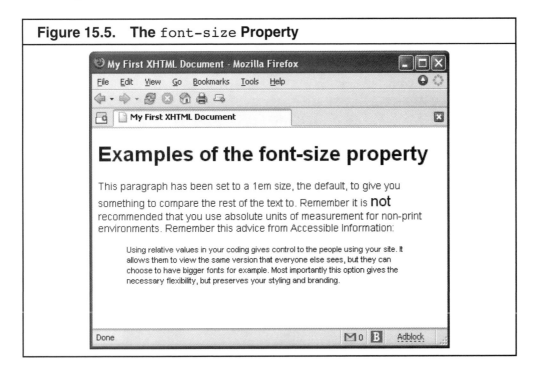

CSS also includes named sizes. These are the CSS equivalent to the seven numeric values for the size attribute on the <font> element. Those seven values are: xx-small, x-small, small, medium, large, x-large, xx-large. medium is considered to be whatever the current default size is.

Additionally you can use the values of larger or smaller, to increase or decrease the size of text one step higher or lower than the current setting.

```
<head>
<style type="text/css">
body {font-size: 1em}
</style>
```

```
</head>
<body>
<p>This paragraph contains text of the following sizes: <span
style="font-size: xx-small">xx-small </span>, <span style="font-
size: x-small">x-small</span>, <span style="font-size:
small">small</span>, <span style="font-size: medium">medium</
span>, <span style="font-size: large">large</span>, <span
style="font-size: x-large">x-large</span>, and <span style="font-
size: xx-large">xx-large</span>. I've also set some text to be
<span style="font-size: smaller">smaller</span> and <span
style="font-size: larger">larger</span>.</p>
</body>
```

SHORTHAND FOR FONT PROPERTIES

All of the font properties can be shortened to just font instead of specifying each specific type of font property. For example, if you want to set your text to 12pt and bold, you can write your CSS code either of the following ways:

```
.style1    {font-size: 12pt; font-weight: bold}
.style2    {font: 12pt bold}
```

The method used in .style2 is, of course, more efficient.

TEXT-ALIGN

The text-align property is the CSS equivalent of the align="" attribute; aligning the text as the value specifies. The possible values of this property are left (default), right, center, and justify (full justification) (Figure 15.6).

```
<head>
<style type="text/css">
.left      {text-align: left}
.center    {text-align: center}
.right     {text-align: right}
.justify   {text-align: justify}
</style>
</head>
<body>
<p class="left">This paragraph is left justified.</p>
<p class="center">This paragraph is centered.</p>
<p class="right">This paragraph is right justified.</p>
<p class="justify"> This paragraph has full justification. This
paragraph has full justification. This paragraph has full jus-
tification. This paragraph has full justification. This para-
graph has full justification. This paragraph has full
justification.</p>
</body>
```

Figure 15.6. The `text-align` Property

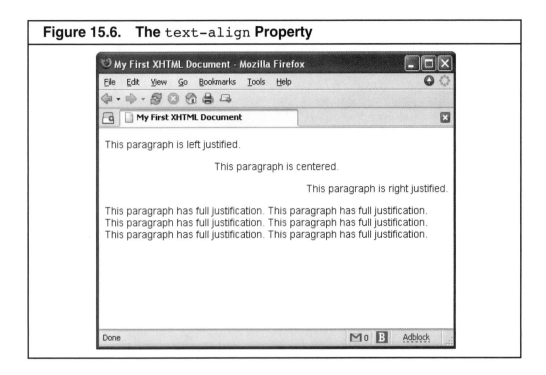

TEXT-DECORATION

There are four possible values for the text-decoration property: `underline` (equivalent of `<u>`), `overline`, `line-through` (equivalent of `<strike>`), and `blink` (Figure 15.7).

NOTE: There was at one time a `<blink>` element in HTML, but due to near universal distaste for this element, it has now disappeared. One wonders why it was ever included in the CSS specification. Luckily, no browser supports it today.

```
<head>
<style type="text/css">
.under  {text-decoration: underline}
.over   {text-decoration: overline}
.strike {text-decoration: line-through}
</style>
</head>
<body>
<p>This paragraph contains text that has been <span
class="under">underlined</span>, <span class="over">overlined</
span>, and <span class="strike">struck out</span>.</p>
</body>
```

Figure 15.7.   The `text-decoration` **Property**

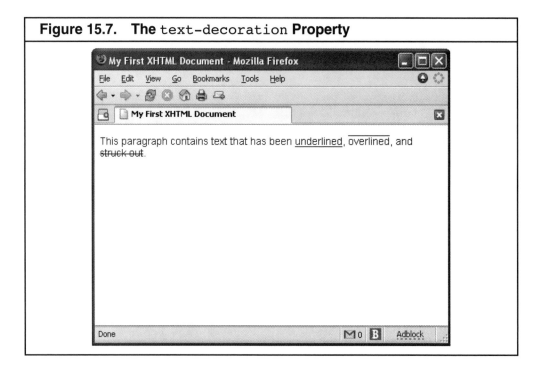

TEXT-INDENT

The `text-indent` property allows authors to indent text, something that Web developers have always wished that HTML/XHTML could do. The important thing to remember is that indentations only affect the first line of an element (a paragraph, for example). If you wish to move every line of a paragraph you need to change the paragraph margins. (Consult Chapter 16 on the "box model" for information on how to do this.) Any of the CSS units of measurement may be used in either a positive or negative amount (Figure 15.8).

```
<head>
<style type="text/css">
p {text-indent: 2em}
</style>
</head>
<body>
<p>Since I have applied the text-indent property to the para-
graph element, the first lines of all paragraphs will be in-
dented 2ems. Suppose you want one paragraph in this document to
not be indented.</p>
<p>This is the issue we need to deal with next.</p>
</body>
```

Figure 15.8. The `text-indent` Property

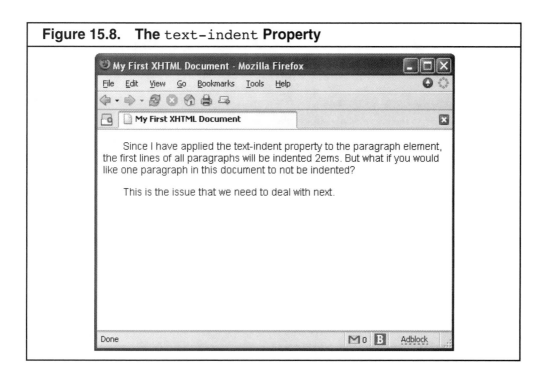

In the previous code example I instructed all paragraphs to be indented 2ems. Suppose, as the example suggests, that I want one of the paragraphs in my document to have no indent. Since we need to have an exception to our rule, the first step is to create a class. Let's assume that we don't want the first paragraph in our document to be indented. We'll create a class named "first" and put in the text-indent property. Let's add the class to the first paragraph.

```
<head>
<style type="text/css">
p       {text-indent: 2em}
.first  {text-indent: }
</style>
</head>
<body>
<p>Since I have applied the text-indent property to the para-
graph element, the first line of all paragraphs will be indented
2ems. Suppose you want one paragraph in this document to not be
indented.</p>
<p>This is the issue we need to deal with next.</p>
</body>
```

The question now becomes "what is the value that needs to be used?" Since we've indented all paragraphs 2ems, let's try subtracting that amount from this class. (Figure 15.9)

```
.first {text-indent: -2em}
```

Figure 15.9.   The `text-indent` Property with a Negative Value

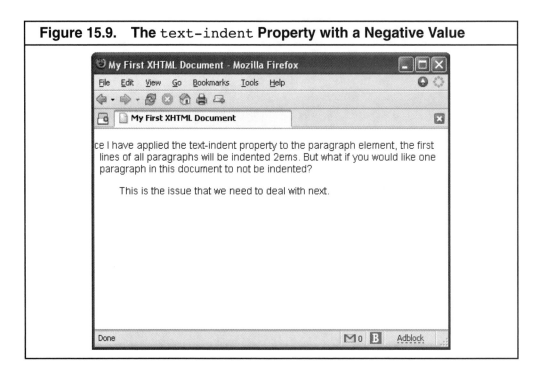

As you can see, this is not the solution we're looking for. In the case of indentations, they are not cumulative. They always start from the point of no indent, or a value of zero. To accomplish our goal, we need to set the value of `text-indent` to zero (Figure 15.10).

```
.first {text-indent: 0}
```

Figure 15.10.   The `text-align` Property with a Zero Value

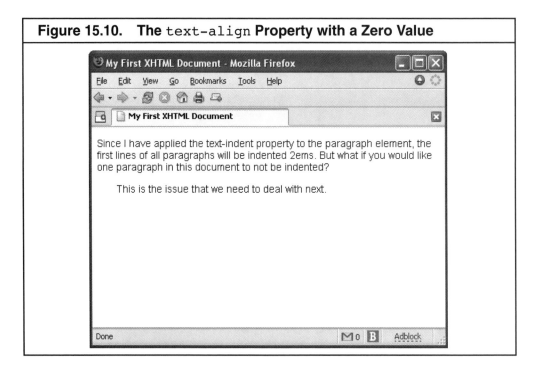

NOTE: When you specify a unit of zero, there is no need to specify which unit of measurement you're using, since zero is the same measurement in all units.

LINE-HEIGHT

The line-height property changes the height of lines within the document. Any of the CSS units of measurement may be used as the value for this property. The following code will give the appearance of a double-spaced document (Figure 15.11).

```
<head>
<style type="text/css">
.double    {line-height: 200%}
</style>
</head>
<body>
<p> This is a single-spaced paragraph. This is a single-spaced
paragraph. This is a single-spaced paragraph. This is a single-
spaced paragraph. This is a single-spaced paragraph. This is a
single-spaced paragraph.</p>
<p class="double"> This is a double-spaced paragraph. This is a
double-spaced paragraph. This is a double-spaced paragraph. This
is a double-spaced paragraph. This is a double-spaced paragraph.
This is a double-spaced paragraph. This is a double-spaced para-
graph. This is a double-spaced paragraph. This is a double-
spaced paragraph. This is a double-spaced paragraph.</p>
<p> This is a single-spaced paragraph. This is a single-spaced
paragraph. This is a single-spaced paragraph. This is a single-
spaced paragraph. This is a single-spaced paragraph. This is a
single-spaced paragraph.</p>
</body>
```

Figure 15.11.   The line-height **Property**

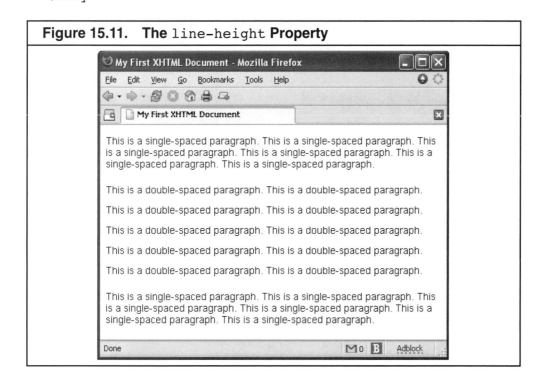

letter-spacing **AND** word-spacing

The letter-spacing property specifies the distance between letters within a word and the word-spacing property specifies the spacing between words. The BCR Web site (www.bcr.org) pages have a green headline at the top of most pages in which the letters are double-spaced the letters and the words are quadruple-spaced. When they created this design, these properties were not well supported they wrote them using HTML only (Figure 15.12).

```
<p><b>R e f e r e n c e    D a t a b a s e
s</b></p>
```

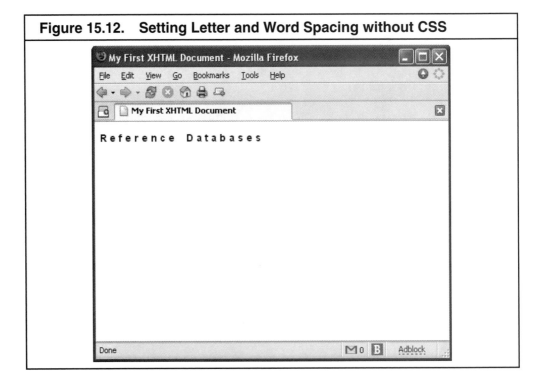

Figure 15.12.   Setting Letter and Word Spacing without CSS

The problems with manually spacing out your letters and words are numerous. Firstly, all of those non-breaking-space character entities are distracting and add a considerable amount of unnecessary code. Secondly, and more importantly, by adding all of those spaces, the words are no longer technically words and will not be indexed properly by any search engine. In the case of text-to-speech browsers, each letter would be spoken individually.

If I were to re-create this using today's CSS, here's what I'd do instead (Figure 15.13).

```
<head>
<style type="text/css">
h1 {letter-spacing: 1em; word-spacing: 2em;
    font-weight: bold; font-size: 90%}
</style>
</head>
```

```
<body>
<h1 id="headline">Reference Databases</h1>
</body>
```

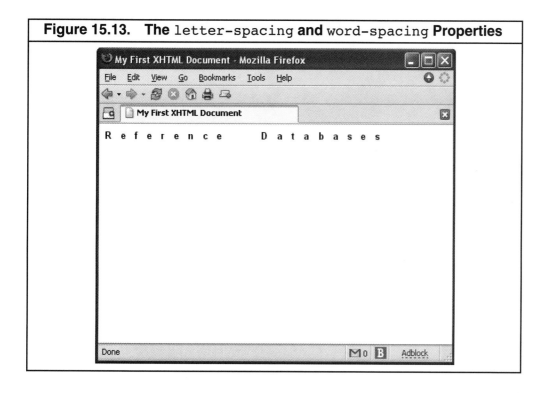

Figure 15.13. The `letter-spacing` **and** `word-spacing` **Properties**

NOTE: I changed from a paragraph to a heading to make the content of the element more semantically correct. A headline should be coded as a heading.

TEXT-TRANSFORM

The `text-transform` property allows you to control the case of text regardless of how it is typed. The possible values are uppercase (display in all uppercase characters,) lowercase (display in all lowercase characters,) and capitalize (capitalize the first letter of every word).

This does not seem especially useful unless you consider potential uses in text-to-speech. For example, you may wish to have a word displayed in all capital letters but a text-to-speech program may treat words that are all uppercase as acronyms and read their letters instead. By typing the word in lowercase in your code but using the `text-transform` to display the word in all uppercase, you get the correct display and allow text-to-speech programs to still read the word as a word, not as a series of letters (Figure 15.14).

```
<head>
<style type="text/css">
.upper   {text-transform: uppercase}
.lower   {text-transform: lowercase}
```

```
.caps {text-transform: capitalize}
</style>
</head>
<body>
<p class="upper">this paragraph has been converted to uppercase.
</p>
<p class="lower">This paragraph has been converted to LOWERCASE.
</p><p class="caps">This paragraph has been capitalized.</p>
</body>
```

Figure 15.14.   The `text-transform` Property

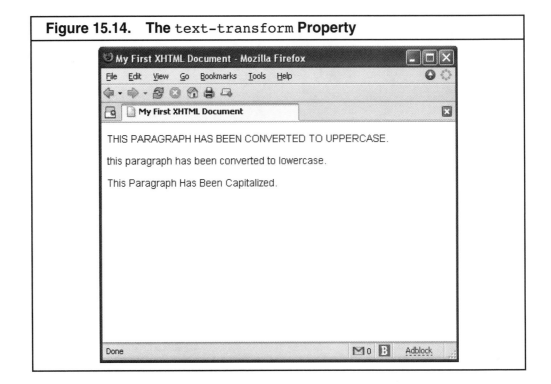

16

The Box Model

In CSS, the box model is what controls the size of items along with both the margins and padding of those items. In addition to that, once you have an understanding of the box model, you can start to move those boxes around the screen, placing them where you want them to be displayed to the user.

WHAT IS THE BOX MODEL?

Every item within a document has an invisible box around it—each letter, each word, and each block-level element. Recall the discussion of the `<div>` element. I described the purpose of the `<div>` element as placing a box around a group of items in order to have an effect on that group as a single unit.

The box model describes how to manipulate that box in regard to its content, its padding, its border, and its margins.

WHAT DOES THE BOX MODEL LOOK LIKE?

The W3C created the following graphic in order to visually illustrate the box model and its components. Let's take a look at it and then I'll describe each of its parts (Figure 16.1).

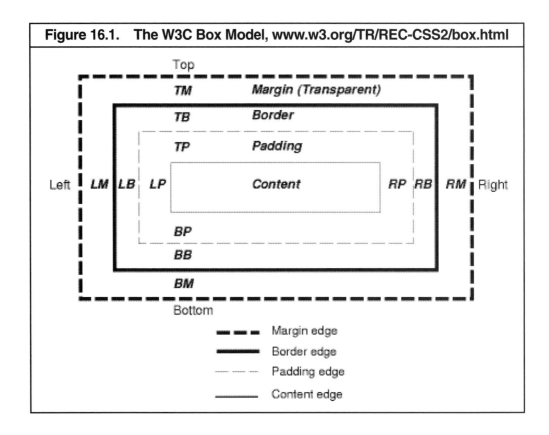

Figure 16.1.   The W3C Box Model, www.w3.org/TR/REC-CSS2/box.html

THE LAYERS

The content contains all of the "rendered items" within a box—the content of the box. If a paragraph has only text, the content of the paragraph is the text. If the paragraph contains text and an image, the content is the text and the image. However, if the paragraph contains some text and an image that was, via CSS, not displayed, then only the text would be considered content.

The padding of an item is the space between the content and the border of the box. By default, borders are not displayed and the difference between a box's padding and its margin seems indistinguishable. Once a border is displayed, this difference becomes clearer. We'll do this later in the chapter.

Envision the border of a box as the box itself, which contains both padding and content. Each item has one of these boxes, but, by default, the box is not displayed.

The margin of the box sits outside of the box's border and establishes the space between this box and adjacent boxes.

Each of the layers may be manipulated as a single item or broken down into each of their four sides. For example, you may set a single value for the margin of a box, thereby applying that value to all four sides of the box, or you may treat each of the four margins (`margin-top`, `margin-right`, `margin-bottom`, and `margin-left`) individually.

EDGES

- *Content edge.*
  Surrounds the rendered content of the box. This item has no width.
- *Padding edge.*
  Surrounds the padding of the box. If there is a zero padding on the box then the padding edge is the same as the content edge
- *Border edge.*
  Surrounds the border of the box. If there is no border on the box (width of zero), then the border edge is the same as the padding edge.
- *Margin edge.*
  Surrounds the margin of the box. If the margin is set to zero, then the margin edge is the same as the padding edge.

The fact that each of these edges, if they have a width of zero, automatically matches up with the previous edge is known as collapsing. In other words, the total width of an item is the sum of the width of the content and all the edges. If a particular edge has no width, it will collapse back onto the width of the previous edge, working inward.

PUTTING THE BOX MODEL TO WORK

Let's put together an example of how we can apply the box model to our document. To keep things simple, we'll use the following document, which contains only one paragraph. We'll manipulate the padding, border, and margin of the paragraph (Figure 16.2).

```
<!DOCTYPE html PUBLIC "-//W3C//DTD XHTML 1.0 Transitional//EN"
"http://www.w3.org/TR/xhtml1/DTD/xhtml1-transitional.dtd">
<html xmlns="http://www.w3.org/1999/xhtml" lang="en"
xml:lang="en">
<head>
<title>An Introduction to RSS</title>
<meta http-equiv="Content-Type" content="text/html; charset=utf-
8" />
<style type="text/css">
</style>
</head>
<body>
<p class="boxModel">RSS is an XML-based (eXtensible Markup Lan-
guage) language used to describe the content of an article.
Another way to describe an RSS file is that it is just raw meta
data (data about data) about a particular document. If you have
created a Web page, you should be familiar with the &lt;meta&gt;
tag. This meta data usually includes information such as a
brief description of the document and keywords that should be
used to index the document. RSS takes that to the next level.</p>
</body>
</html>
```

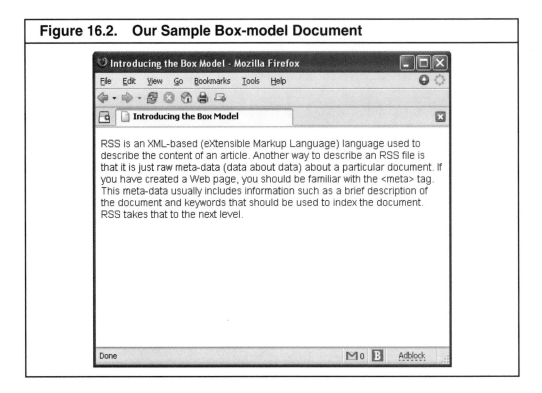

Figure 16.2.   Our Sample Box-model Document

BORDERS

Until you have the border of an item turned on and visible, the concepts of padding and margin are unclear. Turning on the border for this paragraph will make it easier for me to cover the other topics. There are three properties are available for the border: `width`, `color`, and `style`. Without specifying all three properties, the border will not appear. I will review each property individually and show code examples, but there won't be any . screenshot until the end, since there won't be anything to look at until then.

border_width

The border-width property specifies the thickness of the border. This property can have any of the following values:

- `thin`
  To be established by the browser
- `medium`
  Thicker than the `thin` value; also to be established by the browser.
- `thick`
  Thicker than the `medium` value; also to be established by the browser.
- `length`
  An author-specified value using any of the available CSS units of measurements.

Use of the property border-width will set the value for all four sides of the box. You can also use any or all of the following properties to specify values for individual sides: `border-top-width`, `border-right-width`, `border-bottom-width`, `border-left-width`

To set a 2px-thick border around a box we could use either of the following lines of code:

```
.boxModel {border-width: 2px}
.boxModel {border-top-width: 2px; border-right-width: 2px;
          border-bottom-width: 2px;
          border-left-width: 2px}
```

The first is clearly the more efficient option. However, if we wanted to give the feeling of a drop-shadow by establishing a 2px border along only the right and bottom edges of the box, we would need to specify the appropriate sides accordingly.

```
.boxModel {border-right-width: 2px;
          border-bottom-width: 2px;}
```

border_color

The `border-color` property specifies the color of the displayed border. All the CSS color specification methods are available to this property. As with the `border-width` property, use of `border-color` will specify all four sides of the border and side-specific properties are available.

```
.boxModel {border-color: #f00}
.boxModel {border-top-color: red; border-right-color: blue; border-bottom-color: green; border-left-color: yellow}
```

border-style

The `border-color` property specifies the type of border you want to display. There are ten available values:

Table 16.1: Values for Border-style. www.w3.org/TR/REC-CSS2/box.html

none	No border. This value forces the computed value of "border-width" to be "0."
hidden	Same as "none," except in terms of border conflict resolution for table elements.
dotted	The border is a series of dots.
dashed	The border is a series of short line segments.
solid	The border is a single line segment.
double	The border is two solid lines. The sum of the two lines and the space between them equals the value of "border-width."
groove	The border looks as though it were carved into the page.
ridge	The opposite of "groove": the border looks as though it were coming out of the canvas.
inset	The border makes the entire box look as though it were embedded in the canvas.
outset	The opposite of "inset": the border makes the entire box look as though it were emerging from the page.

As with the previous border properties, use of `border-style` specifies the same style for all four sides. The properties for each individual side are also available.

```
.boxModel {border-style: dashed}
.boxModel {border-top-style: solid; border-right-style:
        dotted; border-bottom-groove: green;
        border-left-style: inset}
```

Combining these three properties

Now that we've covered all three properties let's take a look at two examples (Figures 16.3 and 16.4).

```
<style type="text/css">
.boxModel {border-width: 2px; border-color: #f00;
        border-style: dashed}
</style>
```

Figure 16.3.   Our Document with a 2px, Red, Dashed Border

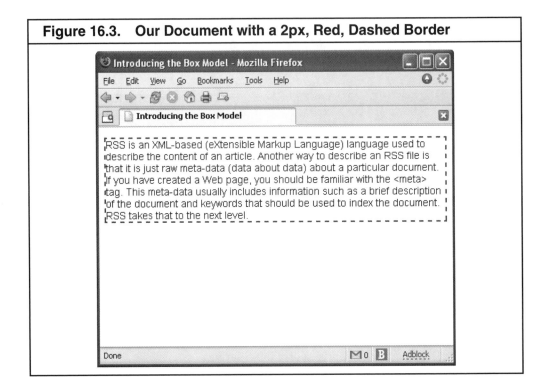

```
<style type="text/css">
.boxModel {border-width: 10px; border-color: green; border-style:
outset}
</style>
```

Figure 16.4.   Our Document with a 10px, Green, Outset Border

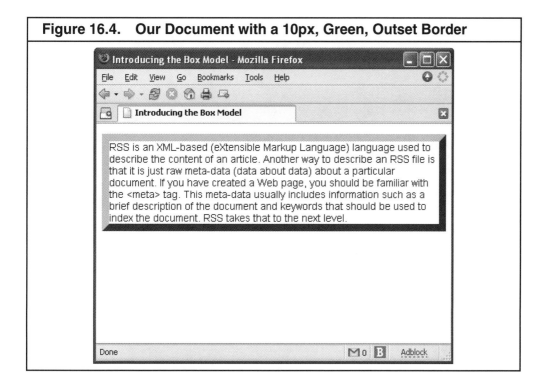

BORDER SHORTHAND

You can abbreviate your border properties as long as you want to specify the same values for all four sides of the border. However, suppose for some reason we want different styles, sizes, and colors for all four sides. Take a look at the following code.

```
.boxModel {border-top-width: 2px; border-top-color: red;
          border-top-style: solid;
          border-right-width: .5in; border-right-color:
          green; border-right-style: dashed;
          border-bottom-width: thick; border-bottom-color:
          black; border-bottom-style: groove;
          border-left-width: 1cm; border-left-color: blue;
          border-left-style: dotted}
```

Now look at the following, more compact option:

```
.boxModel {border-top: 2px red solid;
          border-right: .5in green dashed;
          border-bottom: thick black groove;
          border-left: 1cm blue dotted}
```

I've compressed each of the three properties down into the border-*side* properties. Browsers today are intelligent enough to know that, in this example, 2px implies border-width, red implies border-color, and solid implies border-style. With this in mind we can replace . . .

```
.boxModel {border-width: 2px; border-color: #f00; border-style:
dashed}
```

. . . with . . .

```
.boxModel {border: 2px #f00 dashed}
```

NOTE: When abbreviating your border code, the three values may be provided in any order. Therefore, the following three examples will yield the same result.

```
.boxModel {border: 2px #f00 dashed}
.boxModel {border: #f00 dashed 2px}
.boxModel {border: dashed 2px #f00}
```

PADDING

Before we continue let's check our code to see where we are (Figure 16.5).

```
<!DOCTYPE html PUBLIC "-//W3C//DTD XHTML 1.0 Transitional//EN"
"http://www.w3.org/TR/xhtml1/DTD/xhtml1-transitional.dtd">
<html  xmlns="http://www.w3.org/1999/xhtml"  lang="en"
xml:lang="en">
<head>
<title>An Introduction to RSS</title>
<meta http-equiv="Content-Type" content="text/html; charset=utf-
8" />
<style type="text/css">
.boxModel {border: 2px #f00 dashed}
</style>
</head>
<body>
<p class="boxModel"> RSS is an XML-based (eXtensible Markup
Language) language used to describe the content of an article.
Another way to describe an RSS file is that it is just raw
metadata (data about data) about a particular document. If you
have created a Web page, you should be familiar with the
&lt;meta&gt; tag. This metadata usually includes information
such as a brief description of the document and keywords that
should be used to index the document. RSS takes that to the
next level.</p>
</body>
</html>
```

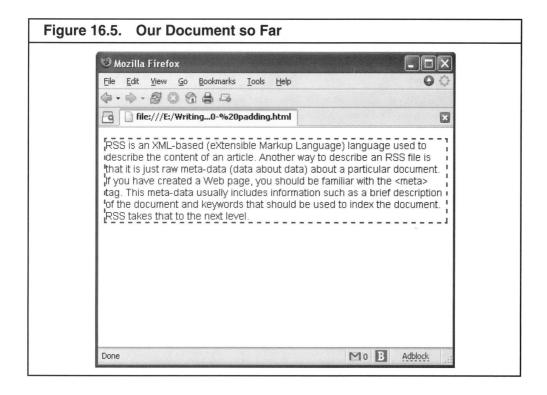

Figure 16.5. Our Document so Far

As described earlier, a box's padding is the space between the content (our words in this case) and the inside of the border edge. At the moment, this is set to the default of no padding; {padding: 0}. This is why, especially along the inside-left edge of our box, the text is bumping up against our border.

NOTE: Although this does not seem to be occurring along the other three inside edges of our box, it is. It doesn't appear to be happening on the left because of word wrapping and some built-in spacing.

The value for padding may be any of the standard CSS units of measurement or a percentage of the parent element (in this case, the body of the document).

```
.boxModel {border: 2px #f00 dashed; padding: 10px}
```

By specifying the property of padding we have mandated that all four sides of the box should have the same padding, 10px (Figure 16.6).

Figure 16.6. The `padding` **Property**

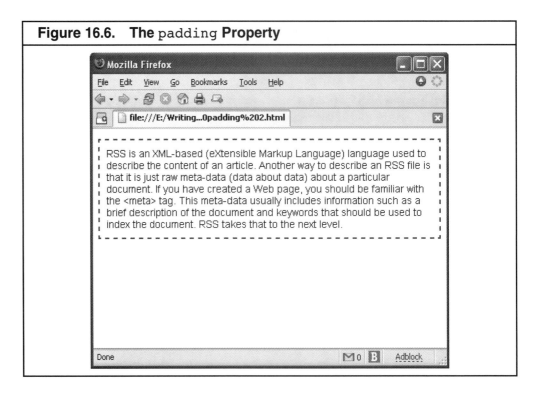

We can also specify values for padding for each individual side (Figure 16.7).

```
.boxModel {border: 2px #f00 dashed; padding-top: 10px;
          padding-right: 15px; padding-bottom: 20px;
          padding-left: 25px}
```

Figure 16.7. Setting Different `padding` **Values on each side of the Box**

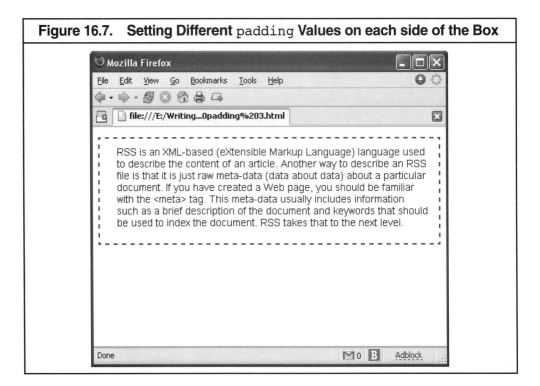

NOTE: There is a method for abbreviating padding values. Since the method for doing this is the same as for abbreviating the values for margin, I'll cover that at the end of the chapter.

MARGINS

Margins work similarly to padding in that they set the width of part of a box. The difference is that in the case of margins, the affected area is outside of the border instead of inside. The margin of a particular item varies depending on the type of element. Inline elements by default have no margins while block-level elements typically have built-in top margins of one line (as with paragraphs and headings), but some have none (as with `<div>`s).

If we were to add a margin property with the value of 1in, we would create one-inch margins on all four sides of our paragraph. (I've added two more paragraphs to better show the application of the margin to the top and bottom edges of our paragraph) (Figure 16.8).

```
<!DOCTYPE html PUBLIC "-//W3C//DTD XHTML 1.0 Transitional//EN"
"http://www.w3.org/TR/xhtml1/DTD/xhtml1-transitional.dtd">
<html  xmlns="http://www.w3.org/1999/xhtml"  lang="en"
xml:lang="en">
<head>
<title>An Introduction to RSS</title>
<meta http-equiv="Content-Type" content="text/html; charset=uft-
8" />
<style type="text/css">
.boxModel {border: 2px #f00 dashed; padding: 10px;
          margin: 1in}
</style>
</head>
<body>
<p>New paragraph.</p>
<p class="boxModel"> RSS is an XML-based (eXtensible Markup
Language) language used to describe the content of an article.
Another way to describe an RSS file is that it is just raw
metadata (data about data) about a particular document. If you
have created a Web page, you should be familiar with the
&lt;meta&gt; tag. This metadata usually includes information
such as a brief description of the document and keywords that
should be used to index the document. RSS takes that to the
next level.</p>
<p>New paragraph.</p>
</body>
</html>
```

Figure 16.8.   The `margin` **Property**

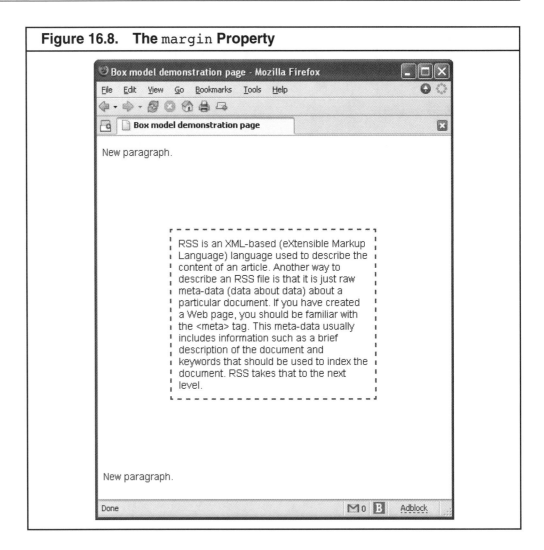

As with all the other properties in the box model, margins can be specified individually. The following code sets 2 percent top and bottom margins and 10 percent left and right margins on the body of the document (Figure 16.9).

```
body {margin-top: 2%; margin-right: 10%; margin-bottom: 2%;
      margin-left: 10%}
```

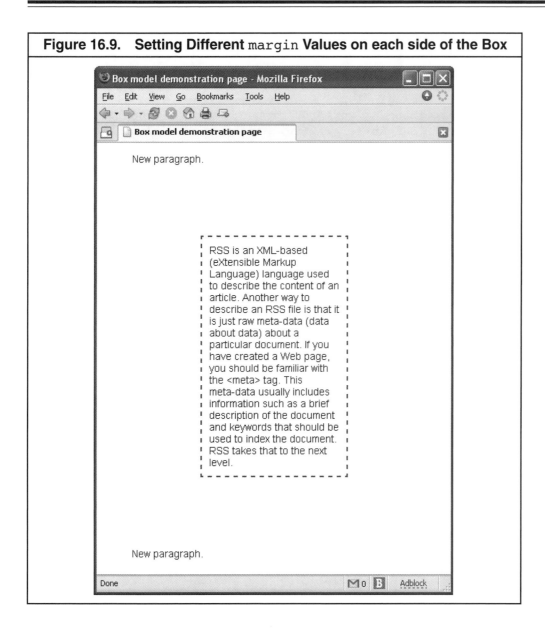

Figure 16.9. Setting Different `margin` Values on each side of the Box

The method for further abbreviating the coding of margin properties will be discussed at the end of the chapter.

An important note about margins

Margins, especially when based on percentages, are based on the available space. Another way to look at it is that any margins set on a parent will be inherited by the child. Let's look at the following example in which we set margins on both the body (the parent) and the paragraph (the child) (Figure 16.10).

```
<!DOCTYPE html PUBLIC "-//W3C//DTD XHTML 1.0 Transitional//EN"
"http://www.w3.org/TR/xhtml1/DTD/xhtml1-transitional.dtd">
<html xmlns="http://www.w3.org/1999/xhtml" lang="en" xml:lang="en">
```

```
<head>
<title></title>
<meta http-equiv="Content-Type" content="text/html; charset=utf-8" />
<style type="text/css">
body      {margin-left: 1in; margin-right: 1in}
.boxModel {border: 2px #f00 dashed; padding: 10px;
          margin-left: .5in; margin-right: .5in}
</style>
</head>
<body>
<p>New paragraph.</p>
<p class="boxModel"> RSS is an XML-based (eXtensible Markup Lan-
guage) language used to describe the content of an article.
Another way to describe an RSS file is that it is just raw
metadata (data about data) about a particular document. If you
have created a Web page, you should be familiar with the
&lt;meta&gt; tag. This metadata usually includes information such
as a brief description of the document and keywords that should
be used to index the document. RSS takes that to the next level.</p>
<p>New paragraph.</p>
</body>
</html>
```

Figure 16.10.   Setting Different `margin` Values for our Document's Body and its Content

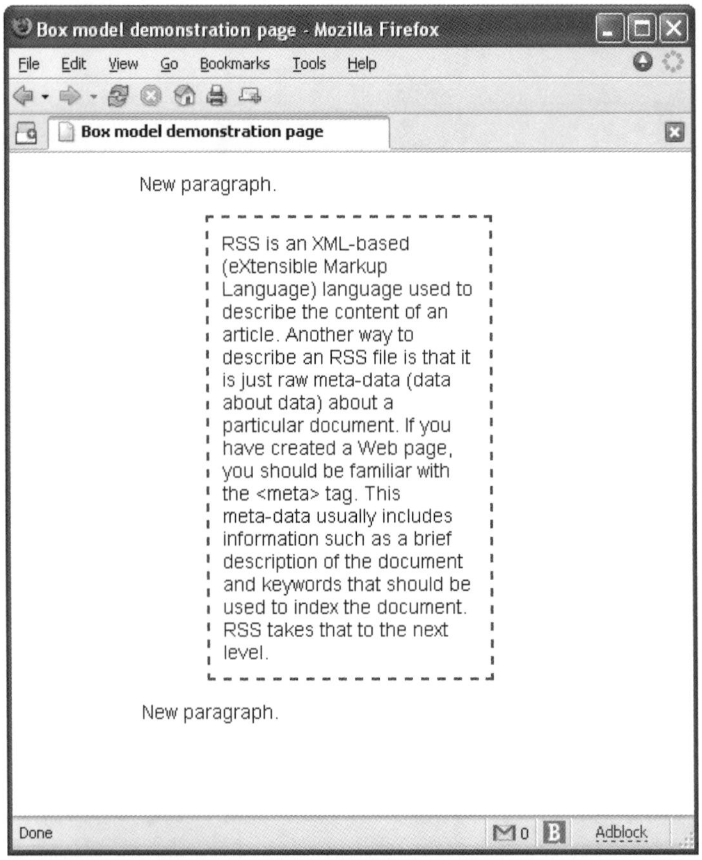

In this case, the left and right margins for the paragraph are set one-half inch from the margin of its parent, which is already one inch from the edge of the browser's window. Therefore the paragraph's left and right margins are a total of 1.5 inches from the edge of the browser window. Margins are cumulative; as you work from parent into child the value of those margins will add to each other.

Using margins to center content

Many current site designs specify for their content a box of a particular width (600 pixels, for example), which should be centered on the page. Using the traditional table-based method, authors would place the content within a table, set its width to 600 pixels, and center the table. The code looks something like this:

```
<table width="600" align="center">
<tr>
<td>
<p class="boxModel">RSS is an XML-based (eXtensible Markup Lan-
guage) language used to describe the content of an article.
Another way to describe an RSS file is that it is just raw
metadata (data about data) about a particular document. If you
have created a Web page, you should be familiar with the
&lt;meta&gt; tag. This metadata usually includes information
such as a brief description of the document and keywords that
should be used to index the document. RSS takes that to the
next level.</p>
</td>
</tr>
</table>
```

However, a problem arises when we attempt to accomplish the same layout without using tables, but instead use CSS and expect it to work in Netscape and Internet Explorer, as well as other Web browsers.

The proper way to center a block of content within a document using CSS is to use the "auto" value on the margin property. The following code will accomplish the same centered result as the table-based code above (Figure 16.11).

```
CSS:
.wrapper {width:600px;margin-left:auto; margin-right: auto}
XHTML:
<div class="wrapper">
<p class="boxModel">RSS is an XML-based (eXtensible Markup Lan-
guage) language used to describe the content of an article.
Another way to describe an RSS file is that it is just raw
metadata (data about data) about a particular document. If you
have created a Web page, you should be familiar with the
&lt;meta&gt; tag. This metadata usually includes information
such as a brief description of the document and keywords that
should be used to index the document. RSS takes that to the
next level.</p>
</div>
```

Figure 16.11.   Centering Content with `margin: auto`

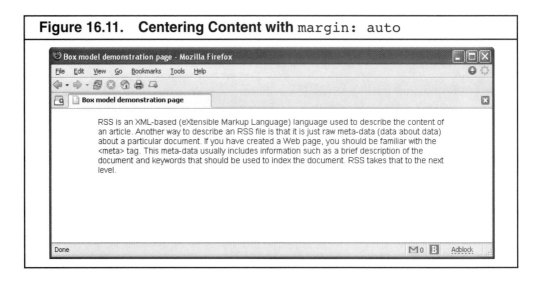

I've named the class "wrapper" because we are wrapping the content within a block. We have set the width of the block to 600 pixels, then directed both the left and right margins to adjust themselves automatically, thus causing the block to appear in the center of the screen. Though this works well in most browsers, including Netscape, Mozilla, Firebird, and Opera, it does not work in Internet Explorer (IE), as that browser does not support the "auto" margin value. Taking this into account, we must circumvent the roadblocks in the individual browsers.

Here is the code that will work in IE (Figure 16.12).

CSS:
```
.wrapper {width:600px; text-align:center}
.content {text-align: left}
```

XHTML:
```
<div class="wrapper">
<div class="content">
<p class="boxModel"> RSS is an XML-based (eXtensible Markup
Language) language used to describe the content of an article.
Another way to describe an RSS file is that it is just raw
metadata (data about data) about a particular document. If you
have created a Web page, you should be familiar with the
&lt;meta&gt; tag. This metadata usually includes information
such as a brief description of the document and keywords that
should be used to index the document. RSS takes that to the
next level.</p>
</div>
</div>
```

Figure 16.12. Centering Content with `text-align: center` **for IE**

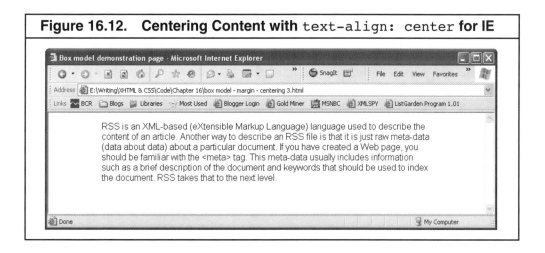

In this case, we've removed the unsupported code and directed the browser to center the content of "wrapper." Not only will this center the content in "wrapper," but it will also center the whole block. This is an incorrect implementation, but that is the format rendered by this code in Internet Explorer. Since we've centered everything within "wrapper," we then create a "content" block in which everything is left-justified. In the end, we are left with a centered block with left-justified content, just as we intended.

The IE version we've just created will not work in the other browsers since they will correctly not center the "wrapper" block, only the block's content. Netscape will display our "wrapper" block along the left edge of the screen. To solve the problem, we need to combine the two sets of code.

CSS:
```
.wrapper  {width:600px;margin-left:auto;
          margin-right:auto;
          text-align:center}
.content {text-align: left}
```

XHTML:
```
<div class="wrapper">
<div class="content">
<p class="boxModel"> RSS is an XML-based (eXtensible Markup Lan-
guage) language used to describe the content of an article.
Another way to describe an RSS file is that it is just raw
metadata (data about data) about a particular document. If you
have created a Web page, you should be familiar with the
&lt;meta&gt; tag. This metadata usually includes information such
as a brief description of the document and keywords that should
be used to index the document. RSS takes that to the next level.</p>
</div>
</div>
```

This code correctly applies the auto-margins in the browsers that understand it, as well as provides the workaround needed for Internet Explorer, rendering the result we want in all current Web browsers.

ABBREVIATING MARGINS AND PADDING

Unless you need to specify individual sides of the box when setting `margins` or `padding`, you can abbreviate the property by using either `margin` or `padding`, respectively. In doing this, you assign a single value to be applied to all four sides. However, there are applications to abbreviating these values. Take a look at the following example:

```
body {margin: 10% 5%}
```

In this example, I've specified two values for margin. When two values are specified, the first will be applied to the top and bottom of the element, while the second value will be applied to the left and right sides of the element.

If we specify three values, the first will be applied to the top, the second to the right and left, and the third will be applied to the bottom. (I've never actually seen this option used in a live Web page, but it is a legal option.)

```
body {margin: 10px 5% 20px}
```

Lastly, we can specify four values.

```
body {margin: .5in 1in 0in 1.5in}
```

When four values are specified, the values are applied in a clockwise order starting with the top of the element: `top`, `right`, `bottom`, `left`.

17

Links

In Chapter 13, I introduced you to the concept of pseudo-selectors, selectors that influence certain sections of an element or are influenced by external factors. The most common use of pseudo-selectors is on hyperlinks. In this chapter, we'll take a detailed look at their application in that situation.

THE ANCHOR PSEUDO CLASSES

Most users are aware, on some level, that hyperlinks have two states—visited and not-visited. This is evidenced by the fact that not-visited links appear in blue and visited links appear in purple on the screen. However, links actually have four different states—not-visited, visited, selected, and hover. I'll describe each of them individually.

- Not-visited (`a:link`).
  These are links that technically have not been visited *recently*, even though most users define them as "not-visited yet." If you were to click on a link and then go back one page, the link will be considered "visited." If you were to never click on that link ever again, eventually (depending on the length of time your browser has been set to keep a history), the link will revert to its "not-visited" state.
- Visited (`a:visited`).
  Similarly, this technically means visited *recently*. As long as a URL is listed in your browser's history, any link to that URL will be considered visited.
- Selected (`a:active`).
  We say that clicking on a link is what "activates" it. This is technically incorrect. It is not the act of pressing the mouse button down over a link that activates it, but the act of pressing down *and then lifting up* off the mouse button over a link

that activates it. The state that the link is in while you're pressing down but before you've lifted up is the selected state.

This also works using the tab and enter keys on your keyboard. If you are on a page, you can use the tab key to move from link to link within that page. Using this method, your enter key becomes the "clicking" method to activate a link. Once you have tabbed to a link but have not yet pressed the enter key, the link is in the selected state. (IE also places a small dotted line around a selected link.)

• Hover (`a:hover`).
  The hover state exists when you have moved your mouse pointer over a link, regardless of whether you've pressed any buttons. By default, browsers will change your mouse pointer to a hand in this state.

Let's look at some examples of how these four states can apply to your design.

```
a {text-decoration: none}
```

In this case I haven't specified a pseudo class, so the property will apply to all states of my hyperlinks. The result of this declaration is to turn off the underlining that browsers automatically add to hyperlinks.

If you would like your hyperlinks to remain blue, regardless of whether or not they've been visited, you would do the following.

```
a:visited {color: blue}
```

Just to be sure you have your bases covered, you would also add the following code, since some browsers automatically treat selected links as visited links, thus turning them purple.

```
a:active   {color: blue}
```

Hover is the state with which designers uaually have the most fun. For example, if I wanted the underlines to appear when the mouse pointer is over a link I can add:

```
a:hover    {text-decoration: underline}
```

Other authors prefer to change the link's color in the hover state:

```
a:hover    {color: red}
```

We can even do both at once.

```
a:hover    {text-decoration: underline; color: red}
```

At the BCR site they have turned off the underlining, and when menu links are hovered they turn yellow and get a little larger. Our code looks like this:

```
#menu a:hover    {color: yellow; text-size: 105%}
```

In this case we've specified only hovered links that are in the area of the page identified as "menu." This prevents the effect from being applied to links in other sections of the page. The possibilities are endless. Try to figure out what each of these examples would do.

```
a:visited {display: none}
a:hover   {display: none}
```

A FEW NOTES ON CODE ORDER

Many new CSS authors stumble into a particular problem when first working with anchor pseudo classes. They write their code and then it won't work. Often, they have forgotten that code order figures within the cascade.

For example:

```
a:hover   {color: red}
a:visited {color: green}
```

Here, visited links will be green even when the user hovers over them. That's because the visited state has precedence over the hover in the cascade.

To solve this problem, commit the following to memory:

link → visited → hover → active

You may find the mnemonic "LoVe HAte" helpful in remembering this order.

18

Lists

In Chapter 6, I mentioned several times that you can use CSS to control the appearance of your lists once you've properly marked them up. In this chapter we'll take one of the examples from Chapter 6 and apply some CSS to change its appearance. We'll also take a look at a completely new way to consider lists from a visual perspective.

Let's take a look at the code we used in Chapter 5 after I turned BCR's main menu into an unordered list (Figure 18.1.)

```
<!DOCTYPE html PUBLIC "-//W3C//DTD XHTML 1.0 Transitional//EN"
"http://www.w3.org/1999/xhtml/DTD/xhtml1-transitional.dtd">
<html xmlns="http://www.w3.org/1999/xhtml" lang="en"
xml:lang="en">
<head>
<title></title>
<meta http-equiv="Content-Type" content="text/html; charset=utf-8" />
<style type="text/css">
</style>
</head>
<body>
<ul>
<li><a href="sitemap/">Site Map</a></li>
<li><a href="/~shoffhin/about/aboutbcr.html">About BCR</a></li>
<li><a href="/~shoffhin/who/">Contact Us</a></li>
<li>Services
 <ul>
 <li><a href="/~bss/oclcsrvs.html">OCLC</a></li>
 <li><a href="/~ids/Reference/">Reference Databases</a></li>
 <li><a href="/~randd/internet.html">Internet</a></li>
 <li><a href="/~bss/cat-tech.html">Cataloging</a></li>
```

```
<li><a href="/~randd/Database-menu.html">Database Creation</a></
li>
 <li><a href="/~bss/rshar.html">Resource Sharing</a></li>
 <li><a href="/~ids/Hardsoft/">Hardware &amp; Software</a></li>
 <li><a href="library-office.html">Library &amp;<br />Office
Supplies</a></li>
 <li><a href="/~ids/Discounts/">Discounts</a></li>
 <li><a href="/~business/">Accounting</a></li>
 <li><a href="/~shoffhin/consult/">Consulting</a></li>
 </ul>
</li>
</ul>
</body>
</html>
```

Figure 18.1.   A Basic List Including a Nested List

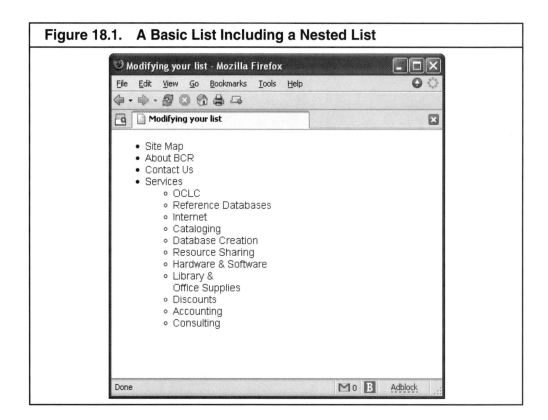

CSS PROPERTIES FOR LISTS

There are only three properties specific to lists, `list-style-type`, `list-style-image`, and `list-style-position`. In this section I'll be covering all three types and how they can be abbreviated. However, these are not the only properties that you'll end up using when manipulating your lists. Properties such as margin, padding, and width will also come into play.

list-style-type

The list-style-type property is the CSS equivalent of the type="" attribute in XHTML. It allows you to specify the type of bullets, if any, to be used on your list. When applying list-style-type to an unordered list, there are four valid properties: disc (Figure 18.2), circle (Figure 18.3), square (Figure 18.4), and none (Figure 18.5).

```
ul {list-style-type: disc}
```

Figure 18.2.   The list-style-type Property with a disc Value

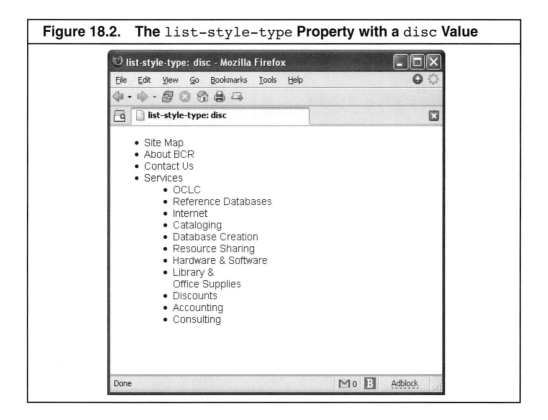

```
ul {list-style-type: circle}
```

Figure 18.3.   The `list-style-type` **Property with a** `circle` **Value**

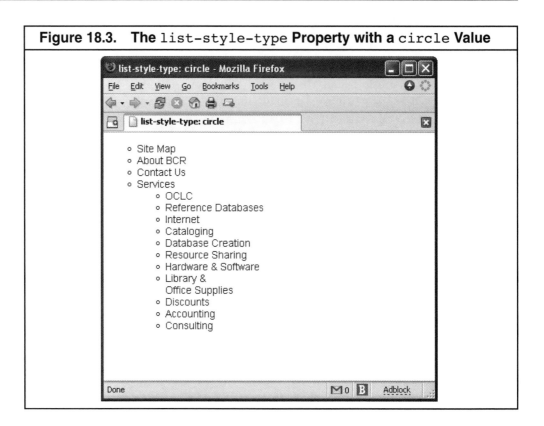

```
ul {list-style-type: square}
```

Figure 18.4.   The `list-style-type` **Property with a** `square` **Value**

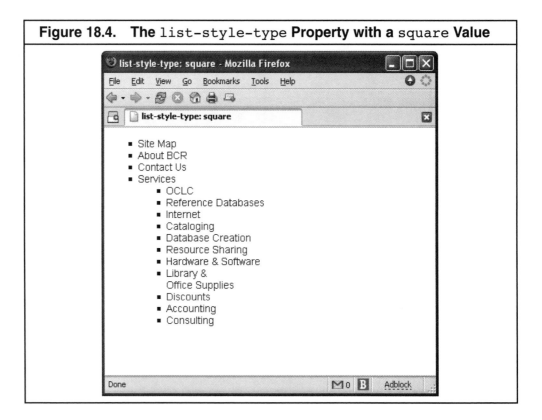

```
ul {list-style-type: none}
```

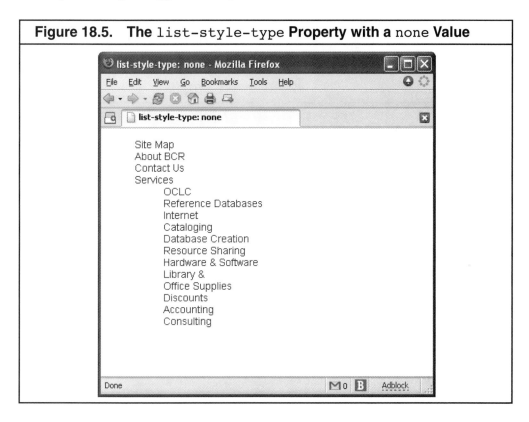

Figure 18.5. The `list-style-type` Property with a `none` Value

When applying `list-style-type` to ordered lists there are 17 different values to choose from, although readers of this book will most likely never use the first six: lower-Roman, upper-Roman, lower-alpha, upper-alpha, decimal, and none. The other 11 are shown in the example below (Figures 18.6 and 18.7).

```
<ol>
 <li style="list-style-type: upper-roman;">upper-roman</li>
 <li style="list-style-type: upper-alpha;">upper-alpha</li>
 <li style="list-style-type: decimal;">decimal</li>
 <li style="list-style-type: lower-roman;">lower-roman</li>
 <li style="list-style-type: lower-alpha;">lower-alpha</li>
 <li style="list-style-type: none;">none &#8212; Despite not show-
ing a number or letter, notice that the counting continues.</li>
 <li style="list-style-type: armenian;">armenian</li>
 <li style="list-style-type: cjk-ideographic;">cjk-ideographic</li>
 <li style="list-style-type: georgian;">georgian</li>
 <li style="list-style-type: hebrew;">hebrew</li>
 <li style="list-style-type: hiragana;">hiragana</li>
 <li style="list-style-type: hiragana-iroha;">hiragana-iroha</li>
 <li style="list-style-type: katakana;">katakana</li>
 <li style="list-style-type: katakana-iroha;">katakana-iroha</li>
 <li style="list-style-type: lower-greek;">lower-greek</li>
 <li style="list-style-type: lower-latin;">lower-latin</li>
```

```
<li style="list-style-type: upper-latin;">upper-latin</li>
<li style="list-style-type: decimal;">Please keep in mind that
some browsers (such as IE6) may not display the characters used in
the above items from 'lower-greek' through 'katakana-iroha'.</li>
</ol>
```

Figure 18.6.   The `list-style-type` Property with the `ol` Values Displayed in Firefox

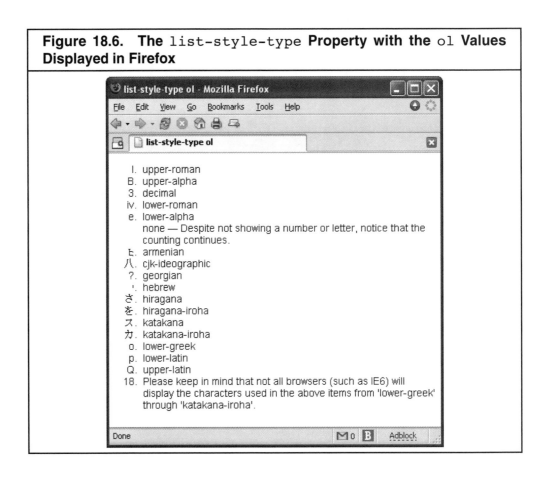

Figure 18.7.   The `list-style-type` Property with the `ol` Values Displayed in IE

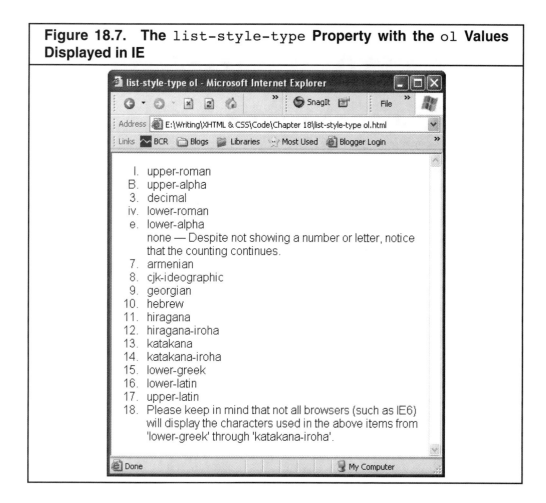

list-style-image

If you have ever used tables to place an image as if it were a bullet on a list, this is the property you've been waiting for. All you need to do is specify the file to be used and the image will be displayed instead of one of the built-in-bullets (Figure 18.8).

```
ul {list-style-image: url(book.gif)}
```

Figure 18.8. An Unordered List with Icons as Bullets

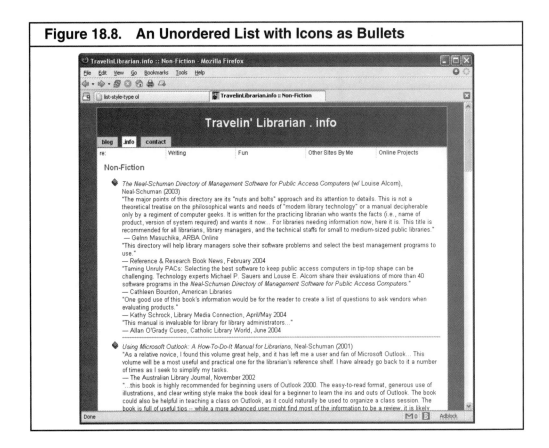

Of course, all of the rules of specifying a URL as discussed in Chapter 13 apply.

list-style-position

The list-style-position property allows you to specify whether the bullets (or numbers/letters) appear outside of the list's margin/content box (the default) or within the list's margin/content box. Below I have created two lists, the first with a value of "outside" and the second with a value of "inside." I've also turned on the lists' borders to better illustrate the bullets' locations (Figure 18.9).

```
<ul style="list-style-position: outside; border: solid 1px black">
<li>This list has a list-style-position of outside which is the
default. Notice how the bullets sit outside the content box and
wrapping occurs to the right of the bullet.</li>
<li>Item</li>
<li>Item</li>
</ul>
<ul style="list-style-position: inside; border: solid 1px black">
<li>This list has a list-style-position of inside. Notice how
the bullets sit inside the content box and wrapping occurs
underneath the bullet.</li>
<li>Item</li>
<li>Item</li>
</ul>
```

Figure 18.9. The `list-style-position` **Property**

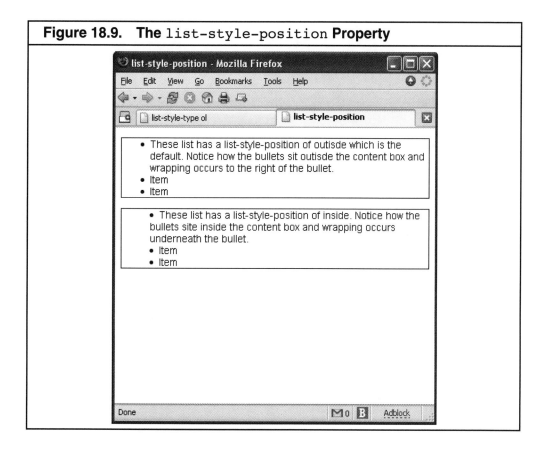

ABBREVIATING WITH `list-style`

As with `border` properties (as discussed in Chapter 16) the list-style properties can be abbreviated. For example, if you want to specify an inside position and upper-Roman numbers you can write it in one of the following two ways.

```
ul {list-style-position: inside;
    list-style-type: upper-alpha}
```

or

```
ul {list-style: inside upper-alpha}
```

Both these lines of CSS will give you the same result but the second is clearly more efficient.

REFORMATTING A LIST

First let's look at our goal (Figure 18.10).

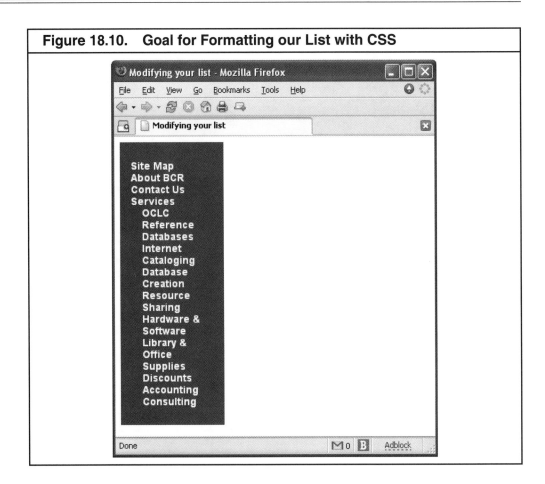

Figure 18.10.　Goal for Formatting our List with CSS

This revised list has a green background, white text, and white hyperlinks that increase slightly in size and turn yellow when hovered over. The lists themselves had no bullets and nested lists are 20 pixels to the right of the master list.

SETTING UP THE BOX

First, let's put our list into a box that we can manipulate. To do this, we put a `<div>` around the list.

```
<!DOCTYPE html PUBLIC "-//W3C//DTD XHTML 1.0 Transitional//EN"
"http://www.w3.org/1999/xhtml/DTD/xhtml1-transitional.dtd">
<html  xmlns="http://www.w3.org/1999/xhtml"  lang="en"
xml:lang="en">
<head>
<title>Modifying your list</title>
<meta http-equiv="Content-Type" content="text/html; charset=utf-
8" />
<style type="text/css">
</style>
</head>
```

```
<div>
<ul>
<li><a href="sitemap/">Site Map</a></li>
<li><a href="/~shoffhin/about/aboutbcr.html">About BCR</a></li>
<li><a href="/~shoffhin/who/">Contact Us</a></li>
<li>Services
 <ul>
 <li><a href="/~bss/oclcsrvs.html">OCLC</a></li>
 <li><a href="/~ids/Reference/">Reference Databases</a></li>
 <li><a href="/~randd/internet.html">Internet</a></li>
 <li><a href="/~bss/cat-tech.html">Cataloging</a></li>
 <li><a href="/~randd/Database-menu.html">Database Creation</a></li>
 <li><a href="/~bss/rshar.html">Resource Sharing</a></li>
 <li><a href="/~ids/Hardsoft/">Hardware &amp; Software</a></li>
 <li><a href="library-office.html">Library &amp;<br />Office
Supplies</a></li>
 <li><a href="/~ids/Discounts/">Discounts</a></li>
 <li><a href="/~business/">Accounting</a></li>
 <li><a href="/~shoffhin/consult/">Consulting</a></li>
 </ul>
</li>
</ul>
</div>
</body>
</html>
```

Next we need to identify this <div> somehow. Since this is the menu for the page and there will be only one, let's use id="menu."

```
<div id="menu">
```

We'll add our CSS one step at a time.

We need to set the width of our <div>. Assuming that we'll be placing this menu off to the side in our final design, we'll assign a width of 200 pixels (Figure 18.11).

```
<style type="text/css">
#menu {width: 200px}
</style>
```

Figure 18.11.   Setting the Width of the List

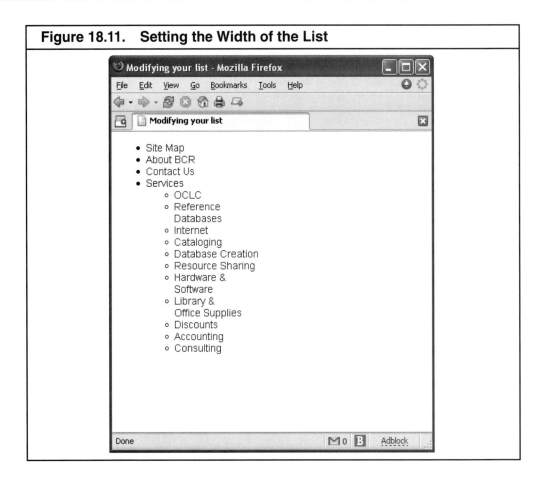

Next, we add a dark green background (Figure 18.12).

```
<style type="text/css">
#menu {width: 200px; background: #063}
</style>
```

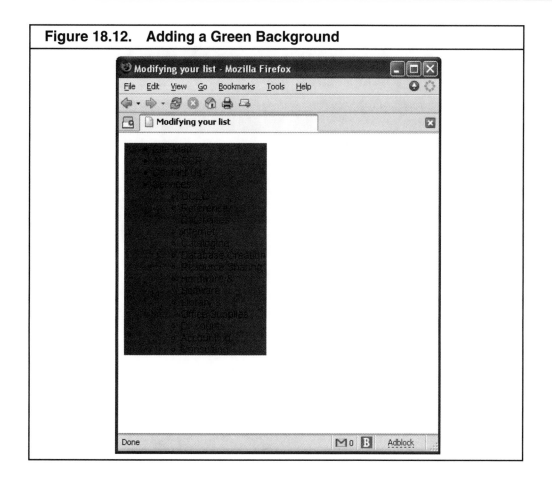

Figure 18.12.   Adding a Green Background

As you can see this has now become illegible with blue links and black text on the dark green background. To increase the visibility of the nonlinked text we'll change its appearance to white and bold (Figure 18.13).

```
<style type="text/css">
#menu {width: 29%; background: #063; color: #fff;
       font-weight: bold}
</style>
```

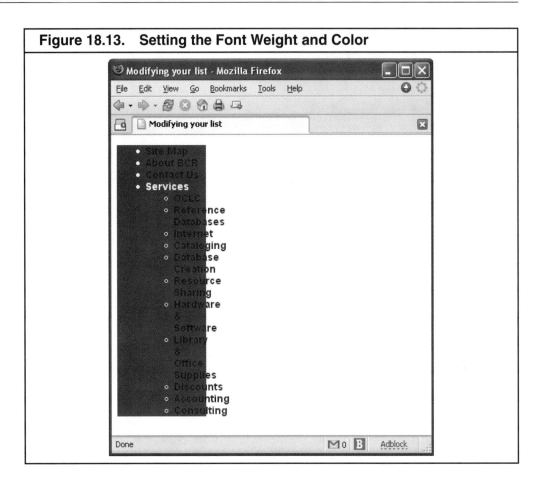

Figure 18.13.   Setting the Font Weight and Color

Our final adjustment to the box itself is to add some padding to keep the text from bumping into the sides of the box.

```
<style type="text/css">
#menu {width: 29%; background: #063; color: #fff;
       font-weight: bold; padding: 10px}
</style>
```

CHANGING THE LINKS

We need to make three changes to the links to accomplish our goal. First, we need to set the link color to white. Assuming that we want only the links within the menu to be white, we need to specify only those links (Figure 18.14).

```
<style type="text/css">
#menu {width: 29%; background: #063; color: #fff;
       font-weight: bold; padding: 10px }
#menu a:link     {color: #fff}
</style>
```

Figure 18.14.   Changing the Link Color

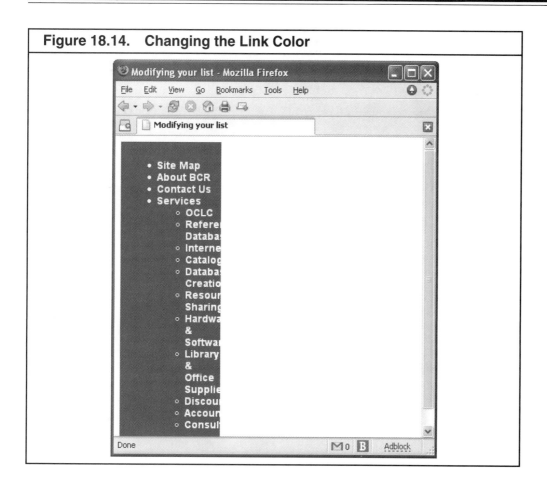

Next we need to ensure that the visited links (but only those within the menu) are also white.

```
<style type="text/css">
#menu {width: 29%; background: #063; color: #fff;
       font-weight: bold; padding: 10px }
#menu a:link     {color: #fff}
#menu a:visited {color: #fff}
</style>
```

Lastly, we'll add the code for the hover effect, changing the links to yellow and making them larger (Figure 18.15).

```
<style type="text/css">
#menu {width: 29%; background: #063; color: #fff;
       font-weight: bold; padding: 10px }
#menu a:link     {color: #fff}
#menu a:visited {color: #fff}
#menu a:hover    {font-size: 105%; color: #ff6}
</style>
```

Figure 18.15. Setting a link hover color and font size change

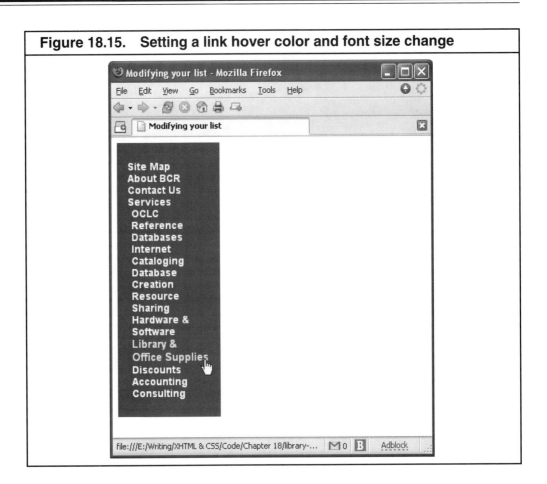

CHANGING THE APPEARANCE OF THE LIST ITEMS

First thing we need to do is turn off the bullets. This can be done by setting the list-style-type to none (Figure 18.16).

```
<style type="text/css">
#menu          {width: 29%; background: #063; color: #fff;
 font-weight: bold; padding: 10px }
#menu a:link    {color: #fff}
#menu a:visited {color: #fff}
#menu a:hover   {font-size: 105%; color: #ff6}
ul  {list-style-type: none}
</style>
```

Figure 18.16. Removing the Bullets

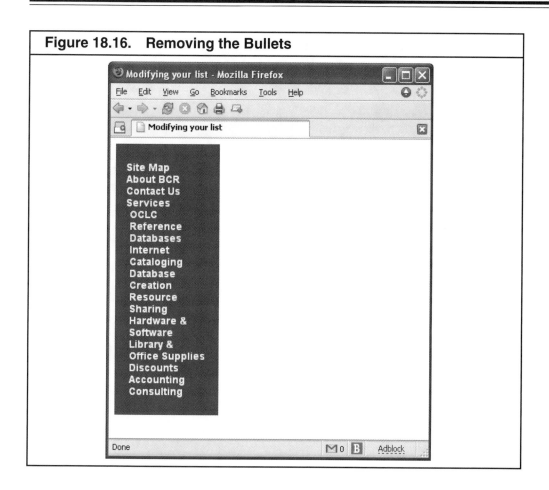

Next, let's move the lists back to the left edge of the box (but not completely to the edge). In order to remove the large left-margin change inherent in lists, we'll set the left margin to zero. Then we can move the list off the left edge of the box by adding a 5 pixel padding on the left (Figure 18.17).

```
<style type="text/css">
#menu             {width: 29%; background: #063; color: #fff;
 font-weight: bold; padding: 10px }
#menu a:link    {color: #fff}
#menu a:visited {color: #fff}
#menu a:hover   {font-size: 105%; color: #ff6}
ul                {list-style-type: none; margin-left: 0px;
 padding-left: 5px}
</style>
```

Figure 18.17.   Adding Some Padding

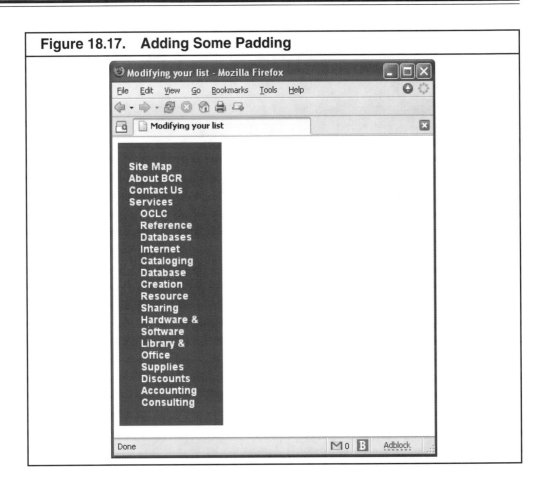

Lastly, we'll set the left margin of the nested list, by setting a 10 pixel left margin on <ul>s when they're children of <ul>s (Figure 18.18).

```
<style type="text/css">
#menu          {width: 29%; background: #063; color: #fff;
      font-weight: bold; padding: 10px }
#menu a:link   {color: #fff}
#menu a:visited {color: #fff}
#menu a:hover  {font-size: 105%; color: #ff6}
ul             {list-style-type: none; margin-left: 0px;
               padding-left: 5px}
ul ul          {margin-left: 10px;}
</style>
```

Figure 18.18. Setting the Left Margin on the Nested List

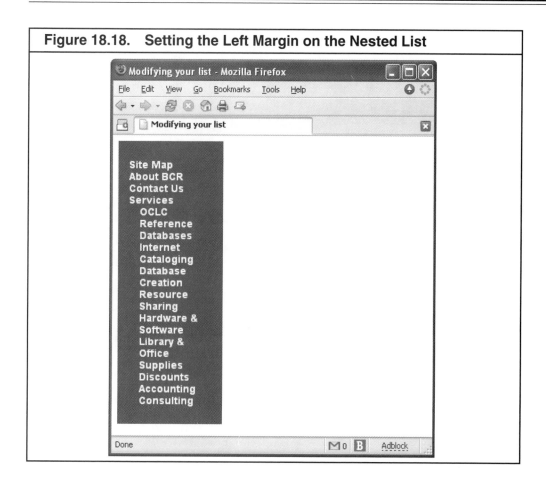

RE-ENVISIONING LISTS

I've come to the conclusion that many years of automatically associating lists with bullets or numbers has limited how people think they can use lists. Even the previous example is pretty straightforward; it's just a list without bullets on a colored background and with some fancy link manipulation. Let's take a look at a completely different way of using a list as a menu.

Here's a simple four-item list we could use as a menu (Figure 18.19).

```
<!DOCTYPE html PUBLIC "-//W3C//DTD XHTML 1.0
Transitional//EN" "http://www.w3.org/1999/xhtml/DTD/xhtml1-
transitional.dtd">
<html xmlns="http://www.w3.org/1999/xhtml" lang="en" xml:lang="en">
<head>
<title>Rethinking lists</title>
<meta http-equiv="Content-Type" content="text/html; charset=utf-
8" />
<style type="text/css">
</style>
</head>
```

```
<body>
<ul>
<li><a href="branches.html">Branches</a></li>
<li><a href="hours.html">Hours</a></li>
<li><a href="staff.html">Staff</a></li>
<li><a href="policies.html">Policies</a></li>
</ul>
</body>
</html>
```

Figure 18.19.   A Basic Four-item List

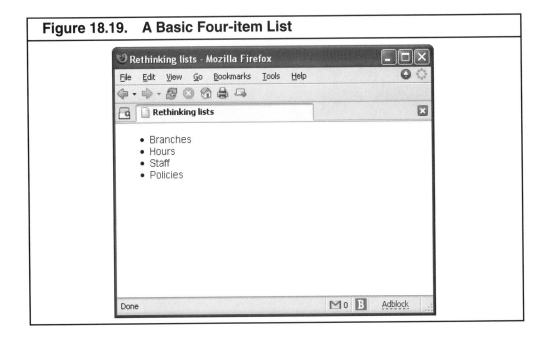

Let's start changing this list by removing the bullets and any margins or padding associated with the list (Figure 18.20).

```
<style type="text/css">
ul {margin: 0; padding: 0; list-style-type: none}
li {margin: 0; padding: 0; list-style-type: none}
</style>
```

Figure 18.20. Setting the Margin and Padding and Removing the Bullets

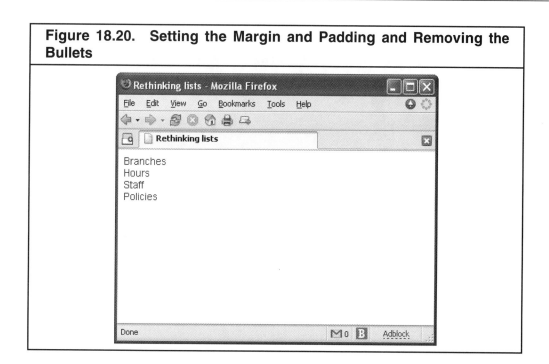

Once we've stripped the list of all of the presentation let's rebuild it into something else—what Web designers call rollover buttons. We'll put each of the list items into boxes of equal size and center the contents. Each item will begin to look like a button (Figure 18.21).

```
<style type="text/css">
ul {margin: 0; padding: 0; list-style-type: none;}
li {margin: 0; padding: 0; list-style-type: none;
    border: 1px solid #000; width: 8em;
    text-align: center}
</style>
```

Figure 18.21.   Adding a Border to each Item

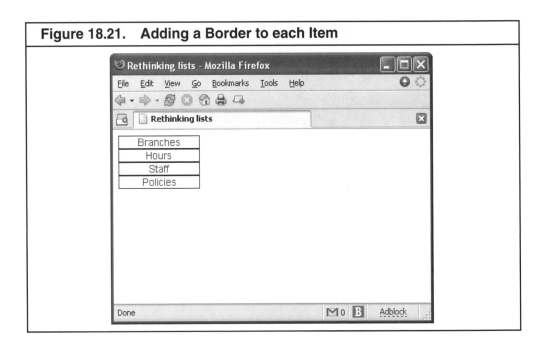

We want to give the boxes some color, but we don't want to change the background color of the items. Let's add a background color to the anchors instead.

```
<style type="text/css">
ul    {margin: 0; padding: 0; list-style-type: none;}
li    {margin: 0; padding: 0; list-style-type: none;
       border: 1px solid #000; width: 8em
       text-align: center }
ul a {color: #fff; background: #6c3;
       text-decoration: none; display: block;
       padding:2px; margin:1px;}
ul a:link, ul a:visited, ul a:active       {color:#fff;}
</style>
```

The selectors in this case have been set to affect only anchors that are children of unordered lists (ul a). If we do not include "ul" in the selector, the code will affect every anchor on the Web page, which is not what we want. We want only to color the text in the list.

In the code, the color property turns the text black against the green set for the background of the anchor. The "text-decoration" property turns off underlining on the anchors.

Setting the display property to block forces the anchor to be treated as content that fills in the entire box we created. Had we not included this setting, the background color would display only behind the linked text and would not fill the entire box.

Lastly, the padding property provides a small bit of space between the edges of the text and the edge of the background color, along with a margin setting that allows a small space between the background color and the box (Figure 18.22).

Figure 18.22.   Adding some Color, Removing the Underlines, and Adding some Padding

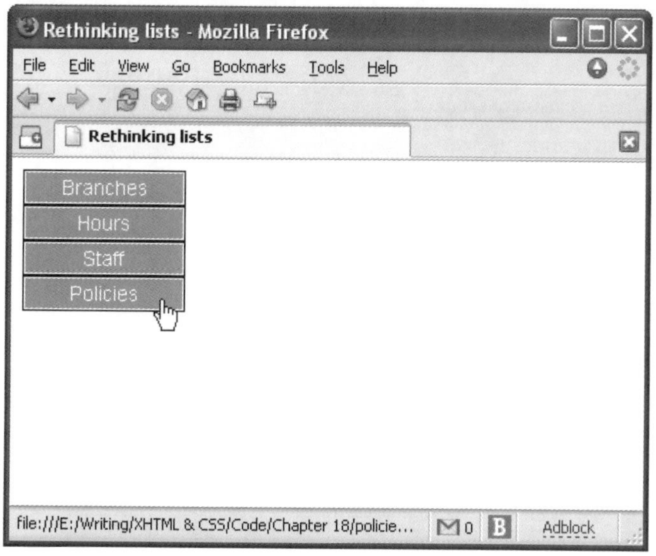

To create the rollover effect, we only need to add one additional line of CSS.

```
<style type="text/css">
ul          {margin: 0; padding: 0; list-style-type: none;}
li          {margin: 0; padding: 0; list-style-type: none;
             border: 1px solid #000; width: 8em;
             text-align: center}
ul a        {color: #fff; background: #6c3;
             text-decoration: none; display: block;
             padding:2px; margin:1px;}
ul a:link,  ul a:visited, ul a:active   {color:#fff;}
ul a:hover {background:#cf9; color: #000}
</style>
```

This changes the background color of the box to a lighter shade of green and the link text to black when the mouse pointer moves over the link (Figure 18.23).

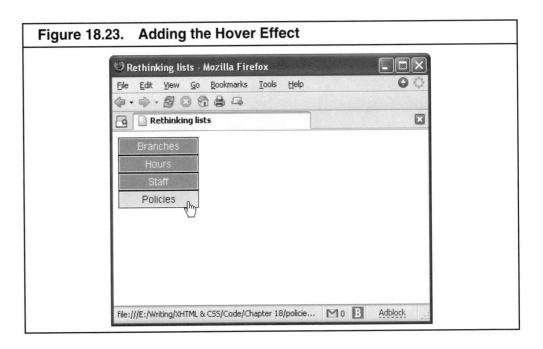

Figure 18.23.   Adding the Hover Effect

There is one small difference between the results in Mozilla-based browsers and in Internet Explorer. In IE, the hover effect works only when the mouse pointer is over the linked text. In Mozilla-based browsers, the hover works whenever the mouse pointer is over any point within the box, not just the linked text.

For more details on the possibilities of combining lists and CSS, and for tools that will help you create the CSS, check out the Max Design Web site at http://css.maxdesign .com.au/.

19

Forms

When we last left our form in Chapter 8, it was functional but not exactly elegant. Everything was justified to the left margin, and all our input boxes were left-justified to their labels. Let's take another look (Figure 19.1).

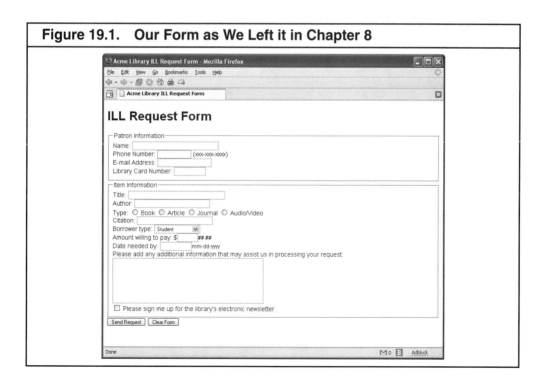

Figure 19.1.   Our Form as We Left it in Chapter 8

```
<!DOCTYPE html PUBLIC "-//W3C//DTD XHTML 1.0
Transitional//EN"  "http://www.w3.org/TR/xhtml/DTD/xhtml1-
transitional.dtd">
<html xmlns="http://www.w3.org/TR/xhtml" lang="en">
<head>
<title>Acme Library ILL Request Form</title>
<meta name="HTTP-Equiv" content="text/html; content="utf-8">
</head>
<body>
<h1>ILL Request Form</h1>
<form method="post" action="/cgi-bin/Yform.cgi">
<input type="hidden" name="recipient" value="msauers@bcr.org" />
<input type="hidden" name="subject" value="ILL Request" />
<input type="hidden" name="sort"value="order:name,phone,email,
card,itemTitle,author,type,citation,borrower,amount,date,
comments,newsletter" />
<input type="hidden" name="required"value="name,phone,card,
itemTitle,author,amount" />
<input type="hidden" name="env_report"value="REMOTE_ADDR,
HHTP_USER_AGENT" />
<input type="hidden" name="title" value="Thank you for submit-
ting your request" />
<input type="hidden" name="return_link_title" value="Back to
the library home page" />
<input type="hidden" name="return_link_url" value="http://
www.bcr.org" />
<input type="hidden" name="courtext1" value="Your request has
been sent to the ILL department for processing. Here is the
information you sent us." />
<input type="hidden" name="courfieldlist" value="yes" />
<input type="hidden" name="courtext2" value="If any of this
information is incorrect please contact the ILL department as
soon as possible so that we may correct the information." />
<input type="hidden" name="courclose" value="Sincerely," />
<input type="hidden" name="myname" value="Michael Sauers, ILL
Department Head" />
<input type="hidden" name="myemail" value="msauers@bcr.org" />
<input type="hidden" name="mywebsite" value="http://www.bcr.org/
" />
<input type="hidden" name="database" value="illdata.txt" />
<input type="hidden" name="delimiter" value="~" />
<fieldset>
<legend>Patron Information</legend>
<label for="name">Name: </label>
<input id="name" type="text" name="name" size="35" /><br />
<label for="phone">Phone Number: </label>
<input id="phone" type="text" name="phone" size="11"
maxlength="11" /> (xxx-xxx-xxxx)<br />
<label for="email">E-mail Address: </label>
<input id="email" type="text" name="email" /><br />
<label for="card">Library Card Number: </label>
<input id="card" type="password" name="card" size="10"
maxlength="10" />
```

```
</fieldset>
<fieldset>
<legend>Item Information</legend>
<label for="itemTitle">Title: </label>
<input id="itemTitle" type="text" name="itemTitle" size="40" /
><br />
<label for="author">Author: </label>
<input id="author" type="text" name="author" size="30" /><br />
Type:
<input id="book" type="radio" name="type" value="book" />
<label for="book">Book</label>
<input id="article" type="radio" name="type" value="article" />
<label for="article">Article</label>
<input id="journal" type="radio" name="type" value="Journal" />
<label for="journal">Journal</label>
<input id="av" type="radio" name="type" value="a/v" />
<label for="av">Audio/Video</label>
<br />
<label for="citation">Citation: </label>
<input id="citation" type="text" name="citation" size="30" /><br />
<label for="borrower">Borrower type: </label>
<select id="borrower" name="borrower">
<option>Adjunct Faculty</option>
<option>Faculty</option>
<option>Staff</option>
<option selected="true">Student</option>
<option>Public</option>
</select>
<br />
<label for="amount">Amount willing to pay: </label>
$<input id="amount" type="text" name="amount" size="5"
maxlength="5" /><small>##.##</small><br />
<label for="date">Date needed by: </label>
<input id="date" type="text" name="date" size="10" maxlength="10"
/><small>mm-dd-yyyy</small><br />
<label for="comments">Please add any additional information that
may assist us in processing your request:</label><br />
<textarea id="comments" name="comments" cols="40" rows="5"></
textarea><br />
<input id="newsletter" type="checkbox" name="newsletter" />
<label for="newsletter">Please sign me up for the library's
electronic newsletter.</label>
</fieldset>
<div>
<input type="submit" value="Send Request" />
<input type="reset" value="Clear Form" />
</div>
</form>
</body>
</html>
```

What we need to do now is to make this form much more visually appealing. Here's our goal (Figure 19.2).

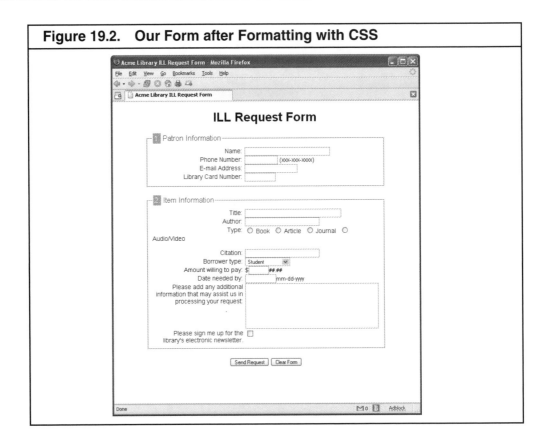

Figure 19.2.   Our Form after Formatting with CSS

DON'T USE TABLES

As previously discussed in Chapter 7, tables should not be used for layout. CSS is more than adequate for the purpose of laying out forms. CSS has actually had this capability since inception, but browser support for the relevant features has been slow to catch up.

LAYOUT

As you can see, we've already taken care of part of our goal by using the `<fieldset>` and `<legend>` elements. Those, as you recall, created the boxes around the two sections of our form and labeled each of those sections.

Here's what we need to accomplish with CSS:

- Increase the size of the `<legend>` text and add the numbers
- Center our `<fieldset>`s on the page
- Increase the spacing both around and within the `<fieldset>`s
- Move our inputs to the right side of the `<fieldset>`s so they all line up on their left edges
- Right-justify our labels so that they all line up to the input boxes.

Let's deal with each of these four items one at a time.

LEGENDS

Since we've used the `<legend>` element, changing the appearance of our legends is just a matter of using legend as a selector and giving it the appropriate declarations. Based on the screenshot of our goal, I have made the text 20 percent larger than normal. All we need to do is add the following (Figure 19.3).

```
legend {font-size: 120%}
```

Figure 19.3.   Increasing the Size of the Legends

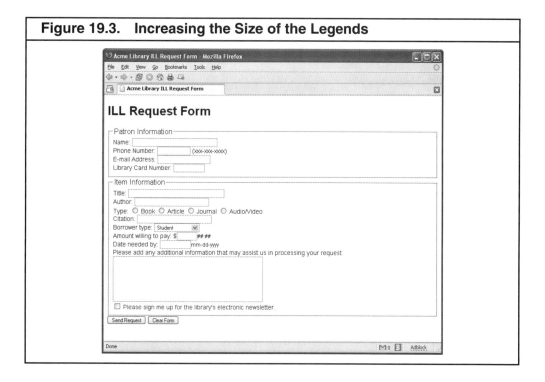

The other thing we need to do to the legend is to add the numbers. The addition of the numbers themselves is just a question of adding "1." and "2." to the appropriate `<label>` content. The formatting of those numbers is slightly more involved.

Since we need to format only a bit of our `<label>` content, we'll create a class and apply it to the appropriate content. In this case we'll need to create a class and apply it with a `<span>`. Here's the markup (Figure 19.4).

```
<legend><span class="number">1.</span> Patron Information</legend>
<legend><span class="number">2.</span> Item Information</legend>
```

Now for the CSS:

```
.number    {background: orange; color: #fff; padding: 2px}
```

Figure 19.4.   Adding Styled Numbers

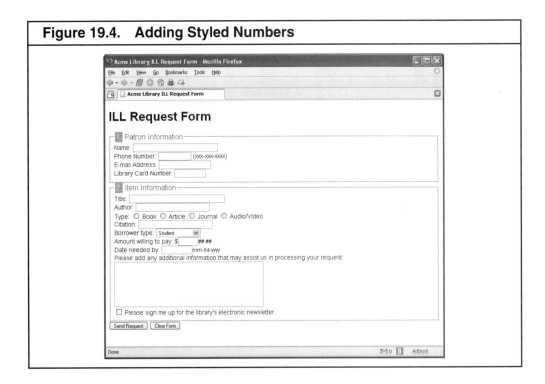

CENTERING THE CONTENT

Our next step is to center all of our content on the page. We're going to break this step down into three smaller ones: the heading, the <fieldset>s, and the buttons.

Centering the heading

Centering our single <h1> is a straightforward job that was discussed back in the text formatting chapter. All we need to do is to add one short line of CSS to take care of that (Figure 19.5)

```
h1 {text-align: center}
```

Figure 19.5.   Centering the Heading

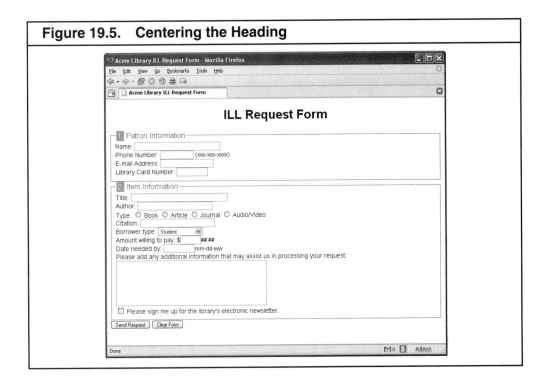

Centering the buttons

Moving the two buttons to the center of the screen is also very straightforward; it's just a matter of adding `text-align: center` to the containing `<div>`. I would *not recommend* simply adding the following line of CSS:

```
div {text-align: center}
```

Even though there is only one `<div>` in this form right now, there is a considerable chance that in the future we might need to add another.

Instead I propose we create a button ID through which we can apply our CSS (Figure 19.6).

CSS:
```
#buttons  {text-align: center}
```

XHTML:
```
<div id="buttons">
```

Figure 19.6. Centering our Buttons

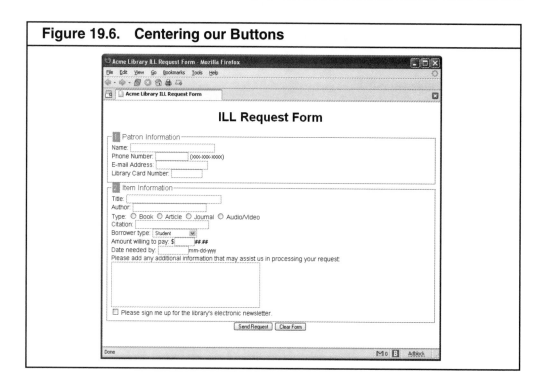

The buttons are still very close to the bottom of our second `<fieldset>`. To move them away from that `<fieldset>` we have two choices—either increase the bottom margin of the `<fieldset>` or increase the top margin of our `<div>`.

In this particular instance the better choice is to increase the top margin of our `<div>`. (We have only one `<div>` and we've already created an ID to apply to it, and, if we increase the bottom margins of `<fieldset>`s they would both be increased accordingly.)

Let's make the change, as shown in Figure 19.7.

```
#buttons   {text-align: center; margin-top: 20px}
```

Figure 19.7.   Adding some Space Above the Buttons

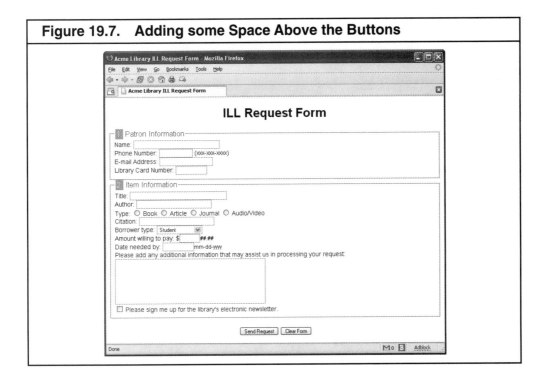

Centering the <fieldset>s

We need to set a width to our <fieldset>s. If we don't, centering the <fieldset>s will prove useless since their widths will be 100 percent of the screen. I've chosen to set my <fieldset>s to take up the middle 80 percent of the available width (Figure 19.8).

```
fieldset   {width: 80%}
```

Figure 19.8.   Setting the Width of the Form

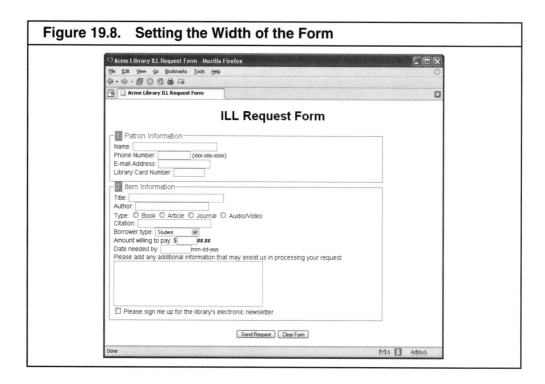

The centering itself is as simple as setting our `<fieldset>`'s left and right margins to a value of `"auto."` (Figure 19.9).

```
fieldset    {width: 80%; margin-left: auto; margin-right: auto}
```

Figure 19.9.   Our Form Centered in Firefox

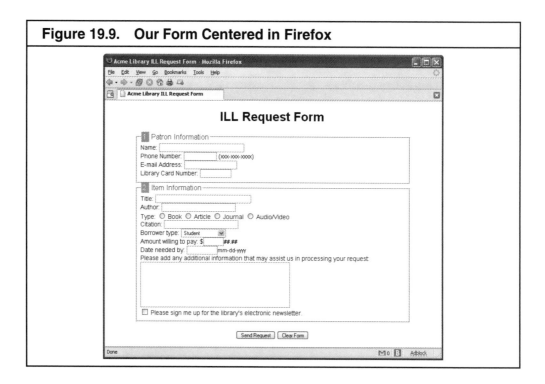

As you can see in this screenshot, Firefox provides the expected result. A problem occurs however, when we look at the same code in Internet Explorer (Figure 19.10).

Figure 19.10. Our Form Not Centered in IE

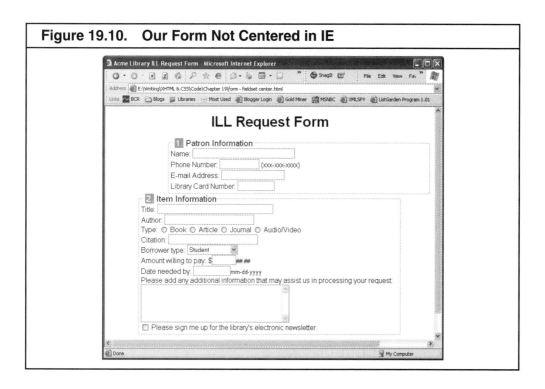

IE fails to properly center our first `<fieldset>`. In order to overcome this problem, we need to revert to placing our content into a wrapper `<div>` and centering that. I'll change the selector now from `fieldset` to `#wrapper`.

```
#wrapper   {width: 80%; margin-left: auto; margin-right: auto}
```

All I need to do now is place a starting `<div id="wrapper">` before the first `<fieldset>` and an ending `</div>` after the last `<fieldset>` to get this to apply. Once I've done that, both Firefox (Figure 19.11) and IE (Figure 19.12) will show the expected results.

```
CSS:
#wrapper   {width: 80%; margin-left: auto;
           margin-right: auto}

XHTML:
<div id="wrapper">
<fieldset>
. . .
</fieldset>
</div>
<div id="buttons">
```

Figure 19.11.   Our Form Still Centered in Firefox

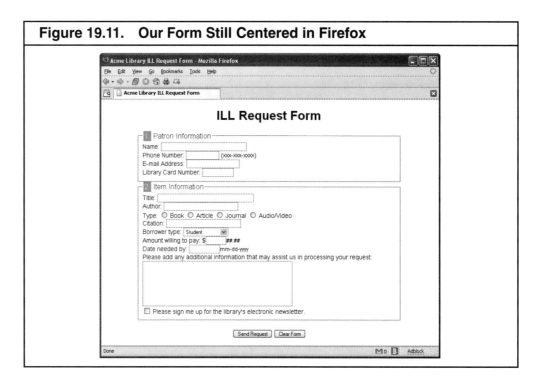

Figure 19.12.   Our Form Now Centered in IE

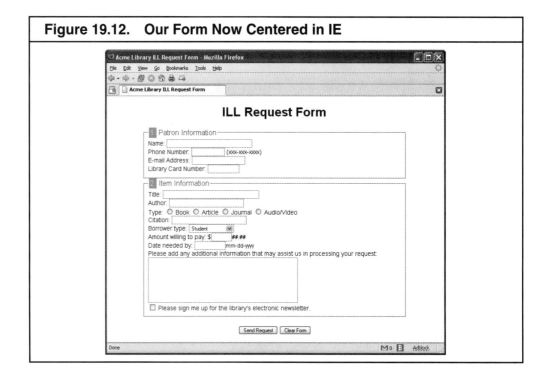

`<fieldset>` SPACING

Setting up the spacing of the `<fieldset>`s is simple. I've decided to assign each `<fieldset>` a 10px padding and 20px margins. This allows for subtle spacing without making it too obvious but without having fields nearly overlapping each other (Figure 19.13).

```
fieldset  {padding: 10px; margin-top: 20px;}
```

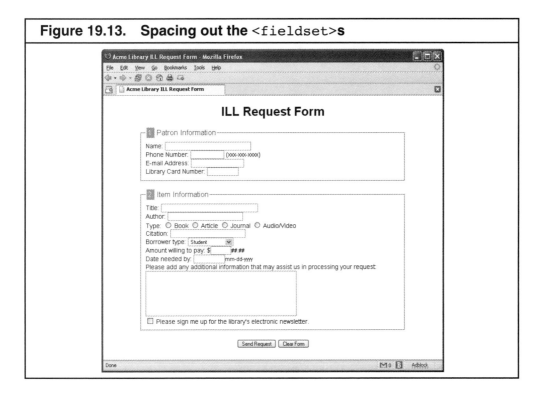

Figure 19.13.   Spacing out the `<fieldset>`s

LINING UP OUR INPUTS AND LABELS

Since we've included the `<label>` element, we can apply our CSS directly instead of adding a set of `<span>`s around all of our label text. There are a couple of steps to this process. The first is to establish a width for the labels. I've decided to allow my labels to occupy 40 percent of the available width. Since we're working within the `<fieldset>`s, that 40 percent is of the width of the `<fieldset>`s, not of the page (Figure 19.14).

```
label {width: 40%}
```

Figure 19.14.   Setting the Width of our Labels

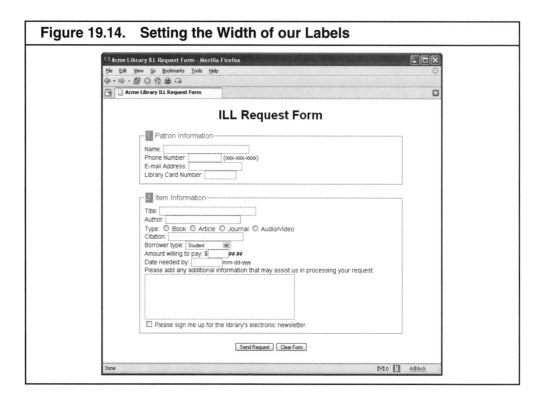

This actually accomplishes nothing by itself. We must specify that the label content appears to the left of the following content. Though the content already appears this way by default, without adding this next bit of code we won't push our nonlabel content off to the right. To do this we tell the labels to float to the left of the rest of the content (Figure 19.15). (I'll be covering the `float` property in the next chapter.)

```
label {width: 40%; float: left}
```

Figure 19.15. Floating our Labels

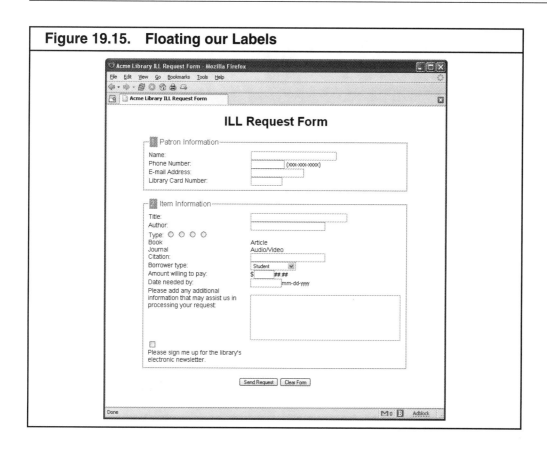

Now, to right-justify the labels, just add a text-align declaration to the label selector (Figure 19.16).

```
label {width: 40%; float: left; text-align: right}
```

Figure 19.16.   Right-justifying our Labels

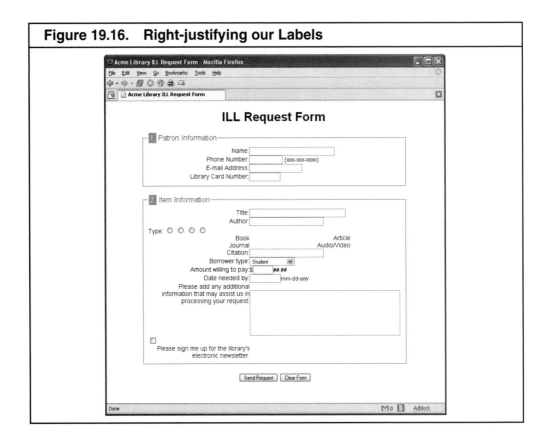

We should make one last adjustment and move the label a little bit away from the fields. We'll add a 5px padding to the right side of our labels (Figure 19.17).

```
label {width: 40%; float: left; text-align: right;
      padding-right: 5px}
```

Figure 19.17.   Adding some Padding to our Labels

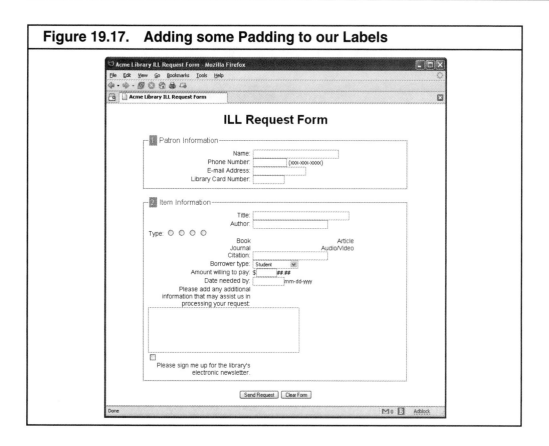

You may have noticed that we're not quite where we need to be. If you haven't noticed it yet, take another look at the form. The problem here is that we have four labels, one for each radio button on which we've set a width, float, and alignment. We want all of them to appear on one line.

Aligning the radio buttons is a multistep process. We start by telling this portion of the form to ignore any CSS we applied to label. In other words, we will create an exception. To do this we need to create a class or an ID. Since this is the only exception, we'll create an ID.

Before we create the ID, we should first determine where to put the ID. In this case we'll need to put "Type:" and its associated radio buttons into a <div>. This will allow us to identify the area we wish to change. Let's revise our code as follows.

```
<div id="type">
Type:
<input id="book" type="radio" name="type" value="book" />
<label for="book">Book</label>
<input id="article" type="radio" name="type" value="article" />
<label for="article">Article</label>
<input id="journal" type="radio" name="type" value="Journal" />
<label for="journal">Journal</label>
<input id="av" type="radio" name="type" value="a/v" />
<label for="av">Audio/Video</label>
</div>
```

Now we need to create some CSS to say that we want to undo everything we did to all of our labels on the labels within the `<div>` with an ID of `"type."` Here's the CSS:

```
#type label    {float: none; width: 0px; text-align: left}
```

This undoes the float, turns off the previously assigned width of 40 percent, and resets the alignment to left for any label within our "type" `<div>`.

The next step is to make sure that the page treats "Type:" as it does the rest of our official `<label>`s. Since we need to treat this item of text differently from others (because it is not enclosed within a `<label>` element) we need to create another exception. In this case since we're working inline, we'll put "Type:" within a span. This time I'll use a class, since there is the chance that we could create another situation like this one in the future if we were to add to our form. (You could use an ID also. Neither choice is wrong in this situation.)

```
<div id="type">
<span class="label">Type:</span>
<input id="book" type="radio" name="type" value="book" />
```

Consider what we need to do to this "label". We need to make it look like the other `<label>`s. We need to give it a width of 40 percent, float it to the left, right justify it, and give it a right padding of 5px. We've already written a declaration to cover that for the `<label>` elements. Instead of rewriting all that code, we can just add the selector for this instance to the existing declaration.

```
label, #type .label  {width: 40%; float: left;
                       text-align: right; padding-right: 5px}
```

In English, this directs the browser to apply that declaration to all <label> elements, and to any item classified as "label" that appears within anything identified as "type." Here's the result in Internet Explorer (Figure 19.18)

Figure 19.18.   The Result in FireFox

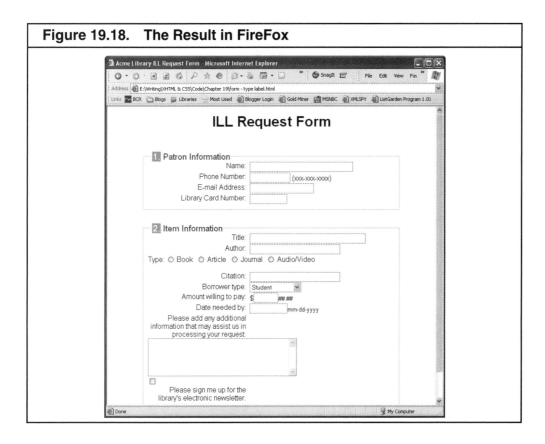

Unfortunately, here's the result in Fire Fox (Figure 19.19).

Figure 19.19.   The Results in IE

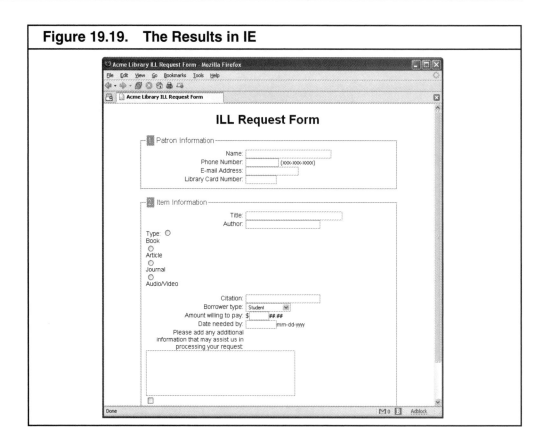

What is happening is that IE is treating the labels as block-level elements, thus putting each of them on its own line. To move them all back onto a single line we need to tell the browser to treat all `<label>`s within this `<div>` as inline elements.

```
#type label {float: none; width: 0px; text-align: left;
             display: inline}
```

Once we do this, the problem disappears (Figure 19.20).

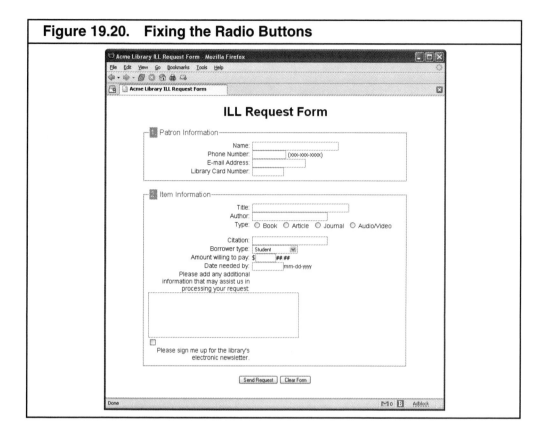

Figure 19.20.   Fixing the Radio Buttons

A FEW LAST ITEMS

As you can see, we still have to deal with two final problems, our `<textarea>` and our checkbox. Let's look at these.

To fix the problem with the `<textarea>` first we need to get rid of the `<br />` sits between the `<label>` and the `<textarea>`.

```
<label for="comments">Please add any additional information that
may assist us in processing your request:</label>
<textarea id="comments" name="comments" cols="40" rows="5"></
textarea><br />
```

Now our checkbox is in an odd location. To make sure it appear *after* the comments box, we need to add `clear="both"` to the `<br />` following our `<textarea>` (Figure 19.21).

```
</textarea><br clear="both" />
```

Figure 19.21.   Clearing the `<textarea>`

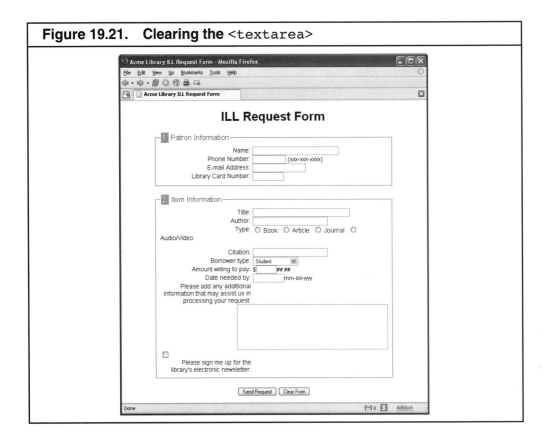

We still have one problem that can be solved by modifying the markup—the `<textarea>` is too wide. To fix this, change the value for the `cols` attribute from 40 to 35 and the `<textarea>` will fall into place (Figure 19.22).

```
<textarea id="comments" name="comments" cols="35" rows="5"></
textarea>
```

Figure 19.22. Shrinking the Width of our `<textarea>`

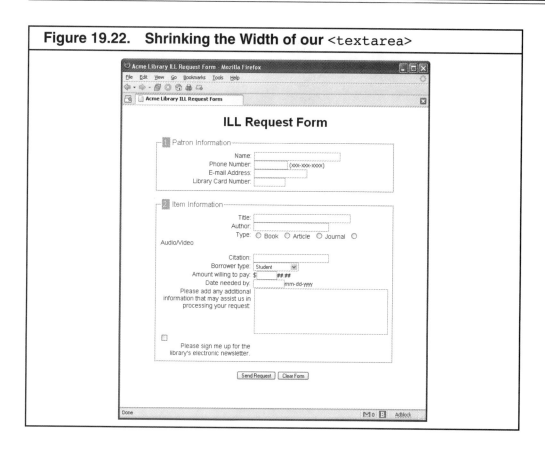

The solution to our problem with the checkbox is an XHTML one, not a CSS one. Our form has had the `<label>` on the left and the `<input>` on the right, *except* in this case. Here the checkbox is on the left while the text in on the right. The simplest solution is to just swap those two lines of code so that it better fits with our existing CSS (Figure 19.23).

```
<textarea id="comments" name="comments" cols="40" rows="5"></
textarea><br />
<label for="newsletter">Please sign me up for the library's
electronic newsletter.</label>
<input id="newsletter" type="checkbox" name="newsletter" />
</fieldset>
<insert screenshot>
```

Figure 19.23.   Our Fixed Checkbox

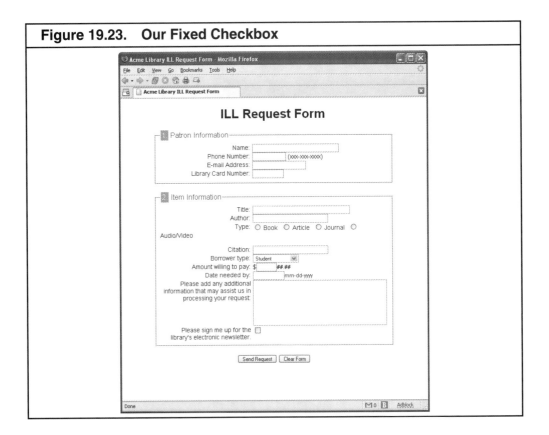

THE COMPLETE REVISED CODE

For your reference, here is the complete revised code for our form. I've embedded the CSS for ease of presentation. Of course, you can move it to a separate file and link it as appropriate.

```
<!DOCTYPE html PUBLIC "-//W3C//DTD XHTML 1.0 Transitional//EN"
"http://www.w3.org/TR/xhtml/DTD/xhtml1-transitional.dtd">
<html xmlns="http://www.w3.org/TR/xhtml" lang="en">
<head>
<title>Acme Library ILL Request Form</title>
<meta name="HTTP-Equiv" content="text/html; content="utf—8">
<style type="text/css">
legend     {font-size: 120%; color: red}
.number    {background: orange; color: #fff; padding: 2px}
h1         {text-align: center}
#buttons   {text-align: center; margin-top: 20px}
#wrapper   {width: 80%; margin-left: auto; margin-right: auto}
fieldset   {padding: 10px; margin-top: 20px;}
label, #type .label   {width: 40%; float: left;
                       text-align: right; padding-right: 5px}
#type label {float: none; width: 0px; text-align: left; display:
inline}
```

```
</style>
</head>
<body>
<h1>ILL Request Form</h1>
<form method="post" action="/cgi-bin/Yform.cgi">
<input type="hidden" name="recipient" value="msauers@bcr.org" />
<input type="hidden" name="subject" value="ILL Request" />
<input type="hidden" name="sort" value="order:name,phone,email,
card,itemTitle,author,type,citation,borrower,amount,date,
comments,newsletter" />
<input type="hidden" name="required" value="name,phone,card,
itemTitle,author,amount" />
<input type="hidden" name="env_report" value="REMOTE_ADDR,
HHTP_USER_AGENT" />
<input type="hidden" name="title" value="Thank you for submitting
your request" />
<input type="hidden" name="return_link_title" value="Back to
the library home page" />
<input type="hidden" name="return_link_url" value="http://
www.bcr.org" />
<input type="hidden" name="courtext1" value="Your request has
been sent to the ILL department for processing. Here is the
information you sent us." />
<input type="hidden" name="courfieldlist" value="yes" />
<input type="hidden" name="courtext2" value="If any of this
information is incorrect please contact the ILL department as
soon as possible so that we may correct the information." />
<input type="hidden" name="courclose" value="Sincerely," />
<input type="hidden" name="myname" value="Michael Sauers, ILL
Department Head" />
<input type="hidden" name="myemail" value="msauers@bcr.org" />
<input type="hidden" name="mywebsite" value="http://www.bcr.org/
" />
<input type="hidden" name="database" value="illdata.txt" />
<input type="hidden" name="delimiter" value="~" />
<div id="wrapper">
<fieldset>
<legend><span class="number">1.</span> Patron Information</legend>
<label for="name">Name: </label>
<input id="name" type="text" name="name" size="35" /><br />
<label for="phone">Phone Number: </label>
<input id="phone" type="text" name="phone" size="11" maxlength="11" />
(xxx-xxx-xxxx)<br />
<label for="email">E-mail Address: </label>
<input id="email" type="text" name="email" /><br />
<label for="card">Library Card Number: </label>
<input id="card" type="password" name="card" size="10"
maxlength="10" />
</fieldset>
<fieldset>
<legend><span class="number">2.</span> Item Information</legend>
<label for="itemTitle">Title: </label>
```

```
<input id="itemTitle" type="text" name="itemTitle" size="40" /
><br />
<label for="author">Author: </label>
<input id="author" type="text" name="author" size="30" /><br />
<div id="type">
<span class="label">Type:</span>
<input id="book" type="radio" name="type" value="book" />
<label for="book">Book</label>
<input id="article" type="radio" name="type" value="article" />
<label for="article">Article</label>
<input id="journal" type="radio" name="type" value="Journal" />
<label for="journal">Journal</label>
<input id="av" type="radio" name="type" value="a/v" />
<label for="av">Audio/Video</label>
</div>
<br />
<label for="citation">Citation: </label>
<input id="citation" type="text" name="citation" size="30" /><br />
<label for="borrower">Borrower type: </label>
<select id="borrower" name="borrower">
<option>Adjunct Faculty</option>
<option>Faculty</option>
<option>Staff</option>
<option selected="true">Student</option>
<option>Public</option>
</select>
<br />
<label for="amount">Amount willing to pay: </label>
$<input id="amount" type="text" name="amount" size="5"
maxlength="5" /><small>##.##</small><br />
<label for="date">Date needed by: </label>
<input id="date" type="text" name="date" size="10" maxlength="10"
/><small>mm-dd-yyyy</small><br />
<label for="comments">Please add any additional information that
may assist us in processing your request:</label>
<textarea style="" id="comments" name="comments" cols="35"
rows="5"></textarea><br clear="both" />
<label for="newsletter">Please sign me up for the library's
electronic newsletter.</label>
<input id="newsletter" type="checkbox" name="newsletter" />
</fieldset>
</div>
<div id="buttons">
<input type="submit" value="Send Request" />
<input type="reset" value="Clear Form" />
</div>
</form>
</body>
</html>
```

20

Positioning

WHAT IS POSITIONING?

There are two ways to approach positioning content within a document when using CSS: floating and positioning. Using floating, you take your content and send it to one side or the other of the window and have the rest of your content flow around it. Positioning allows you to specifically direct the item to appear in a particular location within the document, either relative to its original location or at specific coordinates within the window.

The material in this chapter can get very complicated. In the interest of keeping to the mission of this book—teaching the essentials—I've decided to focus more on the concept of floating than on positioning. Floating causes fewer cross-browser annoyances than positioning does in today's browsers. This chapter will provide a basic understanding of both concepts but you will need to do more research if you intend to use them extensively. (An excellent tutorial can be found at BrainJar.com <www.brainjar.com/css/positioning/default.asp>).

FLOATING CONTENT

The premise of floating content in CSS is similar to using an align attribute on an image in XHTML. (In fact, you can use the CSS float property to replace the align attribute on an image.) The difference is that in CSS you can float anything, whereas in XHTML you can only give this effect to an image.

What floating content does is to take the content out of the page's flow and place it to either the left or the right side, thus forcing the adjacent content to wrap around the floated content. The following are three different ways you can take advantage of the float property: drop-caps, figures and sidebars, and columns.

DROP-CAPS

Drop-caps are typically used in books to decorate the first letter of a chapter. These letters, usually capitals, are significantly larger than the rest of the text in the chapter; they do not extend above the top of the text on the first line, and are sometimes decorated, perhaps as simply as being displayed in a different font.

Here's a screenshot of what we'll accomplish in this example (Figure 20.1).

Figure 20.1.   A Drop-cap

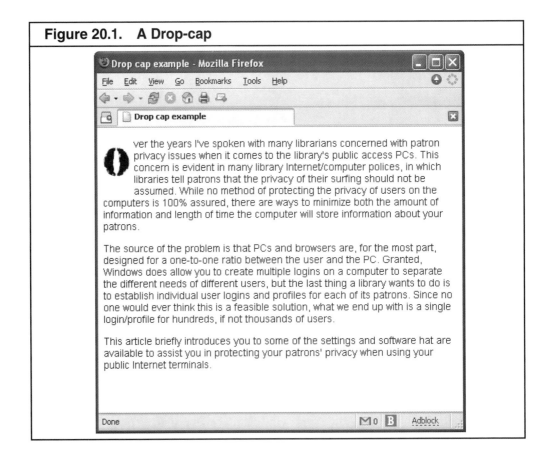

(The complete code for this result is at the end of this section.)

To do this, we first need to specify that we want to change only the first letter of the first paragraph of our document. Here's the CSS code I'll use to do this.

```
p.start:first-letter  { }
```

This selector may look confusing at first. The first thing to note is that `:first-letter` is a pseudo-selector, similar to `:visited` on an anchor. In this case we're specifying that the following declaration will affect only the first letter of something. Translated into English, this selector reads "the first letter of any paragraph classified as "start." (I've used a class instead of an ID just in case we decide to add another drop-cap elsewhere within the document.)

We can start building the declaration by changing the font of the letter. I've selected the font "rubber stamp let," which happens to be on my computer. If you do not have this font you'll want to select a different one (Figure 20.2).

```
p.start:first-letter    {font-family: "rubber stamp let"}
```

Figure 20.2.   Changing the Font of our First Letter

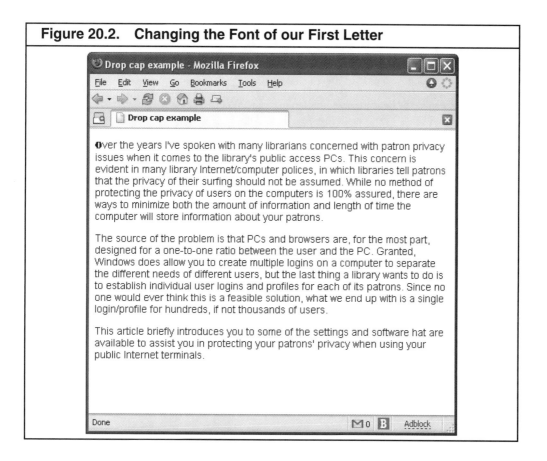

Next we'll increase the size of the letter, in this case to 400 percent. Depending on the font you select, how much you need to increase the font-size to yield the same effect will vary (Figure 20.3).

```
p.start:first-letter    {font-family: "rubber stamp let";
                         font-size: 400%}
```

Figure 20.3.   Increasing the Size of our First Letter

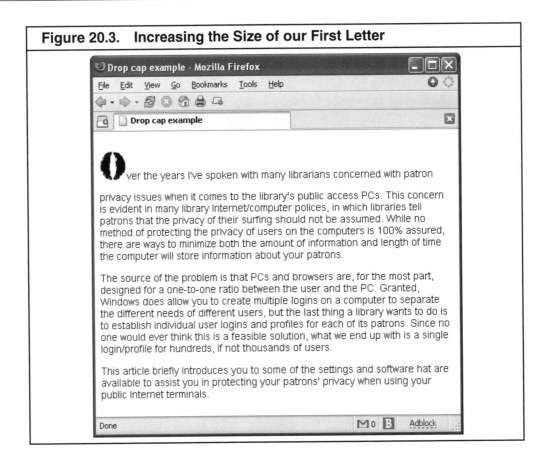

We now have a big letter in the font we'd like but as you can see, the baseline of this letter is aligning with the rest of the text on that line. What we need to do is have the letter lower itself on the line and have the rest of the text wrap around it. This is where the float property becomes useful.

The float property has two values you can choose from: left and right. In this case, left is the appropriate choice. (If you're not sure why, try using the right value and see what happens.) (See Figure 20.4.)

```
p.start:first-letter   {font-family: "rubber stamp let";
                        font-size: 400%; float: left}
```

Figure 20.4.   Floating our First Letter to the Left

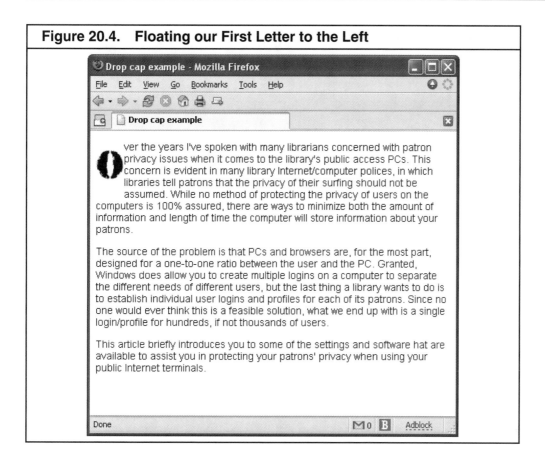

As a final touch, I'll give the letter some right-padding just to space it out from the rest of the paragraph (Figure 20.5).

```
p.start:first-letter   {font-family: "rubber stamp let";
                        font-size: 400%; float: left;
                        padding-right: 5px}
```

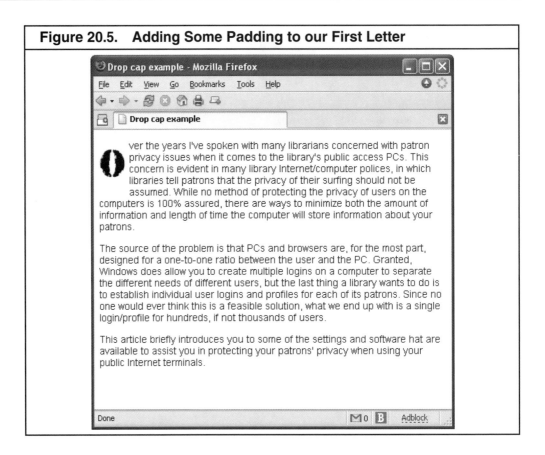

Figure 20.5.   Adding Some Padding to our First Letter

With that last change we have the effect we're looking for. Here's the complete code for the document.

```
<!DOCTYPE html PUBLIC "-//W3C//DTD XHTML 1.0 Transitional//EN"
"http://www.w3.org/1999/xhtml/DTD/xhtml1-transitional.dtd">
<html xmlns="http://www.w3.org/1999/xhtml" lang="en" xml:lang="en">
<head>
<title>Drop cap example</title>
<meta http-equiv="Content-Type" content="text/html; charset=utf-8" />
<style type="text/css">
p.start:first-letter  {font-family: "rubber stamp let";
                       font-size: 400%; float: left;
                       padding-right: 5px}
</style>
</head>
<body>
<p class="start">Over the years I've spoken with many librarians
concerned with patron privacy issues when it comes to the library's
public access PCs. This concern is evident in many library Internet/
computer polices, in which libraries tell patrons that the privacy
of their surfing should not be assumed. While no method of protect-
ing the privacy of users on the computers is 100% assured, there
are ways to minimize both the amount of information and length of
time the computer will store information about your patrons.</p>
<p>The source of the problem is that PCs and browsers are, for
```

the most part, designed for a one-to-one ratio between the user and the PC. Granted, Windows does allow you to create multiple logins on a computer to separate the different needs of different users, but the last thing a library wants to do is to establish individual user logins and profiles for each of its patrons. Since no one would ever think this is a feasible solution, what we end up with is a single login/profile for hundreds, if not thousands, of users. </p>
<p>This article briefly introduces you to some of the settings and software that are available to assist you in protecting your patrons' privacy when using your public Internet terminals. </p>
</body>
</html>

SIDEBARS

Let's take what we just learned by creating a drop-cap and apply that to a different situation. Both figures and sidebars use the same basic CSS code, but a figure has a graphic with a caption while a sidebar is just text. (Of course, these features can be mixed and matched, depending on your design requirements.)

A sidebar example

First, let's take a look at what we're hoping to accomplish (Figure 20.6).

Figure 20.6.   A Sidebar

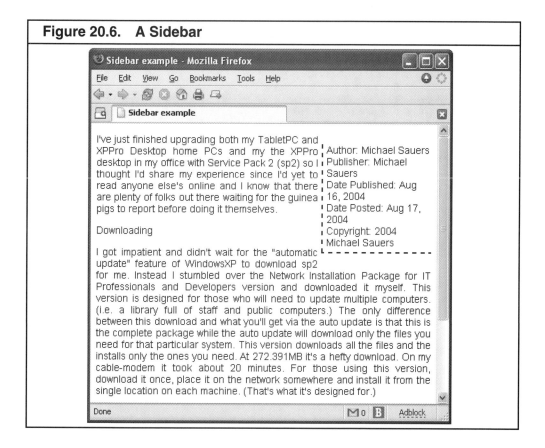

In this example, we have a main body of text, but a sidebar with different text. This text has both a dashed border on both the left and the bottom to separate it from the main body text. (The complete code for this result is at the end of this section. For now we'll just examine the CSS specific to this result.)

Let's look at each step in creating this design. First, we need to add some CSS to set full justification on the body of the document (Figure 20.7).

```
body {text-align: justify}
```

Figure 20.7.   Fully Justifying our Text

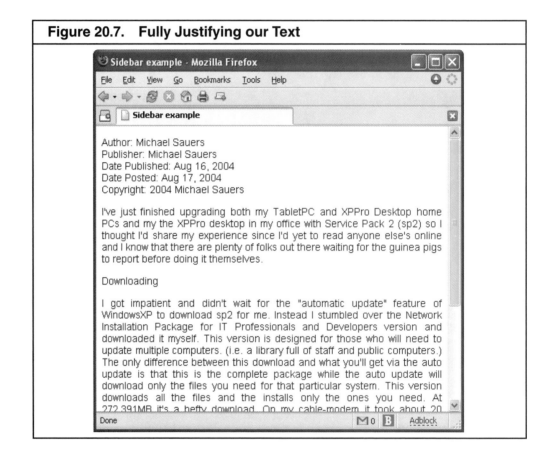

Next we identify the appropriate paragraph containing the sidebar text as having a class of sidebar. (I've used a class here in case I'd want to add another sidebar later in the document.)

An important point to make here is that when you are floating part of your document and leaving the rest in its default location, you need to code the floated content immediately before the content you want to wrap around it. In this case, since we intend for the top of the floated sidebar to align with the top of the first paragraph, we need to code the sidebar immediately before the first paragraph. If we wanted to align the top of the sidebar with the top of the second paragraph we'd need to code the first paragraph, then the sidebar, then the second paragraph. (Remember, text-to-speech browsers will read your content in the *order coded*, not the order presented, so place your sidebars carefully in your code.)

To identify my sidebar I've added <p class="sidebar"> to my XHTML. The next CSS step is to create the sidebar selector.

```
body {text-align: justify}
.sidebar {}
```

The first thing we should do to the sidebar is to give it a specific width. Without specifying a width, the sidebar will default to the width of its content, which in many cases will be the width of the window, completely negating the point of floating the information off to the side (Figure 20.8).

```
body       {text-align: justify}
.sidebar   {width: 150px}
```

Figure 20.8.   Setting the Width of our Sidebar

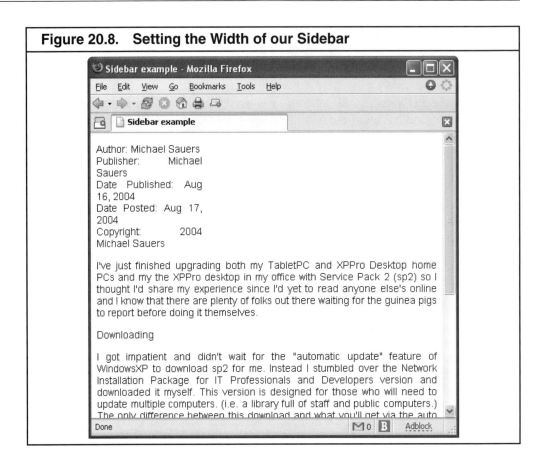

Next let's move the content by instructing it to float off to the right (Figure 20.9).

```
body        {text-align: justify}
.sidebar    {width: 150px; float: right}
```

Figure 20.9.   Floating our Sidebar to the Right

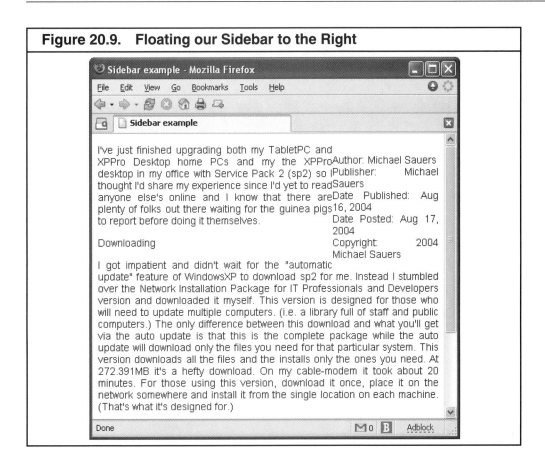

Looking back at our original screenshot, you may notice that the content of the sidebar is left-justified. All we need to do is add a text-align property to make that happen (Figure 20.10).

```
body      {text-align: justify}
.sidebar  {width: 150px; float: right; text-align: left}
```

Figure 20.10.   Left-justifying our Sidebar Text

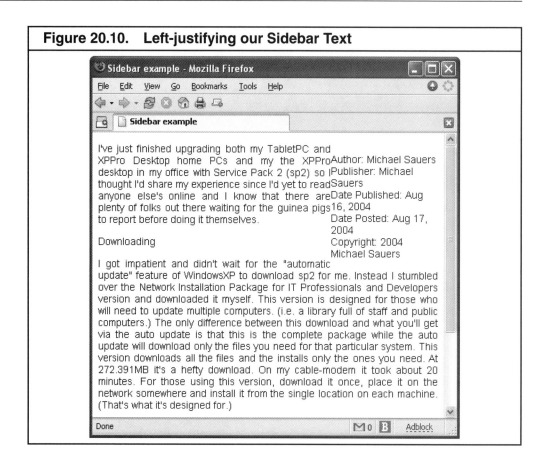

The next step is to add the border on the left and bottom sides (Figure 20.11).

```
body       {text-align: justify}
.sidebar   {width: 150px; float: right; text-align: left;
            border-left: 2px black dashed;
            border-bottom: 2px black dashed}
```

Figure 20.11.   Adding a Right and Bottom Border to our Sidebar

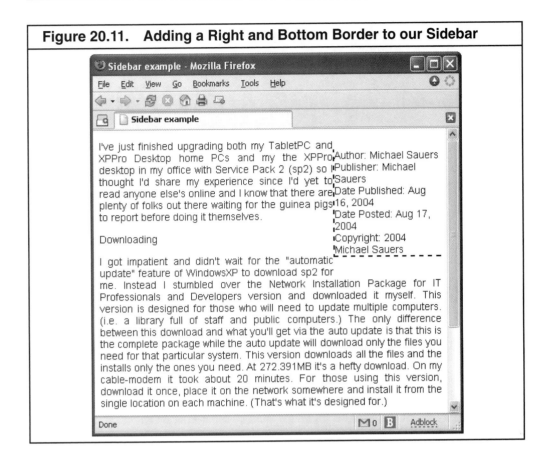

For some fine-tuning of the spacing I've added some left and bottom padding to move the sidebar content away from its border and a small left margin to move the border away from the body content (Figure 20.12).

```
body       {text-align: justify}
.sidebar   {width: 150px; float: right; text-align: left;
            border-left: 2px black dashed;
            border-bottom: 2px black dashed;
            padding-left: 5px; padding-bottom: 5px;
            margin-left: 5px}
```

Figure 20.12. Adding some Padding to and Increasing the Left Margin of our Sidebar

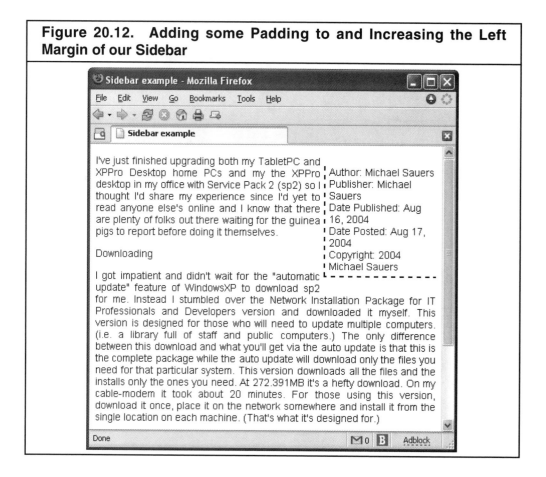

Here's the complete code:

```
<!DOCTYPE html PUBLIC "-//W3C//DTD XHTML 1.0 Transitional//EN"
"http://www.w3.org/1999/xhtml/DTD/xhtml1-transitional.dtd">
<html  xmlns="http://www.w3.org/1999/xhtml"  lang="en"
xml:lang="en">
<head>
<title>Sidebar example</title>
<meta http-equiv="Content-Type" content="text/html; charset=utf-
8" />
<style type="text/css">
body      {text-align: justify}
.sidebar  {width: 150px; float: right; text-align: left;
           border-left: 2px black dashed;
           border-bottom: 2px black dashed;
           padding-left: 5px; padding-bottom: 5px;
           margin-left: 5px}
</style>
</head>
<body>
<p class="sidebar">Author: Michael Sauers<br />Publisher: Michael
Sauers <br />Date Published: Aug 16, 2004<br />Date Posted: Aug
17, 2004 <br />Copyright: 2004 Michael Sauers </p>
```

```
<p>I've just finished upgrading both my TabletPC and XPPro
Desktop home PCs and my XPPro desktop in my office with Service
Pack 2 (sp2) so I thought I'd share my experience since I'd yet
to read anyone else's online and I know that there are plenty
of folks out there waiting for the guinea pigs to report before
doing it themselves.</p>
<p>Downloading</p>
<p>I got impatient and didn't wait for the "automatic update"
feature of WindowsXP to download sp2 for me. Instead I stumbled
over the Network Installation Package for IT Professionals and
Developers version and downloaded it myself. This version is
designed for those who will need to update multiple computers.
(I.e., a library full of staff and public computers.) The only
difference between this download and what you'll get via the
auto update is that this is the complete package while the auto
update will download only the files you need for that particu-
lar system. This version downloads all the files and the in-
stalls only the ones you need. At 272.391MB it's a hefty download.
On my cable-modem it took about 20 minutes. For those using
this version, download it once, place it on the network some-
where and install it from the single location on each machine.
(That's what it's designed for.)</p>
<p>Installation</p>
<p>The installation itself took a total of just 16 minutes on
my desktop. The uncompress and install itself took 11 minutes
while the reboot and post-install functions took five minutes.
(I forgot to time the install on my Tablet but it wasn't much
longer than that. The additional time would be a result of the
fact that the Tablet gets a few more updates than a regular
desktop.) </p>
</body>
</html>
```

Figures

A figure is coded similarly to a sidebar in that they both float off to one side, but in this case we're floating a graphic with a caption, so the requirements are slightly different. (Again, the full code with markup is after the completed example.)

Let's take a look at what we're designing this time (Figure 20.13).

Figure 20.13.   **A Figure**

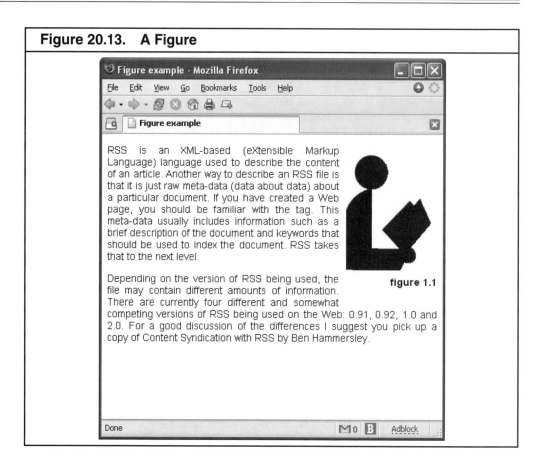

In this example, we've floated an image and a caption to the right, but there is no border and the caption is both bolded and right-justified to the image. Here's the CSS we need to add.

As with the sidebar example, we'll set the body to full justification and assign a class to the paragraph containing the figure and its caption. For these steps, we need to include the following CSS and XHTML (Figure 20.14).

```
CSS:
body   {text-align: justify}
.figure   {}

XHTML:
<p class="figure">
```

Figure 20.14. Getting Started with our Figure

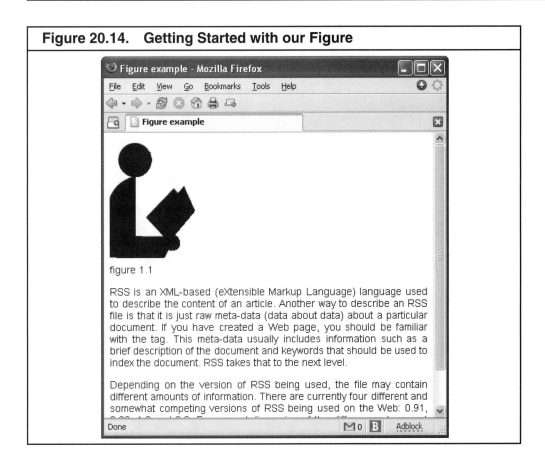

In this situation I am not going to specify a width. First, if the document has multiple figures, each of their contained images will be of different widths. (If all of your images in all of your figures are of the same width, feel free to add a width property to your figure class.) Second, my captions will be short and never longer than the width of the image. (If this is not true for a particular figure, feel free to set a width for the paragraph as an inline style on the paragraph itself.) By holding this width to no larger than the width of the image, we cause the caption text to wrap appropriately under the image.

The next step in this case is to move the figure off to the right (Figure 20.15).

```
body       {text-align: justify}
.figure    {float: right}
```

Figure 20.15.   Floating our Figure

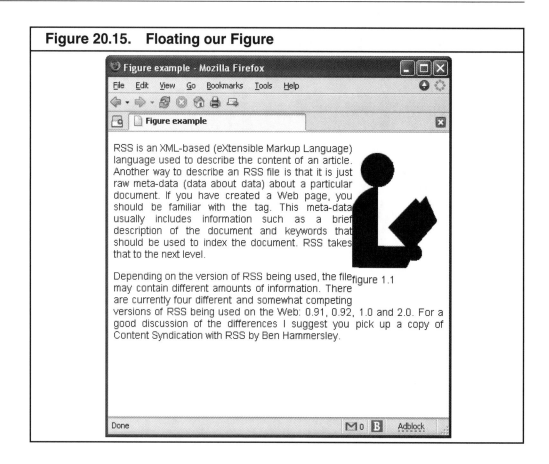

Now we need to bold and right-justify the text (Figure 20.16).

```
body       {text-align: justify}
.figure    {float: right; text-align: right;
            font-weight: bold}
```

Figure 20.16. Aligning and Bolding our Figure's Caption

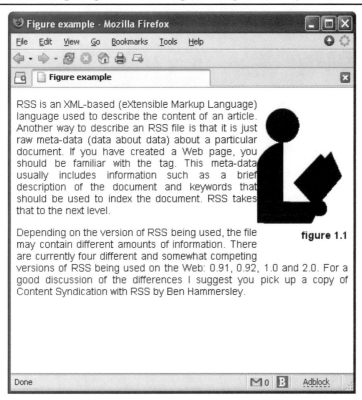

Lastly, we'll add some padding to provide space between the figure's content and the body text (Figure 20.17).

```
body       {text-align: justify}
.figure    {float: right; text-align: right;
            font-weight: bold; padding-left: 10px;
            padding-bottom: 5px}
```

Figure 20.17.   Adding some Padding to our Figure

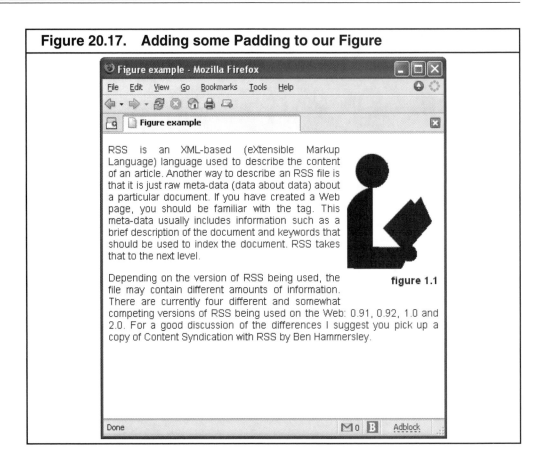

Now we have our figure looking the way we want it. Here's the full code.

```
<!DOCTYPE html PUBLIC "-//W3C//DTD XHTML
1.0 Transitional//EN" "http://www.w3.org/1999/xhtml/DTD/xhtml1-
transitional.dtd">
<html  xmlns="http://www.w3.org/1999/xhtml"  lang="en"
xml:lang="en">
<head>
<title>Figure example</title>
<meta http-equiv="Content-Type" content="text/html; charset=utf-
8" />
<style type="text/css">
body      {text-align: justify}
.figure   {float: right; text-align: right;
           font-weight: bold; padding-left: 10px;
           padding-bottom: 5px;}
</style>
</head>
<body>
<p class="figure"><img src="library.gif" alt="Library Symbol"
/><br />figure 1.1</p>
<p>RSS is an XML-based (eXtensible Markup Language) language
used to describe the content of an article. Another way to de-
scribe an RSS file is that it is just raw metadata (data about
data) about a particular document. If you have created a Web
```

page, you should be familiar with the <meta> tag. This metadata usually includes information such as a brief description of the document and keywords that should be used to index the document. RSS takes that to the next level.</p>

<p>Depending on the version of RSS being used, the file may contain different amounts of information. There are currently four different and somewhat competing versions of RSS being used on the Web: 0.91, 0.92, 1.0 and 2.0. For a good discussion of the differences I suggest you pick up a copy of Content Syndication with RSS by Ben Hammersley.</p>

</body>
</html>

COLUMNS

There are several different ways to use CSS to create columns, thus avoiding the use of tables in your markup. The use of floats is one of those methods.

Take a look at the following code. It's a bit long, but for this example to work well, I need a lot of content (Figure 20.18).

```
<!DOCTYPE html PUBLIC "-//W3C//DTD XHTML
1.0 Transitional//EN" "http://www.w3.org/1999/xhtml/DTD/xhtml1-
transitional.dtd">
<html xmlns="http://www.w3.org/1999/xhtml" lang="en" xml:lang="en">
<head>
<title>Creating columns using CSS floats</title>
<meta http-equiv="Content-Type" content="text/html; charset=utf-8" />
<style type="text/css">
</style>
</head>
<body>
<div id="left">
<p><b>Don't Doesn't Work</b></p>
<p><i>The opinions expressed in this article are the author's
alone and do not reflect the opinions of The Bibliographical
Center for Research, The Aurora Public Library or The Arapahoe
Library District.</i></p>
<p>Back in 1991 I was taking an American literature class at
SUNY Brockport. We had read the assigned book for the week, Upton
Sinclair's The Jungle, and the instructor asked us why Sinclair
had started a novel that contained so much horror, sadness and
despair with a happy scene of a wedding reception. What she
expected to hear from me was something about the contrast between
their work and non-work lives. My answer to her was that Sinclair
just wanted to hook the reader so they would read the rest of the
book; starting out the novel on a depressing note would not
encourage readers to continue reading. I'm sure that every American
literature professor is rolling their eyes, or rolling over in
their grave over my analysis of the opening of this book, but I
still stick by this theory.1 Looking back on this situation I can
see the early formation of my distinct lack of support for over-
analyzing problems. In my life I've come to realize that too many
people over-analyze a problem when trying to come up with a
```

solution, when many times the answer is straightforward or already exists. I believe this applies to the "problems" associated with providing Internet access to patrons in public libraries. [Please note: In this article I am specifically dealing only with public libraries. I do accept that in private institutions, schools and higher education that the situation is different and a different solution may need to be provided.] </p>

<p>For the past eleven years, through graduate school, my period as an independent consultant in Las Vegas, NV, board member of the Aurora Public Library, reference desk volunteer at the Arapahoe Library District and the past seven years as the Internet Trainer for the Bibliographical Center for Research (BCR), I have been keeping an eye on the state of Internet access policies in public libraries in the U.S. I've read literally hundreds of policies, looking at them from both the point of view of a librarian, board member and a patron. I've talked to librarians, library staff, directors and board members. We discussed the issues involved and the policies that have been created. We've talked informally and in a classroom environment in my Internet Access Policies workshop. I've heard the horror stories and the success stories. I've heard about the patrons causing trouble and I've heard about the librarians having to do battle with their board, city or county in order just to provide access in the first place. I'm tempted to say that I've heard it all and that you couldn't tell me something new, but I know better than that. </p>

<p>From all of this input I've come to this simple conclusion: a public library's Internet access policy is pointless and its creation was a waste of time that could have better been spent working on the library's budget. I will admit that the discussion that happens during the creation of a policy (assuming discussion happened and that the policy was not set by decree) is worthy of the time taken, since it raises many important issues. (The policy of whether or not to filter, especially in light of CIPA, is not an issue I'll be addressing in this article. I'll be focusing on other issues that sit outside of the filtering debate.) The policy itself, however, I'll show is not. Many of you may believe my opinion to be extreme, but give me the chance to convince you. </p>

<p>One of the points that I make in my class and book titled Using the Internet as a Reference Tool is that computers—and the Internet—are just tools that we already have the necessary skills to use. It is simply the application of those skills that we, as librarians, need to work on. The fact that the information is electronically accessed is irrelevant to the issue. I hold that this is also true when it comes to patron access to that information. </p>

<p>Today, a significant majority of Internet access policies contain a list of things that the patron cannot do or cannot access. No porn, no chat, no e-mail; "research only."2 All this accomplishes is to turn the library staff into computer police. Staffs are busy enough as it is trying to assist patrons. They do not have the time, or in many cases the desire, to be controlling what they can and cannot do. I would even argue that we do not have the authority to say what information a patron can and cannot access. </p>

<p>This is not to say that I support letting the patrons do whatever they want, without consequences. Illegal is illegal.

However, let's for a moment take the computer out of the picture. For example, would you, as a librarian look over the shoulder of a patron to see whether the book they were reading was "appropriate?"3 No librarian I've ever asked has answered yes to this question. However, when it comes to what the patron is viewing on the computer, many librarians seem to be willing to do exactly that. I've even recently read a policy that stated "All Internet users must have a current library card, or pay $2.00/hour for use." Now, when I'm traveling and I walk into a library in another town, no one has yet to charge me for taking a book off the shelf and reading it in the library. Yet when it comes to the computers I'll be charged for using them? Why the discrepancy? </p>

<p>Does your library have a behavior policy? If you do, chances are good that this policy is rather generic and states that patrons should not perform any action that causes a disturbance for other library patrons, whether through action or speech. If a group of teens are talking in the library loud enough to disturb other patrons, they are asked to quiet down. If they are holding a normal conversation, not disturbing anyone else, they are left alone.4</p>

<p>Well, why can't this behavioral policy, which has been in most libraries for years, be applied to the use of the Internet? Stated another way: as long as the patron isn't bothering anyone, why can't we just leave him or her alone? When their actions elevate to the level of causing a disturbance then, and only then, should the librarian become involved. I am still not encouraging allowing everything. Illegal is still illegal and should be dealt with appropriately, by reporting the problem to the appropriate authorities. </p>

</div>

<div id="right">

<p>I believe that use of this policy in this way has several benefits for the library. First, this reduces the need for library staff to act as police. With this policy, library staff can assist patrons when they ask for it, or become involved when there is a perceived problem. No problem or request, no involvement. </p>

<p>Second, by using a behavioral policy, this gives the library additional flexibility than a "this is what you can't do" policy. If the policy states "no porn" and the student is doing a report on modern erotic art, the librarian is, by policy, forced to prevent the patron from doing their work. By treating it as a behavioral issue, the librarian, in most cases, will not become involved at all. If, however, another patron complains about what that student is looking at on their screen, the librarian can use their professional judgment in balancing the needs of the student against the complaint made and deal with the situation as he or she sees fit. </p>

<p>The other problem that may arise from having a "don't" list is that of exceptions. The moment a librarian creates an exception for one patron they open the door for other patrons to complain with "But you let them do it. Why won't you let me?" When your policy has flexibility built in, you're on much better footing when dealing with such a situation. </p>

<p>Several libraries use this method of dealing with potential problems in their library. In all of the cases I've encountered, the libraries have reported significant success with the method and are glad they chose to use their existing policy this way. </p>

```
<p>Conclusion:<br />
In many libraries today policies regarding Internet access by
patrons have been over-analyzed and over-thought. The result of
this has been to turn library staff into a police force, reducing
the time available to perform many other important tasks. In
these cases the computer is being treated differently than other
library resources. By removing the computer from the equation,
most libraries will realize that they already have a policy on
library behavior that can be applied to computer and Internet
access related problems. This policy method removes the need for
library staff to be police and gives that staff additional flex-
ibility to deal with problems as they arise.</p>
<hr />
<p>Endnotes:<br />
1. Actually, since I've become a published author myself I've modi-
fied this theory somewhat. I no longer believe that it was Sinclair's
idea to start with a happy scene. More likely it was his publisher
or editor that suggested it. "Uh, Up, can I call you Up? No? Well,
Mr. Sinclair, we love the book and plan to publish it for you, we'd
just like you to make a few changes. First, take out all the
socialism. The political climate just isn't right. Okay? Also, the
beginning's a bit of a downer. Could you add a chapter at the
beginning that hooks the reader? Maybe a wedding reception . . . " </p>
<p>2. I find the concept of "research only" on a public library
computer to be contradictory to the library's mission. For any-
one that believes a "research only" policy is a good one I ask
this: what is the "research" value of Danielle Steel books?
Public libraries have always had an entertainment value and the
computers in the library should be no different. Also, by saying
"research only" we have now assigned ourselves the job of deter-
mining whether or not what the patron is doing is research.
Something I don't believe we have the right to do. </p>
<p>For those librarians concerned with limited number of comput-
ers and giving those that need access the access, I am in full
support of time limits on the computers. This gives every patron
a fair chance to use the available computers and do what they
need to do. What they do with their time however, is not our
business unless it causes a disturbance. </p>
<p>3. We have a "banned book week." Why don't we have a "Banned
Web Site Week." Here is another example of how we treat computers
differently from other library resources. </p>
<p>4. Many libraries also completely ban cell phone use in the
library. The trouble is, it's the behavior of the cell phone
user, the not cell phone itself that's the problem. I was once
told to leave a library with my cell phone because I was using
it. I had left it on vibrate and was whispering into the phone.
Trouble is, I was having trouble hearing the person on the other
end due to the gaggle of young girls "doing their homework" at a
table ten feet away from me. I was asked to stop what I was doing
yet they were not despite the fact that they were causing more of
a disturbance than I was. </p>
</div>
</body>
</html>
```

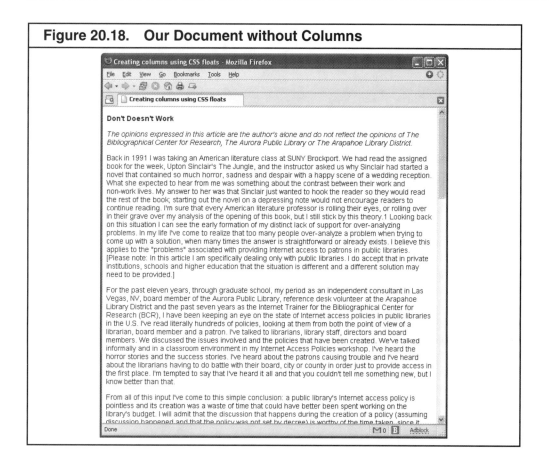

Figure 20.18. Our Document without Columns

The important part of this code is not the content itself. The important lines are the following:

```
<div id="left">
. . .
</div>
<div id="right">
. . .
</div>
```

This document contains 20 paragraphs of body content. The first ten are in the `<div>` with an ID of "left." The last ten are in a `<div>` with an ID of "right." Now that my content has been placed into two different boxes, the key is to size and place those boxes to fit my two-column design.

At this point it is obvious that we need to float something but, which of the two `<div>`s should we float? The problem is that the two `<div>`s do not have the same amount of content and therefore will be different lengths. If we were to float the right `<div>` the content of the left `<div>` would wrap around it. We could float the left `<div>` but what if we later edit our document and add more content on the right? If the right `<div>` were to become the larger of the two, it would start to wrap around the content of the left `<div>`. The solution, then, is to float *both* of the `<div>`s.

Before we can do this, we must assign a width to each of our `<div>`s. Unless you have very specific size requirements, the best approach is to give these widths a percentage value. This will keep our columns flexible and allow them to adjust to the available window space. I suggest setting each of the `<div>`s to a 48 percent width (Figure 20.19).

```
#left  {width: 48%}
#right {width: 48%}
```

Figure 20.19.   Setting the Width of our Columns

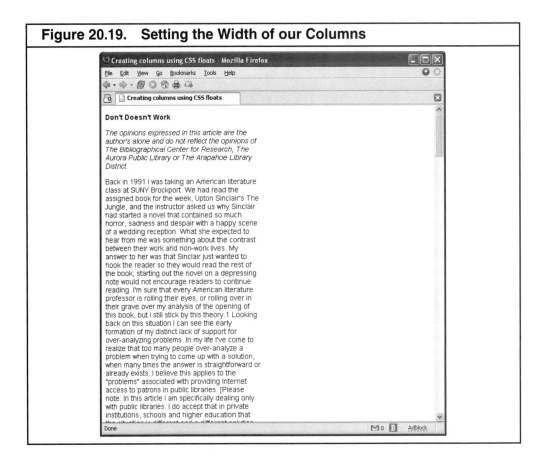

What we need to do next is to float each of our `<div>`s accordingly (Figure 20.20).

```
#left  {width: 48%; float: left}
#right {width: 48%; float: right}
```

Figure 20.20. Floating our Columns

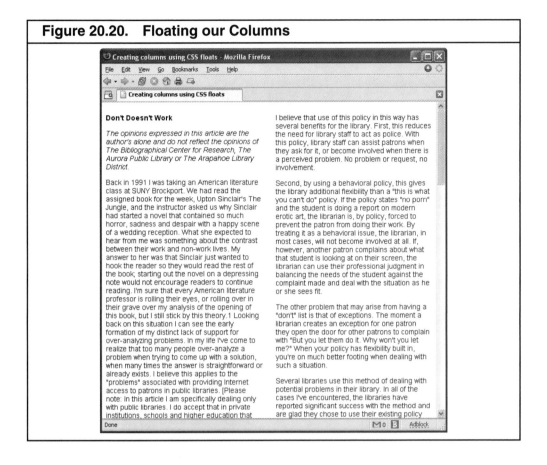

If you're wondering why I didn't set the widths to 50 percent each, take a look at this screenshot and see what that would do (Figure 20.21).

Figure 20.21. Our Columns with 50 Percent Widths in IE.

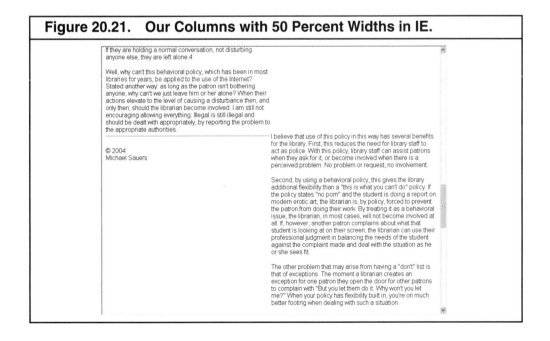

When we set the combined widths to equal to (or greater than) 100 percent, we're not taking into account the padding and margins automatically built into our `<div>`s by the browser. Once that tiny bit of spacing is added, the total becomes larger than 100 percent. Since the `<div>`s are not allowed to overlap, the right `<div>` will start in the first location where there is space which is below the left `<div>`.

Now that we have two columns, let's try putting a footer at the bottom of the document. This footer should consist of a horizontal rule and a paragraph containing a copyright statement and your name. From a markup perspective, since we want the footer to appear after both of our columns, we need to add the following to our code.

```
</div>
<hr />
<p>&copy; 2004<br />
Michael Sauers</p>
</body>
</html>
```

Before we look at the results, ask yourself where this new content is going to appear? When you have the answer in your head, look at the following screenshot and see if it matches your answer (Figure 20.22).

Figure 20.22.   Our Footer Displayed in the Wrong Location on the Screen

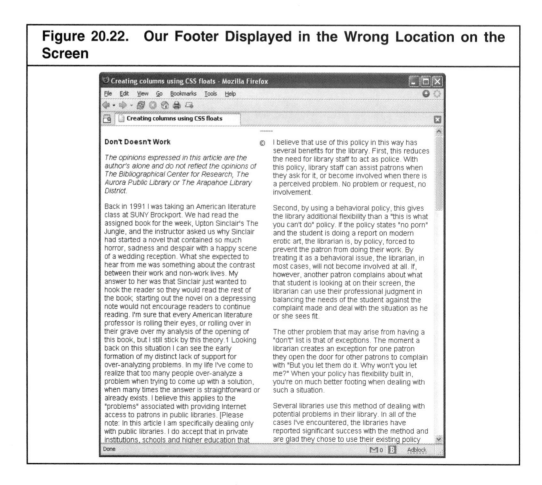

The key is to remember that, when you float something, you take it out of the normal flow of the document. The cursor is left wherever it was before, but moved out of the way of the floated content, since overlaps are not allowed.

Picture your cursor in the upper-left corner of the window. Now place the content in the left `<div>` and then picture where the cursor has been moved to. It will now be on the first line of the window but just to the right of the left `<div>`. This is exactly where the `<hr>` is being displayed. The rest of the content is being displayed in that gutter because that's where the cursor is. It's moving vertically because this content cannot overlap the right `<div>` and is therefore printing where there is room, forced lower and lower on the page.

The solution to this problem is both elegant and simple. What we need to do is add just one line of markup and CSS. Take a look at the following.

```
</div>
<br style="clear: both" />
<hr />
```

What we've done is insert a line break but, using some inline CSS, told the browser to keep breaking until it can clear all content on both the left and right sides. (This is the CSS equivalent of the `clear` attribute.) With this addition we finally have the result we want (Figure 20.23).

Figure 20.23.   Our Footer Where it Should Be

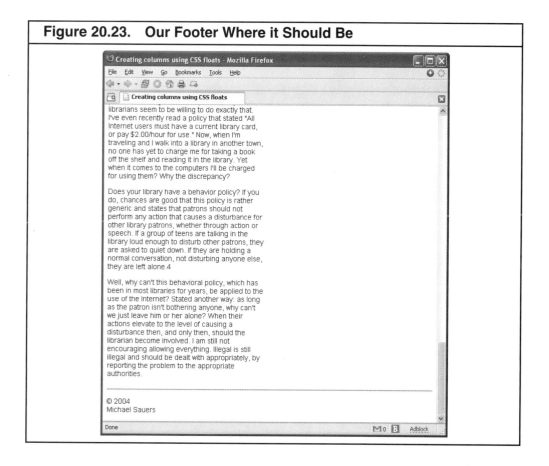

Here is the completed code for this example.

```
<!DOCTYPE html PUBLIC "-//W3C//DTD XHTML
1.0 Transitional//EN" "http://www.w3.org/1999/xhtml/DTD/xhtml1-
transitional.dtd">
<html xmlns="http://www.w3.org/1999/xhtml" lang="en" xml:lang="en">
<head>
<title>Columns using floats.</title>
<meta http-equiv="Content-Type" content="text/html; charset=utf-8" />
<style type="text/css">
#left {width: 48%; float: left}
#right{width: 48%; float: right}
</style>
</head>
<body>
<div id="left">
<p><b>Don't Doesn't Work<b></p>
<p><i>The opinions expressed in this article are the author's
alone and do not reflect the opinions of The Bibliographical
Center for Research, The Aurora Public Library or The Arapahoe
Library District.</i></p>
<p>Back in 1991 I was taking an American literature class at SUNY
Brockport. We had read the assigned book for the week, Upton
Sinclair's The Jungle, and the instructor asked us why Sinclair
had started a novel that contained so much horror, sadness and
despair with a happy scene of a wedding reception. What she
expected to hear from me was something about the contrast between
their work and non-work lives. My answer to her was that Sinclair
just wanted to hook the reader so they would read the rest of the
book; starting out the novel on a depressing note would not
encourage readers to continue reading. I'm sure that every American
literature professor is rolling their eyes, or rolling over in
their grave over my analysis of the opening of this book, but I
still stick by this theory.1 Looking back on this situation I can
see the early formation of my distinct lack of support for over-
analyzing problems. In my life I've come to realize that too many
people over-analyze a problem when trying to come up with a
solution, when many times the answer is straightforward or al-
ready exists. I believe this applies to the "problems" associ-
ated with providing Internet access to patrons in public libraries.
[Please note: In this article I am specifically dealing only with
public libraries. I do accept that in private institutions, schools
and higher education that the situation is different and a dif-
ferent solution may need to be provided.] </p>
<p>For the past eleven years, through graduate school, my period
as an independent consultant in Las Vegas, NV, board member of
the Aurora Public Library, reference desk volunteer at the Arapahoe
Library District and the past seven years as the Internet Trainer
for the Bibliographical Center for Research (BCR), I have been
keeping an eye on the state of Internet access policies in public
libraries in the U.S. I've read literally hundreds of policies,
looking at them from both the point of view of a librarian, board
member and a patron. I've talked to librarians, library staff,
directors and board members. We discussed the issues involved
```

and the policies that have been created. We've talked informally
and in a classroom environment in my Internet Access Policies
workshop. I've heard the horror stories and the success stories.
I've heard about the patrons causing trouble and I've heard about
the librarians having to do battle with their board, city or
county in order just to provide access in the first place. I'm
tempted to say that I've heard it all and that you couldn't tell
me something new, but I know better than that. </p>
<p>From all of this input I've come to this simple conclusion: a
public library's Internet access policy is pointless and its creation was a waste of time that could have better been spent
working on the library's budget. I will admit that the discussion
that happens during the creation of a policy (assuming discussion
happened and that the policy was not set by decree) is worthy of
the time taken, since it raises many important issues. (The policy
of whether or not to filter, especially in light of CIPA, is not
an issue I'll be addressing in this article. I'll be focusing on
other issues that sit outside of the filtering debate.) The policy
itself, however, I'll show is not. Many of you may believe my
opinion to be extreme, but give me the chance to convince you. </p>
<p>One of the points that I make in my class and book titled Using
the Internet as a Reference Tool is that computers—and the Internet—
are just tools that we already have the necessary skills to use.
It is simply the application of those skills that we, as librarians, need to work on. The fact that the information is electroni-
cally accessed is irrelevant to the issue. I hold that this is
also true when it comes to patron access to that information. </p>
<p>Today, a significant majority of Internet access policies con-
tain a list of things that the patron cannot do or cannot access. No
porn, no chat, no e-mail; "research only."2 All this accomplishes
is to turn the library staff into computer police. Staffs are busy
enough as it is trying to assist patrons. They do not have the time,
or in many cases the desire, to be controlling what they can and
cannot do. I would even argue that we do not have the authority to
say what information a patron can and cannot access. </p>
<p>This is not to say that I support letting the patrons do
whatever they want, without consequences. Illegal is illegal.
However, let's for a moment take the computer out of the picture.
For example, would you, as a librarian look over the shoulder of a
patron to see whether the book they were reading was "appropriate?"3 No librarian I've ever asked has answered yes to this
question. However, when it comes to what the patron is viewing on
the computer, many librarians seem to be willing to do exactly
that. I've even recently read a policy that stated "All Internet
users must have a current library card, or pay $2.00/hour for
use." Now, when I'm traveling and I walk into a library in another
town, no one has yet to charge me for taking a book off the shelf
and reading it in the library. Yet when it comes to the computers
I'll be charged for using them? Why the discrepancy? </p>
<p>Does your library have a behavior policy? If you do, chances are
good that this policy is rather generic and states that patrons
should not perform any action that causes a disturbance for other
library patrons, whether through action or speech. If a group of
teens are talking in the library loud enough to disturb other

patrons, they are asked to quiet down. If they are holding a normal conversation, not disturbing anyone else, they are left alone.4</p>
<p>Well, why can't this behavioral policy, which has been in most libraries for years, be applied to the use of the Internet? Stated another way: as long as the patron isn't bothering anyone, why can't we just leave him or her alone? When their actions elevate to the level of causing a disturbance then, and only then, should the librarian become involved. I am still not encouraging allowing everything. Illegal is still illegal and should be dealt with appropriately, by reporting the problem to the appropriate authorities. </p>
</div>
<div id="right">
<p>I believe that use of this policy in this way has several benefits for the library. First, this reduces the need for library staff to act as police. With this policy, library staff can assist patrons when they ask for it, or become involved when there is a perceived problem. No problem or request, no involvement. </p>
<p>Second, by using a behavioral policy, this gives the library additional flexibility than a "this is what you can't do" policy. If the policy states "no porn" and the student is doing a report on modern erotic art, the librarian is, by policy, forced to prevent the patron from doing their work. By treating it as a behavioral issue, the librarian, in most cases, will not become involved at all. If, however, another patron complains about what that student is looking at on their screen, the librarian can use their professional judgment in balancing the needs of the student against the complaint made and deal with the situation as he or she sees fit. </p>
<p>The other problem that may arise from having a "don't" list is that of exceptions. The moment a librarian creates an exception for one patron they open the door for other patrons to complain with "But you let them do it. Why won't you let me?" When your policy has flexibility built in, you're on much better footing when dealing with such a situation. </p>
<p>Several libraries use this method of dealing with potential problems in their library. In all of the cases I've encountered, the libraries have reported significant success with the method and are glad they chose to use their existing policy this way. </p>
<p>Conclusion:
In many libraries today policies regarding Internet access by patrons have been over-analyzed and over-thought. The result of this has been to turn library staff into a police force, reducing the time available to perform many other important tasks. In these cases the computer is being treated differently than other library resources. By removing the computer from the equation, most libraries will realize that they already have a policy on library behavior that can be applied to computer and Internet access related problems. This policy method removes the need for library staff to be police and gives that staff additional flexibility to deal with problems as they arise.</p>
<hr />
<p>Endnotes:
1. Actually, since I've become a published author myself I've modi-

```
fied this theory somewhat. I no longer believe that it was Sinclair's
idea to start with a happy scene. More likely it was his publisher
or editor that suggested it. "Uh, Up, can I call you Up? No? Well,
Mr. Sinclair, we love the book and plan to publish it for you, we'd
just like you to make a few changes. First, take out all the social-
ism. The political climate just isn't right. Okay? Also, the beginning's
a bit of a downer. Could you add a chapter at the beginning that
hooks the reader? Maybe a wedding reception . . . " </p>
<p>2. I find the concept of "research only" on a public library
computer to be contradictory to the library's mission. For any-
one that believes a "research only" policy is a good one I ask
this: what is the "research" value of Danielle Steel books?
Public libraries have always had an entertainment value and the
computers in the library should be no different. Also, by saying
"research only" we have now assigned ourselves the job of deter-
mining whether or not what the patron is doing is research.
Something I don't believe we have the right to do. </p>
<p>For those librarians concerned with limited number of comput-
ers and giving those that need access the access, I am in full
support of time limits on the computers. This gives every patron
a fair chance to use the available computers and do what they
need to do. What they do with their time however, is not our
business unless it causes a disturbance. </p>
<p>3. We have a "banned book week." Why don't we have a "Banned
Web Site Week." Here is another example of how we treat computers
differently from other library resources. </p>
<p>4. Many libraries also completely ban cell phone use in the
library. The trouble is, it's the behavior of the cell phone user,
the not cell phone itself that's the problem. I was once told to
leave a library with my cell phone because I was using it. I had
left it on vibrate and was whispering into the phone. Trouble is, I
was having trouble hearing the person on the other end due to the
gaggle of young girls "doing their homework" at a table ten feet
away from me. I was asked to stop what I was doing yet they were
not despite the fact that they were causing more of a disturbance
than I was. </p>
</div>
<br style="clear: both" />
<hr />
<p>&copy; 2004<br />
Michael Sauers</p>
</body>
</html>
```

Before we leave the subject of floats, I want to address one additional benefit to using CSS floats to create columns instead of tables. You don't have to code the content displayed on the left first. (We ran into this issue with sidebars.)

When you have a document with a menu on the left and narrative content on the right, using a table would require you to code the menu first and the narrative content second. Due to the way tables are coded, there is no way to avoid this. If you think this problem is immaterial, consider your users with accessibility issues.

For example, a text-to-speech browser will read the document in code order. If your document is coded using a table, the browser will read your menu first and then the narrative content. If you use CSS floats instead, you can code the narrative content first and the menu second, yet still have the menu displayed on the left side of the screen for visually oriented browsers.

Look at the following code and its resulting browser display (Figure 20.24).

```
<!DOCTYPE html PUBLIC "-//W3C//DTD XHTML 1.0 Transitional//EN"
"http://www.w3.org/1999/xhtml/DTD/xhtml1-transitional.dtd">
<html xmlns="http://www.w3.org/1999/xhtml" lang="en" xml:lang="en">
<head>
<title>A menu coded second yet displayed on the left.</title>
<meta http-equiv="Content-Type" content="text/html; charset=utf-
8" />
<style type="text/css">
#left   {width: 18%; float: left}
#right  {width: 79%; float: right}
ul      {margin: 0; padding: 0; list-style-type: none;}
li      {margin: 0; padding: 0; list-style-type: none;
        border: 1px solid #000; width: 100%;
        text-align: center}
ul a    {color: #fff; background: #6c3;
        text-decoration: none; display: block;
        padding:2px; margin:1px;}
ul a:link       {color:#fff;}
ul a:visited    {color:#fff;}
ul a:active     {color:#fff;}
ul a:hover      {background:#cf9; color: #000}
</style>
</head>
<body>
<div id="right">
<p>This is contained within &lt;div id="right"&gt; but coded
first.</p>
<p><b>Don't Doesn't Work<b></p>
<p><i>The opinions expressed in this article are the author's
alone and do not reflect the opinions of The Bibliographical
Center for Research, The Aurora Public Library or The Arapahoe
Library District.</i></p>
<p>Back in 1991 I was taking an American literature class at
SUNY Brockport. We had read the assigned book for the week,
Upton Sinclair's The Jungle, and the instructor asked us why
Sinclair had started a novel that contained so much horror,
sadness and despair with a happy scene of a wedding reception.
What she expected to hear from me was something about the
contrast between their work and non-work lives. My answer to
her was that Sinclair just wanted to hook the reader so they
would read the rest of the book; starting out the novel on a
depressing note would not encourage readers to continue read-
ing. I'm sure that every American literature professor is roll-
ing their eyes, or rolling over in their grave over my analysis
of the opening of this book, but I still stick by this theory.1
Looking back on this situation I can see the early formation of
my distinct lack of support for over-analyzing problems. In my
life I've come to realize that too many people over-analyze a
problem when trying to come up with a solution, when many times
```

the answer is straightforward or already exists. I believe this applies to the "problems" associated with providing Internet access to patrons in public libraries. [Please note: In this article I am specifically dealing only with public libraries. I do accept that in private institutions, schools and higher education that the situation is different and a different solution may need to be provided.] </p>

<p>For the past eleven years, through graduate school, my period as an independent consultant in Las Vegas, NV, board member of the Aurora Public Library, reference desk volunteer at the Arapahoe Library District and the past seven years as the Internet Trainer for the Bibliographical Center for Research (BCR), I have been keeping an eye on the state of Internet access policies in public libraries in the U.S. I've read literally hundreds of policies, looking at them from both the point of view of a librarian, board member and a patron. I've talked to librarians, library staff, directors and board members. We discussed the issues involved and the policies that have been created. We've talked informally and in a classroom environment in my Internet Access Policies workshop. I've heard the horror stories and the success stories. I've heard about the patrons causing trouble and I've heard about the librarians having to do battle with their board, city or county in order just to provide access in the first place. I'm tempted to say that I've heard it all and that you couldn't tell me something new, but I know better than that. </p>

<p>From all of this input I've come to this simple conclusion: a public library's Internet access policy is pointless and its creation was a waste of time that could have better been spent working on the library's budget. I will admit that the discussion that happens during the creation of a policy (assuming discussion happened and that the policy was not set by decree) is worthy of the time taken, since it raises many important issues. (The policy of whether or not to filter, especially in light of CIPA, is not an issue I'll be addressing in this article. I'll be focusing on other issues that sit outside of the filtering debate.) The policy itself, however, I'll show is not. Many of you may believe my opinion to be extreme, but give me the chance to convince you. </p>

<p>One of the points that I make in my class and book titled Using the Internet as a Reference Tool is that computers—and the Internet—are just tools that we already have the necessary skills to use. It is simply the application of those skills that we, as librarians, need to work on. The fact that the information is electronically accessed is irrelevant to the issue. I hold that this is also true when it comes to patron access to that information. </p>

<p>Today, a significant majority of Internet access policies contain a list of things that the patron cannot do or cannot access. No porn, no chat, no e-mail; "research only."2 All this accomplishes is to turn the library staff into computer police. Staffs are busy enough as it is trying to assist patrons. They do not have the time, or in many cases the desire, to be controlling what they can and cannot do. I would even argue that we do not have the authority to say what information a patron can and cannot access. </p>

<p>This is not to say that I support letting the patrons do what-

ever they want, without consequences. Illegal is illegal. However, let's for a moment take the computer out of the picture. For example, would you, as a librarian look over the shoulder of a patron to see whether the book they were reading was "appropriate?"3 No librarian I've ever asked has answered yes to this question. However, when it comes to what the patron is viewing on the computer, many librarians seem to be willing to do exactly that. I've even recently read a policy that stated "All Internet users must have a current library card, or pay $2.00/hour for use." Now, when I'm traveling and I walk into a library in another town, no one has yet to charge me for taking a book off the shelf and reading it in the library. Yet when it comes to the computers I'll be charged for using them? Why the discrepancy? </p>

<p>Does your library have a behavior policy? If you do, chances are good that this policy is rather generic and states that patrons should not perform any action that causes a disturbance for other library patrons, whether through action or speech. If a group of teens are talking in the library loud enough to disturb other patrons, they are asked to quiet down. If they are holding a normal conversation, not disturbing anyone else, they are left alone.4</p>

<p>Well, why can't this behavioral policy, which has been in most libraries for years, be applied to the use of the Internet? Stated another way: as long as the patron isn't bothering anyone, why can't we just leave him or her alone? When their actions elevate to the level of causing a disturbance then, and only then, should the librarian become involved. I am still not encouraging allowing everything. Illegal is still illegal and should be dealt with appropriately, by reporting the problem to the appropriate authorities. </p>

<p>I believe that use of this policy in this way has several benefits for the library. First, this reduces the need for library staff to act as police. With this policy, library staff can assist patrons when they ask for it, or become involved when there is a perceived problem. No problem or request, no involvement. </p>

<p>Second, by using a behavioral policy, this gives the library additional flexibility than a "this is what you can't do" policy. If the policy states "no porn" and the student is doing a report on modern erotic art, the librarian is, by policy, forced to prevent the patron from doing their work. By treating it as a behavioral issue, the librarian, in most cases, will not become involved at all. If, however, another patron complains about what that student is looking at on their screen, the librarian can use their professional judgment in balancing the needs of the student against the complaint made and deal with the situation as he or she sees fit. </p>

<p>The other problem that may arise from having a "don't" list is that of exceptions. The moment a librarian creates an exception for one patron they open the door for other patrons to complain with "But you let them do it. Why won't you let me?" When your policy has flexibility built in, you're on much better footing when dealing with such a situation. </p>

<p>Several libraries use this method of dealing with potential problems in their library. In all of the cases I've encountered,

the libraries have reported significant success with the method and are glad they chose to use their existing policy this way. </p>
<p>Conclusion:
In many libraries today policies regarding Internet access by patrons have been over-analyzed and over-thought. The result of this has been to turn library staff into a police force, reducing the time available to perform many other important tasks. In these cases the computer is being treated differently than other library resources. By removing the computer from the equation, most libraries will realize that they already have a policy on library behavior that can be applied to computer and Internet access related problems. This policy method removes the need for library staff to be police and gives that staff additional flexibility to deal with problems as they arise.</p>
<hr />
<p>Endnotes:
1. Actually, since I've become a published author myself I've modified this theory somewhat. I no longer believe that it was Sinclair's idea to start with a happy scene. More likely it was his publisher or editor that suggested it. "Uh, Up, can I call you Up? No? Well, Mr. Sinclair, we love the book and plan to publish it for you, we'd just like you to make a few changes. First, take out all the socialism. The political climate just isn't right. Okay? Also, the beginning's a bit of a downer. Could you add a chapter at the beginning that hooks the reader? Maybe a wedding reception . . . " </p>
<p>2. I find the concept of "research only" on a public library computer to be contradictory to the library's mission. For anyone that believes a "research only" policy is a good one I ask this: what is the "research" value of Danielle Steel books? Public libraries have always had an entertainment value and the computers in the library should be no different. Also, by saying "research only" we have now assigned ourselves the job of determining whether or not what the patron is doing is research. Something I don't believe we have the right to do. </p>
<p>For those librarians concerned with limited number of computers and giving those that need access the access, I am in full support of time limits on the computers. This gives every patron a fair chance to use the available computers and do what they need to do. What they do with their time however, is not our business unless it causes a disturbance. </p>
<p>3. We have a "banned book week." Why don't we have a "Banned Web Site Week." Here is another example of how we treat computers differently from other library resources. </p>
<p>4. Many libraries also completely ban cell phone use in the library. The trouble is, it's the behavior of the cell phone user, the not cell phone itself that's the problem. I was once told to leave a library with my cell phone because I was using it. I had left it on vibrate and was whispering into the phone. Trouble is, I was having trouble hearing the person on the other end due to the gaggle of young girls "doing their homework" at a table ten feet away from me. I was asked to stop what I was doing yet they were not despite the fact that they were causing more of a disturbance than I was. </p>

```
</div>
<div id="left">
<ul>
<li><a href="#">"Don't Doesn't Work"</a></li>
<li><a href="#">"Protecting Patron Privacy on Public PCs" </a></li>
<li><a href="#">"Installing Windows XP Service Pack 2: One Librarian's Experience" </a></li>
<li><a href="#">"Set Up Multiple Identities In Outlook Express" </a></li>
<li><a href="#">"An Introduction to RSS" </a></li>
<li><a href="#">"An Introduction to XHTML" </a></li>
<li><a href="#">"Style Guidance" </a></li>
<li><a href="#">"Return to Sender: Solid State Software" </a></li>
<li><a href="#">"Electronic Mailing List Netiquette" </a></li>
<li><a href="#">"Internet Owner's Manual: What is Not Indexed by Search Engines?" </a></li>
</ul>
</div>
</body>
</html>
```

Figure 20.24.   A Menu Coded Second but Displayed on the Left

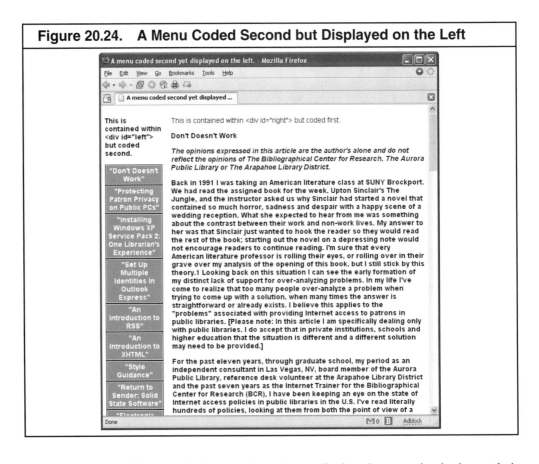

As you can see, I have my left and right columns displayed appropriately due to their respective float properties. However, the right column has been coded first, thereby causing text-to-speech browsers to read the right column first.

POSITIONING CONTENT

When it comes to having exact control over the position of an element, CSS has the options for you. Some browsers have minor problems with some of what I'm going to present in this section, but many of these problems can be overcome with minor adjustment to your code. I'll focus on how they're supposed to work and provide examples that I know will work in today's browsers.

The main CSS property we need to focus on is the `position` property. This property tells the browser which type of positioning you want to use. Once you've established that, it is then a matter of specifying where you want the content positioned. The values for the position property are `static`, `relative`, `absolute`, `fixed`, and `inherit`.

Once you have selected a position type, you must then provide the new location of the item using one or more of the location properties: `top`, `left`, `bottom`, and `right`. Each of the properties' values may be in any of the CSS units of measurement as discussed in Chapter 14. Since all of my examples will be screen-based, I'll be using pixels.

Let's look at examples of each of the four position types.

position: static

This static position instructs the browser to display the item in the location it would use as part of the normal flow of this document. This is the default position type, so it would rarely be used by a Web designer.

position: relative

If you set the position type as relative, you may then move the element from the position that it would occupy had you not positioned it. In the following example, the key is to focus on the declaration for the `.book img` selector. In this case I've moved the book's cover image up and to the left of its usual position to cause it to overlap the border (Figure 20.25).

```
<!DOCTYPE html PUBLIC "-//W3C//DTD XHTML 1.0
Transitional//EN" "http://www.w3.org/1999/xhtml/DTD/xhtml1-
transitional.dtd">
<html xmlns="http://www.w3.org/1999/xhtml" lang="en" xml:lang="en">
<head>
<title>A menu coded second yet displayed on the left.</title>
<meta http-equiv="Content-Type" content="text/html; charset=utf-
8" />
<style type="text/css">
.book      {border: 1px solid #6c3; width: 225px;
            height160px; padding-left: 5px;
            padding-top: 10px;
            padding-right: 10px; margin-left: 20px}
.book img {position: relative; left: -14px; top: -20px;
 float:    left}
.title     {font-style: italic}
</style>
</head>
<body>
```

```
<div class="book">
<p><img src="scepters.jpg" alt="Scepters" />
<span class="title">Scepters</span><br />L. E. Modesitt, Jr.</p>
</div>
</body>
</html>
```

Figure 20.25.　The position **Property with a** relative **Value**

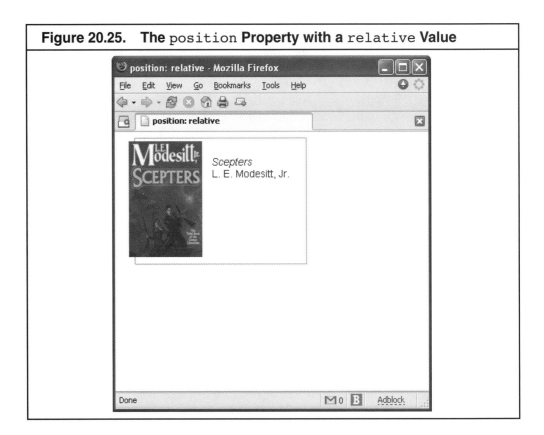

POSITION: ABSOLUTE

The absolute position type allows you to specify exactly where in the document you want a particular element to be placed. When position is set to absolute, you must the specify the x and y coordinates of the upper-left corner of the element. These coordinates may be specified by using any pair of the top, left, bottom, and right properties. Here are a few examples, each of which assumes that there is a paragraph of text and the book cover graphic used in the relative positioning example (Figure 20.26).

```
img {position: absolute; top: 0; left: 0}
```

Figure 20.26. The `position` **Property with an** `absolute` **Value Placing the Image in the Upper Left Corner of the Browser Window**

In this example, I've specified that the upper-left corner of the image should appear zero pixels from the top of the window and zero pixels from the left of the window. You should note that the absolute position type does allow for content overlap. The overlap problem in this example can be corrected by adding a `margin-left` to the paragraph that is larger than the width of the image (Figure 20.27).

```
img {position: absolute; top: 0; right: 0}
```

Figure 20.27.   The `position` **Property with an** `absolute` **Value Placing the Image in the Upper Right Corner of the Browser Window**

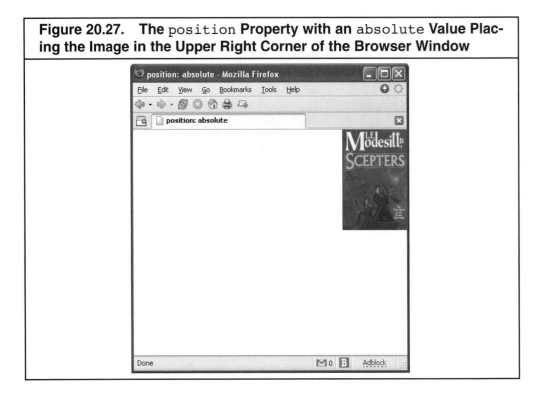

In this example, I've directed the upper-left corner of the image to appear zero pixels from the top and zero pixels from the right. However, the absolute positioning type cannot force the element off the screen, so the right position is automatically shifted to the left equal to the width of the image (Figure 20.28).

```
img {position: absolute; bottom: 100px; left: 300px}
```

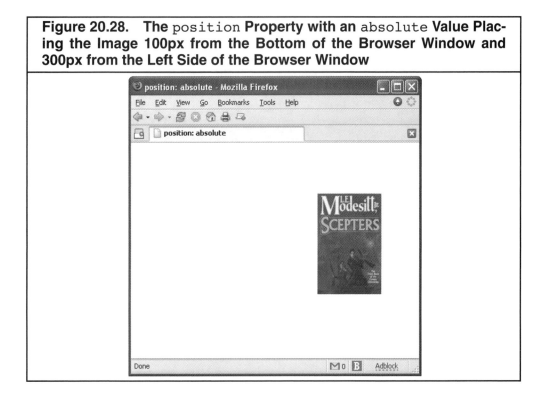

Figure 20.28. The `position` **Property with an** `absolute` **Value Placing the Image 100px from the Bottom of the Browser Window and 300px from the Left Side of the Browser Window**

In this third example, I've placed the upper-left corner of the image 100 pixels from the bottom of the window and 300 pixels from the left side of the window. If I were to add additional text to this document, the image would continue to overlap that content.

position: fixed

The fixed position places an element in the document in the same manner as the absolute positioning type. The singular difference is that the position of the element is "fixed" on the screen. In other words, if the document moves (scrolls), the item will not scroll with it; it will remain in place. Absolutely positioned elements will scroll with the document.

position: inherit

The CSS specification lists this as a valid value for the position property. One might assume this means that the element is to inherit its position from its parent. However, unlike inheriting other properties such as font or color, this seems illogical. Unfortunately, though the W3C does list this as a value, it provides no explanation of its purpose.[1]

POSITIONING IN THE THIRD DIMENSION:

`z-index: ±n`

Although absolute positioning of an element might seem handy at first, there is the significant problem of content overlap. In the previous examples there is little chance of wanting that overlap, even if we could send the image behind the text. Suppose our image were more of a watermark. We might want that image to be placed in a particular location on the screen, displayed behind the text.

NOTE: Depending on your design and the image, setting the image as a background might be a better choice. However, background does not allow for pixel-perfect positioning.

CSS includes a property known as z-index, which allows you to specify a stack order for positioned elements. The value for z-index may be any positive or negative number. Elements that have not been positioned are considered to have a z-index of zero. Therefore items with a lower z-index value will be behind other items while those with higher values will be in front of other elements (Figure 20.29).

Here's a small modification of the first position: absolute example with the addition of a z-index: −1 on the positioned element.

```
<!DOCTYPE html PUBLIC "-//W3C//DTD XHTML 1.0 Transitional//EN"
"http://www.w3.org/1999/xhtml/DTD/xhtml1-transitional.dtd">
<html xmlns="http://www.w3.org/1999/xhtml" lang="en" xml:lang="en">
<head>
<title>A menu coded second yet displayed on the left.</title>
<meta http-equiv="Content-Type" content="text/html; charset=utf-8" />
<style type="text/css">
img {position: absolute; top: 0; left: 0; z-index: -1}
</style>
</head>
<body>
<h1><img src="scepters.jpg" alt="Scepters" /><i>Scepters</i> by
L. E. Modesitt, Jr.</h1>
</div>
</body>
</html>
```

Figure 20.29.   Using z-index **to Overlap Content**

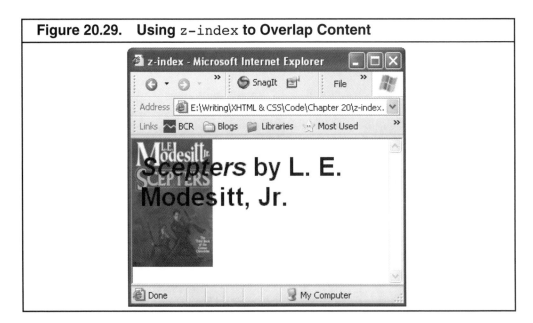

As you can see, the image is now behind the text.

NOTE

1. The position property specification can be found at www.w3.org/TR/REC-CSS2/visuren.html#positioning-scheme

21

Media Types

Although media types are extremely powerful, unfortunately all of their power lies in their potential. Today, very few browsers support CSS media types, and those that do support a very small subset of what's available. In this chapter, I'll mainly discuss the possibilities and will give you real-life examples whenever possible.

WHAT ARE MEDIA TYPES?

The authors of CSS considered the fact that, when you separate content from style, you have extensive flexibility in how you present that content. The ability to include multiple alternative style sheets is just one of those ways. Another way to enhance flexibility is to consider that you may be presenting your content on different platforms. When you consider multiple platforms, you may need to consider alternate styles.

When displaying on a screen, a document is considered a single entity; hence the concept of scrolling. However, once you move to a printed environment, you now have discrete units—pages—in which to work. When the document is converted to speech, it is once again a single entity, but speed, volume, and pitch suddenly become factors. These are the issues that CSS media types attempt to deal with.

CSS defines ten different media types.[1] They are:

- `all`
  Suitable for all devices. This is the default media type. Everything we've done so far has been applied as if the media type were specified as "all."
- `aural`
  Intended for speech synthesizers.
- `braille`
  Intended for braille tactile feedback devices.

- `embossed`
  Intended for paged braille printers.
- `handheld`
  Intended for handheld devices (typically small screen, monochrome, and with limited bandwidth).
- `print`
  Intended for paged, opaque material and for documents viewed on screen in print preview mode.
- `projection`
  Intended for projected presentations (for example, projectors or print to transparencies).
- `screen`
  Intended primarily for color computer screens.
- `tty`
  Intended for media using a fixed-pitch character grid, such as teletypes, terminals, or portable devices with limited display capabilities. Authors should not use pixel units with the `"tty"` media type.
- `tv`
  Intended for television-type devices (low resolution, color, limited-scrollability screens, available sound).

If you read the specifications for the properties that can be applied to each of the media types, you will notice that most properties are not listed as applying to a particular media type. Instead they apply to a particular media group. This is because in many circumstances, a particular property can apply to more than one of the above-listed types.

The media groups are as follows.[2]

- *continuous* or *paged.*
  "Both" means that the property in question applies to both media groups.
- *visual, aural,* or *tactile.*
- *grid* (for character grid devices), or *bitmap.*
  "Both" means that the property in question applies to both media groups.
- *interactive* (for devices that allow user interaction), or *static* (for those that don't).
  "Both" means that the property in question applies to both media groups.
- *all* (includes all media types)

Table 21.1 shows which media types belong to which groups.[3]

Table 21.1.
Relationship Between Media Groups and Media Types

	Media Groups			
Media Types	continuous/paged	visual/aural/tactile	grid/bitmap	interactive/static
aural	continuous	aural	N/A	both
braille	continuous	tactile	grid	both
emboss	paged	tactile	grid	both
handheld	both	visual	both	both
print	paged	visual	bitmap	static
projection	paged	visual	bitmap	static
screen	continuous	visual	bitmap	both
tty	continuous	visual	grid	both
tv	both	visual, aural	bitmap	both

ONE BRIEF EXAMPLE

Before we move on to specifying media types within CSS code, let's look at a brief example of why you might want to specify different styles for different platforms.

This is the home page for the Bobby, an accessibility testing service (Figure 21.1).

Figure 21.1. The Bobby Home Page as Displayed in a Browser

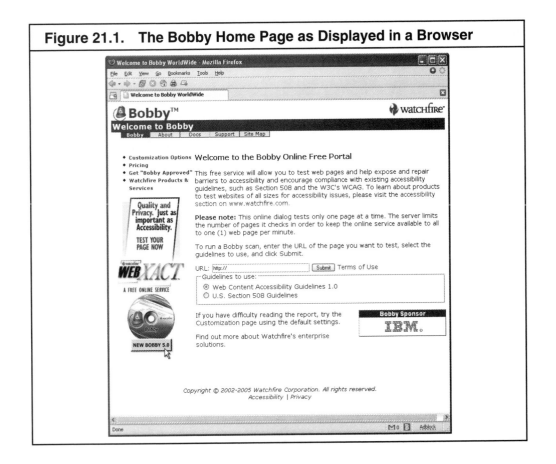

Using a browser that supports the print media type (Firefox), let's look at the print preview of the same page (Figure 21.2).

Figure 21.2.   The Bobby Home Page as Printed

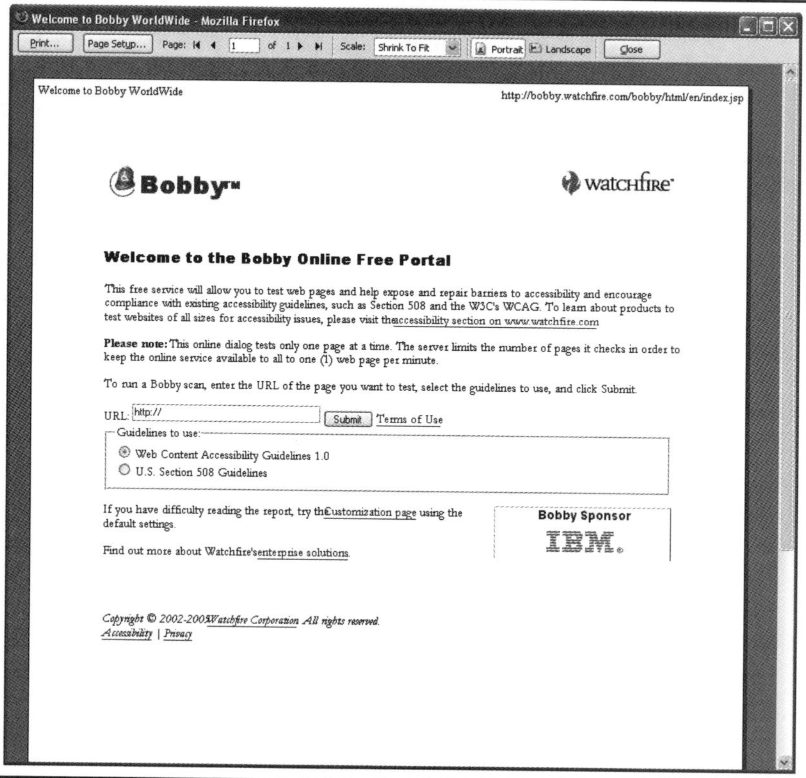

See the difference? In this case, some of what is displayed on the screen; the advertisements, the menu, and the navigation bar are not being sent to the printer. This is accomplished with the addition of just three lines of CSS code.

SPECIFYING MEDIA TYPES

You have two options as to how to specify that your styles only apply to a particular media type. You can specify within the CSS itself or you can use the XHTML `media=""` attribute. We'll look at the attribute method first.

THE MEDIA ATTRIBUTE

The media attribute is used when linking to a CSS file. For example, if you write one CSS file for all media types but also write a separate CSS file to apply just to printing, you can link to both of them in the following manner:

```
<link rel="stylesheet" type="text/css" href="style.css" />
<link rel="stylesheet" type="text.css" href="print.css"
media="print" />
```

In this example, the `style.css` file will apply to all media types, including print, since "all" is the default media type. The `print.css` file will only apply when sending the document to a printer.

If you want to specify that `style.css` only applies to screens and handheld devices, while retaining `print.css` for the print media you can adjust your code as follows:

```
<link rel="stylesheet" type="text/css" href="style.css"
media="screen, handheld" />
<link rel="stylesheet" type="text.css" href="print.css"
media="print" />
```

As you see, you can create a comma-delimited list within the media attribute to apply it to multiple media types.

THE @MEDIA RULE

The `@media` rule is the method for specifying a particular media type with the CSS itself. Here's what the code looks like:

```
@media mediatype      {
    all selectors and declarations that apply
                    }
```

NOTE: As with all CSS code, this could be written as one line. However, since this code includes nested braces, writing the code in with the spacing shown above is common practice for ease of reading and editing.

So, If I had a CSS file in which I wanted to add just a few additional lines that only applied to the print media type, my CSS would look like this:

```
body {color: white; background: black}
@media print            {
    body {color: black; background: white}
                    }
```

This example will yield white text on a black background in all media types (the default) except the print media type, which will have black text on a white background.

THE PRINT MEDIA TYPE IN MORE DETAIL

Since the print media type is the only one that currently has any significant support in today's browsers and typically holds the most interest for today's Web authors, we'll examine it a little further here. Keep in mind that, as of this writing, not all of the page-specific properties were supported. Be sure to test any of the following that you decide to integrate into your site.

INSERTING PAGE BREAKS

One of the most interesting aspects of the print media type is the ability to control where page breaks occur within a document. Let's say you have a rather long document broken into multiple sections, and each section starts with a Level 2 heading. (Level 2 would be for the "title" of the document.) By adding the following to your CSS, you would ensure (in browsers that support this feature) that each "section" of the document starts on a new piece of paper.

```
@media print     {
    h2 {page-break-before: always}
                    }
```

Table 21.2 shows the three page-related properties and Table 21.3 shows the available values for those properties.

Table 21.2
The page properties

page-break-before	auto | always | avoid | left | right | inherit
page-break-after	auto | always | avoid | left | right | inherit
page-break-inside	avoid | auto | inherit

Table 21.3
The Available Values for the page Properties

auto	Neither force nor forbid a page break before (after, inside) the generated box. (default)
always	Always force a page break before (after) the generated box.
avoid	Avoid a page break before (after, inside) the generated box.
left	Force one or two page breaks before (after) the generated box so that the next page is formatted as a left page.
right	Force one or two page breaks before (after) the generated box so that the next page is formatted as a right page.

NOTE: The paged media types allow for specifying if a page should be a "left" page or a "right" page. This is used when you intend the printed output to be double-sided and bound together. For example, for the purposes of binding, you might want a left page to have a wider right margin while a right page would have a larger left margin taking into account where the pages will be physically bound.

HIDING FROM THE PRINTER

This particular item is not specific to the print media type. This is probably the most commonly used declaration within print style sheets today. For example, if you have a `<div id="menu">` in your document and you want that section not to appear on the printed version of the document, you would include the following within your print styles.

```
#menu {display: none}
```

WIDOW AND ORPHAN CONTROL

In text documents, "widows" are a few lines of a paragraph that are at the bottom of one page with the rest of the paragraph on the next, while orphans are a few lines of a paragraph at the top of a page while the rest of the paragraph is on the previous page. Through the use of the widows and orphans properties you can control how many lines of a paragraph are allowed to be separated from the rest of the paragraph or even prevent this separation entirely.

The following code allows four lines to be separated while preventing the separation of only one, two, or three lines.

```
@media print    {
   body {widows: 4; orphans 4}
                   }
```

This example prevents widows and orphans altogether.

```
@media print    {
   body {widows: 0; orphans 0}
                   }
```

THE @PAGE RULE

The @page rule allows you to set the dimensions and margins of a "page box" to be placed on the printed sheet of paper. For example, the following specifies that the document should be formatted on an 8.5"×11" page with one-inch margins.

```
@page {size: 8.5in 11in; margin: 1in}
```

In this example, the content of the document will be printed within these dimensions and margins regardless of the physical size of the sheet of paper being printed on.

Setting the page size

When you set the dimensions of the page using the size property, you have five options for the value of size.

- auto
  The default setting which allows the browser to determine the page's size and orientation
- *n n*
  Specifes the dimensions of the page in width and height. All of the standard values of measurements are available
- portrait
  Overrides the browser and sets the page to where the long size of the page is vertical
- landscape
  Overrides the browser and sets the page to where the long size of the page is horizontal.

Mis-matched dimensions?

Current browsers don't much little support for the @page rule. When that support does arrive, consider what happens when the page box is significantly larger or smaller than the printed sheet of paper. This is the course of action the W3C suggests.

> *Rendering page boxes that do not fit a target sheet*
> If a page box does not fit the target sheet dimensions, the user agent may choose to:
>
> • Rotate the page box 90° if this will make the page box fit.
> • Scale the page to fit the target.
>
> The user agent should consult the user before performing these operations.
>
> *Positioning the page box on the sheet*
> When the page box is smaller than the target size, the user agent is free to place the page box anywhere on the sheet. However, it is recommended that the page box be centered on the sheet since this will align double-sided pages and avoid accidental loss of information that is printed near the edge of the sheet.

NOTES

1. www.w3.org/TR/REC-CSS2/media.html
2. ibid.
3. ibid.

Index

About the Author

Michael Sauers of Aurora, Colorado, is the Internet Trainer for the Bibliographical Center for Research, a multistate nonprofit regional library consortium. For BCR, Michael travels extensively throughout twelve states training librarians and others how to use the Internet and its related technologies. His live and online classes range in topics from basic Internet use to Web design and accessible technology. Michael has given presentations at national conferences including ALA Annual and Computers in Libraries.

Prior to joining BCR in 1997 he was an independent consultant and trainer in Las Vegas, Nevada. He has also worked for both the New York State Library and the New York State Assembly. He earned his Masters of Library Science from the University at Albany (SUNY) in 1995.

Michael has published five previous titles, *Microsoft FrontPage 2000 Advanced Topics*, *XHTML Essentials*, *Using the Internet as a Reference Tool: A How-To-Do-It Manual for Librarians* (Neal-Schuman, 2001), and *Using Microsoft Outlook: A How-To-Do-It Manual and CD-ROM Tutorial* (Neal-Schuman, 2001). He co-authored with Louise Alcorn *The Neal-Schuman Directory of Management Software for Public Access Computers* (Neal-Schuman, 2003).